Certification Study Companion Series

The Apress Certification Study Companion Series offers guidance and hands-on practice to support technical and business professionals who are studying for an exam in the pursuit of an industry certification. Professionals worldwide seek to achieve certifications in order to advance in a career role, reinforce knowledge in a specific discipline, or to apply for or change jobs. This series focuses on the most widely taken certification exams in a given field. It is designed to be user friendly, tracking to topics as they appear in a given exam. Authors for this series are experts and instructors who not only possess a deep understanding of the content, but also have experience teaching the key concepts that support readers in the practical application of the skills learned in their day-to-day roles.

More information about this series at https://link.springer.com/bookseries/17100

Google Cloud Platform (GCP) Professional Cloud Network Engineer Certification Companion

Learn and Apply Network Design Concepts to Prepare for the Exam

Dario Cabianca

Apress®

Google Cloud Platform (GCP) Professional Cloud Network Engineer Certification Companion: Learn and Apply Network Design Concepts to Prepare for the Exam

Dario Cabianca
Georgetown, KY, USA

ISBN-13 (pbk): 978-1-4842-9353-9
https://doi.org/10.1007/978-1-4842-9354-6

ISBN-13 (electronic): 978-1-4842-9354-6

Managing Director, Apress Media LLC: Welmoed Spahr
Acquisitions Editor: Joan Murray
Development Editor: Laura Berendson
Editorial Assistant: Gryffin Winkler

Cover image designed by Isaac Soler at eStudioCalamar

Distributed to the book trade worldwide by Springer Science+Business Media New York, 1 New York Plaza, 1 FDR Dr, New York, NY 10004. Phone 1-800-SPRINGER, fax (201) 348-4505, e-mail orders-ny@springer-sbm.com, or visit www.springeronline.com. Apress Media, LLC is a California LLC and the sole member (owner) is Springer Science + Business Media Finance Inc (SSBM Finance Inc). SSBM Finance Inc is a **Delaware** corporation.

For information on translations, please e-mail booktranslations@springernature.com; for reprint, paperback, or audio rights, please e-mail bookpermissions@springernature.com.

Apress titles may be purchased in bulk for academic, corporate, or promotional use. eBook versions and licenses are also available for most titles. For more information, reference our Print and eBook Bulk Sales web page at http://www.apress.com/bulk-sales.

Printed on acid-free paper

To Margie, my sound and complete love.

Table of Contents

About the Author

Dario Cabianca is a computer scientist (PhD, University of Milan), author, and cloud architect. He has worked with a variety of global enterprises for more than two decades and possesses more than 11 cloud certifications. He used his own fail-proof techniques to prepare and pass GCP, Azure, and AWS exams. He is excited to share his knowledge to help readers of his study companion book prepare for the GCP Professional Cloud Network Engineer certification exam and also come away equipped with the necessary tools and knowledge to be confident and successful on the job.

About the Technical Reviewer

Raymond Blum leads a global team of Google engineers that develops tools to support emerging platforms and architectures. Based in New York, he was previously a site reliability engineer at Google, helping to ensure that Gmail, Ads, and other Google services were always available and safe. A passionate champion of dependable infrastructure, Raymond has contributed to Data Integrity best practices published by Google and by the Association for Computing Machinery.

In previous lives, Raymond developed software for media and financial companies and ran an Internet service hosting company. In what spare time exists, he reads everything that he can and makes friends with robots.

Acknowledgments

This book is the result of the study, work, and research I accomplished over the past two years. I could not have written this book without the help of family, friends, colleagues, and experts in the field of computer networks and computer science.

When my friend, former colleague, and author Tom Nelson first introduced me to Apress in August 2021, I had no idea I was about to embark on this wonderful journey.

First and foremost, I am grateful to my wife Margie, who carefully created a conducive space at home so I could stay focused on this work and prepare quality content for this book (not an easy task with my two young sons Joseph and Samuele eager to learn networks from their dad).

The team at Apress has been phenomenal for accommodating my schedule a few times and for providing the necessary guidance in a timely manner. Thanks to Gryffin Winkler, Raymond Blum, Laura Berendson, Joan Murray, and Jill Balzano. Without your prompt and careful assistance, this work would not have been possible.

Every concept I explained in the book is the product of scientific curiosity, theory, practice, and experience I acquired through my professional and academic career.

I was inspired by the idea of a Virtual Private Cloud (VPC) network intended as a *logical routing domain*, as clearly described by Emanuele Mazza in the presentation he gave in the "VPC Deep Dive and Best Practices" session at Google Cloud Next 2018. Not only did this concept consolidate my understanding of VPCs—whose scope extends the boundaries of zones and regions—but it naturally helped build more knowledge touching a significant number of exam objectives.

I am also grateful to Luca Prete for his article "GCP Routing Adventures (Vol. 1)" he posted on Medium, which helped me explain in a simple yet comprehensive way the concept of BGP (Border Gateway Protocol) routing mode, as it pertains to VPCs.

The section about VPC Service Controls implementation required extra work due to the sophistication of this unique capability offered by GCP. The article "Google Cloud VPC-Service Controls: Lessons Learned" posted on Medium by my friend Andrea Gandolfi was instrumental in helping me set the context and document the key features of this product. Thanks Andrea for your great article!

A number of other friends and former colleagues helped me develop my knowledge on some of the objectives of the exam. These include Daniel Schewe, Ali Ikram, Rajesh Ramamoorthy, Justin Quattlebaum, Stewart Reed, Stephen Beasey, Chris Smith, Tim DelBosco, and Kapil Gupta. Thanks to all of you for your constructive feedback and the methodical approach you shared during our problem solving discussions.

Last, I cannot express enough words of gratitude for the Late Prof. Giovanni Degli Antoni (Gianni), who guided me through my academic career in the University of Milan, and my beloved parents Eugenia and Giuseppe, who always supported me in my academic journey and in life.

Introduction

This book is about preparing you to pass the Google Cloud Professional Cloud Network Engineer certification exam and—most importantly—to get you started for an exciting career as a Google Cloud Platform (GCP) network engineer.

There are a number of professional cloud certifications covering a broad array of areas. These certifications are offered by all three leading public cloud providers in the world, that is, Amazon Web Services (AWS), Microsoft Azure, and Google Cloud Platform. These areas include cloud architecture, cloud engineering and operations (also known as DevOps), data engineering, cloud security, and cloud networking. Among all these areas, the *network* is the key element of the infrastructure your workloads use to deliver business value to their users. Think about it. Without the network—whether it be physical or virtual, covering a local or wide area (LAN and WAN, respectively)—there is no way two (or more) computers can communicate with each other and exchange data. Back in the 1990s, the former Sun Microsystems (later acquired by Oracle) introduced a slogan, "the Network is the Computer," to emphasize that computers should be networked or—to an extreme—they are not computers. This slogan was ahead of its time and put an emphasis on the nature of distributed systems, where the parts of a system are not concentrated into one single unit (computer), but they are spread across multiple units (computers). This slogan originated when cloud computing didn't exist. Yet, in my opinion, it is still real and is agnostic to where your workloads operate, that is, in your company's data centers, in GCP (or other clouds), or both. The fundamental difference between computer networking in the data centers (also referred to as traditional networking or on-premises networking) and in the cloud is that the cloud makes all things "more distributed." In fact, if you leverage the capabilities offered by the cloud, it's easier to design and implement *recovery-oriented architectures* for your workloads, which help you mitigate the risks of single point of failures (SPFs) by enabling self-healing functionality and other fault tolerance techniques. The cloud—when properly used—can address many other concerns that apply to software and hardware distributed systems. Don't worry! Throughout this book, I will teach you what "more distributed" means and how the users of your workloads can benefit from it. This brings us to who this book is for.

This book is intended for a broad audience of cloud solution architects (in any of the three public cloud providers), as well as site reliability, security, network, and software engineers with foundational knowledge of Google Cloud and networking concepts. Basic knowledge of the OSI model, the RFC 1918 (private address space) paper, the TCP/IP, the TLS (or SSL), and the HTTP protocols is a plus, although it is not required.

I used the official exam guide to organize the content and to present it in a meaningful way. As a result, the majority of the chapters are structured to map one to one with each exam objective and to provide detailed coverage of each topic, as defined by Google. The exposition of the content for most of the key topics includes a theoretical part, which is focused on conceptual knowledge, and a practical part, which is focused on the application of the acquired knowledge to solve common use cases, usually by leveraging reference architectures and best practices. This approach will help you gradually set context, get you familiarized with the topic, and lay the foundations for more advanced concepts.

Given the nature of the exam, whose main objective is to teach you how to design, engineer, and architect efficient, secure, and cost-effective network solutions with GCP, I have developed a bias for diagrams, infographic content, and other illustrative material to help you "connect the dots" and visually build knowledge.

Another important aspect of the exposition includes the use of the Google Cloud Command Line Interface (gcloud CLI) as the main tool to solve the presented use cases. This choice is deliberate, and the rationale about it is twofold. On the one side, the exam has a number of questions that require you to know the gcloud CLI commands. On the other side, the alternatives to the gcloud CLI are the console and other tools that enable Infrastructure as Code (IaC), for example, HashiCorp Terraform. The former leverages the Google Cloud user interface and is subject to frequent changes without notice. The latter is a product that is not in the scope of the exam.

A Google Cloud free account is recommended to make the best use of this book. This approach will teach you how to use the gcloud CLI and will let you practice the concepts you learned. Chapter 1 will cover this setup and will provide an overview of the exam, along with the registration process. If you want to become an expert on shared Virtual Private Cloud (VPC) networks, I also recommend that you create a Google Workspace account with your own domain. Although this is not free, the price is reasonable, and you will have your own organization that you can use to create multiple GCP users and manage IAM (Identity and Access Management) policies accordingly.

In Chapter 2, you will learn the important factors you need to consider to design the network architecture for your workloads. The concept of a Virtual Private Cloud (VPC) network as a *logical routing domain* will be first introduced, along with a few reference topologies. Other important GCP constructs will be discussed, for example, projects, folders, organizations, billing accounts, Identity and Access Management (IAM) allow policies, and others, to help you understand how to enable separation of duties—also known as *microsegmentation*—effectively. Finally, an overview of hybrid and multi-cloud deployments will be provided to get you familiarized with the GCP network connectivity products.

Chapter 3 is your VPC "playground." In this chapter, you'll use the gcloud CLI to perform a number of operations on VPCs and their components. You will learn the construct of a subnetwork, intended as a partition of a VPC, and you will create, update, delete, and peer VPCs. We will deep dive in the setup of a shared VPC, which we'll use as a reference for the upcoming sections and chapters. The concepts of Private Google Access and Private Service Connect will be introduced and implemented. A detailed setup of a Google Kubernetes Engine (GKE) cluster in our shared VPC will be implemented with examples of internode connectivity. The fundamental concepts of routing and firewall rules will be discussed, with emphasis on their applicability scope, which is the entire VPC.

Chapter 4 will be entirely focused on the implementation of VPC Service Controls. This is a topic I have been particularly interested in covering as a separate chapter, because of its level of sophistication and because the literature available is dispersed in multiple sources. The chapter provides two deep dive examples of VPC Service Controls using a shared VPC, including their important dry-run mode feature.

Chapter 5 will cover all the load balancing services you need to know to pass the exam, beginning from the nine different "flavors" of GCP load balancers. A number of deep dive examples on how to implement global, external HTTP(S) load balancers with different backend types will be provided. You will become an expert at choosing the right load balancer based on a set of business and technical requirements, which is exactly what you are expected to know during the exam and at work.

Chapter 6 will cover advanced network services that provide additional security capabilities to your workloads. These are Cloud DNS, Cloud NAT, and Packet Mirroring.

In Chapter 7, you will learn how to implement the GCP products that enable hybrid and multi-cloud connectivity. These include the two "flavors" of Cloud Interconnect (Dedicated and Partner) and the two flavors of Cloud VPN (HA and Classic).

The last chapter (Chapter 8) concludes our study by teaching you how to perform network operations as a means to proactively support and optimize the network infrastructure you have designed, architected, and implemented.

Each chapter (other than Chapter 1) includes at the end a few questions (and the correct answers) to help you consolidate your knowledge of the covered exam objective.

As in any discipline, you will need to supplement what you learned with experience. The combination of the two will make you a better GCP network engineer. I hope this book will help you achieve your Google Cloud Professional Cloud Network Engineer certification and, most importantly, will equip you with the tools and the knowledge you need to succeed at work.

CHAPTER 1

■ ■■ ■

Exam Overview

You are starting your preparation for the Google Professional Cloud Network Engineer certification. This certification validates your knowledge to implement and manage network architectures in Google Cloud.

In this chapter, we will set the direction on getting ready for the exam. We will outline resources that will aid you in your learning strategy. We will explain how you can obtain access to a free tier Google Cloud account, which will allow you to practice what you have learned. We will provide links to useful additional study materials, and we will describe how to sign up for the exam.

Exam Content

The Google Cloud Professional Cloud Network Engineer certification is designed for individuals who would like to validate their knowledge of network infrastructure and services in Google Cloud. You are expected to have a thorough understanding of the following subject areas:

- Virtual Private Cloud (VPC) networks
- Routing
- Network services
- Hybrid and multi-cloud interconnectivity
- Network operations

The exam does not cover cloud service fundamentals, but some questions on the exam assume knowledge of these concepts. Some of the broad knowledge areas that you are expected to be familiar with are

- Compute infrastructure concepts, for example, virtual machines, containers, container orchestration, serverless compute services
- Site Reliability Engineering (SRE) concepts
- Familiarity with Google Cloud Storage classes
- Familiarity with the TCP and HTTP(S) protocols
- Familiarity with security topics such as Identity and Access Management (IAM), endpoint protection, and encryption in transit
- Basic knowledge of DevOps best practices

© Dario Cabianca 2023

D. Cabianca, *Google Cloud Platform (GCP) Professional Cloud Network Engineer Certification Companion*, Certification Study Companion Series, https://doi.org/10.1007/978-1-4842-9354-6_1

Exam Subject Areas

The main subject areas that are covered on the exam are listed in Table 1-1.

Table 1-1. *Exam subject areas*

Domain
Designing, planning, and prototyping a Google Cloud network
Implementing Virtual Private Cloud (VPC) instances
Configuring network services
Implementing hybrid interconnectivity
Managing, monitoring, and optimizing network operations

Google doesn't provide their weighting ranges, nor does it tell you how you scored in each domain. The outcome of the exam is pass/fail and is provided immediately upon submitting your exam.

You are expected to learn all topics according to the exam study guide that are included in this study companion.

Exam Format

The exam consists of 50–60 questions with a time length of two hours, all of which are in one of the following formats:

- **Multiple choice:** Select the most appropriate answer.
- **Multiple select:** Select all answers that apply. The question will tell you how many answers are to be selected.

As long as you come well prepared to take the exam, you should be able to complete all questions within the allotted time. Some questions on the exam may be unscored items to gather statistical information. These items are not identified to you and do not affect your score.

The registration fee for the Google Professional Cloud Network Engineer certification exam is $200 (plus tax where applicable).

For the latest information about the exam, navigate to the Google Cloud Certifications page at the following URL: `https://cloud.google.com/certification/cloud-network-engineer`.

Supplementary Study Materials

To be well prepared for this exam, you will utilize this study companion as well as other materials, including hands-on experience, on-demand training courses, the Google Cloud documentation, and other self-study assets.

While this study companion provides enough information to help you prepare for all topics that are covered on the exam, you may wish to supplement your learning materials with additional free self-study resources:

- You may enroll in the Google Cloud Innovator learning platform at `https://cloud.google.com/innovators` and review the learning tracks.

- You should also sign up for a Google Cloud free tier account at `https://cloud.google.com/free`.

Sign Up for a Free Tier

Google Cloud offers a free tier program with the following benefits:

- 20+ free products for all customers

- $300 in free credits for new customers

- Additional free credits for businesses

There is no charge to use the 20+ products up to their specified free usage limit. The free usage limit does not expire, but is subject to change. Keep in mind that even with a free tier account, you are still required to provide a valid credit card, although charges start after you use your allotted $300 credit or after 90 days.

To sign up, visit `https://cloud.google.com/free`.

Register for the Exam

To register for the exam, you need to create a Google Cloud Webassessor account (unless you already have one) for exams in English by visiting `https://webassessor.com/googlecloud`.

Scroll down and click as indicated in Figure 1-1.

Please log in with your Google Cloud Webassessor account to see our catalog and register for an exam.

| Login |
| Password |

Forgot password?

LOGIN

Make sure you review the retake policy and recertification eligibility criteria before you take an exam. There is a limit on the number of times you can take the exam and a waiting period between attempts (even if you are taking the same exam in a different language). It is the user's responsibility to adhere to these terms and conditions to avoid possible suspension or rejection of exam results.

Don't have an account?

Click here to create a Google Cloud Webassessor account for exams in English.

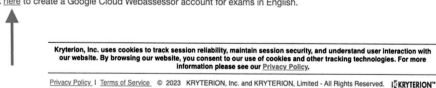

Kryterion, Inc. uses cookies to track session reliability, maintain session security, and understand user interaction with our website. By browsing our website, you consent to our use of cookies and other tracking technologies. For more information please see our Privacy Policy.

Privacy Policy | Terms of Service © 2023 KRYTERION, Inc. and KRYTERION, Limited - All Rights Reserved. ⦗KRYTERION™

Figure 1-1. *Signing up for Webassessor*

Fill out the form and click "Save" as indicated in Figure 1-2.

Powered By

Login:		Save	Cancel

Must be alphanumeric characters and NOT an email address. If you have ever used Webassessor before, your login for Google Cloud exams must be unique

Password:

The password must be at least 8 characters long and contain at least one uppercase character, one lowercase character, one digit, and one special character: !@#$£%^&*()[] (e.g., "johnSmith6$")

Re-Enter Password

Legal First Name:

When taking an exam at a testing center, the name on your two forms of identification must match exactly (characters included) with your name as specified below. Additionally, all identification must be current. Expired identification will not be accepted.

Legal Last Name (if no last name enter a period "."):

Email Address:

Primary Phone:

Address Line 1:

Address Line 2:

City:

Province/State: N/A

Postal Code:

Country: United States

Figure 1-2. *Creating a Webassessor account*

Upon creating your Webassessor account, you are all set and you can schedule your exam.

Schedule the Exam

Visit https://webassessor.com/googlecloud and log in. Then click the "REGISTER FOR AN EXAM" button as indicated in Figure 1-3.

Powered
By

Receipts   Register For An Exam   My Assessments   **Home**

You last logged in 12 August 2022 at 6:32AM MST.

Make sure you review the retake policy and recertification eligibility criteria before you take an exam. There is a limit on the number of times you can take an exam and a waiting period between attempts (even if you are taking the same exam in a different language). It is your responsibility to adhere to these terms and conditions to avoid possible suspension or rejection of exam results.

Launching your online exam? Due to high volume, you may experience additional wait time (15-20 mins) before connecting with a proctor. Do not disconnect. We appreciate your patience!

REGISTER FOR AN EXAM

Kryterion, Inc. uses cookies to track session reliability, maintain session security, and understand user interaction with our website. By browsing our website, you consent to our use of cookies and other tracking technologies. For more information please see our Privacy Policy.

Privacy Policy | Terms of Service   © 2023   KRYTERION, Inc. and KRYTERION, Limited - All Rights Reserved.   K KRYTERION™

Figure 1-3. *Registering for the exam*

Scroll down until you find the Google Cloud Certified Professional Cloud Network Engineer (English) exam in the list as indicated in Figure 1-4. You will see a "Buy Exam" blue button. In my case, since I am already certified the button is unavailable. Click the "Buy Exam" button.

Google Cloud Certified - Professional Cloud Network Engineer (English)	This is the Google Cloud Certified - Professional Cloud Network Engineer exam. Please refer to the exam guide for current topics that may appear on the exam. You may attempt an exam at a test center or online and each attempt regardless of delivery method or language counts toward the total permissible attempts and the waiting period between attempts still applies (see our Retake Policy).		*multiple*	
Google Cloud Certified - Professional Cloud Network Engineer (English)	Pre-requisites:: Retake Policy :		Onsite Proctored	USD 200.00
Google Cloud Certified - Professional Cloud Network Engineer (English)	Pre-requisites:: Retake Policy :		Remote Proctored	USD 200.00

Figure 1-4. *Selecting the exam*

You will be asked whether you want to take the exam at a test center (Onsite Proctored) or online at home (Remote Proctored). Select your preferred choice.

Regardless of where you will take the exam, you will need to present a government-issued identification (ID) before you start your exam.

If you will take your exam online at your home, you will also need a personal computer or a mac that has a reliable webcam and Internet connection and a suitable, distraction-free room or space where you will be taking your exam.

■ **Tip** If you take your exam online, make sure you use your own personal computer or mac to take the exam. Do not attempt to take the exam using your company's laptop or a computer in the office. This is because a company-owned computer typically uses a VPN (virtual private network) client and software to provide an extra layer of protection to prevent corporate data exfiltration. This software generates issues with the software you need to download and install in order to take your exam.

Depending on your selection, the next screen asks you to select a test center location as indicated in Figure 1-5.

Receipts   **Register For An Exam**   My Assessments   Home

Choose options below to narrow down the list of testing centers displayed.

Country: United States	Province/State: Kentucky	City: All	OR
Postal Code [ ] Range 10 miles			Search

Select the Testing Center where you wish to take the test.

AVAILABLE TESTING CENTERS

	Testing Location Name	Address	City	Province/State	Country	Map	Important Location Information
☐	Ashland Community and Technical College	1400 College Drive, Goodpaster Bldg Room G101	Ashland	Kentucky	United States	Map	⊖
☐	Southcentral Kentucky Community and Tech College	1127 Morgantown Road, KATI Campus	Bowling Green	Kentucky	United States	Map	⊖
☐	Elizabethtown Community & Technical College	610 College Street Road, Assessment Center, Room 129RPC	Elizabethtown	Kentucky	United States	Map	⊖
☐	Gateway Community and Technical College	500 Technology Way	Florence	Kentucky	United States	Map	⊖
☐	Northern Kentucky University Testing Services	1 Nunn Drive, 101 University Center	Highland Heights	Kentucky	United States	Map	⊖
☐	Jefferson Community and Technical College	110 W. Chestnut St, Chestnut Hall, Room 301	Louisville	Kentucky	United States	Map	⊖

Figure 1-5. *Selecting a test center*

Upon selecting a test center, you will be prompted to choose the date and time of your exam, agree to the Google Cloud's certification terms and conditions, and acknowledge your selections as indicated in Figure 1-6.

Figure 1-6. *Selecting date and time*

Finally, you will be directed to check out where you will pay your exam fee ($200 plus taxes).

Rescheduling and Cancellation Policy

If you need to make any changes to your scheduled exam date or time, you need to log in to your Webassessor account and click Reschedule or Cancel next to your scheduled exam.

For onsite exams scheduled at a testing center, a late rescheduling or cancellation fee is applied if you update your registration less than 72 hours before your scheduled exam start time.

For online proctored exams taken remotely, a late rescheduling or cancellation fee is applied if you update your registration less than 24 hours before your scheduled exam start time.

Exam Results

You are expected to take the exam at the scheduled place and time. After the completion of the exam, you will immediately receive a Pass/Fail result.

If you achieve a Pass result, your transcript will record the exam as **Pass**, and a few days later (it may take a week or even longer), you will receive an email confirming the result, which includes a link to a Google Cloud Perks website where you can select a gift.

If you fail, your transcript will record the exam as **Fail**, and you will also receive an email to confirm the result. Don't give up if you don't pass the exam on your first try. Review all the study materials again, taking into consideration any weak areas that you have identified after reviewing your scoring feedback, and retake the exam.

Retake Policy

If you don't pass an exam, you can take it again after 14 days. If you don't pass the second time, you must wait 60 days before you can take it a third time. If you don't pass the third time, you must wait 365 days before taking it again.

All attempts, regardless of exam language and delivery method (onsite or online testing), count toward the total permissible attempts, and the waiting period between attempts still applies. Circumventing this retake policy by registering under a different name or any other means is a violation of the Google Cloud Exam Terms and Conditions and will result in a denied or revoked certification.

Summary

In this chapter, we covered all the areas that will help prepare you for the Google Professional Cloud Network Engineer certification exam. We provided an overview of the exam content and the type of questions you will find on the exam. We explained how to access free training resources from Google Cloud and how to sign up for a free tier Google Cloud account. The free tier account will allow you to gain hands-on experience working with Google Cloud.

The next chapter will provide an introduction to the Google Cloud networking capabilities and services to get you started on your Google Cloud Network Engineer learning journey.

CHAPTER 2

■ ■ ■

Designing, Planning, and Prototyping a Google Cloud Network

Like in a data center, computers are physically interconnected with cables, and data are transmitted across the network(s) using bridges, repeaters, switches, and routers; in the cloud, the compute elements of your workload—for example, Compute Engine instances (commonly known as virtual machines—VMs), Google Kubernetes Engine (GKE) nodes, Cloud Run container instances, App Engine instances—are also interconnected, but using a different technology, that is, *software-defined networking*.

Software-defined networking (SDN) is an approach to networking that uses software-based controllers or application programming interfaces (APIs) to communicate with underlying hardware infrastructure and direct traffic on a network.

The key difference between SDN and traditional networking is infrastructure: SDN is software-based as suggested by its name, while traditional networking is hardware-based. Because the control plane is software-based, SDN is much more flexible than traditional networking. As a result, SDN allows administrators to control the network, change configuration settings, provision resources, and increase network capacity—all from a centralized user interface, without the need for more hardware.

In this chapter, you will be introduced to the building blocks of a network in Google Cloud.

We will start by addressing the overall network architecture, which is intended to help you answer your "why" questions. Every aspect of the Google Cloud network(s) that you will architect, design, build, and maintain must tie to one (or more) of the areas covered in the overall network architecture. These areas include high availability, fault tolerance, security, performance, cost, and others.

Then, you will learn how to design a Google Cloud network and how to pick and choose each component based on your workloads' requirements and the preceding areas.

Next, you will learn how to apply these concepts to the design of hybrid and multi-cloud networks, which are prevalent nowadays. The Google Cloud network connectivity products will be introduced, and their applicability and scope will be explained with a number of reference architectures.

Finally, container networking will be presented, and you will see how Google Cloud provides native networking capabilities that address most of the container networking concerns.

Designing an Overall Network Architecture

The most important component of your network architecture in the Google Cloud Platform (GCP) is the *Virtual Private Cloud* (VPC).

A VPC is a virtual version of a physical network. Unlike other public clouds, VPC networks are global resources, that is, a single VPC can span multiple regions without communicating over the public Internet. This means you can connect and manage resources distributed across the globe from a single Google Cloud project. You can also create multiple, isolated VPC networks in a single project (Figure 2-1).

© Dario Cabianca 2023
D. Cabianca, *Google Cloud Platform (GCP) Professional Cloud Network Engineer Certification Companion*, Certification Study Companion Series, https://doi.org/10.1007/978-1-4842-9354-6_2

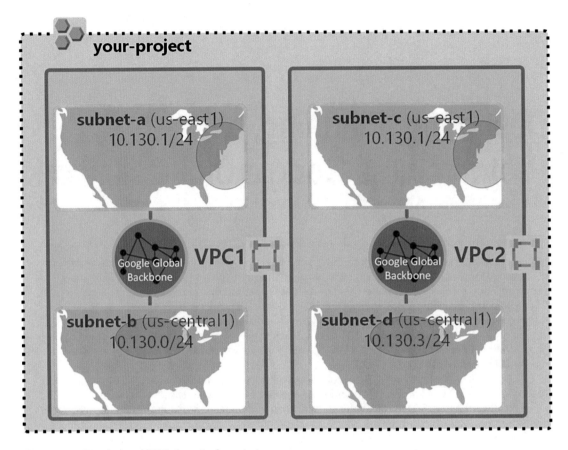

Figure 2-1. *Two isolated VPCs in a single project*

VPC networks themselves do not define IP address ranges. Instead, each VPC network is comprised of one or more partitions called *subnets*. Each subnet in turn defines one or more IP address ranges. Subnets are regional resources; each subnet is explicitly associated with a single region.

All compute resources of your workload rely on a VPC network's routing capabilities for communication. The VPC connects—by default—the resources to each other. Additionally, the VPC can be connected to other VPCs in GCP, on-premises networks, or the Internet. However, this external form of communication does not happen by default. You have to explicitly configure it.

The design of your overall network architecture is the result of your workload business and technical requirements:

- Do you need zonal, regional, or global (multi-regional) redundancy for the resources (e.g., compute, storage, etc.) in your workload?

- Are high performance and low latency must-have characteristics of your workload?

- Does your workload use sensitive data that must be protected in transit, in use, and at rest?

- Does your workload need to operate in a hybrid environment (i.e., some components of your workload are located on-premises—in your data center—other components are located in GCP, and others might even be located in other public clouds)?

- What's your trade-off between cost and the other nonfunctional requirements earlier?

The following sections provide the rationale behind the architectural decisions you need to make when you design your network in GCP.

High Availability, Failover, and Disaster Recovery Strategies

Two key factors in designing the network architecture of your workload are resilience and high availability. The network architecture of your workload will vary if your workload serves during peak time a few dozen concurrent requests originating from a single region, as opposed to several thousand concurrent requests from multiple regions with an expected 99.99% availability and very low-latency response (e.g., submilliseconds).

In the former scenario, you will not need to worry about multi-regional failover because one of your business requirements states your visitors originate from a single region. In the latter scenario, multi-regional failover and a selection of highly performant cloud services will be required to meet the requirements of global, high availability as well as low latency.

To learn how to design your workload overall network architecture for resilience—disaster recovery—and high availability, we need first to introduce a few terms.

Disaster Recovery

Disaster recovery (DR) is a key element of a business continuity plan, which involves a set of policies and procedures to enable the recovery of vital technology infrastructure and systems following a natural or a human-induced disaster.

High Availability

High availability (HA) is a characteristic of a system which aims to ensure an agreed level of operational performance, usually uptime (i.e., availability), for a higher than normal period.

Service Level Indicator

A Service Level Indicator (SLI) is a metric which is used to quantify an important aspect of your workload level of service.

Availability is one of the most used SLIs and is defined as the fraction of the time that a service is usable, for example, 99%.

Durability is another common SLI, which indicates the probability that data will be retained over a long period of time.

Other examples of SLIs include

- **Request latency**: Indicates how long it takes to return a response to a request.

- **Error rate**: Fraction between erroneous requests and all requests received.

- **System throughput**: Typically measured in requests per second. The measurements are often aggregated: that is, raw data is collected over a measurement window and then turned into a rate, average, or percentile.

Service Level Objective

A Service Level Objective (SLO) is a target value or range of values for a service level that is measured by an SLI. A natural structure for SLOs is thus

$$\text{lower bound} \leq \text{SLI} \leq \text{upper bound}$$

Recovery Time Objective

Recovery Time Objective (RTO) is a time objective which denotes the maximum tolerable length of time that your workload can be offline. This value is usually defined as part of a larger service level agreement (SLA). For example, an RTO equal to 60 minutes indicates that according to your business continuity plan, your workload must be back online within 60 minutes after a major incident causing your workload to go offline has occurred.

Recovery Point Objective

Recovery Point Objective (RPO) is another time objective which denotes the maximum tolerable length of time during which data might be lost from your workload due to a major incident. For example, an RPO equal to five minutes indicates that according to your business continuity plan, you can afford to lose up to five minutes of data in order for your workload to operate in an acceptable way.

The smaller your RTO and RPO values are (i.e., the faster your workload must recover from an interruption), the more your workload will cost to run, as illustrated in Figure 2-2.

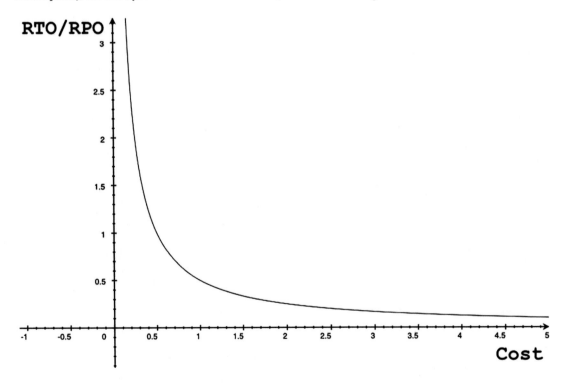

Figure 2-2. *Recoverability cost based on RTO/RPO*

Architecting Your Network for Resilience and High Availability

Now that you are familiar with basic Site Reliability Engineering (SRE) terms, let's see how your workload requirements are mapped to SLOs and how SLOs can be used to define the topology of your network.

The requirements your workload need to fulfill will ultimately translate into one or more SLOs. SLOs are a means to define thresholds—a lower bound and an upper bound for a given SLI, for example, availability, which are intended to determine whether a service is deemed to perform in an acceptable manner with respect to a given metric.

Once your SLOs are defined, for example:

- Availability > 99.99%

- RTO < 4 hours

- RPO < 2 hours

- Request latency < 100 milliseconds

your job as a network engineer is to guide the architecture team in the selection of the appropriate Google Cloud network services that will help you meet your workload SLOs. While traditional network designs focus on techniques to improve the availability of single components at a time, cloud-native designs focus instead on the composition of components—network services being some but not all of them—to achieve your workload SLOs.

Composition is important because without it, your workload availability cannot exceed that of the GCP products it uses; in fact, unless your application never fails, it will have lower availability than the underlying GCP products.

Figure 2-3 shows how you choose the GCP services you need to consider to meet your workload availability and disaster recovery requirements.

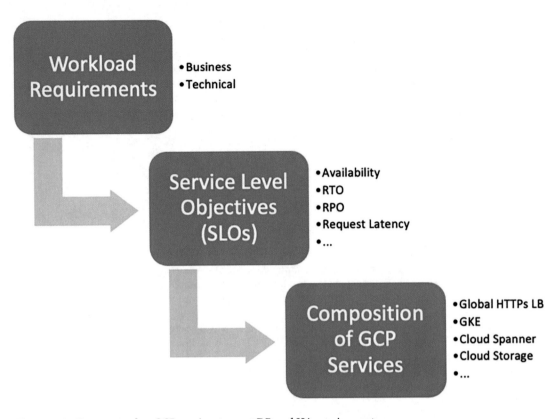

Figure 2-3. *Process to select GCP services to meet DR and HA requirements*

You may be wondering how do you select which GCP services you need to use in order to meet your workload SLOs? To answer this question, you need to understand how the availability SLI is related to zones and regions. Google Cloud generally designs products to deliver the levels of availability for zones and regions (Table 2-1).

Table 2-1. *Availability design goals for zonal and regional GCP services*

GCP Service Locality	Examples	Availability Design Goal	Implied Downtime
Zonal	Compute Engine, Persistent Disk	99.9%	8.75 hours/year
Regional	Regional Cloud Storage, Replicated Persistent Disk, Regional Google Kubernetes Engine	99.99%	52 minutes/year

As a result, the selection of the GCP services for your workload is based upon the comparison of the GCP availability design goals against your acceptable level of downtime, as formalized by your workload SLOs.

For example, if your workload has an availability SLO greater than 99.99%, you'll probably want to exclude zonal GCP services because zonal GCP services are guaranteed an availability of 99.9% only, as indicated in Table 1-1.

While best practices on how to architect a workload for resilience, high availability, and performance on GCP are out of the scope of this book, it is important that you understand how your workload SLOs—RPO, RTO for DR, and availability for HA—drive the selection and the composition of GCP services in order to meet your workload business and technical requirements.

Figure 2-4 illustrates how GCP compute, storage, and network services are broken down by locality (zonal, regional, multi-regional).

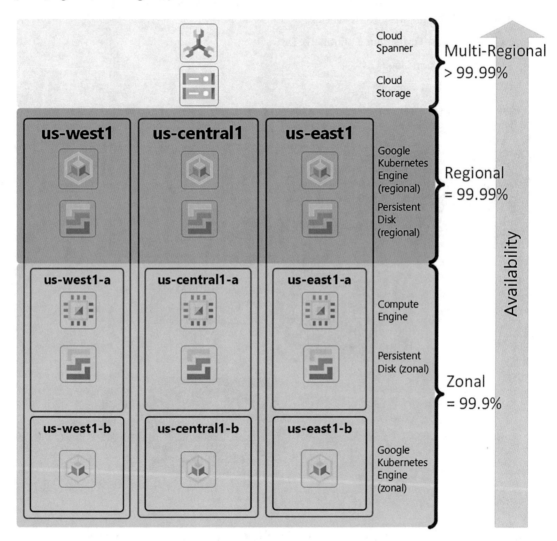

Figure 2-4. *Breakdown of main GCP services by locality*

For further details, refer to https://cloud.google.com/architecture/disaster-recovery.

DNS (Domain Name System) Strategy

In a hybrid topology comprised of resources deployed on-premises and one or more public clouds, DNS records for internal (RFC 1918) resources often need to be resolved across environments. On-premises DNS records are usually administered using an authoritative DNS server, such as BIND in UNIX/Linux environments or Active Directory in Microsoft Windows environments.

The DNS strategy of your workload overall network architecture revolves around where you want the resolution of your DNS internal records to occur:

- On-premises using your authoritative DNS servers

- On GCP using Cloud DNS

- Both (hybrid approach)

Figure 2-5 shows the tasks you need to complete to execute an effective DNS strategy for your workload overall network architecture.

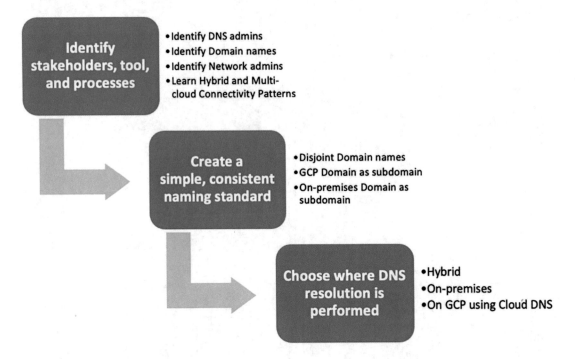

Figure 2-5. *DNS strategy process*

Using Hybrid DNS Resolution with Two Authoritative DNS Systems

This is the preferred approach with two authoritative DNS systems, as illustrated in Figure 2-6:

- Authoritative DNS resolution for your private Google Cloud environment gcp. dariokart.com is accomplished by Cloud DNS.

- Authoritative DNS resolution for your on-premises environment corp.dariokart.com is hosted by existing DNS servers on-premises.

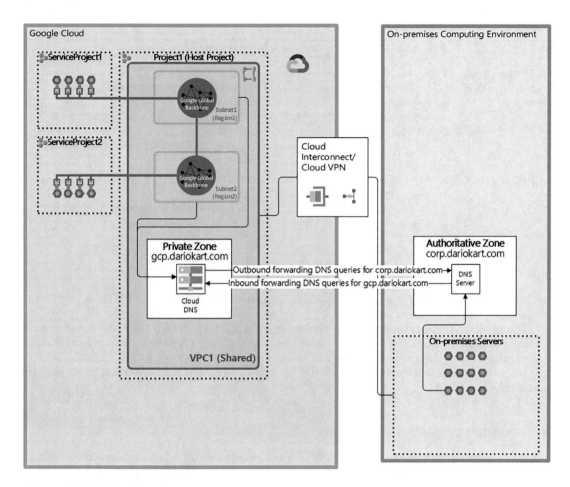

Figure 2-6. *Hybrid DNS resolution*

Using Nonhybrid DNS Resolution

Alternatively, you can either use your existing on-premises DNS authoritative server to resolve all your DNS records or move the resolution to GCP using Cloud DNS.

Whether your DNS authoritative server is located on-premises or on GCP, this approach is suboptimal. Table 2-2 explains why.

Table 2-2. *DNS resolution on-premises vs. GCP*

DNS Resolution	Advantage(s)	Disadvantage(s)
On-premises (your authoritative DNS server)	• Fewer changes • Leverages existing tools • Uses deny lists to filter individual DNS requests on-premises	• DNS requests from GCP have higher latency • Dependency with on-premises for DNS operations • Difficult to integrate "elastic" compute resources • Incompatibility with Dataproc and other services
GCP (Cloud DNS)	• No need to maintain HA DNS server on-premises • Centralized logging and monitoring with Cloud DNS	• DNS requests from on-premises have higher latency • Requires a reliable connection to your VPC network for name resolution

Security and Data Exfiltration Requirements

Another factor that you need to account for in designing an overall network architecture for your workload is the protection of your workload sensitive data.

Security controls need to be enforced to prevent unauthorized identities (e.g., users or service accounts) from accessing your workload sensitive data. These may be in the form of perimeter controls, Identity and Access Management (IAM) controls, or your workload-specific security controls.

In this section, you will learn what you need to do in order to effectively prevent exfiltration of sensitive data from your workload.

VPC Service Perimeter

With a VPC *service perimeter*, you can lock down GCP services similar to how firewalls protect your VMs.

Since any GCP service can be consumed in the form of one or more REST (Representational State Transfer) API calls (HTTP requests), by limiting access to who can consume the APIs for which GCP service, you are essentially establishing a *logical* perimeter for GCP service access. With a VPC service perimeter, you can force one or more GCP APIs to be accessed only by a limited number of authorized GCP projects.

Any API request coming from entities outside the service perimeter is unauthorized and will result in a 403 HTTP Status Code—Forbidden.

This approach is an effective way to mitigate the risk of data exfiltration because constraints are introduced at the data (the object containing sensitive information), the API (the action or the verb to act on the data), and most importantly the actor (or the subject), that is, the identity who is attempting to exfiltrate the data.

Figure 2-7 illustrates some of the most common use cases where data exfiltration can be prevented by using a VPC service perimeter. More details will be covered in the next chapters.

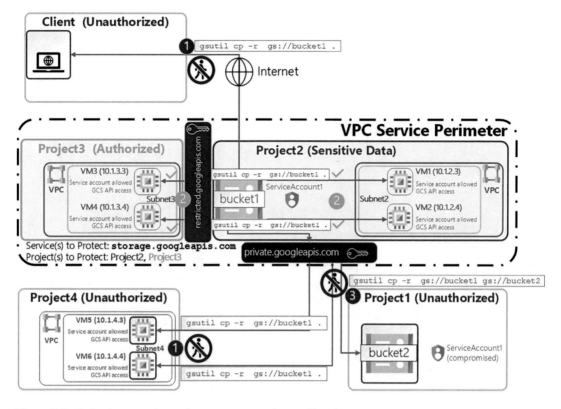

Figure 2-7. *Enforcing a service perimeter to prevent data exfiltration*

These are

1. Access from the Internet or from unauthorized VPC networks

2. Access from authorized VPC networks to GCP resources (e.g., VMs) in authorized projects

3. Copy data with GCP service to service calls, for example, from bucket1 to bucket2

Load Balancing

Just like a VPC is a software-defined network, which provides routing among its components, a cloud load balancer is a software-defined, fully distributed managed service. Since it is not hardware-based, you don't have to worry about managing a physical load balancing infrastructure.

A load balancer distributes inbound traffic across multiple compute elements of your workload—that is, backends. By spreading the load, a load balancer reduces the risk that your workload experiences performance issues.

Figure 2-8 illustrates an example of a logical architecture of a load balancer, where the specific backends are VMs (Compute Engine instances), Google Kubernetes Engine (GKE) clusters, and Google Cloud Storage buckets. Notice how the interaction from the load balancer frontend and its backends is mediated by a *backend service* component, whose intent is to decouple the load and direct it to a given backend.

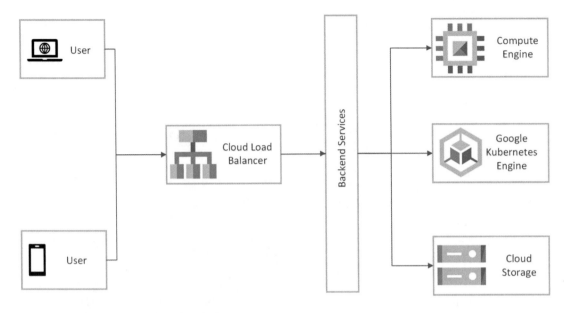

Figure 2-8. *Overview of a cloud load balancer*

In designing an overall network architecture, another important decision you need to make is whether *cost* or *performance*—you can't have both; otherwise, you need to revise your requirements with your stakeholders—are key factors as directed by your workload requirements.

Load balancing is part of a group of GCP network services. The service itself comes in different flavors depending on how important cost or performance is relevant to your workload.

In this section, we will describe how cost and performance impact the selection of the load balancer that best suits your workload requirements. Chapter 5 will provide all the necessary details you need to know to implement a performant, resilient, modern, cost-effective, and secure load balancing solution for your workload.

Unlike other public cloud providers, GCP offers *tiered* network services.

As illustrated in Figure 2-9, the *premium tier* leverages Google's highly performant, highly optimized, global backbone network to carry traffic between your users and the GCP region where the frontend services of your workload's load balancer are located—in our example *us-central1*. The public Internet is only used to carry traffic between the user's Internet Service Provider (ISP) and the closest Google network ingress point, that is, Google Edge Point of Presence (PoP).

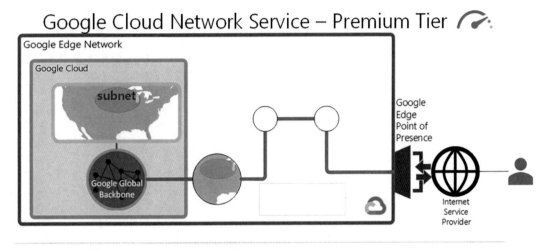

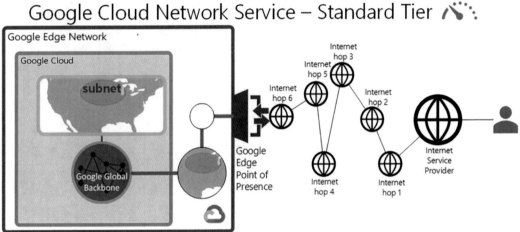

Figure 2-9. *Network service tiers overview*

Conversely, the *standard tier* leverages the public Internet to carry traffic between your workload GCP services and your users. While the use of the Internet provides the benefit of a lower cost when compared to using the Google global backbone (premium tier), choosing the standard tier results in lower network performance and availability similar to other public cloud providers.

Think of choosing between premium and standard tiers as booking a rail ticket. If cost is your main concern and travel time is not as important, you should consider traveling with a "standard" train that meets your budget. Otherwise, if travel time is critical and you are willing to pay extra, you should consider traveling with a high-speed train, which leverages state-of-the-art high-speed rail infrastructure, that is, premium tier.

21

Table 2-3 shows a comparison between the two network tiers.

Table 2-3. GCP network tiers at a glance

Category	Premium Tier	Standard Tier
Performance	High performance, low latency	Lower performance, higher latency
Cost	Varies by region (egress only is charged)	Lower cost
Network Services Locality	Global, e.g., global load balancers (single VIP (Virtual IP Address) with backends in multiple regions)	Regional (one VIP per region)
Service Level	Global SLA	Regional SLA

As explained, the rationale about choosing premium tier instead of standard tier for your load balancer (and other network services) is mainly driven by performance and cost.

If performance and reliability are your key drivers, then you should opt for a load balancer that utilizes the premium tier.

If cost is your main driver, then you should opt for a load balancer that utilizes the standard tier.

The decision tree in Figure 2-10 will help you select the network tier that best suits the load balancing requirements for your workload.

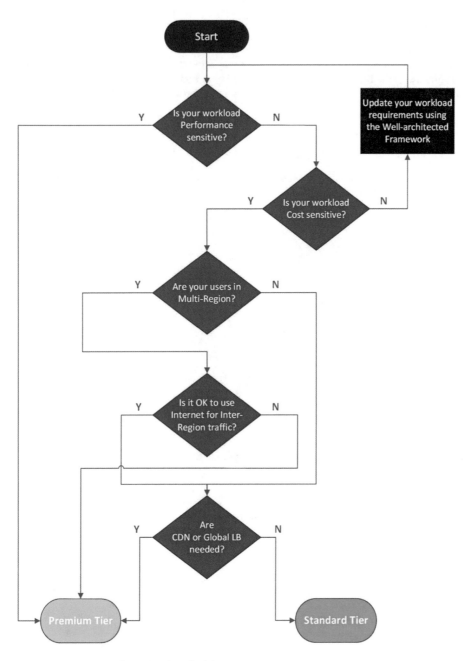

Figure 2-10. *Network service tiers decision tree*

Applying Quotas per Project and per VPC

One of the drivers that helps shape your workload overall network architecture is definitely cost. Cost is everywhere: you pay for infrastructure (physical or virtual), you pay for software (commercial off the shelf or do-it-yourself), and you pay for the life cycle of your software and your infrastructure.

One of the benefits of the cloud is that you can limit the cost of your resource usage by specifying quotas.

Container Networking

Containers have been around for a while. As a developer, containers give you the benefit of *portability* by allowing you to package your workload and its dependencies as a small unit (in the order of MB) or container.

Google Cloud allows you to deploy your containers using one of these three container services (Figure 2-11).

Google
Kubernetes
Engine

Cloud Run

Compute
Engine

Figure 2-11. *GCP container services*

You choose your container service that best fits your workload business and technical requirements based on how much infrastructure you are willing to manage. The goal is to reduce time-to-market, with fast and agile delivery of products and services for your workload, then let GCP manage and scale the containers for you using Cloud Run, which is a managed serverless compute platform for containers.

Conversely, if your business and technical requirements compel you to exercise more control on your container infrastructure, then Google Kubernetes Engine (GKE, i.e., managed Kubernetes service) or Google Compute Engine (you manage all the container infrastructure and the workloads running in your containers) are options to consider.

GKE sits in the middle between Cloud Run and Google Compute Engine. As a result, it provides the right mix of manageability and network controls you need in order to properly design your workload network architecture.

In this section, we will focus on GKE, and we will address some of the architectural choices you will need to make when designing an overall network architecture for your workload.

Google Kubernetes Engine

As the inventor of Kubernetes, Google Cloud offers a fully managed Kubernetes service, which takes care of scheduling and scaling your containers while monitoring their health and state. We will assume the reader has a basic knowledge of containers and container orchestration using Kubernetes. The infographic in Figure 2-12 provides an overview of the key Kubernetes constructs using GKE and how they relate to each other from a network perspective.

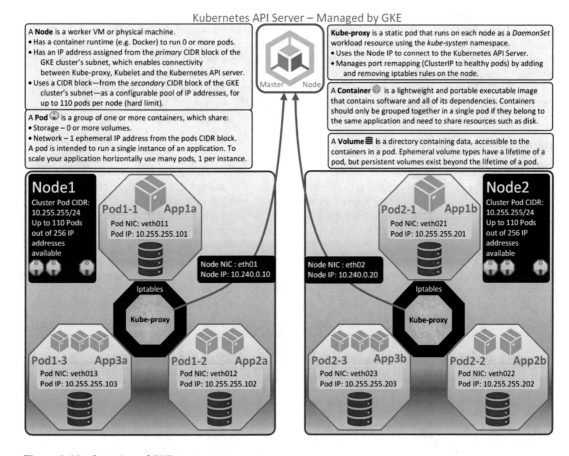

Figure 2-12. *Overview of GKE components*

Planning IP Address Allocation for Services, Pods, and Nodes

So, you chose to use GKE as compute service for your workload, and you also understood at a high level what its components do and how they interact with each other. Now, the question is how do you design your workload overall network architecture using GKE? And, most importantly, where do you start?

As always, your workload business and technical requirements will drive the design of your workload architecture. And, just like for an *Infrastructure as a Service* approach, where you start from a predefined number of VMs, which will scale in and out (horizontally) or up and down (vertically) based on expected demand, with GKE you will also need to size your cluster.

Kubernetes has introduced the construct of a *Horizontal Pod Autoscaler* (HPA) to manage horizontal scaling of your workload.

■ **Note**   To learn more about HPA, use the official Kubernetes reference: `https://kubernetes.io/docs/tasks/run-application/horizontal-pod-autoscale/`.

As per the preceding Kubernetes documentation, an HPA *automatically scales the number of pods in a replication controller, deployment, replica set, or stateful set based on observed CPU utilization (or, with custom metrics support, on some other application-provided metrics)*. This shifts your focus on properly planning for expansion (or reduction) of your pods, thereby addressing the problem of exhausting the IP address originally allocated to your pods.

One of the best practices to properly plan IP allocation for your pods, services, and nodes is to use VPC-native clusters, which as of the writing of this book are enabled by default.

Using VPC-Native Clusters

GKE clusters are very dynamic systems. Pods and their constituents (e.g., containers, volumes, etc.) are ephemeral entities, which are created, scheduled, consumed, and ultimately terminated by Kubernetes during its orchestration process. Any pod in a cluster is designed to be able to communicate with any other pod in the cluster (without Network Address Translation (NAT)), whether it be in the same node or in a different node that belongs to your GKE cluster. As your cluster scales out in response to high demand, new pods are created and new routes are consumed, thereby rapidly approaching the quota per project.

When the *route quota* is reached, just like for other quotas GCP returns a "quota exceeded" error message.

With VPC-native clusters, you no longer need to worry about running out of route quotas in response to scaling, nor do you need to worry about running out of IP addresses for your pods and services.

This is because in a VPC-native cluster, pod and service IP addresses are reserved in the VPC network *before* the pods are created in your cluster.

In VPC-native clusters, IP ranges are allocated in accordance with the following scheme:

- Nodes use the subnet's primary IP range, which is required at creation time.

- Pods use one of the subnet's secondary IP ranges.

- Services use another secondary IP range.

All these three IP ranges must be disjoint, that is, they cannot overlap. You have the option to let GKE manage them for you, when you create your cluster, or you can manage them yourself.

Finally, with VPC-native clusters, your pods and services are more closely integrated with your VPC network than using route-based clusters. This allows for advanced VPC capabilities like shared VPC, container-native load balancing, and many others. Let's touch base on container-native load balancing and why this capability is relevant to your workload's overall network architecture. We will learn in detail how the other capabilities work in the upcoming chapters.

Using Container-Native Load Balancing

Your workload compute elements constitute what is commonly known as a *backend*, which is a component of your architecture responsible for serving incoming requests. These may be in the form of HTTPS requests, TCP requests, or requests using other protocols. If your workload serves HTTP or HTTPS traffic, container-native load balancing is definitely a "bonus" that you can—and should—benefit from when using VPC-native clusters. Let's see why.

In the enterprise world, a frontend system is often placed in front of your backends to ensure incoming requests for a service are equally distributed across each compute element of your backends, whether they be VMs (Compute Engine instances in GCP) or pods in a GKE cluster.

Traditional load balancing capabilities were provided in GKE on a per-node (VM) basis. This was due to the fact that traditional load balancers didn't have a way to recognize pods. In the absence of a way to recognize and group pods as a backend, the load balancer used a *managed instance group* (MIG) to group VMs. Kubernetes ingress objects in GKE leveraged the managed instance group as backend and used an HTTPS load balancer to perform load balancing to nodes in the cluster.

■ **Note** To learn more about ingress, use the official Kubernetes reference: `https://kubernetes.io/docs/concepts/services-networking/ingress/`.

Iptable rules programmed on each node routed requests to the pods. This approach was effective for small clusters serving a limited number of incoming requests, but it turned out to be inefficient for larger clusters due to suboptimal data paths with unnecessary hops between nodes.

As new nodes (VMs) were added in response to increasing incoming requests, the load balancer attempted to equally distribute the load across the nodes. However, if connections were heavily reused (e.g., HTTP/2), then requests were served by older nodes. As a result, a number of pods remained underutilized, while others became overutilized. This imbalance scenario was caused by a mismatch between connections and requests, as illustrated in Figure 2-13.

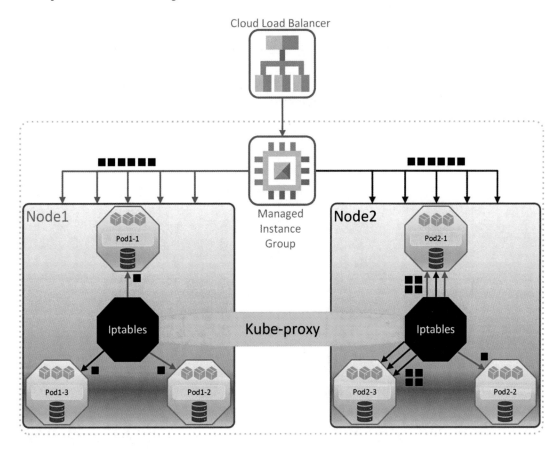

Figure 2-13. *Traditional container load balancing*

There are two ways to address this issue:

- **Complex**: Ensure connections are recycled periodically; however, even after recycling your requests periodically, the load balancer will still have to use iptables to access the pods.

- **Simple**: Use container-native load balancing.

With container-native load balancing, an abstraction layer *network endpoint group* (NEG) is introduced to efficiently mediate the interaction between the load balancer and the cluster pods. This is because a network endpoint group is fully integrated with the Kubernetes ingress controller running on GKE, thereby eliminating the need of Iptables. As a result, the HTTPS load balancer has direct visibility to the pods in your GKE cluster, allowing for

- Accurate load balancing

- Accurate health checks (because pods are sending their health information to the load balancer directly)

- No double-hop traffic (because iptables are no longer needed)

- Visibility and traceability (because the load balancer has direct visibility to the pods, not just the nodes)

Figure 2-14 shows how container-native load balancing leverages the network endpoint group construct to accurately balance incoming HTTP(S) traffic directly to pods instead of VMs.

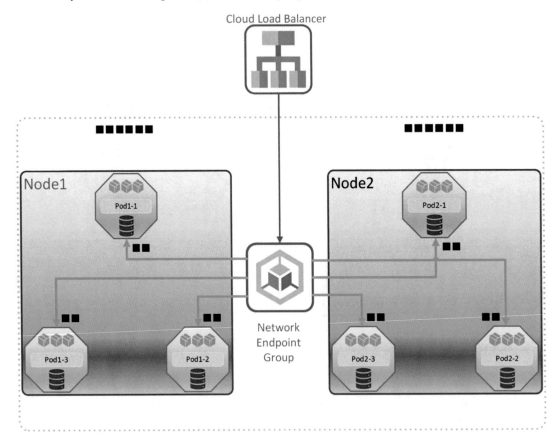

Figure 2-14. *Container-native load balancing*

SaaS, PaaS, and IaaS Services

The cloud compute model you choose is another factor that can impact the design of your workload overall network architecture. The infographic in Figure 2-15 will help you decide when one model is more suitable than another based on velocity (e.g., time-to-market) or flexibility.

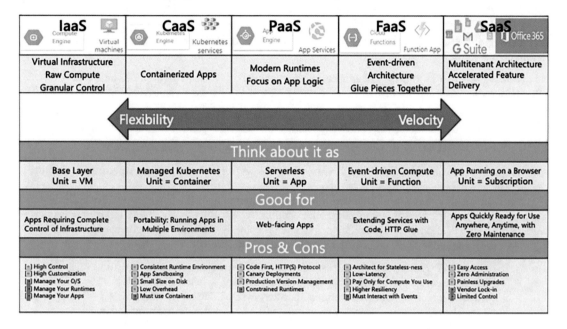

Figure 2-15. *Overview of cloud compute models*

Designing Virtual Private Cloud (VPC) Instances

A VPC is a logical isolation of a section of your cloud and is the cloud equivalent of a traditional network that you would build in your data center, but with the extremely important benefit of running on infrastructure *highly optimized* for

- Scale

- Performance

- Reduced network cost

A Google Cloud VPC uses state-of-the-art network infrastructure, which gives you access to the highly optimized and highly available *Google global backbone.*

The Google global backbone enables billion-user services like google.com (search), Gmail, Google Maps, YouTube, and many more.

Table 2-4 shows how a Google Cloud VPC is different from other public cloud providers' VPCs.

Table 2-4. *GCP Virtual Private Cloud differentiating capabilities*

Global Features	Shareable Features	Private Features
Single VPC across multiple regions	Single VPC for an entire organization, isolated within projects	Private access to Google APIs and services
No cross-region VPNs required	Firewall rules, routes, VPNs configured once	VPC Service Controls for enhanced perimeter security
No peering of regional VPCs required	RFC 1918 IP address space managed centrally	No need for public IP addresses to access Google APIs and services

VPC Specifications

A VPC is intended to be a *logical routing domain*, which allows implicit connectivity among any compute resource hosted in one of its partitions or *subnets*.

A compute resource can be a VM (also known as a Compute Engine instance), a pod in a GKE cluster, an App Engine flexible environment instance, or any other GCP product built using VMs. From now on, we will use the terms "VM" and "Compute Engine instance" or simply "instance" interchangeably.

VPCs are designed in accordance with the following specifications:

1. **Global**: VPCs are global resources, that is, they can span across multiple regions. VPCs are composed of a number of IP range partitions—denoted by CIDR blocks—which are known as subnets. The acronym "CIDR" stands for *Classless Inter-domain Routing*. More information on CIDR block notation is provided in the following section.

2. **Regional subnets**: Subnets are regional resources, that is, a subnet is limited to one region.

3. **Firewall rules**: Traffic to and from compute resources (e.g., VMs, pods) is controlled by firewall rules, which are defined on a per-VPC basis.

4. **Implicit connectivity**: Compute resources hosted in a (subnet of a) VPC are allowed to communicate with each other by default, unless otherwise specified by a "deny" firewall rule. Implicit connectivity among compute resources in a VPC occurs using RFC 1918 IPv4 addresses. More information on RFC 1918 is provided in the following section.

5. **Implicit encryption in transit**: Not only does a VPC network provide implicit connectivity between compute resources (e.g., VMs) hosted in its subnets, but this connectivity is *automatically encrypted* for you. Put differently, VM-to-VM connections within VPC networks and peered VPC networks are automatically authenticated and encrypted at layer 3 (network layer of the OSI model). You don't have to check a box to enable encryption in transit between VMs.

6. **Private Google API access**: Compute resources in a VPC can consume Google APIs without requiring public IPs, that is, without using the Internet.

7. **IAM**: Like any other GCP resources, VPCs can be administered using Identity and Access Management (IAM) roles.

8. **Shared VPC**: An organization can use a Shared VPC to keep a VPC network in a common host project. Authorized IAM identities from other projects in the same organization can create resources that use subnets of the Shared VPC network.

9. **VPC peering**: VPCs can be securely connected to other VPCs in different projects or different organizations using VPC peering. Traffic is always encrypted and stays in the Google global backbone without traversing the Internet.

10. **Secure hybrid connectivity**: VPCs can be securely connected to your on-premises data center (hybrid connectivity) or other clouds (multi-cloud connectivity) using Cloud VPN or Cloud Interconnect. More details will be provided in Chapter 7.

11. **No multicast support**: VPCs do not support IP multicast addresses within the network. In other words, in a VPC packets can only be sent from one sender to one receiver, each identified by their IP address.

Subnets

When you create a VPC, you don't need to specify an IP range just for the VPC. Instead, you use subnets to tell which partition of your VPC is associated to which IP range. As per the VPC specifications, remember that subnets are regional resources, while VPCs are global.

■ **Note** From now on, we will be using the terms "IP range" and "CIDR block" interchangeably. For more information about CIDR block notation, refer to `https://tools.ietf.org/pdf/rfc4632.pdf`.

Each subnet must have a primary IP range and, optionally, one or more secondary IP ranges for alias IP. The per-network limits describe the maximum number of secondary ranges that you can define for each subnet. Primary and secondary IP ranges must be RFC 1918 addresses.

■ **Note** RFC 1918 is the official *Address Allocation for Private Internets* standard. In the next sections, when we discuss connectivity with respect to IP addressing, we will be using the terms "private" and "internal" interchangeably to signify RFC 1918 connectivity. While you don't need to read the whole document, section 3 is recommended (`https://datatracker.ietf.org/doc/html/rfc1918#section-3`).

For your convenience and to help you acquire more familiarity with the CIDR block IPv4 notation, a table that maps block size (number of IP addresses) to the number of blocks is shown in Figure 2-16.

Notation	# Addresses	# Blocks	a,b,c,d Assignments		Examples
a.b.c.d/32	1	4294967296			Host route
a.b.c.d/31	2	2147483648	d=2n	n=0,..,127	Point-to-point link
a.b.c.d/30	4	1073741824	d=4n	n=0,..,63	
a.b.c.d/29	8	536870912	d=8n	n=0,..,31	
a.b.c.d/28	16	268435456	d=16n	n=0,..,15	
a.b.c.d/27	32	134217728	d=32n	n=0,..,7	
a.b.c.d/26	64	67108864	d=64n	n=0,..,3	
a.b.c.d/25	128	33554432	d=128n	n=0,1	
a.b.c.0/24	256	16777216			Class C block
a.b.c.0/23	512	8388608	c=2n	n=0,..,127	
a.b.c.0/22	1024	4194304	c=4n	n=0,..,63	
a.b.c.0/21	2048	2097152	c=8n	n=0,..,31	
a.b.c.0/20	4096	1048576	c=16n	n=0,..,15	
a.b.c.0/19	8192	524288	c=32n	n=0,..,7	
a.b.c.0/18	16384	262144	c=64n	n=0,..,3	
a.b.c.0/17	32768	131072	c=128n	n=0,1	
a.b.0.0/16	65536	65536			Class B block
a.b.0.0/15	131072	32768	b=2n	n=0,..,127	
a.b.0.0/14	262144	16384	b=4n	n=0,..,63	
a.b.0.0/13	524288	8192	b=8n	n=0,..,31	
a.b.0.0/12	1048576	4096	b=16n	n=0,..,15	
a.b.0.0/11	2097152	2048	b=32n	n=0,..,7	
a.b.0.0/10	4194304	1024	b=64n	n=0,..,3	
a.b.0.0/9	8388608	512	b=128n	n=0,1	
a.0.0.0/8	16777216	256			Class A block and largest IANA block
a.0.0.0/7	33554432	128	a=2n	n=0,..,127	
a.0.0.0/6	67108864	64	a=4n	n=0,..,63	
a.0.0.0/5	134217728	32	a=8n	n=0,..,31	
a.0.0.0/4	268435456	16	a=16n	n=0,..,15	
a.0.0.0/3	536870912	8	a=32n	n=0,..,7	
a.0.0.0/2	1073741824	4	a=64n	n=0,..,3	
a.0.0.0/1	2147483648	2	a=128n	n=0,1	
0.0.0.0/0	4294967296	1			Entire IPv4 Internet and default route

Figure 2-16. *Classless Inter-domain Routing (CIDR) blocks in IPv4 notation*

IP Address Management and Bring Your Own IP (BYOIP)

VMs can have internal IP addresses or external IP addresses. The terms *internal* and *external* denote whether the VM communicates with other VMs or services using private (RFC 1918) IP addresses or the Internet, respectively.

External IP Addresses

You can assign an external IP address to a VM or a forwarding rule if the VM needs to communicate with

- The Internet

- Resources in another network (VPC)

- Services other than Compute Engine (e.g., APIs hosted in other clouds)

Resources from outside a VPC network can address a specific resource in your VPC by using the resource's external IP address. The interaction is allowed as long as firewall rules enable the connection. We will provide detailed information of firewall rules in the upcoming sections. For the time being, think of a firewall rule as a means to inspect traffic and determine whether traffic is allowed or denied based on origin, destination, ports, and protocols.

In other words, only resources with an external IP address can send and receive traffic directly to and from outside your VPC.

Compute Engine supports two types of external IP addresses:

- **Static external IP addresses**: For VMs, static external IP addresses remain attached to stopped instances until they are removed. Static external IP addresses can be either regional or global:

  - Regional static external IP addresses allow resources of that region or resources of zones within that region to use the IP address.

  - Global static external IP addresses are available only to global forwarding rules, used for global load balancing. You can't assign a global IP address to a regional or zonal resource.

- **Ephemeral external IP addresses**: Ephemeral external IP addresses are available to VMs and forwarding rules. Ephemeral external IP addresses remain attached to a VM instance only until the VM is stopped and restarted or the instance is terminated. If an instance is stopped, any ephemeral external IP addresses that are assigned to the instance are released back into the general Compute Engine pool and become available for use by other projects. When a stopped instance is started again, a new ephemeral external IP address is assigned to the instance.

Internal IP Addresses

Just like for external IP addresses, Compute Engine supports static and ephemeral internal IP addresses:

- **Static internal IP addresses**: Static internal IP addresses are assigned to a project long term until they are explicitly released from that assignment and remain attached to a resource until they are explicitly detached from the resource. For VM instances, static internal IP addresses remain attached to stopped instances until they are removed.

- **Ephemeral internal IP addresses**: Ephemeral internal IP addresses are available to VM instances and forwarding rules. Ephemeral internal IP addresses remain attached to VM instances and forwarding rules until the instance or forwarding rule is deleted. You can assign an ephemeral internal IP address when you create a resource by omitting an IP address specification in your request and letting Compute Engine randomly assign an address.

The infographic in Figure 2-17 illustrates the external and internal IP address concepts for two VPCs in the same project.

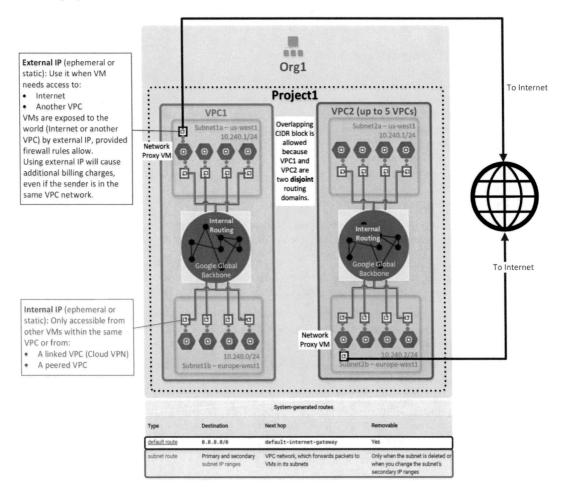

Figure 2-17. *Two VPCs in the same project connected to the Internet*

Standalone vs. Shared VPC

Another important factor you need to consider during your VPC design is how you want to enable separation of duties (or concerns).

From one side, a standalone VPC might be a reasonable option for your use case because your organization is small, with a low growth rate, and you have a central team that manages the network and the security of all your workloads.

The extreme opposite is a large organization, with high growth rate and multiple lines of businesses (LOBs), which requires a high degree of separation of duties.

In the next sections, you will learn what design considerations you need to account for to determine whether to choose a standalone or a shared VPC.

Additionally, you will learn the most common "flavors" of a shared VPC and what each flavor is best suited for.

Standalone

Start with a single VPC network for resources that have common requirements.

For many simple use cases, a single VPC network provides the features that you need while being easier to create, maintain, and understand than the more complex alternatives. By grouping resources with common requirements and characteristics into a single VPC network, you begin to establish the VPC network border as the perimeter for potential issues.

For an example of this configuration, see the single project, single VPC network reference architecture: https://cloud.google.com/architecture/best-practices-vpc-design#single-project-single-vpc.

Factors that might lead you to create additional VPC networks include scale, network security, financial considerations, compliance, operational requirements, and Identity and Access Management (IAM).

Shared

The Shared VPC model allows you to export subnets from a VPC network in a *host project* to other *service projects* in the same organization or tenant.

■ **Note**   The term "organization" dates a while back when the Lightweight Directory Access Protocol (LDAP) was invented. In this context, we use this term to denote the root node of the Google Cloud resource hierarchy. All resources that belong to an organization are grouped under its root node. We will use the terms "organization" and "tenant" interchangeably. For more information, see https://cloud.google.com/resource-manager/docs/cloud-platform-resource-hierarchy.

If your use case requires cross-organizational private connectivity, then VPC network peering is an attractive option to consider. In this section, we will focus on Shared VPC connectivity, which by definition pertains to connectivity in the context of a single organization.

With Shared VPC, VMs in the service projects can connect to the shared subnets of the host project.

Use the Shared VPC model to centralize the network administration presented when multiple teams work together, for example, the developers for an N-tier application.

For organizations with a large number of teams, Shared VPC provides an effective means to extend the architectural simplicity of a single VPC network across multiple teams.

In this scenario, network policy and control for all networking resources are centralized and easier to manage. Service project departments can configure and manage their compute resources, enabling a clear separation of concerns for different teams in the organization.

Resources in service projects can communicate with each other more securely and efficiently across project boundaries using internal (RFC 1918) IP addresses. You can manage shared network resources—such as subnets, routes, and firewalls—from a central host project, so you can enforce consistent network policies across the projects.

Multiple vs. Single

Single and multiple VPC common use cases are provided as reference architectures as follows.

Single VPC in Single Host Project

As illustrated in Figure 2-18, this initial reference architecture includes all of the components necessary to deploy highly available architectures across multiple regions, with subnet-level isolation and a 99.99% SLA (multi-regional SLA) connecting to your on-premises data centers.

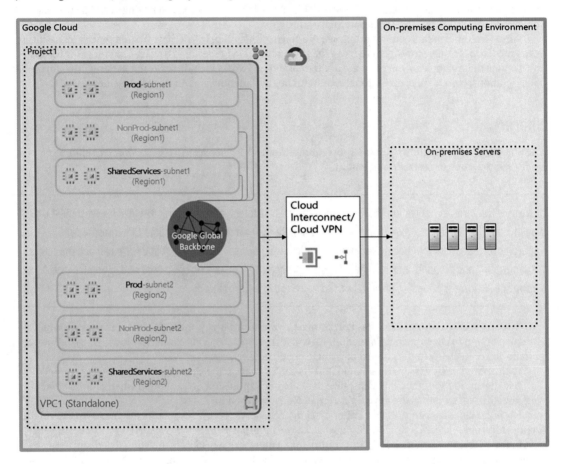

Figure 2-18. *Single VPC in a single host project*

Single Shared VPC with Multiple Service Projects

Extending the previous reference architecture, this approach lets administrators delegate administrative responsibilities—such as creating and managing instances—to service project administrators while allowing host project administrators centralized control over network resources like subnets, routes, and firewall rules.

Figure 2-19 shows an example of a single shared VPC with built-in redundancy for production, non-production, and shared services workload deployments.

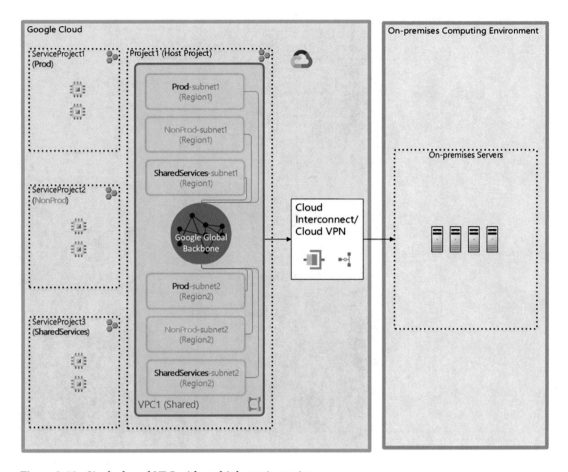

Figure 2-19. *Single shared VPC with multiple service projects*

Multiple Shared VPCs with Multiple Service Projects

In accordance with the principle of separation of duties, we can further isolate resources by creating separated, shared VPCs: one shared VPC for production and another shared VPC for non-production environments, each hosted in their own separate host project. Figure 2-20 illustrates such architecture for VPC isolation, which builds on GCP's high availability, failover, and disaster recovery strategies while separating production from non-production.

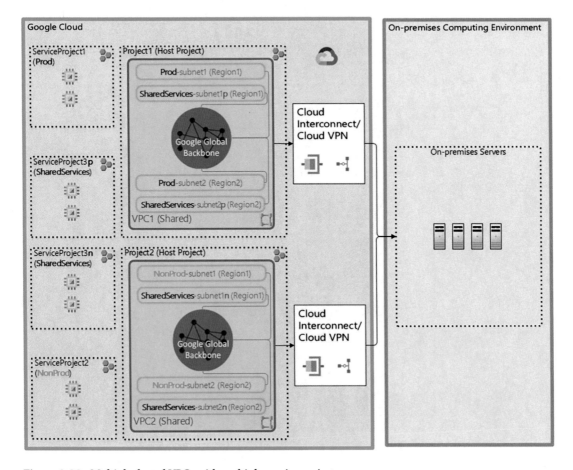

Figure 2-20. *Multiple shared VPCs with multiple service projects*

There are many reasons to consider VPC isolation, including

- Audit requirements (such as HIPAA (Health Insurance Portability and Accountability Act))

- Quota considerations between environments

- Another layer of logical isolation

Regional vs. Multi-regional

Your workload business requirements will help you determine how *resilient* your network architecture needs to be. Remember, we discussed in the "High Availability, Failover, and Disaster Recovery Strategies" section how SLIs and SLOs are derived by your business continuity and availability requirements and how these metrics (SLIs) and their respective tolerance thresholds (SLOs) help you shape the most suitable overall network architecture and the most appropriate selection of services (zonal, regional, multi-regional).

The good news is that in either scenarios, for example, highly resilient architectures (multi-regional VPCs, with multi-regional services) or lowly resilient architectures (multi-zonal, with regional services), Google Cloud has the right combination of products and services that meet your business continuity and availability requirements.

Another key factor that makes your life easier in designing VPC instances is the fact that Google Cloud VPCs are *global* resources, which by definition span multiple regions without using the Internet and—most importantly—without you having to worry about connecting them somehow (e.g., using IPsec VPN tunnels, Interconnect, or other means). This is a remarkable advantage, which will simplify your VPC network design and will reduce implementation costs.

Regarding operational costs, you need to consider that—unlike ingress—egress traffic is charged, and the amount of these charges depends on a number of factors including

- Whether traffic uses an internal or an external IP address

- Whether traffic crosses zones or regions

- Whether traffic stays within the Google Global Backbone or it uses the Internet

---

■ **Note**   For more information about VPC pricing, refer to the official Google Cloud page: `https://cloud.google.com/vpc/pricing`.

VPC Network Peering

VPC network peering allows you to extend the advantages of private (RFC 1918) connectivity beyond the boundaries of a single organization. With this model, you can design a *hub and spoke* topology where the hub hosts common core services in the same VPC, also known as the *producer VPC*. Typical core services include authentication, directory services, proxies, and others, which are cross-cutting in nature and thereby are suitable for consumption at scale across different enterprises.

The producer VPC exposes common core services to a number of consumers, which use their own VPC networks—*consumer VPCs*—and are "peered" with the producer VPC. Consumer VPCs may be hosted in their own project or even in separate organizations (tenants) from the producer VPC one.

For the sake of designing VPC networks, peering provides the unique advantage of letting you use internal IP address (RFC 1918) connectivity between peered VPCs. Traffic between peered VPCs stays in the Google Global Backbone network, that is, it does not traverse the Internet.

By using an internal IP address instead of external IP address, or VPN connectivity between your VPCs, you get the following benefits:

- **Lower latency**: Internal connectivity leverages the Google Global Backbone network, which is highly optimized for scale, performance, and cost.

- **Higher security**: No need to traverse the Internet to connect your VPCs.

- **Lower cost**: No egress charges because you are not using external IP addresses.

Typical use cases include

- **Software as a Service (SaaS)**: Cross-cutting, SaaS services can be privately exposed to a number of consumers within and across organizations.

- **Native tenant isolation**: Since VPC network peering is a *nontransitive* relation, a consumer can only access resources in the producer VPC. A consumer cannot access resources in another consumer's VPC network.

Examples

Figure 2-21 illustrates how SaaS and native tenant isolation work.

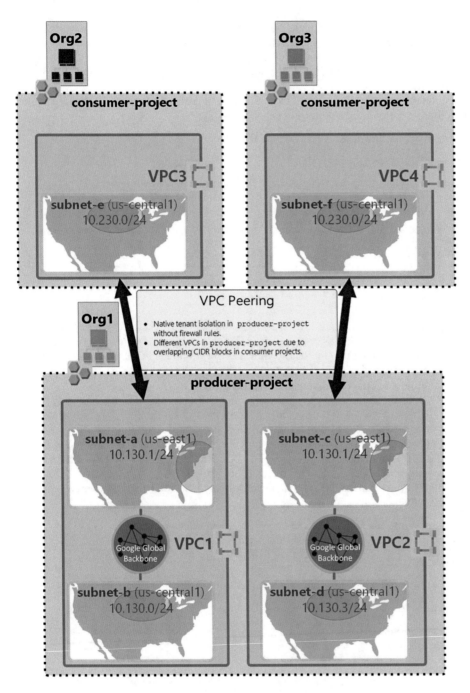

Figure 2-21. *Cross-organizational VPC network peering*

We have two consumers, each hosted in their own organization (tenant), which require the same group of SaaS services. Since the consumers have no knowledge of each other—yet they need common, cross-cutting SaaS services offered by the "blue" tenant (Org1)—in this scenario their VPCs have a subnet with an overlapping private CIDR block, that is, 10.130.1/24.

Note that this wouldn't have happened had the two consumers been part of the same tenant (or organization).

SaaS services are deployed in the producer VPCs, which are hosted in the "blue" organization (Org1).

Since the two consumers have an overlapping CIDR block, the producer project requires two VPCs. The same VPC cannot be peered with multiple consumers that use overlapping IP addresses.

The consumer in the "green" tenant (Org3) can consume SaaS services deployed in a subnet in VPC2.

Likewise, the consumer in the "red" tenant (Org2) can consume SaaS services deployed in a subnet in VPC1.

As a result, the consumer in the "green" tenant cannot access resources hosted in the "red" tenant. Conversely, the consumer in the "red" tenant cannot access resources hosted in the "green" tenant. This demonstrates the concept of native tenant isolation.

The infographic in Figure 2-22 shows a holistic view of all the constructs we reviewed so far, including IP addresses, subnets, VPCs, routes, and peered VPCs.

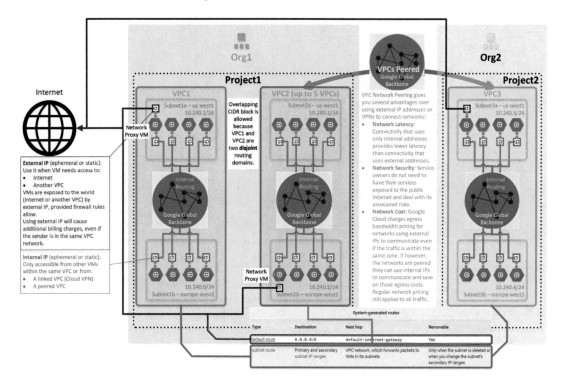

Figure 2-22. *Cross-organizational peered VPCs, with a network proxy*

The example in Figure 2-23 illustrates how VPC network peering can be used in conjunction with shared VPC. Two isolated environments (i.e., production and non-production) require common shared services, which are deployed in a producer VPC (VPC3 in Project3) and are peered with the production VPC and the non-production VPC (consumer VPCs). The consumer VPCs are two shared VPCs, which expose their subnets to a number of service projects (for the sake of simplicity, only one service project has been displayed, but the number can—and should—be greater than one).

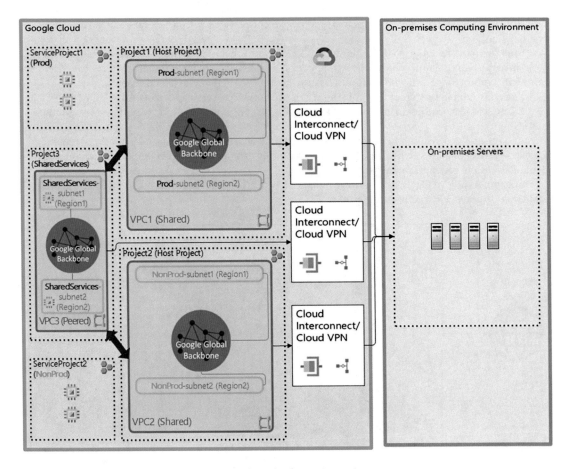

Figure 2-23. *Multiple shared, peered VPCs with multiple service projects*

This reference architecture provides the dual benefit of promoting reuse of common capabilities (e.g., common, cross-cutting, SaaS services) through VPC network peering and separating concerns through shared VPCs.

Firewalls

Similarly to your data center's DMZ (demilitarized zone), each VPC network has a built-in firewall that blocks all incoming (ingress) traffic from outside of the VPC to its VMs and compute resources (e.g., GKE pods, etc.). You can configure *firewall rules* to override this default behavior, which is designed to protect your VPC from untrusted clients in the outside world, that is, the Internet, other VPCs, or other sources located in other clouds or on-premises.

Unlike traditional DMZs—as shown in Figure 2-24—where a cluster of firewalls separates each trusted zone, GCP firewalls are *globally distributed* to allow for resilience and scalability. As a result, there are no choke points and no single point of failures. GCP firewalls are characterized by the following:

- **VPC scope**: By default, firewall rules are applied to the whole VPC network.

- **Network tag scope**: Filtering can be accomplished by applying firewall rules to a set of VMs by tagging the VMs with a *network tag*.

- **Service account scope**: Firewall rules can also be applied to a set of VMs, which are associated to a specific *service account*. You will need to indicate whether or not the service account and the VMs are billed in the same project, and choose the service account name in the source/target service account field.

- **Internal traffic**: You can also use firewall rules to control internal traffic between VMs by defining a set of permitted source machines in the rule.

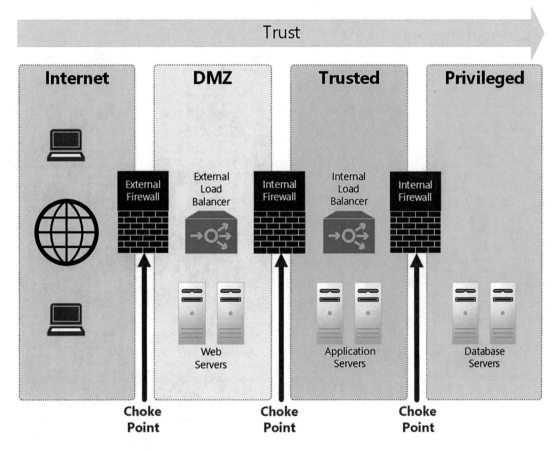

Figure 2-24. *Traditional network security architecture*

Firewall rules are a flexible means to enforce network perimeter control by using ingress/egress directions, allow/deny actions with priorities (0 highest priority, 65535 lowest priority), and an expressive way to denote your sources and targets in the form of CIDR blocks, network tags, or service accounts.

■ **Exam tip**   You cannot delete the implied rules, but you can override them with your own rules. Google Cloud always blocks some traffic, regardless of firewall rules; for more information, see blocked traffic: https://cloud.google.com/vpc/docs/firewalls#blockedtraffic.

To monitor which firewall rule allowed or denied a particular connection, see Firewall Rules Logging: https://cloud.google.com/vpc/docs/firewall-rules-logging.

Example

The example in Figure 2-25 illustrates how two firewall rules can be used to

1. Allow a Global HTTPS load balancer Front End (GFE) to access its backend, represented by a management instance group with VMs denoted by the web-server network tag

2. Deny the Global HTTPS load balancer Front End (GFE) direct access to the VMs in a database server farm, denoted by the db-server network tag

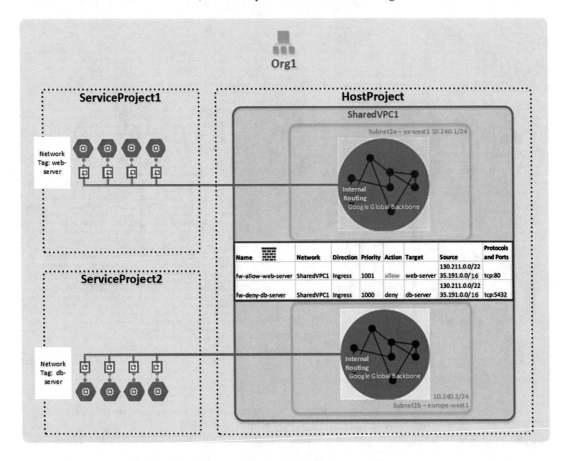

Figure 2-25. *Example of firewall rules in a multitier application*

Notice the separation of concerns achieved by using a shared VPC model, where the backend instances are billed in their own service project ServiceProject1, which is connected to the shared VPC SharedVPC1 hosted in HostProject.

Likewise, the database instances are billed in their own service project ServiceProject2, which is also connected to the shared VPC.

The host project handles the network administration of the subnets exposed to the two service projects. This includes the network security aspects, which are described by the two aforementioned firewall rules. The firewall table in the figure is deliberately extended to the width of the shared VPC to emphasize its global distribution scope, which applies to the entire VPC network.

More details about firewall configurations and how to effectively use them to secure the perimeter of your VPC will be provided in the next chapters.

Custom Routes

One common problem you need to address when designing your VPC network instances is how to link them together efficiently and securely.

In your data center, network interconnectivity requires switches, hubs, bridges, and routers, to name a few. All these hardware components need to be multiplied as the number of networks grows in response to increasing traffic. As the networks grow, the associated capital and operational costs may grow disproportionately.

Google Cloud Platform leverages *software-defined routing* to address these problems. By design, every VPC network uses a scalable, distributed, virtual routing mechanism, which is defined as a *routing table* and operates at the VPC network level, just like firewall rules.

Moreover, each VM has a *controller*, which is a built-in component aware of all the routes from the VPC routing table. Each packet leaving a VM is delivered to the appropriate next hop of an applicable route based on a routing order. When you add or delete a route, the set of changes is propagated to the VM controllers by using an eventually consistent design.

VPCs come with *system-generated* routes, which are automatically created for you by GCP and provide internal routing connectivity among its subnets using the highly performant Google Global Backbone network and egress routing connectivity to the Internet via a default Internet gateway.

■ **Note**   You still need to create an external IP address if your VMs need access to the Internet. Also, consider extra cost for traffic egressing your VMs.

Additionally, when you establish a peering connection between two VPCs, peer routes are automatically created to allow the two VPCs to communicate privately (RFC 1918).

Finally, for any other scenarios where system-generated or peer routes are not suitable to meet your workload requirements—for example, hybrid or multi-cloud workloads—GCP allows you to create your own custom routes. These can be of type *static* or *dynamic*. The former type (static route) supports a predefined number of destinations and is best suited for simple network topologies that don't change very often. The latter type (dynamic route) leverages a new resource, that is, *Cloud Router*, which is intended to add and remove routes automatically in response to changes. Cloud Router leverages the Border Gateway Protocol (BGP) to exchange routes with a peer of a BGP session. More information will be provided in the next chapter.

Figure 2-26 summarizes the different types of routes.

Route Category	Route Type	Next Hop	Notes
System-generated	Default	default-internet-gateway 0.0.0.0/0 for IPv4 ::/0 for IPv6	Applies to the whole VPC. You can delete the default route **to completely isolate your network from the internet.**
	Subnet	VPC Forwards packets to VMs and internal load balancers (ILBs) in the VPC	Applies to the whole VPC. Created automatically.
Custom	Static	Valid static route next hop: 1. next-hop-gateway, i.e. default-internet-gateway 2. next-hop-instance, i.e. a VM's hostname and zone 3. next-hop-ilb, i.e. the IP address of an Internal Load Balancer 4. next-hop-address, i.e. the internal primary IP address of a VM 5. next-hop-vpn-tunnel, i.e. VPN Gateway's hostname and region	Consider using next-hop-ilb instead of next-hop-instance or next-hop-address for reliability as an ILB uses health checks to route packets to healthy VMs. **VMs are zonal resources.** If next hop refers to a VM in another region, egress cost and latency are added.
	Dynamic	Peered BGP session on a **Cloud Router**	Routes are added and removed *automatically* by Cloud Routers in your VPC. **Destinations always represent CIDR blocks outside your VPC**, received from a peered BGP.
Peer	Subnet	Peered VPC Forwards packets to VMs and internal load balancers (ILBs) in the peered VPC	No Overlapping subnet IP ranges between two peered VPCs.
	Custom	Next hop in the peered VPC network	Custom static or custom dynamic route in a network connected using VPC Network Peering.

Figure 2-26. *Route types*

Designing a Hybrid and Multi-cloud Network

Unless you work in a startup, or your IT department is mature enough to have executed (or is in the process of executing) a program to successfully migrate all your workloads to the cloud, the infrastructure that makes your workload run is likely located in a number of data centers. These may be owned (or leased) by your company or a public cloud provider. These data centers ideally should be geographically distributed in the proximity of your customers.

Because workloads, infrastructure, and processes are unique to each company, a hybrid strategy must be adapted to specific needs. As a result, the terms *hybrid cloud* and *multi-cloud* are sometimes used inconsistently.

Within the context of GCP, the term hybrid cloud denotes a setup in which common or interconnected workloads are deployed across multiple computing environments, one hosted in a public cloud and at least one being private in your data center, that is, *on-premises.*

The term multi-cloud denotes setups that combine at least two public cloud providers, including potentially private computing environments.

Figure 2-27 shows the difference between hybrid and multi-cloud topologies.

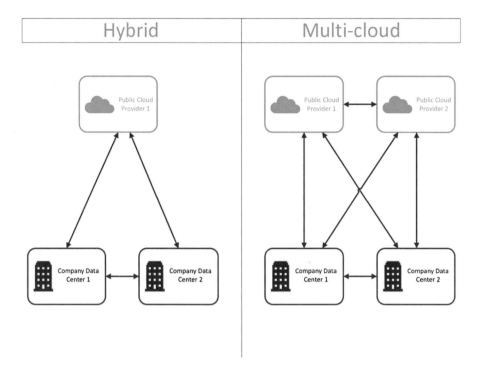

Figure 2-27. *Comparison between hybrid and multi-cloud topologies*

Notice how connectivity is allowed between public cloud providers in a multi-cloud topology. An example is Cloud VPN, which can be configured to establish IPsec tunnels between GCP and Amazon Web Services. You will learn more about Cloud VPN in the upcoming sections.

Drivers for Hybrid and Multi-cloud Networks

A hybrid or multi-cloud topology is rarely a goal in itself, but rather a means of meeting business requirements. Choosing the right hybrid or multi-cloud topology therefore requires first clarifying these requirements.

Business Requirements

Common requirements and drivers from the business side include

- Reducing capex or general IT spending

- Increasing flexibility and agility to respond better to changing market demands

- Building out capabilities, such as advanced analytics services, that might be difficult to implement in existing environments

- Improving quality and availability of service

- Improving transparency regarding costs and resource consumption

- Complying with laws and regulations about data sovereignty

- Avoiding or reducing vendor lock-in

Development Requirements

From a development standpoint, common requirements and drivers include

- Automating and accelerating workload rollouts to achieve faster *time-to-market* and shorter cycle times

- Leveraging APIs and services to increase development velocity

- Accelerating the provisioning of compute and storage resources

Operational Requirements

Common requirements and drivers to consider from the operations side include

- Ensuring consistent authentication, authorization, auditing, and policies across computing environments

- Using consistent tooling and processes to limit complexity

- Providing visibility across environments

Architectural Requirements

On the architecture side, the biggest constraints often stem from existing systems and can include

- Dependencies between workloads

- Performance and latency requirements for communication between systems

- Dependencies on hardware or operating systems that might not be available in the public cloud

- Licensing restrictions

Overall Goals

The goal of a hybrid and multi-cloud strategy is to meet these requirements with a plan that describes

- Which workload should be run in or migrated to each computing environment

- Which pattern to apply across multiple workloads

- Which technology and network topology to use

Any hybrid and multi-cloud strategy is derived from the business requirements. However, how you derive a usable strategy from the business requirements is rarely clear. The workloads, architecture patterns, and technologies you choose not only depend on the business requirements but also influence each other in a cyclic fashion. The diagram represented in Figure 2-28 illustrates this cycle.

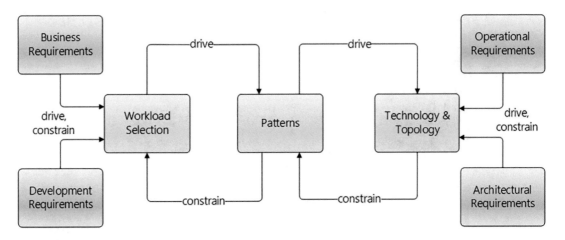

Figure 2-28. *Workload refinement cycle*

Designing a Hybrid and Multi-cloud Strategy

There is no *one-size-fits-all* approach that allows you to meet the business requirements for all the workloads in your enterprise.

Instead, you need to pursue a methodical approach, which starts by defining a clear vision of your future (computing environment) state and progressively selects the relevant, common characteristics of the workloads that are deemed as the "best fits" to be migrated or rearchitected for GCP. These common, relevant characteristics are called *patterns* and are used to derive the network topologies for the "best fits." The topologies will be further refined based on workload priorities.

The natural progression of this approach is illustrated in Figure 2-29. Keep in mind that this is not intended to be a prescriptive way to create your hybrid and multi-cloud strategy. Rather, it allows you to get started and think about your computing environment's current and future states along with a well-defined path on how to get there.

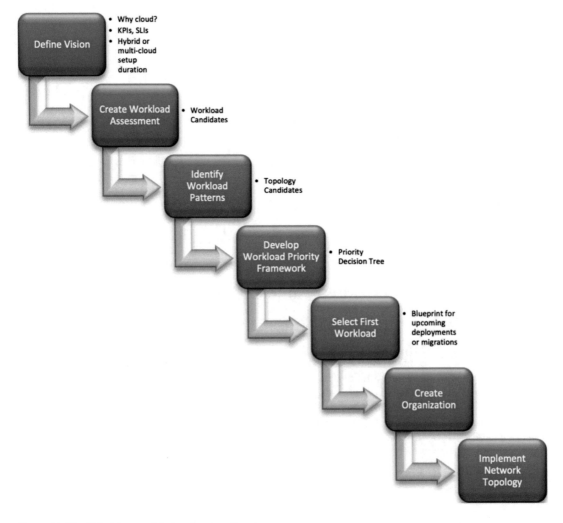

Figure 2-29. *Hybrid vs. multi-cloud rationalization process*

So, you've done your research using the rationalization process we just described and determined that some of your workloads—for the time being—need to operate in a hybrid (or multi-cloud) network. Now what?

Assuming you already have created your organization in GCP, the next step is to *implement* your hybrid (or multi-cloud) network topology, and to do that, you need to decide how your company's on-premises data center(s) will connect to GCP.

GCP offers a number of options, and the choice you need to make depends on

- **Latency**: For example, do you need high availability and low latency (e.g., < 2 milliseconds) for your workload?

- **Cost**: For example, is cost a priority, or are you willing to pay more for lower latency, stronger security, and better resilience?

- **Security**: For example, do you need to fulfill security requirements due to compliance?

- **Resilience**: For example, how resilient does your workload need to be?

In the upcoming sections, we will review these design options in detail, emphasizing the trade-offs you will need to make when choosing one vs. the other.

The visual illustrated in Figure 2-30 will serve as a reference. Don't worry about understanding each concept just yet. At the end of the section, it will all make sense. Chapter 7 will cover the implementation details for each solution in depth.

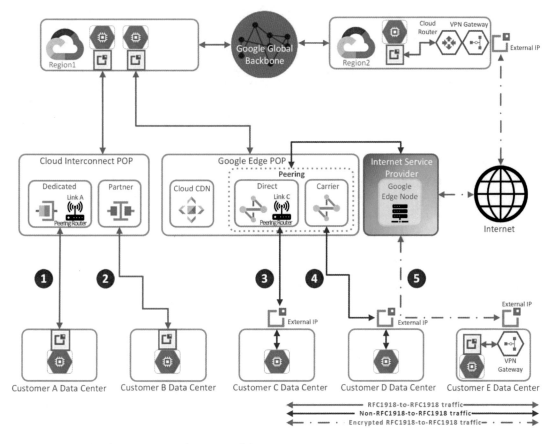

Figure 2-30. *Hybrid connectivity reference model*

Dedicated Interconnect vs. Partner Interconnect

If your workload requires low latency and private-to-private address connectivity (i.e., RFC 1918 IP address space for all its components), then Cloud Interconnect is the option for you.

A typical use case could be the migration to the cloud of an application used *internally* in your company. The users are company employees, internal to your company's organization. Due to regulatory requirements, some components—for example, some database and the hardware security module (HSM)—cannot be migrated to GCP. Other components instead, for example, the frontend and some APIs, can be migrated.

A key factor in this use case is the fact that this application is internal, that is, all users will access the application from the company's network (e.g., RFC 1918 IP address space) or its extension to GCP. No access from the Internet or other external networks is allowed.

Another key factor is the fact that you need fast connectivity between your company's data center and GCP to effectively leverage the HSM in order to authenticate users and authorize their access to the requested resource.

With Cloud Interconnect, traffic between your on-premises computing environment and GCP does not traverse the Internet. Instead, a physical link connects your company's data centers to a Google Point of Presence (PoP), which is your entry point to the closest region and the Google Global Backbone network.

This link can be directly installed or facilitated by a service provider.

In the former scenario—Dedicated Interconnect, solution 1—customer A's network must physically meet the Google Global Backbone network entry point in a supported colocation facility, also known as a Cloud Interconnect PoP. This means customer A's peering router will be installed in the Cloud Interconnect PoP in order to establish the physical link, which comes in two flavors, that is, 10 Gbps or 100 Gbps pipes.

In the latter scenario—Partner Interconnect, solution 2—customer B uses a service provider to connect to the Google Global Backbone network. This may be for a number of reasons, for example, cost, that is, customer B is not willing to lease space in the colocation facility and maintain networking equipment. Instead, customer B would rather use a *managed* service provided by a partner.

■ **Note** Cloud Interconnect does not encrypt traffic. To help secure communication between workloads, consider using Transport Layer Security (TLS).

Direct vs. Carrier Peering

Now, imagine the application we used before grows in popularity and needs to be upgraded to support external users, who will access it from the Internet. This new use case will require internal access from your company's network and external access from the Internet.

We learned that with Cloud Interconnect internal users can access the application from the company's network, all of them using RFC 1918 IP address space. What about external users who need access from the Internet? This is where *peering* comes into play.

With a peering connection, your non-RFC 1918 workloads—that is, workloads whose components need to expose or consume public endpoints—are designed to be as close as possible to your customers. As a result, you deliver a better customer experience because your customers experience low latency and fast recoveries from component failures (better resilience).

Peering is similar to Cloud Interconnect in that your on-premises resources are connected to GCP without traversing the Internet.

However, with peering your hybrid application is connected a step closer to your external users because the link established between your company's network and the entry point (also known as exchange or cloud onramp) to the Google Global Backbone occurs in a Google Edge PoP, which is one of the many locations worldwide where Google connects to the Internet.

■ **Note** On the Internet, every network is assigned an autonomous system number (ASN) that encompasses the network's internal network infrastructure and routes. Google's primary ASN is 15169.

There are two ways a network can connect to Google without using RFC 1918 IP addresses:

1. **IP transit**: Buy services made available by an Internet Service Provider (ISP), which is connected to Google (ASN 15169).

2. **Peering**: Connect directly to Google (ASN 15169) in one of the Google Edge PoPs around the world.

As you can imagine, peering offers lower latency because you avoid the ISP mediation. Therefore, if your workload requires high-throughput, low-latency, non-RFC 1918 connectivity, then peering is your best choice.

Just like Interconnect, peering comes in two flavors, direct and carrier.

Direct peering is best suited when your company already has a footprint in one of Google's PoPs, for example, it already uses a Dedicated Interconnect circuit.

Carrier peering is best suited when your company chooses to let a carrier manage a peering connection between its network and GCP.

In our reference model, solutions 3 and 4 show how customers C and D connect to GCP using direct and carrier peering, respectively.

IPsec VPN

Both Interconnect and peering leverage connectivity between your company's data centers and a GCP PoP without using the Internet. This is a great benefit in terms of performance and security. By using a dedicated communication channel, whether directly or using a carrier, you avoid extra hops while minimizing the chances of data exfiltration.

However, this comes at the expense of high costs. As of the writing of this book, a 10 Gbps circuit price is $2.328 per hour using Dedicated Interconnect. A 100 Gbps circuit price is $18.05 per hour. Additionally, you need to account for costs related to VLAN (Virtual Local Area Network) attachments (which is where your traffic exchange link is established), as well as egress costs from your VPCs to your company's data centers on-premises.

If you are looking for a more cost-effective solution for your private-to-private workloads and are willing to sacrifice performance and security for cost, then a virtual private network (VPN) IPsec tunnel is the way to go.

GCP offers a service called Cloud VPN, which provides just that. With Cloud VPN, your on-premises resources can connect to the resources hosted in your VPC using a tunnel that traverses the Internet. RFC 1918 traffic is encrypted and routed to its RFC 1918 destination via a router on-premises and a router on GCP.

If you need resilience in addition to cost-effectiveness, GCP offers a highly available VPN solution, called HA VPN, which comes with 99.99% uptime.

A complete setup of an HA VPN will be covered in Chapter 7.

Bandwidth and Constraints Provided by Hybrid Connectivity Solutions

Architecting your hybrid solution can be a daunting task. This is because, by definition, *hybrid* means grouping things of a different type into one and, most importantly, making them work together, which can be the hard part when multiple technologies and teams are involved.

One thing to remember is that a hybrid network architecture is rarely your future state architecture. Rather, a hybrid topology is a part of a transitional architecture. Put differently, it is an architecture that—for the time being—will be good enough to meet your workload(s) business and technical requirements: it will get you there, but it is not your future state architecture, which should be developed using a *cloud-native* approach.

■ **Note** What does "cloud-native" really mean? There is not a definitive answer, but a general consensus instead. If you want to learn my understanding of "cloud-native," see www.linkedin.com/pulse/cloud-native-api-driven-approach-coding-dna-dario-cabianca/.

Nevertheless, GCP provides a number of hybrid and multi-cloud network connectivity products, and your job as a GCP network engineer is to help your company's network engineering team pick and choose which product best suits your company's short- and long-term visions.

The decision tree in Figure 2-31 can help you determine the first selection of GCP network connectivity products that fit your workload network requirements.

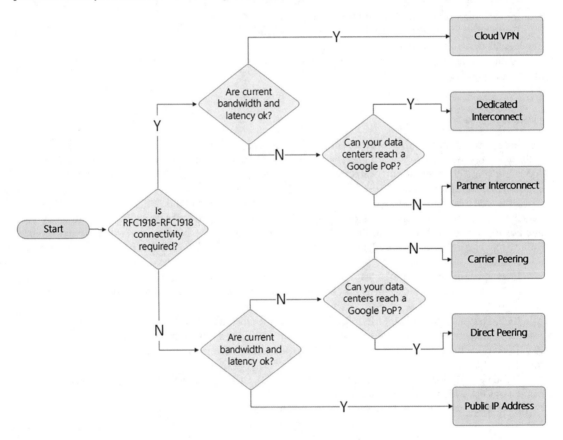

Figure 2-31. *GCP hybrid connectivity product decision tree*

Depending on the specifics of your workload's network requirements, you might end up using a combination of products.

A detailed comparison among them is displayed in Figure 2-32.

Google Cloud Hybrid and Multi-cloud Network Connectivity Products

	Public IP Address	Cloud VPN	Direct Peering	Carrier Peering	Dedicated Interconnect	Partner Interconnect
RFC1918-to-RFC1918 connectivity	No	Yes	No	No	Yes	Yes
SLA	• Internet: No SLA • Service Provider (last-mile) SLA	• Internet: No SLA • GCP: >=99.99% HA VPN or >=99.9% Classic VPN • Service Provider (last-mile) SLA	More info at: https://peering.google.com/#/options/peering	More info at: https://peering.google.com/#/options/peering	GCP: >=99.9% or >=99.99% based on regional or multi-regional design	• GCP: >=99.9% or >=99.99% based on regional or multi-regional design • Partner SLA
Bandwidth	Depends on Service Provider	Each IPsec tunnel: • =< 3-Gbps (sum of ingress and egress)	10 or 100-Gpbs	Depends on Partner's services availability	Each Connection: • 1x, …, or 8x 10-Gbps • 1x, or 2x 100-Gbps	Each VLAN attachment: • 50-Mbps to 50-Gbps (Max) based on Partner's availability
Security	Traffic traverses the Internet	Traffic traverses the Internet, but is encrypted between VPN endpoints	Direct physical connection to Google	Indirect physical connection to Google (via Partner)	• Traffic does not traverse the Internet • Direct physical connection to Google	• Traffic does not traverse the Internet • Indirect physical connection to Google (via Partner)
Cost	External IP Address cost	• Cloud VPN cost (does not reduce egress cost) • On-premises VPN cost	• Direct Peering cost • Co-location fees and routing hardware	• Carrier Peering cost • Partner fees	• Dedicated Interconnect cost • Co-location fees and routing hardware	• Partner Interconnect cost • Partner fees
Support	• Internet: none • Service Provider support	• Internet: none • Service Provider (last mile) support • GCP: based on support package	Peering technical requirements must be met	Peering technical requirements must be met	GCP: based on support package	Partner support
Delay, Jitter, Packet loss	Internet-dependent	Internet-dependent	Depends on GCP, and On-premises network performance	Depends on GCP, On-premises, and Partner network performance	Depends on GCP, and On-premises network performance	Depends on GCP, On-premises, and Partner network performance

Figure 2-32. *GCP hybrid connectivity product comparison*

Cloud Router

Cloud Router was briefly presented in the "Custom Routes" section, when the definition of *dynamic route* was introduced. In this and the upcoming sections, we will learn more about this product and why it represents an integral component of your multi-cloud and hybrid strategy.

First and foremost, let's summarize a few important concepts we already know about Virtual Private Cloud (VPC) networks and how a Google Cloud VPC is different from other public cloud providers' VPC networks.

VPC Routing

A VPC is a logical routing domain, because

1. *By design, it provides internal routing connectivity between all its subnets in any region.*

2. Internal connectivity means RFC 1918 IP addressing, that is, traffic stays within the Google Global Backbone and does not traverse the Internet.

3. *A VPC lives within one (and one only) project*, which represents a container you use for billing, securing, and grouping the Google Cloud resources for your workload.

4. *A project may have more than one VPC.* In this case, the VPCs within your project are completely **disjoint** from each other, and their subnets might even have overlapping CIDR ranges, as shown in Figure 2-33. Still, they wouldn't be able to connect to each other—unless you choose to do so (e.g., using an IPsec VPN tunnel and a NAT to disambiguate the overlapping CIDR ranges).

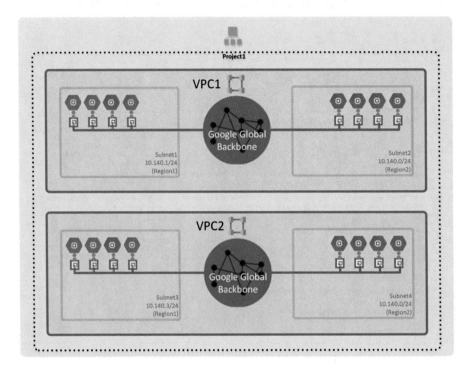

Figure 2-33. *Two VPCs in the same project with overlapping CIDR 10.140.0/24*

Cloud Router Overview

Cloud Router is a fully managed, distributed, software-defined service, intended to advertise custom dynamic routes among autonomous systems (AS) using the Border Gateway Protocol (BGP).

■ **Note** An autonomous system (AS) is defined as a connected group of one or more IP prefixes run by one or more network operators, which has a **single** and **clearly defined** routing policy (`https://datatracker.ietf.org/doc/html/rfc1930#section-3`).

The goal of a Cloud Router is twofold. A Cloud Router exports internal routes outside its VPC. Conversely, a Cloud Router imports external routes inside its VPC, based on information exchanged with its BGP peer. The BGP peer can be located in Google Cloud, on-premises, or in another cloud.

An important Cloud Router's feature is that its behavior is controlled by a property of the VPC where it lives, that is, the *dynamic routing mode* property. As we will learn later, if the VPC operates in *global* dynamic routing mode, then all its Cloud Routers advertise to their BGP peers subnet routes from subnets in all regions spanned by the Cloud Routers' VPC.

In contrast, Cloud Routers in a VPC configured with *regional* dynamic route mode are limited to advertising only subnet routes from subnets in the same region of the Cloud Routers.

Figure 2-34 demonstrates this concept by showing how CloudRouter1 in GCP's Region1 advertises routes from Region1 and Region2 to its on-premises PeerRouter1 counterpart and how it imports routes from PeerRouter1 related to the two on-premises data centers.

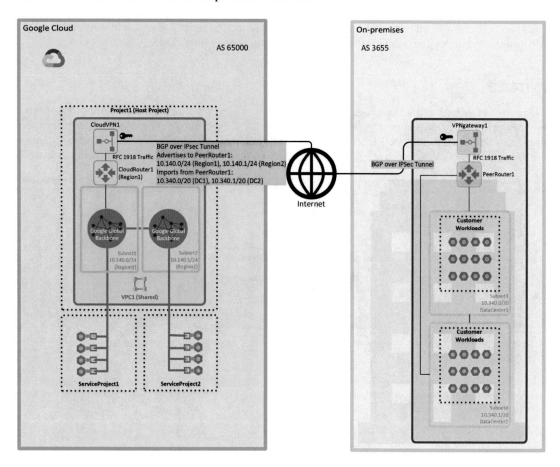

Figure 2-34. *Cloud Router in a VPC configured with global dynamic routing*

Multi-cloud and Hybrid Topologies

Connecting your company's data centers to GCP and other clouds in a secure, performant, and reliable manner is key to any successful hybrid and multi-cloud deployment. The choice of what hybrid and multi-cloud topology you use has a direct impact on the ability of your workloads to meet their business and technical requirements.

■ **Note**   The term "topology" derives from the Greek words *topos* and *logos*, which mean "locus" (i.e., the place where something is situated or occurs) and "study," respectively. Therefore, in the context of network engineering, a topology is a blueprint for networks, whose logical or physical elements are combined in accordance with a given pattern.

In the next sections, we will review a few hybrid and multi-cloud network topologies, which will help you execute your workload migration or modernization strategy. The term "private computing environment" will be used to denote your company on-premises data centers or another cloud.

Mirrored

In a mirrored topology, as the name suggests, you mirror your cloud computing environment into your private one. Notice in Figure 2-35 how your workload infrastructure is located in its own shared VPC, which is separated from its automation components (CI/CD (Continuous Integration/Continuous Deployment) pipelines). These are located in another VPC, which connects to your private computing environment using RFC 1918 IP space.

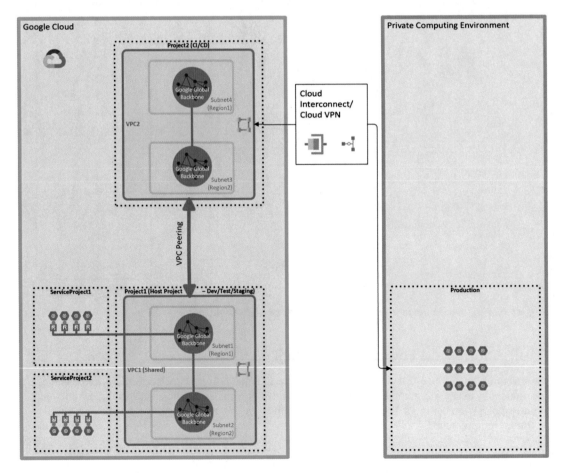

Figure 2-35. *Reference architecture for mirrored topology*

Eventually, the production network will "relocate" to a VPC in Google Cloud when the migration of your workload is completed.

Meshed

A meshed topology is the simplest way to extend your network from your company's data center(s) into Google Cloud or from another public cloud provider. The outcome of this topology is a network that encompasses all your computing environments, whether they be in Google Cloud, on-premises, or in other clouds.

This topology is best suited when your hybrid or multi-cloud workloads require private addressing (RFC 1918 IP addresses), cross-environment connectivity.

The design in Figure 2-36 shows an example of a meshed topology that connects a Google Cloud VPC (VPC1) to a VPC in another cloud (VPC2) by leveraging a Dedicated Cloud Interconnect link.

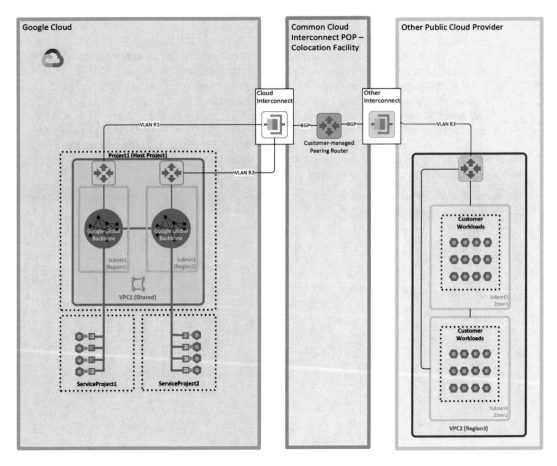

Figure 2-36. *Design of a meshed topology using Dedicated Interconnect*

Let's point out a few important details specific to this design:

1. A peering router must be physically installed in a common Cloud Interconnect Point of Presence (PoP) facility and configured with two local address links:

    a. A link to Google Cloud

    b. A link to the desired public cloud provider

2. You (the customer) are responsible for installing, configuring, and maintaining the peering router. A similar design is available for Partner Interconnect connectivity, whereas the partner manages the router, and the router can be virtualized.

3. Make sure VPC1 and VPC2 have no overlapping CIDRs. Otherwise, a NAT (Network Address Translation) router will be required.

4. A VLAN attachment is a construct that tells your Cloud Router which VPC network can be reached through a BGP session. Once a VLAN attachment is associated to a Cloud Router, it automatically allocates an ID and a BGP peering IP address, which are required for your peering router (in the common Cloud Interconnect PoP facility) to establish a BGP session with it. If your VPC is configured with *global dynamic routing*, any Cloud Router in the VPC automatically advertises to your peering router (over a BGP session) the VPC subnets that are in other regions. Put differently, this setup (global dynamic routing) is a cost-effective way to interconnect your multi-cloud VPCs because you only need one Cloud Router in your VPC, which leverages the Google Global Backbone to advertise to its counterpart—that is, the peering router—*all routes for all* subnets located in any region of your VPC.

An alternative design is to leverage a virtual private network (VPN) IPsec tunnel to connect VPC1 and VPC2 as illustrated in Figure 2-37.

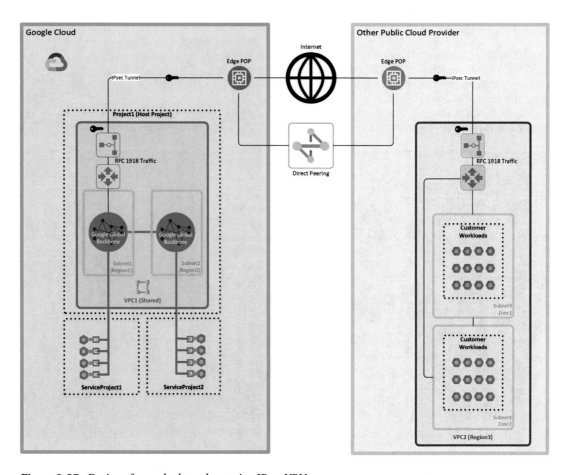

Figure 2-37. *Design of a meshed topology using IPsec VPN*

As you learned before, a key difference between Interconnect and IPsec VPN is that the latter uses the Internet or direct peering as a communication channel.

As a result, a secure tunnel between the two clouds must be established in order to ensure authentication, confidentiality, and integrity of the data exchanged between the components of your multi-cloud workload. This is where Cloud VPN and its counterpart peer VPN gateway in the other public cloud provider come into play.

The two VPN gateways need to expose a public IP address in order to communicate over the Internet (or direct peering), and they also need to be configured to establish a security association between them. A security association may include attributes such as cryptographic algorithm and mode, traffic encryption key, and parameters for the network data to be passed over the connection. More details about this setup will be provided in Chapter 7.

Additionally, if VPC1 has been configured to use global dynamic routing mode, only one Cloud Router is needed. In the other public cloud provider, you should expect one VPN gateway per region.

Gated Egress

A gated topology is intended to privately expose APIs to your workloads.

With a *gated egress* topology, you want to expose APIs to your GCP workloads, which act as consumers. This is typically achieved by deploying an API gateway in your private computing environment to act as a *façade* for your workloads within.

Figure 2-38 displays this setup, with the API gateway acting as a façade and placed in the private computing environment, whereas the consumers are GCP VMs hosted in service projects of a shared VPC.

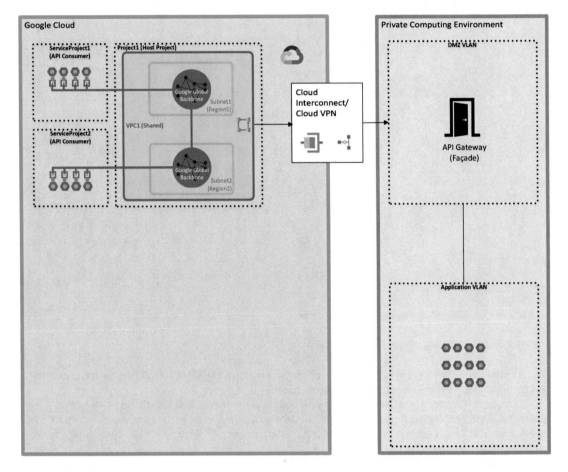

Figure 2-38. *Reference architecture for gated egress topology*

All traffic uses RFC 1918 IP addresses, and communication from your private computing environment to GCP (i.e., ingress with respect to GCP) is not allowed.

Gated Ingress

Conversely, a *gated ingress* topology is intended to expose APIs to your private computing environment workloads, which act as consumers.

As illustrated in Figure 2-39, this time the API gateway is deployed in GCP and consists of a group of VMs (or virtual network appliances), each equipped with two network interfaces:

1. **eth0**: Connected to a Transit VPC, which receives incoming RFC 1918 traffic from the private computing environment

2. **eth1**: Connected to a Shared VPC, where your workloads operate

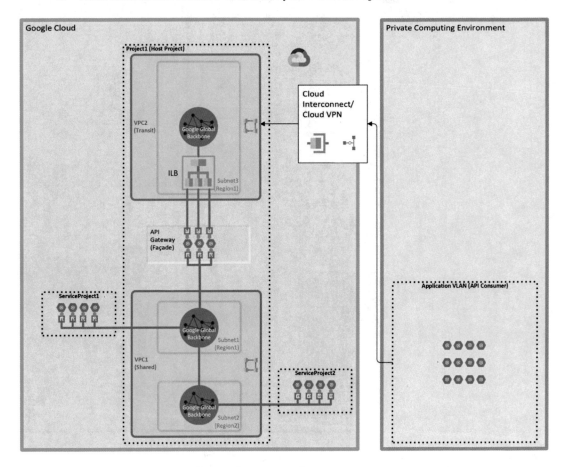

Figure 2-39. *Reference architecture for gated ingress topology*

An internal load balancer (ILB) is placed in the Transit VPC to balance incoming traffic across the VMs.

All traffic uses RFC 1918 IP addresses, and communication from GCP to your private computing environment (i.e., egress with respect to GCP) is not allowed.

Gated Ingress and Egress

This topology lets your workloads take advantage of the gated egress and gated ingress benefits at the same time. As a result, it is best suited when your hybrid or multi-cloud workloads need to consume cross-boundaries APIs, but they also expose APIs as well.

All inbound and outbound traffic—with respect to GCP—uses RFC 1918 IP addresses, and firewall rules need to be configured in the Transit VPC and in the DMZ VLAN (also known as Perimeter VLAN) to only allow API consumption and nothing else.

Figure 2-40 shows this setup, which is obtained by combining gated egress (Figure 2-38) and gated ingress (Figure 2-39).

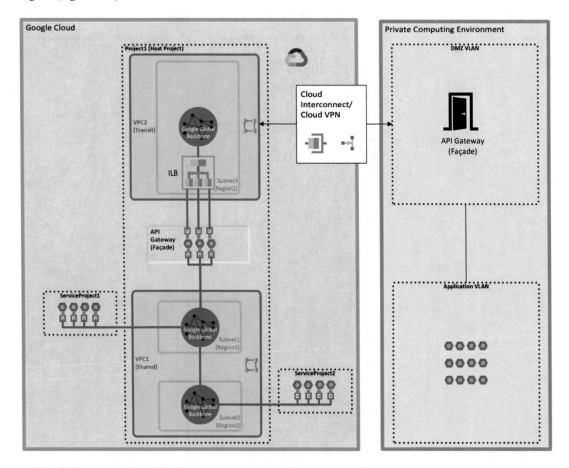

Figure 2-40. *Reference architecture for gated egress and ingress topology*

Handover

This topology is best suited for hybrid or multi-cloud analytics workloads. The approach leverages the broad spectrum of big data services offered by Google Cloud in order to ingest, store, process, analyze, and visualize data originated in your private compute environment.

Since there is no private connectivity requirement across environments, it is recommended to use direct or carrier peering connectivity, which provides high throughput and low latency.

Data pipelines are established to load data (in batches or in real time) from your private compute environment into a Google Cloud Storage bucket or a Pub/Sub topic. GCP workloads (e.g., Hadoop) process the data and deliver it in the proper format and channel.

To prevent data exfiltration, it is also recommended to create a VPC service perimeter—as shown in Figure 2-41—that protects the projects and the service APIs and allows access to the ETL (Extract Transform Load (Data)) workloads responsible for data ingestion and processing.

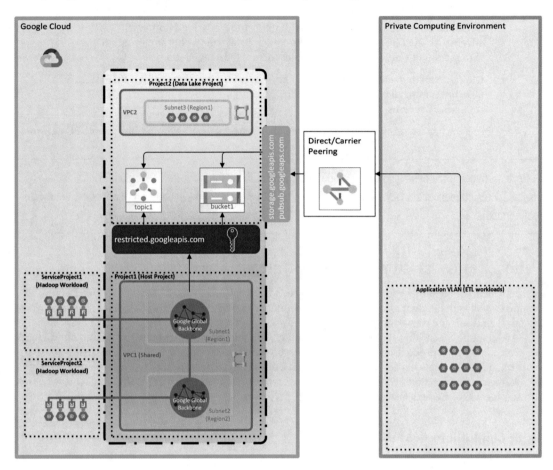

Figure 2-41. *Reference architecture for handover topology*

Regional vs. Global VPC Routing Mode

You learned in the "Meshed" section that a VPC network can be configured to use regional (default) or global dynamic routing modes.

This feature controls the behavior of *all* the Cloud Routers created in your VPC, by determining whether or not they should take advantage of the Google Global Backbone in the way they advertise subnet routes to their BGP peer counterparts.

This feature is toggled with the bgp-routing-mode flag in the gcloud compute networks [create | update] commands:

```
gcloud compute networks create NAME [--bgp-routing-mode=MODE; default="regional"]
[--description=DESCRIPTION] [--mtu=MTU] [--range=RANGE] [--subnet-mode=SUBNET_MODE] [GCLOUD_
WIDE_FLAG ...]
```

As you learned in the "Custom Routes" section, each VM has a built-in controller, which is aware of all the routes in the VPC routing table. The value you assign to the `bgp-routing-mode` flag will update the controller for each VM in the VPC as explained in the following text.

`MODE` value must be one of

- **Regional**: This is the default option. With this setting, all Cloud Routers in this VPC advertise to their BGP peers subnets from their local region only and program VMs with the router's best-learned BGP routes in their local region only.

- **Global**: With this setting, all Cloud Routers in this VPC advertise to their BGP peers all subnets from all regions and program VMs with the router's best learned BGP routes in all regions.

You can set the `bgp-routing-mode` flag any time, that is, while creating or updating your VPC network.

■ **Note** Changing the dynamic routing mode has the potential to interrupt traffic in your VPC or enable/disable routes in unexpected ways. Carefully review the role of each Cloud Router before changing the dynamic routing mode.

Failover and Disaster Recovery Strategy

A product like Cloud Router with its unique ability to advertise subnet routes across the regions of your VPC empowers you with the right tool to develop your workload resilience and high availability strategy in a cost-effective, efficient, and easy-to-implement manner.

Additionally, when you supplement Cloud Router with the proper selection of hybrid and multi-cloud network connectivity products we reviewed before, you are off to developing a resilient, robust, secure, performant, and scalable network architecture with a differentiated level of sophistication.

In the next two sections, we will present two reference topologies aimed at helping you achieve failover, disaster recovery, and high availability (HA) for your workloads.

High Availability (HA) VPN

A high availability VPN topology provides failover, disaster recovery, and up to 99.99% availability by duplicating the number of IPsec tunnels between your Cloud VPN instances and their corresponding peer VPN gateways.

There is no single reference HA VPN topology. Rather, there are a few variations to this approach, which are based upon the specifics of your private computing environment.

A reference topology is illustrated in Figure 2-42.

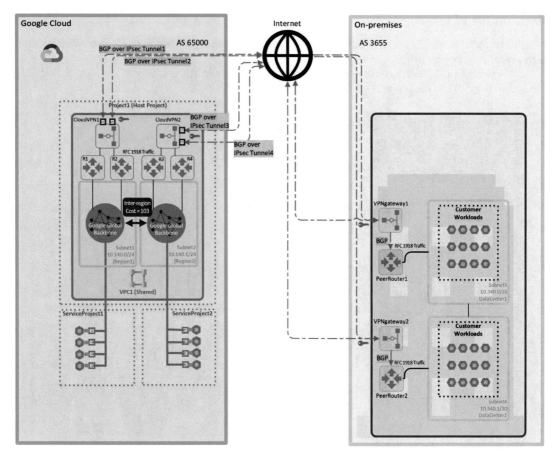

Figure 2-42. *Two peer HA VPN topology with 99.99% availability*

A few points to highlight are described as follows:

1. VPC1 is configured to use global dynamic routing mode.

2. Each Google Cloud region has its own Cloud VPN instance (defined in this use case as HA VPN Gateway), that is, CloudVPN1 and CloudVPN2.

3. CloudVPN1 and CloudVPN2 have two external IP addresses each, one per IPsec tunnel.

4. Each on-premises data center has its own VPN Gateway, that is, VPNgateway1 and VPNgateway2.

5. As we will see in the next section, an Inter-region cost is automatically added for optimal path selection. For the time being, think of this Inter-region cost as a "toll" you have to pay when your traffic is routed to another region (or continent). More details will be provided in Chapters 3 and 7.

Redundant VPC

A redundant VPC leverages a combination of Interconnect links and IPsec tunnels to achieve failover and high availability for your hybrid workloads.

The example in Figure 2-43 illustrates a reference topology of a hybrid setup, where a multi-regional VPC is extended to two data centers on-premises.

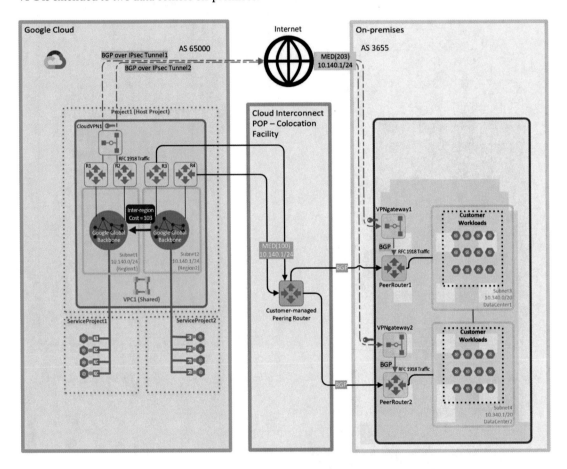

Figure 2-43. *Redundant VPC exhibiting egress route advertisement*

The setup uses two Dedicated Interconnect links as a primary connection and two IPsec tunnels as a secondary connection in the event the customer-managed peering router becomes unavailable.

For egress route advertisement, there are a number of important points to highlight:

1. The four Cloud Router instances R1, R2, R3, R4 are distributed in two regions.

2. VPC1 is configured to use global dynamic routing mode.

3. As a result of point #2, R1, R2, R3, R4 advertise routes for all VPC subnets, that is, Subnet1 in Region1, Subnet2 in Region2.

4. R3, R4 advertise routes using Dedicated Interconnect. This is the primary network connectivity product selected for this reference topology.

5. R1, R2 advertise routes using Cloud VPN. This is the secondary (backup) network connectivity product selected for this reference topology.

6. Cloud Router instances are automatically configured to add an *Inter-region cost* when they advertise subnet routes for subnets *outside* of their region. This value (e.g., 103 in our reference topology) is automatically added to the advertised route priority—the MED (Multi-exit Discriminator). The higher the MED, the lower the advertised route priority. This behavior ensures optimal path selection when multiple routes are available.

7. When the on-premises BGP peer routers `PeerRouter1` and `PeerRouter2` learn about `Subnet2` routes in `Region2`, they favor routes using Dedicated Interconnect rather than VPN because—as stated in point #6—routes advertised by R3, R4 using Dedicated Interconnect have MED values (100) lower than MED values for routes advertised by R1, R2 (203=100+103), resulting in higher priorities.

Let's review now how this reference topology provides failover and disaster recovery for ingress route advertisement.

In this scenario (Figure 2-44), the advertised route priority can be left equal (e.g., MED=100) for all advertised on-premises subnet routes.

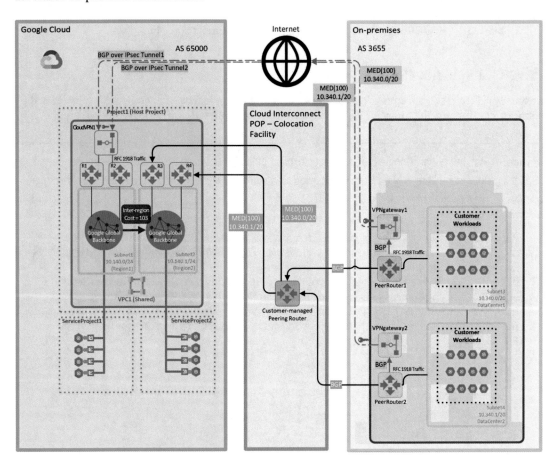

Figure 2-44. *Redundant VPC exhibiting ingress route advertisement*

By using the same MED, Google Cloud automatically adds that Inter-region cost (103) when R1, R2 in Region1 program routes in VPC1 whose destinations are in Subnet2 ranges.

As a result, on-premises route advertisements are load-balanced across the four instances of Cloud Router, that is, R1, R2 (in Region1) and R3, R4 (in Region2). However, if the destination is an IP range in Subnet2, that is, 10.140.1/24, then Interconnect links are favored because they have a lower MED, resulting in higher priority.

Accessing Google Services/APIs Privately from On-Premises Locations

Google services are exposed in the form of application programming interfaces (APIs), which are consumed over the Internet, for example, storage.googleapis.com, bigtable.googleapis.com, bigquery. googleapis.com, etc.

This setup requires that your workload uses at least a VM (or another type of compute service) with an external IP address. Exposing your workloads to the Internet always presents at a minimum security risks and unpredictable latency due to the ever-evolving topology of the Internet and the massive amount of data that traverses its many nodes.

What if you want to mitigate these security risks and latency concerns by *choosing not to use external IP addresses*?

This is where **Private Google Access** and **Private Service Connect** come into play.

Private Google Access

Private Google Access is a feature of a VPC subnet, which enables VMs (or other compute resources) in the subnet to consume eligible Google APIs and services *from their internal (RFC 1918) IP address*.

■ **Note**   Most, but not all, Google Cloud services expose their API for internal access. The list of supported services can be found here: https://cloud.google.com/vpc/docs/configure-private-service-connect-apis#supported-apis.

Put differently, *a VM no longer needs an external IP address in order to consume Google APIs and services, provided the subnet it belongs to has been configured to use Private Google Access and a few DNS and route configurations are made.*

In Figure 2-45, an on-premises network is connected to a shared VPC (VPC1) through a Cloud VPN tunnel. Traffic from on-premises hosts to Google APIs travels through the IPsec tunnel to VPC1 and then is sent through a custom route (goto-apis), which uses the default Internet gateway as its next hop (step 1). This next hop allows traffic to leave the VPC network and be delivered to private.googleapis.com (199.36.153.8/30).

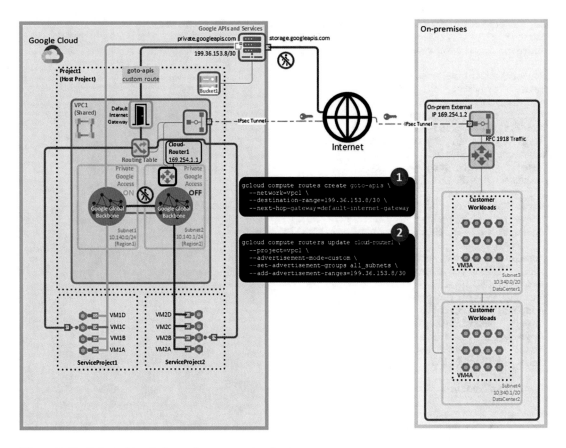

Figure 2-45. *Private Google Access for on-premises hosts*

Keep in mind that with this setup, the on-premises DNS server has to be configured to map
`*.googleapis.com` requests to `private.googleapis.com`, which resolves to the 199.36.153.8/30 IP
address range.

You can resolve the `private.googleapis.com` and `restricted.googleapis.com` domains from any
computer connected to the Internet, as shown in Figure 2-46.

```
DariosMacStudio:~ dariocabianca$ nslookup private.googleapis.com
Server:         fe80::cab4:22ff:fec8:78c%17
Address:        fe80::cab4:22ff:fec8:78c%17#53

Non-authoritative answer:
Name:   private.googleapis.com
Address: 199.36.153.10
Name:   private.googleapis.com
Address: 199.36.153.8
Name:   private.googleapis.com
Address: 199.36.153.9
Name:   private.googleapis.com
Address: 199.36.153.11

DariosMacStudio:~ dariocabianca$ nslookup restricted.googleapis.com
Server:         fe80::cab4:22ff:fec8:78c%17
Address:        fe80::cab4:22ff:fec8:78c%17#53

Non-authoritative answer:
Name:   restricted.googleapis.com
Address: 199.36.153.5
Name:   restricted.googleapis.com
Address: 199.36.153.6
Name:   restricted.googleapis.com
Address: 199.36.153.4
Name:   restricted.googleapis.com
Address: 199.36.153.7

DariosMacStudio:~ dariocabianca$ ▌
```

Figure 2-46. *The public DNS A records for* private.googleapis.com *and* restricted.googleapis.com

Also, the Cloud Router instance CloudRouter1 has to be configured to advertise the 199.36.153.8/30 IP address range through the Cloud VPN tunnel by using a custom route advertisement (step 2). Traffic going to Google APIs is routed through the IPsec tunnel to VPC1.

There are a few additional points to highlight:

1. VM1A, VM1B, VM1C, VM1D can access Bucket1 by consuming the private. googleapis.com endpoint. This is because they all share access to subnet1, which is configured to allow Private Google Access.

2. VM2B can also access Bucket1 by consuming the private.googleapis.com endpoint. This time—as you may have noticed—VM2B shares access to subnet2, which is configured to *deny* Private Google Access. However, VM2B can leverage its external IP address to access Bucket1. Even with its external IP address, traffic remains within Google Cloud without traversing the Internet.

3. All VMs that share access to subnet2 and do not have an external IP address (i.e., VM2A, VM2C, VM2D) cannot access Bucket1. This is because subnet2 is configured to *deny* Private Google Access.

Private Service Connect

An alternative and fully managed approach to privately exposing Google APIs and services to your hybrid or multi-cloud workload is a network service called **Private Service Connect (PSC)**.

Unlike Private Google Access, PSC leverages one or more endpoints in your VPC (instead of using the VPC's default Internet gateway) to forward requests to Google APIs and services. Traffic from on-premises consumers still travels through your VPC network using a VPN tunnel or a Cloud Interconnect VLAN attachment, but this time an *IP forwarding rule* instead of the default Internet gateway is used to route traffic to its final destination, that is, a Google API or a service your on-premises component needs to consume.

The PSC endpoint mentioned earlier is a construct which acts a *frontend* to the service your hybrid or multi-cloud workload needs to consume (in this case, a Google API or service). This endpoint uses a single (i.e., `w.x.y.z/32`) IPv4 address *disjoint* from the ranges of the VPC subnets in order to forward incoming traffic to the destined Google API or service.

You will learn in Chapter 3 how to implement a PSC to allow a workload to consume Google APIs and services privately. For the time being, all you need to understand is that the PSC endpoint does the "magic" by letting Google take care of forwarding packets to the desired API or a service. You no longer need to worry about configuring routes, ensuring no IP spaces overlap, controlling Network Address Translation (NAT), and all other network-centric concerns because PSC abstracts these network-centric concerns for you. With PSC, all you do is just configure a route to the PSC endpoint, and Google manages the rest for you.

Figure 2-47 shows the previous example updated with a PSC endpoint.

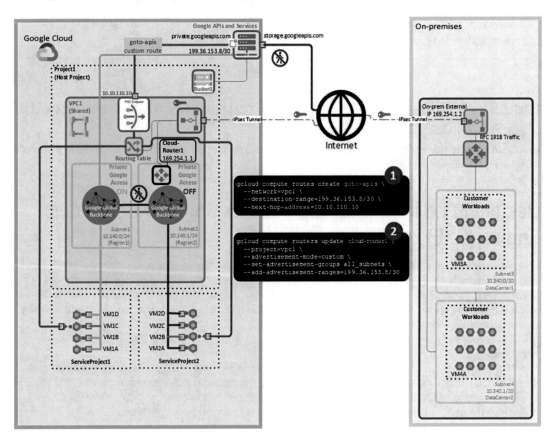

Figure 2-47. *Private Service Connect for on-premises hosts*

Similarly to the Private Google Access example, a new custom route goto-apis must be created, this time by setting the --next-hop-address flag to the PSC endpoint IPv4 address *10.10.110.10* instead of the default Internet gateway, which has been removed. CloudRouter1 must subsequently advertise this newly created custom route so that its on-premises peer router is aware of it.

Also, the PSC endpoint must be located in the VPC connected to the on-premises network—in this example, VPC1. This is another requirement for on-premises VMs, for example, VM3A, VM4A, to consume data stored in Bucket1 using the PSC endpoint.

Finally, you must configure your on-premises DNS so that it can make queries to your private DNS zones. If you've implemented the private DNS zones using Cloud DNS, then you need to complete the following steps:

1. In VPC1, create an inbound server policy.

2. In VPC1, identify the inbound forwarder entry points in the regions where your Cloud VPN tunnels or Cloud Interconnect attachments (VLANs) are located.

3. Configure on-premises DNS name servers to forward the DNS names for the PSC endpoints to an inbound forwarder entry point *in the same region* as the Cloud VPN tunnel or Cloud Interconnect attachment (VLAN) that connects to VPC1.

■ **Note**   With PSC, the target service or API does not need to be hosted or managed by Google. A third-party service provider can be used instead. This point and the fact that PSC is fully managed make PSC the recommended way to let workloads consume services and APIs privately.

IP Address Management Across On-Premises Locations and Cloud

When your workload operates in a hybrid or multi-cloud topology, you need to make sure that the IP ranges you choose for the subnets of your VPCs do not overlap with each other and most importantly do not overlap with your on-premises networks.

Designing an IP Addressing Plan for Google Kubernetes Engine (GKE)

When it comes to using IP addresses with GKE, you will have to address a supply and demand challenge.

On the supply side, organizations are running low on IP addresses because of large on-premises networks and constantly evolving multi-cloud deployments that use RFC 1918 IP addresses. On the demand side, GKE clusters are very dynamic systems by nature and result in quick consumption of IP addresses by resources such as pods, nodes, and services.

As a result, a risk of exhausting IP addresses has become more and more prevalent during GKE deployments.

Moreover, the work required to manage IP addresses can be substantial, particularly in hybrid deployments where cloud architects and network architects operate in different teams.

There's no question that managing IP addresses in GKE can be challenging. While there's no silver bullet for solving IP exhaustion, GKE offers a number of ways to address this problem.

GKE VPC-Native Clusters

First and foremost, you should use GKE VPC-native clusters instead of route-based clusters. You learned the basics about GKE VPC-native clusters in the "Container Networking" section.

A cluster that uses *alias IP address ranges* is called a VPC-native cluster. A cluster that uses custom static routes in a VPC network is called a route-based cluster.

Let's revisit how IP addresses are used by GKE in VPC-native clusters.

When you create a VPC-native cluster, you specify a subnet in your VPC network:

```
gcloud container clusters create CLUSTER_NAME \
    --region=COMPUTE_REGION \
    --enable-ip-alias \
    --create-subnetwork name=SUBNET_NAME,range=NODE_IP_RANGE \
    --cluster-ipv4-cidr=POD_IP_RANGE \
    --services-ipv4-cidr=SERVICES_IP_RANGE
```

A VPC-native GKE cluster uses three unique subnet IP address ranges:

1. It uses the *subnet's primary* IP address range, that is, NODE_IP_RANGE, for all node IP addresses.

2. It uses *one secondary* IP address range, that is, POD_IP_RANGE, for all pod IP addresses.

3. It uses *another secondary* IP address range, that is, SERVICES_IP_RANGE, for all service (cluster IP) addresses.

Since VPC-native clusters are designed to reserve pod IP addresses *before* the pods are created—in the preceding gcloud command by using the --cluster-ipv4-cidr flag—you are already off to a great start in the design of the IP addresses plan for your GKE cluster.

Figure 2-48 shows how the aforementioned three subnet IP ranges are allocated with respect to worker nodes, pods, and services.

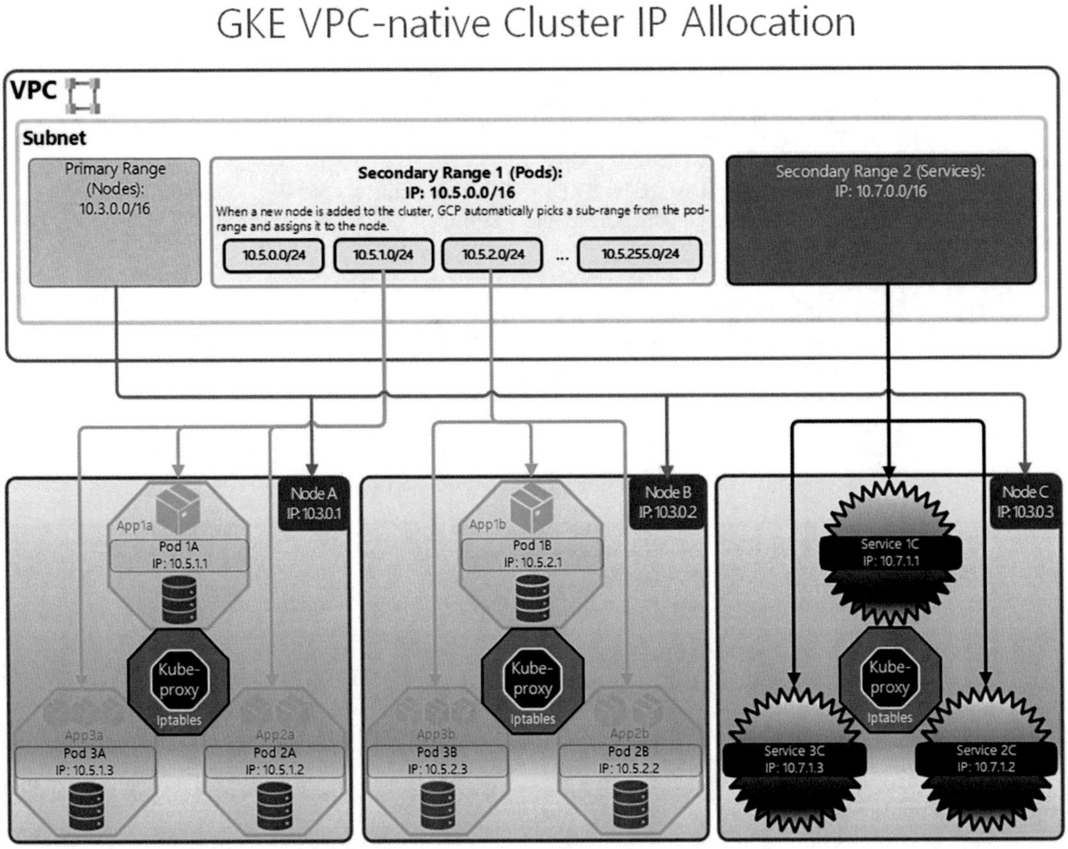

GKE VPC-native Cluster IP Allocation

Figure 2-48. *IP address allocation in a GKE VPC-native cluster*

An early allocation of IP ranges for the pods in your cluster has a twofold benefit: preventing conflict with other resources in your cluster's VPC network and allocating IP addresses efficiently. For this reason, VPC-native is the default network mode for all clusters in GKE versions 1.21.0-gke.1500 and later.

Optimizing GKE IP Ranges

So now that you have chosen to use VPC-native clusters, how do you go about deciding how much IP space your GKE cluster *effectively* needs?

To answer this question, you need to do an exercise of capacity planning to estimate the current and the future demand for your cluster. A key factor in this estimation process is *extensibility*, that is, you will want to plan for expansion of the computing resources your GKE cluster is made of, whether they be more nodes, more pods, or more services.

At the same time, you will also want to mitigate the risk of IP address exhaustion by making sure whatever masks you choose for your cluster nodes, pods, and services are not too big for what your workload really needs.

In CIDR notation, the mask is denoted by the digit after the "/", that is, /x where $0 \leq x \leq 32$.

Flexible Pod Density

A differentiating feature of GKE—when compared to other managed Kubernetes offerings from other public cloud providers—is its ability to let you configure the pod density per worker node on an as-needed basis. *Wouldn't it be nice to be able to tell GKE that after further revisions your workload running on a standard, VPC-native GKE cluster no longer needs the default value of a maximum of 110 pods per node?*

The pod density of a cluster is configurable using the --default-max-pods-per-node flag when you create a new GKE VPC-native cluster:

```
gcloud container clusters create your-cluster \
  --enable-ip-alias \
  --cluster-ipv4-cidr 10.0.0.0/24 \
  --services-ipv4-cidr 10.4.0.0/25 \
  --create-subnetwork name='your-subnet',range=10.4.32.0/28 \
  --default-max-pods-per-node 16 \
  --zone us-west1-a
```

Assuming you have proper IAM permissions, the preceding code will create a new subnet your-subnet in the zone us-west1-a and a standard GKE cluster, which is VPC-native because the flag --enable-ip-alias is set—resulting in two secondary ranges in the subnet your-subnet, one for the pod IPs and another for the service IPs.

The cluster will use the IP range 10.4.32.0/28 for its worker nodes, the IP range 10.0.0.0/24 for its pods, and the IP range 10.4.0.0/25 for its services.

Finally, each worker node will host no more than 16 pods, as illustrated in Figure 2-49.

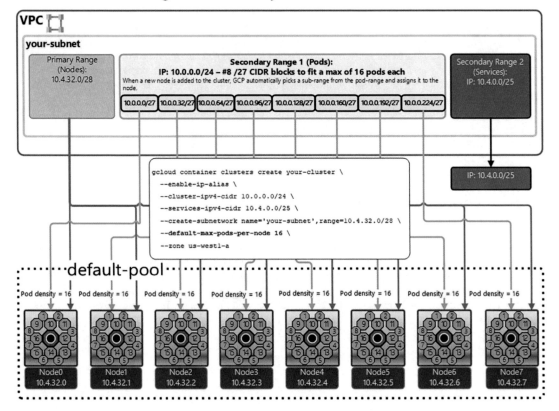

Figure 2-49. *Flexible pod density configuration at cluster creation*

Now, let's say you want to decrease the pod density from 16 to 8. This may be because your performance metrics showed you don't actually need 16 pods per node to meet your business and technical requirements. Reducing the pod density will allow you to make better use of your preallocated IP range 10.0.0.0/24 for pods.

You can reduce the pod density from 16 to 8 by creating a *node pool* in your existing cluster:

```
gcloud container node-pools create your-node-pool \
    --cluster your-cluster \
    --max-pods-per-node 8
```

The preceding code overrides the previously defined cluster-level default maximum of 16 pods per node with a new value of 8 pods per node.

In Figure 2-50, you can visually spot how the reduction of pods' density applies to the newly created node pool.

Overriding Pod density of a Cluster by creating a Node Pool

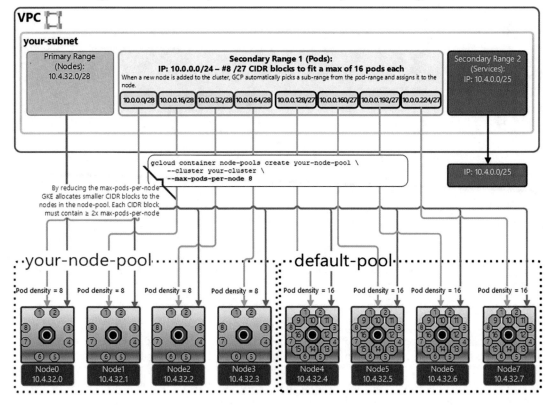

Figure 2-50. *Flexible pod density configuration by adding a node pool*

When you introduce node pools to reduce the pod density of an existing cluster, GKE automatically assigns a smaller CIDR block to each node in the node pool based on the value of max-pods-per-node. In our example, GKE has assigned /28 blocks to Node0, Node1, Node2, Node3.

■ **Exam tip**   You can only set the maximum number of pods per node at cluster creation or after creating a cluster by using a node pool.

Expanding GKE IP Ranges

In the previous section, you learned how to use the flexible pod density GKE feature to efficiently allocate RFC 1918 IP addresses for the pods, the services, and the nodes of your GKE cluster.

In this section, we will introduce a different approach: instead of using the existing IP range, let's find a way to add new CIDR blocks to the pool of IP addresses for your GKE cluster.

Non-RFC 1918

The first way to expand your GKE cluster's IP ranges is by using non-RFC 1918 reserved ranges.
Figure 2-51 shows this list of non-RFC 1918 ranges.

CIDR block	Description
100.64.0.0/10	Shared address space RFC 6598
192.0.0.0/24	IETF protocol assignments RFC 6890
192.0.2.0/24 (TEST-NET-1) 198.51.100.0/24 (TEST-NET-2) 203.0.113.0/24 (TEST-NET-3)	Documentation RFC 5737
192.88.99.0/24	IPv6 to IPv4 relay (deprecated) RFC 7526
198.18.0.0/15	Benchmark testing RFC 2544
240.0.0.0/4	Reserved for future use (Class E) as noted in RFC 5735 and RFC 1112. Some operating systems do not support the use of this range, so verify that your OS supports it before creating subnets that use this range.

Figure 2-51. *Non-RFC 1918 reserved CIDR blocks*

From a routing perspective, these IP addresses are treated like RFC 1918 addresses (i.e., 10.0.0.0/8, 172.16.0.0/12, 192.168.0.0/16), and subnet routes for these ranges are exchanged by default over VPC peering.

However, since these addresses are reserved, they are not advertised over the Internet, and when you use them, the traffic stays within your GKE cluster and your VPC network.

Privately Used Public IP (PUPI)

Another way to expand your GKE cluster's IP ranges is by using *privately used public IPs*. As the name suggests, these are IP addresses that are normally routable on the Internet (hence their designation as *public*), but in this context are used privately in a VPC network.

When you use these addresses as subnet ranges, Google Cloud does not announce these routes to the Internet and does not route traffic from the Internet to them.

Unlike non-RFC 1918, subnet routes for privately used public addresses are not exchanged over VPC peering by default. Put differently, peer VPC networks must be explicitly configured to import them in order to use them.

Last, make sure that these IP addresses don't overlap with any of your VPC primary and secondary subnet ranges.

Public and Private Cluster Nodes

By default, you can configure access from the Internet to your cluster's workloads. Routes are not created automatically.

Private clusters assign internal IP addresses to nodes and pods. As a result, your workloads are completely isolated from the Internet.

Unlike public clusters, private clusters' control planes can be accessed by a public endpoint and a private endpoint. Your workload security requirements drive the decision on who can access your private cluster control plane and from where.

Control Plane Public vs. Private Endpoints

The last aspect you need to consider when designing an IP addressing plan for GKE is access to the GKE control plane.

Think of the control plane as the brain of your GKE cluster, where all decisions are made to allocate, schedule, and dispose of resources for your containerized workload (e.g., worker nodes, pods, volumes, etc.).

Conversely, think of the data plane as the body of your GKE cluster, where the actual work happens by letting the pods in your worker node(s) compute, process, and store your workload data.

What does "access to the GKE control plane" really mean?

To answer this question, you need to decide *who* is authorized to access the control plane and from *where*. The first concern—the "who"—is a security concern, which is an important area of a broader topic, that is, Identity and Access Management (IAM), and will not be covered in this book. This book focuses on the networking aspects of your GCP workload. As a result, this section will cover the "where," which is the location of the user requesting access to the control plane, and how the request reaches its destination and is eventually fulfilled.

Private GKE clusters expose their control plane using a public and a private endpoint. This feature, combined with the fact that all worker nodes do not have external IPs, differentiates private clusters from other GKE clusters.

There are three ways you can access a private cluster endpoint. Let's review them.

Private Cluster with Disabled Public Endpoint

This is the most secure private cluster configuration, where the cluster public endpoint is deliberately disabled to protect its control plane from requests originating from the Internet. Figure 2-52 illustrates this configuration.

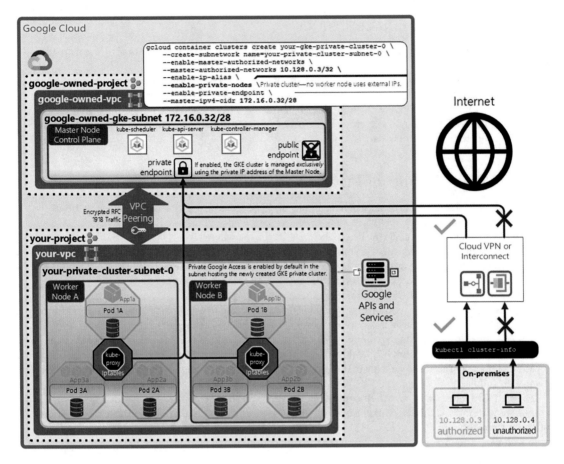

Figure 2-52. *GKE private cluster with disabled public endpoint*

This configuration is achieved by leveraging the `--enable-private-endpoint gcloud container clusters create` flag.

Notice in the figure the only entry point to the cluster control plane is its private endpoint, which is implemented by an internal TCP/UDP network load balancer in the control plane's VPC network.

By default, any worker node, pod, or service in the cluster has access to the private endpoint. In fact, for private clusters, this is the only way worker nodes, pods, and services access the control plane.

In terms of CIDR blocks, with reference to Figure 2-52, `your-private-cluster-subnet-0` primary range, first and secondary ranges are allowed to access the private endpoint. If you want other IP ranges to access the private endpoint, you need to explicitly authorize them by using the `--master-authorized-network` flag, which accepts a comma-delimited list of IP addresses in CIDR notation.

Since the GKE cluster is private and its control plane public endpoint has been disabled, the only CIDR blocks you can specify as values of the `--master-authorized-network` flag are RFC 1918 ranges.

In Figure 2-52, the on-premises VM with internal IP `10.128.0.3` is authorized access, while any other IP address is denied access to the private endpoint control plane.

This configuration is best suited when your GKE workload requires the highest level of restricted access to the control plane by blocking any access from the Internet.

Private Cluster with Limited Public Endpoint Access

There are scenarios where you want to access your private cluster control plane from the Internet, yet in a restrained manner.

You enable access to your cluster's control plane public endpoint by omitting the `--enable-private-endpoint` flag when you create your private cluster, as shown in Figure 2-53.

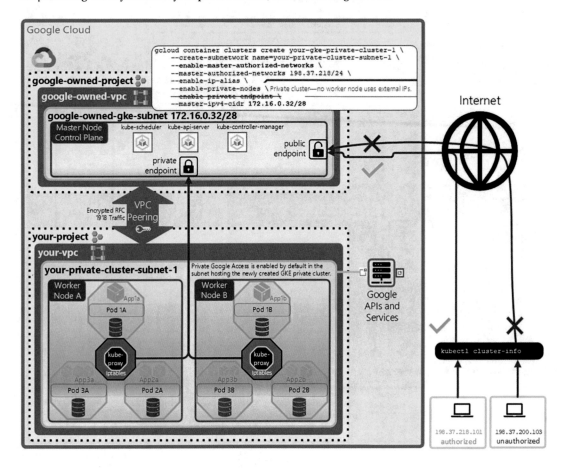

Figure 2-53. *GKE private cluster with limited public endpoint access*

Subsequently, you leverage the `--master-authorized-network` flag to selectively list the CIDR blocks authorized to access your cluster control plane.

Figure 2-53 illustrates this configuration: the non-RFC 1918 CIDR block `198.37.218/24` is authorized access to the control plane, whereas the client `198.37.200.103` is denied access.

This is a good choice if you need to administer your private cluster from source networks that are not connected to your cluster's VPC network using Cloud Interconnect or Cloud VPN.

Private Cluster with Unlimited Public Endpoint Access

This is the least secure configuration in that access to the GKE cluster's control plane is allowed from any IP address (0.0.0.0/0) through the HTTPS protocol.

This configuration can be achieved by using the `--no-enable-master-authorized-networks` flag as indicated in Figure 2-54.

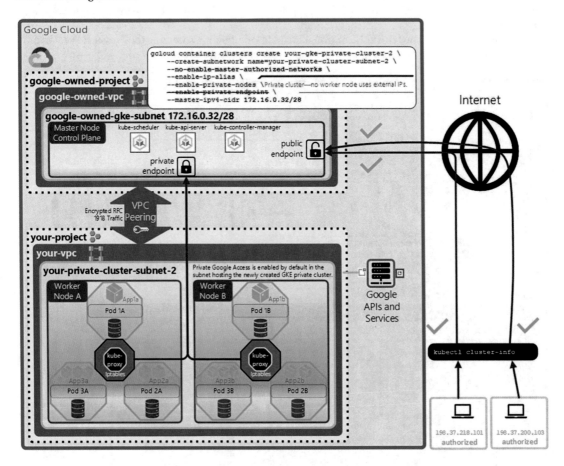

Figure 2-54. *GKE private cluster with unlimited public endpoint access*

Summary

This chapter walked you through the important things you need to consider when designing, planning, and prototyping a network in Google Cloud.

The key drivers that shape the design of the overall network architecture were introduced, that is, high availability, resilience, performance, security, and cost. You learned how tweaking your workload's nonfunctional requirements has an impact on the resulting network architecture.

We introduced the construct of a Virtual Private Cloud network (VPC), along with its foundational components (private and public IP addresses), its location components (subnets, routes), and its security components (firewall rules). You learned how to design VPCs to meet your workload business and technical requirements, by leveraging the global, highly performant, and highly optimized Google Cloud backbone.

Whether your workloads are cloud-native (born in the cloud), or they are being migrated from your company on-premises data centers (hybrid), or even from other clouds (multi-cloud), you learned how Google Cloud provides products, services, and reference architectures to meet your needs.

Last, as the creator of Kubernetes, you learned how Google Cloud offers a diverse set of unique features that help you choose the best network capabilities for your containerized workloads, including VPC-native clusters, container-native load balancing, flexible pod density, and private clusters.

In the next chapter, we will deep dive into VPC networks and introduce the tools you need to build the VPCs for your workloads.

Exam Questions
Question 2.1 (VPC Peering)

Your company just moved to GCP. You configured separate VPC networks for the Finance and Sales departments. Finance needs access to some resources that are part of the Sales VPC. You want to allow the private RFC 1918 address space traffic to flow between Sales and Finance VPCs without any additional cost and without compromising the security or performance. What should you do?

- **A.**　Create a VPN tunnel between the two VPCs.

- **B.**　Configure VPC peering between the two VPCs.

- **C.**　Add a route on both VPCs to route traffic over the Internet.

- **D.**　Create an Interconnect connection to access the resources.

Rationale

A is not correct because VPN will hinder the performance and will add additional cost.

B is CORRECT because VPC network peering allows traffic to flow between two VPC networks over private RFC 1918 address space without compromising the security or performance at no additional cost.

C is not correct because RFC 1918 is a private address space and cannot be routed via public Internet.

D is not correct because Interconnect will cost a lot more to do the same work.

Question 2.2 (Private Google Access)

You are configuring a hybrid cloud topology for your organization. You are using Cloud VPN and Cloud Router to establish connectivity to your on-premises environment. You need to transfer data from on-premises to a Cloud Storage bucket and to BigQuery. Your organization has a strict security policy that mandates the use of VPN for communication to the cloud. You want to follow Google-recommended practices. What should you do?

- **A.**　Create an instance in your VPC with Private Google Access enabled. Transfer data using your VPN connection to the instance in your VPC. Use `gsutil cp files gs://bucketname` and `bq --location=[LOCATION] load --source_format=[FORMAT] [DATASET].[TABLE] [PATH_TO_SOURCE] [SCHEMA]` on the instance to transfer data to Cloud Storage and BigQuery.

B. Use `nslookup -q=TXT spf.google.com` to obtain the API IP endpoints used for Cloud Storage and BigQuery from Google's netblock. Configure Cloud Router to advertise these netblocks to your on-premises router using a flexible routing advertisement. Use `gsutil cp files gs://bucketname` and `bq --location=[LOCATION] load --source_format=[FORMAT] [DATASET]. [TABLE] [PATH_TO_SOURCE] [SCHEMA]` on-premises to transfer data to Cloud Storage and BigQuery.

C. Configure Cloud Router (in your GCP project) to advertise `199.36.153.4/30` to your on-premises router using a flexible routing advertisement (BGP). Modify your on-premises DNS server CNAME entry from `*.googleapis.com` to `restricted.googleapis.com`. Use `gsutil cp files gs://bucketname` and `bq --location=[LOCATION] load --source_format=[FORMAT] [DATASET]. [TABLE] [PATH_TO_SOURCE] [SCHEMA]` on-premises to transfer data to Cloud Storage and BigQuery.

D. Use `gsutil cp files gs://bucketname` and `bq --location=[LOCATION] load --source_format=[FORMAT] [DATASET].[TABLE] [PATH_TO_SOURCE] [SCHEMA]` on-premises to transfer data to Cloud Storage and BigQuery.

Rationale

A is not correct because it adds additional operational complexity and introduces a single point of failure (Instance) to transfer data. This is not Google-recommended practice for on-premises private API access.

B is not correct because these netblocks can change, and there is no guarantee these APIs will not move to different netblocks.

C is CORRECT because it enables on-premises Private Google Access, allowing VPN and Interconnect customers to reach APIs such as BigQuery and Google Cloud Storage natively across an Interconnect/VPN connection. The CIDR block 199.36.153.4/30 is obtained when you try to resolve restricted.googleapis.com. You need this CIDR block when adding a custom static route to enable access to Google-managed services that VPC Service Controls supports. Google Cloud Storage and BigQuery APIs are eligible services to secure the VPC perimeter using VPC Service Controls. Therefore, the CNAME type DNS records should resolve to restricted.googleapis.com.

D is not correct because it will utilize an available Internet link to transfer data (if there is one). This will not satisfy the security requirement of using the VPN connection to the cloud.

CHAPTER 3

■ ■ ■

Implementing Virtual Private Cloud Instances

In the previous chapter, you learned about Virtual Private Cloud networks (VPCs) and how to design one or more VPCs from a set of business and technical requirements for your workload. We showed how every detail of your VPC design and connectivity traces back to one or more requirements.

The well-architected framework was also introduced as a tool to guide you through the GCP services and network tier (premium or standard) decision-making process. Think of the collection of all GCP services, along with their "flavors" and all their possible configurations as a palette. Your workload business requirements will tell you what should be drawn in your painting. Your workload technical requirements will tell you for each element in your painting what mix of color, shade, and pattern to use. The well-architected framework will help you further choose the optimal combination of shapes, colors, shades, and patterns so the final painting will look great.

At this point, the overall network architecture and topology should have been designed. With reference to the painting analogy, you should have your canvas, your shapes, and colors selected.

In this chapter, we will take a step further and will teach you how to build your VPCs, and most importantly we will teach you how to establish connectivity among your VPCs and other networks, in accordance with the topologies developed in Chapter 2.

Configuring VPCs

Whether your workload runs entirely on GCP, in a hybrid, or a multi-cloud environment, you usually start small with a VPC located in a single region.

As your workload gets more hits, incoming traffic increases, and your VPC may need to gradually expand to more zones and eventually to other regions in order for your workload to perform and be resilient.

However, with GCP the original network configuration just seamlessly works. This is because *VPCs are designed for scale and extensibility*.

For example, you can extend the IP address range of a subnet anytime. You can even add a new subnet after a VPC has been created. When you add a new subnet, you specify a name, a region, and at least a primary IP address range according to the subnet rules.

There are some constraints each subnet must satisfy, for example, no overlapping IP address ranges within the same VPC, unique names if the subnets are in the same region and project, and others we will review later. The idea is that you can scale and extend your VPC with little configuration changes and, most importantly, without having the need to recreate it.

© Dario Cabianca 2023
D. Cabianca, *Google Cloud Platform (GCP) Professional Cloud Network Engineer Certification Companion*, Certification Study Companion Series, https://doi.org/10.1007/978-1-4842-9354-6_3

Configuring VPC Resources

There are a number of ways to build and configure VPCs. In this book, you will learn how to build and configure the VPCs for your workloads using the gcloud command-line interface (CLI).

You may wonder why we chose to use the gcloud CLI when there are many other options to build and configure VPCs (and other infrastructure) like Terraform and other tools, including the console.

The main reason is because you are expected to know the gcloud CLI to pass the exam, and not necessarily Terraform or other tools.

Another reason is because the gcloud CLI is easy to use and comes free with your (or your company's) GCP account. It simply runs using a Cloud Shell terminal from a modern browser upon sign-in to the console or from a terminal session in your local machine. The latter requires to install the gcloud CLI.

■ **Note**   To learn how to install the gcloud CLI on your machine, see https://cloud.google.com/sdk/gcloud#download_and_install_the.

Last, the gcloud command line is less likely to change than any other tools—and typically, changes are backward compatible.

Figure 3-1 shows how to check the gcloud CLI version. Google maintains the gcloud CLI and all the software available when you use a Cloud Shell terminal.

```
darioxml@cloudshell:~ (zippy-chariot-334616)$ gcloud version
Google Cloud SDK 383.0.1
alpha 2022.04.26
app-engine-go 1.9.72
app-engine-java 1.9.96
app-engine-python 1.9.100
app-engine-python-extras 1.9.96
beta 2022.04.26
bigtable
bq 2.0.74
bundled-python3-unix 3.8.11
cbt 0.12.0
cloud-build-local 0.5.2
cloud-datastore-emulator 2.2.0
cloud-run-proxy 0.3.0
core 2022.04.26
datalab 20190610
gsutil 5.9
kpt 1.0.0-beta.13
local-extract 1.5.1
minikube 1.25.2
pubsub-emulator 0.6.0
darioxml@cloudshell:~ (zippy-chariot-334616)$ █
```

Figure 3-1. *Using the gcloud CLI from the Google Cloud Shell*

All gcloud commands follow this informal syntax:

```
gcloud <gcp-service-name-singular> <gcp-resource-plural> [<gcp-resource-plural>]
<verb> [flags]
```

In the upcoming sections, you will learn how to create a VPC and how to configure some of its key components, that is, subnets, firewall rules, and routes.

Creating VPCs

In Google Cloud, VPCs come in two flavors: auto mode (default) and custom mode.

Auto-mode VPCs automatically create a subnet in each region for you. You don't even have to worry about assigning an IP range to each subnet. GCP will automatically assign an RFC 1918 IP range from a predefined pool of RFC 1918 IP addresses.

If you want more control in the selection of subnets for your VPC and their IP ranges, then use *custom-mode* VPCs. With custom-mode VPCs, you first create your VPC, and then you manually add subnets to it as documented as follows.

■ **Note**   In GCP, IP ranges are assigned on a per-subnet basis. As a result, you don't need to allocate IP ranges until you add subnets to your custom-mode VPC.

In Figure 3-2, we created our first custom-mode VPC, named your-first-vpc.

```
Welcome to Cloud Shell! Type "help" to get started.
darioxml@cloudshell:~ (zippy-chariot-334616)$ gcloud compute networks create your-first-vpc --subnet-mode=custom
Created [https://www.googleapis.com/compute/v1/projects/zippy-chariot-334616/global/networks/your-first-vpc].
NAME: your-first-vpc
SUBNET_MODE: CUSTOM
BGP_ROUTING_MODE: REGIONAL
IPV4_RANGE:
GATEWAY_IPV4:

Instances on this network will not be reachable until firewall rules
are created. As an example, you can allow all internal traffic between
instances as well as SSH, RDP, and ICMP by running:

$ gcloud compute firewall-rules create <FIREWALL_NAME> --network your-first-vpc --allow tcp,udp,icmp --source-ran
ges <IP_RANGE>
$ gcloud compute firewall-rules create <FIREWALL_NAME> --network your-first-vpc --allow tcp:22,tcp:3389,icmp

darioxml@cloudshell:~ (zippy-chariot-334616)$ []
```

Figure 3-2. *Creating a custom-mode VPC*

■ **Exam tip**   Every Google Cloud new project comes with a default network (an auto-mode VPC) that has one subnet in each region. The subnet CIDR blocks have IPv4 ranges only and are automatically assigned for you. The subnets and all subnet ranges fit inside the 10.128.0.0/9 CIDR block. You will need to remember this CIDR block for the exam. It is best practice to create your own VPCs in custom mode rather than using the built-in default auto-mode VPC. This is because the default VPC is a very large VPC (it has one subnet per region) with little flexibility with respect to CIDR blocks and other networking aspects. Use the default VPC for experimentation only, when you need a VPC "ready-to-go" to quickly test a feature. For all other scenarios, use custom-mode VPCs.

Creating Subnets

As shown in Figure 3-3, to create a subnet you must specify at a minimum the VPCs the subnet is a part of—you learned in Chapter 2 that subnets are partitions of a VPC—as well as the primary IP range in CIDR notation.

```
darioxml@cloudshell:~ (zippy-chariot-334616)$ gcloud compute networks subnets create your-subnet-1 --network=your
-first-vpc --range=192.168.0.0/27
Did you mean region [us-east1] for subnetwork: [your-subnet-1] (Y/n)?  Y

Created [https://www.googleapis.com/compute/v1/projects/zippy-chariot-334616/regions/us-east1/subnetworks/your-su
bnet-1].
NAME: your-subnet-1
REGION: us-east1
NETWORK: your-first-vpc
RANGE: 192.168.0.0/27
STACK_TYPE: IPV4_ONLY
IPV6_ACCESS_TYPE:
INTERNAL_IPV6_PREFIX:
EXTERNAL_IPV6_PREFIX:
darioxml@cloudshell:~ (zippy-chariot-334616)$
```

Figure 3-3. *Creating a subnet*

The gcloud command in Figure 3-3 added to the VPC your-first-vpc a subnet named your-subnet-1 with a primary CIDR block 192.168.0.0/27. Notice that you were asked to specify a region. This happens when the CLI doesn't know what the default region for your account is.

■ **Exam tip**   You cannot use the first two and the last two IP addresses in a subnet's primary IPv4 range. This is because these four IP addresses are reserved by Google for internal use. In our preceding example, you cannot use 192.168.0.0 (network), 192.168.0.1 (default gateway), 192.168.0.30 (reserved by Google for future use), and 192.168.0.31 (broadcast). The same constraint does not apply to secondary IP ranges of a subnet (see the next paragraph for more information about secondary ranges).

In addition to a primary IP range, a subnet can optionally be assigned up to two secondary IP ranges. You learned in Chapter 2 that the first and the second secondary IP ranges are used by GKE to assign IP addresses to its pods and its services, respectively. More information about secondary IP ranges will be provided in the upcoming sections.

Listing Subnets

You can list the subnets of your VPC as displayed in Figure 3-4.

```
darioxml@cloudshell:~ (zippy-chariot-334616)$ gcloud compute networks subnets list --network=your-first-vpc
NAME: your-subnet-1
REGION: us-east1
NETWORK: your-first-vpc
RANGE: 192.168.0.0/27
STACK_TYPE: IPV4_ONLY
IPV6_ACCESS_TYPE:
INTERNAL_IPV6_PREFIX:
EXTERNAL_IPV6_PREFIX:
darioxml@cloudshell:~ (zippy-chariot-334616)$ ▮
```

Figure 3-4. *Listing the subnets in a given VPC*

Listing VPCs

Likewise, you can list the VPCs in your GCP project as shown in Figure 3-5.

```
darioxml@cloudshell:~ (zippy-chariot-334616)$ gcloud compute networks list
NAME: default
SUBNET_MODE: AUTO
BGP_ROUTING_MODE: REGIONAL
IPV4_RANGE:
GATEWAY_IPV4:

NAME: your-first-vpc
SUBNET_MODE: CUSTOM
BGP_ROUTING_MODE: REGIONAL
IPV4_RANGE:
GATEWAY_IPV4:
darioxml@cloudshell:~ (zippy-chariot-334616)$
```

***Figure 3-5.** Listing the VPCs in your GCP project*

Notice the list shows your-first-vpc and the default VPC, which has one subnet in each region.

Deleting VPCs

If you want to delete a VPC, you need to make sure any resource that uses the VPC has been deleted first.

For example, the command in Figure 3-6 fails because your-first-vpc contains the subnet your-subnet-1, which has not been deleted yet.

```
darioxml@cloudshell:~ (zippy-chariot-334616)$ gcloud compute networks delete your-first-vpc
The following networks will be deleted:
 - [your-first-vpc]

Do you want to continue (Y/n)?  Y

ERROR: (gcloud.compute.networks.delete) Could not fetch resource:
 - The network resource 'projects/zippy-chariot-334616/global/networks/your-first-vpc' is already being used by '
projects/zippy-chariot-334616/regions/us-east1/subnetworks/your-subnet-1'

darioxml@cloudshell:~ (zippy-chariot-334616)$
```

***Figure 3-6.** Failed attempt to delete a VPC*

As a result, first we need to delete your-subnet-1, and only afterward we can delete your-first-vpc, as illustrated in Figure 3-7.

```
darioxml@cloudshell:~ (zippy-chariot-334616)$ gcloud compute networks subnets delete your-subnet-1
Did you mean region [us-east1] for subnetwork: [your-subnet-1] (Y/n)?  Y

The following subnetworks will be deleted:
 - [your-subnet-1] in [us-east1]

Do you want to continue (Y/n)?  Y

Deleted [https://www.googleapis.com/compute/v1/projects/zippy-chariot-334616/regions/us-east1/subnetworks/your-su
bnet-1].
darioxml@cloudshell:~ (zippy-chariot-334616)$ gcloud compute networks delete your-first-vpc
The following networks will be deleted:
 - [your-first-vpc]

Do you want to continue (Y/n)?  Y

Deleted [https://www.googleapis.com/compute/v1/projects/zippy-chariot-334616/global/networks/your-first-vpc].
darioxml@cloudshell:~ (zippy-chariot-334616)$ █
```

***Figure 3-7.** Successful attempt to delete a VPC*

Configuring VPC Peering

VPC peering allows a VPC's internal routing capabilities to go beyond the scope of its subnets and reach the subnets of another VPC, also referred to as its *peer* VPC. The two peered VPCs may be in the same projects or different projects or even different organizations.

VPC peering is one of a few ways to interconnect two VPCs. Other ways include external IP addresses, IPsec VPN tunnels, multi-NIC (network interface controller) network virtual appliances (NVAs), and others. When compared to external IP addresses and VPN, VPC peering offers the following advantages:

1) **Lower latency and higher security**: Traffic between two peered VPCs is encrypted by default and always remains in the Google Global Backbone— without traversing the Internet.

2) **Lower cost**: Since two peered VPCs use internal IP addressing to communicate with each other, egress costs are lower than external IP addresses or VPN, which both use connectivity to the Internet.

In the examples in Figures 3-8 to 3-11, you will create two VPCs with two subnets each. You will then create two VMs, one in each VPC. Finally, you will peer the two VPCs and verify that the two VMs can communicate with each other.

```
darioxml@cloudshell:~ (zippy-chariot-334616)$ gcloud compute networks create vpc1 --subnet-mode=custom
Created [https://www.googleapis.com/compute/v1/projects/zippy-chariot-334616/global/networks/vpc1].
NAME: vpc1
SUBNET_MODE: CUSTOM
BGP_ROUTING_MODE: REGIONAL
IPV4_RANGE:
GATEWAY_IPV4:

Instances on this network will not be reachable until firewall rules
are created. As an example, you can allow all internal traffic between
instances as well as SSH, RDP, and ICMP by running:

$ gcloud compute firewall-rules create <FIREWALL_NAME> --network vpc1 --allow tcp,udp,icmp --source-ranges <IP_RA
NGE>
$ gcloud compute firewall-rules create <FIREWALL_NAME> --network vpc1 --allow tcp:22,tcp:3389,icmp

darioxml@cloudshell:~ (zippy-chariot-334616)$ gcloud compute networks subnets create subnet1a --network=vpc1 --re
gion=us-east1 --range=10.240.1.0/28
Created [https://www.googleapis.com/compute/v1/projects/zippy-chariot-334616/regions/us-east1/subnetworks/subnet1
a].
NAME: subnet1a
REGION: us-east1
NETWORK: vpc1
RANGE: 10.240.1.0/28
STACK_TYPE: IPV4_ONLY
IPV6_ACCESS_TYPE:
INTERNAL_IPV6_PREFIX:
EXTERNAL_IPV6_PREFIX:
darioxml@cloudshell:~ (zippy-chariot-334616)$
```

Figure 3-8. *Creating the first VPC and the first subnet*

■ **Note** Unlike default VPCs, custom VPCs require that you explicitly add the default firewall rules to ssh (Secure Shell) or rdp (Remote Desktop Protocol) to the VPC.

```
darioxml@cloudshell:~ (zippy-chariot-334616)$ gcloud compute networks subnets create subnet1b --network=vpc1 --re
gion=us-central1 --range=10.240.3.0/28
Created [https://www.googleapis.com/compute/v1/projects/zippy-chariot-334616/regions/us-central1/subnetworks/subn
et1b].
NAME: subnet1b
REGION: us-central1
NETWORK: vpc1
RANGE: 10.240.3.0/28
STACK_TYPE: IPV4_ONLY
IPV6_ACCESS_TYPE:
INTERNAL_IPV6_PREFIX:
EXTERNAL_IPV6_PREFIX:
darioxml@cloudshell:~ (zippy-chariot-334616)$
```

Figure 3-9. *Creating the second subnet in the first VPC*

```
darioxml@cloudshell:~ (zippy-chariot-334616)$ gcloud compute networks create vpc2 --subnet-mode=custom
Created [https://www.googleapis.com/compute/v1/projects/zippy-chariot-334616/global/networks/vpc2].
NAME: vpc2
SUBNET_MODE: CUSTOM
BGP_ROUTING_MODE: REGIONAL
IPV4_RANGE:
GATEWAY_IPV4:

Instances on this network will not be reachable until firewall rules
are created. As an example, you can allow all internal traffic between
instances as well as SSH, RDP, and ICMP by running:

$ gcloud compute firewall-rules create <FIREWALL_NAME> --network vpc2 --allow tcp,udp,icmp --source-ranges <IP_RA
NGE>
$ gcloud compute firewall-rules create <FIREWALL_NAME> --network vpc2 --allow tcp:22,tcp:3389,icmp
```

Figure 3-10. *Creating the second VPC*

```
darioxml@cloudshell:~ (zippy-chariot-334616)$ gcloud compute networks subnets create subnet2b --network=vpc2 --re
gion=us-central1 --range=10.240.4.0/28
Created [https://www.googleapis.com/compute/v1/projects/zippy-chariot-334616/regions/us-central1/subnetworks/subn
et2b].
NAME: subnet2b
REGION: us-central1
NETWORK: vpc2
RANGE: 10.240.4.0/28
STACK_TYPE: IPV4_ONLY
IPV6_ACCESS_TYPE:
INTERNAL_IPV6_PREFIX:
EXTERNAL_IPV6_PREFIX:
darioxml@cloudshell:~ (zippy-chariot-334616)$ gcloud compute networks subnets create subnet2a --network=vpc2 --re
gion=us-east1 --range=10.240.2.0/28
Created [https://www.googleapis.com/compute/v1/projects/zippy-chariot-334616/regions/us-east1/subnetworks/subnet2
a].
NAME: subnet2a
REGION: us-east1
NETWORK: vpc2
RANGE: 10.240.2.0/28
STACK_TYPE: IPV4_ONLY
IPV6_ACCESS_TYPE:
INTERNAL_IPV6_PREFIX:
EXTERNAL_IPV6_PREFIX:
darioxml@cloudshell:~ (zippy-chariot-334616)$ ▮
```

Figure 3-11. *Creating two subnets in the second VPC*

Now let's create a VM in subnet1a and a VM in subnet2b (Figure 3-12).

```
darioxml@cloudshell:~ (zippy-chariot-334616)$ gcloud compute instances create vm1 --network=vpc1 --subnet=subnet1
a --zone=us-east1-c
Created [https://www.googleapis.com/compute/v1/projects/zippy-chariot-334616/zones/us-east1-c/instances/vm1].
NAME: vm1
ZONE: us-east1-c
MACHINE_TYPE: n1-standard-1
PREEMPTIBLE:
INTERNAL_IP: 10.240.1.4
EXTERNAL_IP: 35.231.202.227
STATUS: RUNNING
darioxml@cloudshell:~ (zippy-chariot-334616)$ gcloud compute instances create vm2 --network=vpc2 --subnet=subnet2
b --zone=us-central1-c
Created [https://www.googleapis.com/compute/v1/projects/zippy-chariot-334616/zones/us-central1-c/instances/vm2].
NAME: vm2
ZONE: us-central1-c
MACHINE_TYPE: n1-standard-1
PREEMPTIBLE:
INTERNAL_IP: 10.240.4.2
EXTERNAL_IP: 35.238.132.176
STATUS: RUNNING
darioxml@cloudshell:~ (zippy-chariot-334616)$
```

Figure 3-12. *Creating two VMs, one in each VPC*

Figure 3-13 shows the current setup. The other three VMs shown in each subnet are for illustrative purposes to emphasize the internal routing capability of a VPC.

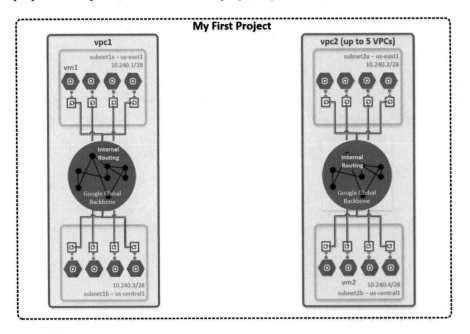

Figure 3-13. *A project containing two VPCs with eight VMs in each VPC*

To test connectivity between the two VMs, we first need to be able to connect to each VM, and for this to happen, we need to create an ingress firewall rule for each VPC to allow access to the VMs using the SSH (Secure Shell) protocol.

Figure 3-14 illustrates the creation of the two firewall rules. Notice the direction (ingress or egress) is omitted because ingress is the default value. Also, as you will learn later in this chapter, firewall rules apply to the entire VPC.

```
darioxml@cloudshell:~ (zippy-chariot-334616)$ gcloud compute firewall-rules create allow-ssh-vpc1 --network=vpc1
--allow=tcp:22,tcp:3389,icmp
Creating firewall...working..Created [https://www.googleapis.com/compute/v1/projects/zippy-chariot-334616/global/
firewalls/allow-ssh-vpc1].
Creating firewall...done.
NAME: allow-ssh-vpc1
NETWORK: vpc1
DIRECTION: INGRESS
PRIORITY: 1000
ALLOW: tcp:22,tcp:3389,icmp
DENY:
DISABLED: False
darioxml@cloudshell:~ (zippy-chariot-334616)$ gcloud compute firewall-rules create allow-ssh-vpc2 --network=vpc2
--allow=tcp:22,tcp:3389,icmp
Creating firewall...working..Created [https://www.googleapis.com/compute/v1/projects/zippy-chariot-334616/global/
firewalls/allow-ssh-vpc2].
Creating firewall...done.
NAME: allow-ssh-vpc2
NETWORK: vpc2
DIRECTION: INGRESS
PRIORITY: 1000
ALLOW: tcp:22,tcp:3389,icmp
DENY:
DISABLED: False
darioxml@cloudshell:~ (zippy-chariot-334616)$ █
```

Figure 3-14. *Enabling* ssh *and* ICMP *(Internet Control Message Protocol) to the two VPCs*

Let's now log in to vm1 and test connectivity to vm2. As you can see in Figure 3-15, the ping command will eventually time out because the two VPCs where vm1 and vm2 reside are completely disjointed.

```
darioxml@cloudshell:~ (zippy-chariot-334616)$ gcloud compute ssh --zone "us-east1-c" "vm1" --project "zippy-char
iot-334616"
Warning: Permanently added 'compute.6669447983170351950' (ECDSA) to the list of known hosts.
Linux vm1 5.10.0-13-cloud-amd64 #1 SMP Debian 5.10.106-1 (2022-03-17) x86_64

The programs included with the Debian GNU/Linux system are free software;
the exact distribution terms for each program are described in the
individual files in /usr/share/doc/*/copyright.

Debian GNU/Linux comes with ABSOLUTELY NO WARRANTY, to the extent
permitted by applicable law.
darioxml@vm1:~$ ping 10.240.4.2
PING 10.240.4.2 (10.240.4.2) 56(84) bytes of data.

^C
--- 10.240.4.2 ping statistics ---
202 packets transmitted, 0 received, 100% packet loss, time 205803ms

darioxml@vm1:~$
```

Figure 3-15. *No connectivity exists between the two VMs.*

Now, let's peer the two VPCs as shown in Figures 3-16 and 3-17.

```
darioxml@cloudshell:~ (zippy-chariot-334616)$ gcloud compute networks peerings create vpc1-vpc2 --network=vpc1 --
peer-network=vpc2
Updated [https://www.googleapis.com/compute/v1/projects/zippy-chariot-334616/global/networks/vpc1].
---
autoCreateSubnetworks: false
creationTimestamp: '2022-05-12T18:20:48.080-07:00'
id: '8676441580175887519'
kind: compute#network
name: vpc1
networkFirewallPolicyEnforcementOrder: AFTER_CLASSIC_FIREWALL
peerings:
- autoCreateRoutes: true
  exchangeSubnetRoutes: true
  exportCustomRoutes: false
  exportSubnetRoutesWithPublicIp: true
  importCustomRoutes: false
  importSubnetRoutesWithPublicIp: false
  name: vpc1-vpc2
  network: https://www.googleapis.com/compute/v1/projects/zippy-chariot-334616/global/networks/vpc2
  state: INACTIVE
  stateDetails: '[2022-05-12T20:56:43.288-07:00]: Waiting for peer network to connect.'
routingConfig:
  routingMode: REGIONAL
selfLink: https://www.googleapis.com/compute/v1/projects/zippy-chariot-334616/global/networks/vpc1
selfLinkWithId: https://www.googleapis.com/compute/v1/projects/zippy-chariot-334616/global/networks/8676441580175
887519
subnetworks:
- https://www.googleapis.com/compute/v1/projects/zippy-chariot-334616/regions/us-central1/subnetworks/subnet1b
- https://www.googleapis.com/compute/v1/projects/zippy-chariot-334616/regions/us-east1/subnetworks/subnet1a
```

Figure 3-16. *Peering vpc1 to vpc2*

```
darioxml@cloudshell:~ (zippy-chariot-334616)$ gcloud compute networks peerings create vpc2-vpc1 --network=vpc2 --
peer-network=vpc1
Updated [https://www.googleapis.com/compute/v1/projects/zippy-chariot-334616/global/networks/vpc2].
---
autoCreateSubnetworks: false
creationTimestamp: '2022-05-12T18:51:51.401-07:00'
id: '7620219451762280280'
kind: compute#network
name: vpc2
networkFirewallPolicyEnforcementOrder: AFTER_CLASSIC_FIREWALL
peerings:
- autoCreateRoutes: true
  exchangeSubnetRoutes: true
  exportCustomRoutes: false
  exportSubnetRoutesWithPublicIp: true
  importCustomRoutes: false
  importSubnetRoutesWithPublicIp: false
  name: vpc2-vpc1
  network: https://www.googleapis.com/compute/v1/projects/zippy-chariot-334616/global/networks/vpc1
  state: ACTIVE
  stateDetails: '[2022-05-12T21:03:05.198-07:00]: Connected.'
routingConfig:
  routingMode: REGIONAL
selfLink: https://www.googleapis.com/compute/v1/projects/zippy-chariot-334616/global/networks/vpc2
selfLinkWithId: https://www.googleapis.com/compute/v1/projects/zippy-chariot-334616/global/networks/7620219451762
280280
subnetworks:
- https://www.googleapis.com/compute/v1/projects/zippy-chariot-334616/regions/us-east1/subnetworks/subnet2a
- https://www.googleapis.com/compute/v1/projects/zippy-chariot-334616/regions/us-central1/subnetworks/subnet2b
```

Figure 3-17. *Peering vpc2 to vpc1*

Vice versa, since the peering relation is symmetrical, we need to peer vpc2 to vpc1.

Once the peering has been established, vm1 can ping vm2 and vice versa, as you can see in Figure 3-18.

```
darioxml@cloudshell:~ (zippy-chariot-334616)$ gcloud compute ssh --zone "us-east1-c" "vm1"  --project "zippy-char
iot-334616"
Linux vm1 5.10.0-13-cloud-amd64 #1 SMP Debian 5.10.106-1 (2022-03-17) x86_64

The programs included with the Debian GNU/Linux system are free software;
the exact distribution terms for each program are described in the
individual files in /usr/share/doc/*/copyright.

Debian GNU/Linux comes with ABSOLUTELY NO WARRANTY, to the extent
permitted by applicable law.
Last login: Fri May 13 03:43:01 2022 from 34.138.252.59
darioxml@vm1:~$ ping 10.240.4.2
PING 10.240.4.2 (10.240.4.2) 56(84) bytes of data.
64 bytes from 10.240.4.2: icmp_seq=1 ttl=64 time=31.6 ms
64 bytes from 10.240.4.2: icmp_seq=2 ttl=64 time=30.6 ms
64 bytes from 10.240.4.2: icmp_seq=3 ttl=64 time=30.6 ms
64 bytes from 10.240.4.2: icmp_seq=4 ttl=64 time=30.6 ms
64 bytes from 10.240.4.2: icmp_seq=5 ttl=64 time=31.9 ms
64 bytes from 10.240.4.2: icmp_seq=6 ttl=64 time=31.9 ms
64 bytes from 10.240.4.2: icmp_seq=7 ttl=64 time=33.3 ms
64 bytes from 10.240.4.2: icmp_seq=8 ttl=64 time=33.2 ms
64 bytes from 10.240.4.2: icmp_seq=9 ttl=64 time=33.2 ms
^C
--- 10.240.4.2 ping statistics ---
9 packets transmitted, 9 received, 0% packet loss, time 8012ms
rtt min/avg/max/mdev = 30.553/31.864/33.260/1.082 ms
darioxml@vm1:~$
```

Figure 3-18. *vm1 connectivity to vm2 established with VPC peering*

The final setup is shown in Figure 3-19.

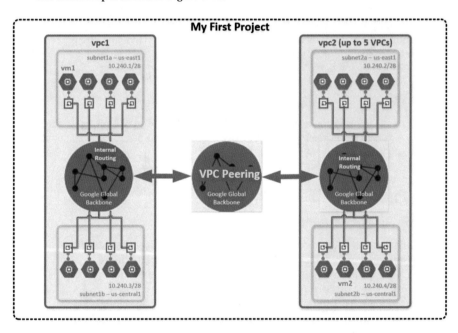

Figure 3-19. *VPC peering between vpc1 and vpc2*

Creating a Shared VPC and Sharing Subnets with Other Projects

Before discussing Shared VPC, let's start by introducing the concept of a project.

Host and Service Project Concepts

A *project* is a container that you use to group and administer the Google Cloud resources for your workload, for example, VMs, VPCs, principals, storage buckets, GKE clusters, cloud SQL databases, and many others. The resources can belong to any service type, for example, compute, network, storage, databases, IAM, etc. In this context, a project is a construct intended to enforce boundaries between resources.

A project is also a unit of billing and a unit of permissions. The former associates one—and one only—billing account to the project, and the latter defines IAM policies for the project. Resource quotas are also managed at a project level.

In order to create a shared VPC, your GCP account must exist in the context of an organization resource. Once an organization is available, you can create a shared VPC in a project called the *host project*.

You then share this VPC with other projects in your organization called *service projects*. Within a service project, you can create VMs (and other compute resources) and connect them to some or all the subnets of the Shared VPC you created in the host project. Since the VMs are created in the service project, the billing account associated to the service project pays for the VMs and the other compute resources connected to the shared subnets.

This construct *host-service* project has the key benefit of letting you scale your organization to thousands of cloud developers by centrally administering your VPCs. This construct also furthers separation of concerns because all developers in your organization will be focusing on the development of their applications—within the boundaries of their own GCP service project—while all network engineers will be focusing on the administration of shared VPCs, within the boundaries of their GCP host project.

Shared VPC Deep Dive

In this section, you will learn how to provision a shared VPC with two subnets. You will configure the first subnet `subnet-frontend` to be accessed by user `joseph@dariokart.com` and the second subnet `subnet-backend` to be accessed by user `samuele@dariokart.com`.

Assigning Roles to Principals

To implement this use case, you will need three principals:

1. A principal with the `compute.xpnAdmin` and `resourcemanager.projectIamAdmin` roles at the organization or folder level. The former role grants permissions to enable a host project and subsequently to attach service projects to the host project. The latter role grants permissions to share all—or a subset of—the existing and future subnets. Additionally, if you want to view your Shared VPC from the console, you need to add a role, which includes the `compute.network.list` permission, for example, `compute.networkViewer`.

2. A principal with the `compute.networkUser` role in the subnet `subnet-frontend` and basic editor role in the service project `frontend-devs`.

3. A principal with the `compute.networkUser` role in the subnet `subnet-backend` and basic editor role in the service project `backend-devs`.

In this exercise, user gianni@dariokart.com will be principal one, that is, a user with Shared VPC administration access at the organization level. Users joseph@dariokart.com and samuele@dariokart.com will be principals two and three, respectively.

Figures 3-21 to 3-23 illustrate the IAM allow policy setup for principal gianni@dariokart.com.

```
itsmedario@cloudshell:~ (vpc-host-nonprod-pu645-uh372)$ gcloud organizations list
DISPLAY_NAME: dariokart.com
ID: 585269232696
```

Figure 3-20. *Getting the organization ID*

```
itsmedario@cloudshell:~ (vpc-host-nonprod-pu645-uh372)$ gcloud organizations add-iam-policy-binding 585269232696
  --member='user:gianni@dariokart.com'  --role="roles/compute.xpnAdmin"
Updated IAM policy for organization [585269232696].
```

Figure 3-21. *Adding* compute.xpnAdmin *role to gianni@dariokart.com*

```
itsmedario@cloudshell:~ (vpc-host-nonprod-pu645-uh372)$ gcloud organizations add-iam-policy-binding 585269232696
  --member='user:gianni@dariokart.com'  --role="roles/resourcemanager.projectIamAdmin"
Updated IAM policy for organization [585269232696].
```

Figure 3-22. *Adding* resourcemanager.projectIamAdmin *role to gianni@dariokart.com*

```
itsmedario@cloudshell:~ (vpc-host-nonprod-pu645-uh372)$ gcloud organizations add-iam-policy-binding 585269232696
  --member='user:gianni@dariokart.com'  --role="roles/compute.networkViewer"
Updated IAM policy for organization [585269232696].
```

Figure 3-23. *Adding* compute.networkViewer *role to* gianni@dariokart.com

Figures 3-24 and 3-25 illustrate the IAM allow policy setup for principals joseph@dariokart.com and samuele@dariokart.com, respectively.

```
itsmedario@cloudshell:~ (vpc-host-nonprod-pu645-uh372)$ gcloud projects add-iam-policy-binding frontend-devs-7734
  --member='user:joseph@dariokart.com' --role='roles/editor'
Updated IAM policy for project [frontend-devs-7734].
bindings:
- members:
  - serviceAccount:service-239408874101@compute-system.iam.gserviceaccount.com
  role: roles/compute.serviceAgent
- members:
  - serviceAccount:239408874101-compute@developer.gserviceaccount.com
  - serviceAccount:239408874101@cloudservices.gserviceaccount.com
  - user:joseph@dariokart.com
  role: roles/editor
- members:
  - user:itsmedario@dariokart.com
  role: roles/owner
etag: BwXhX5-E4-A=
version: 1
itsmedario@cloudshell:~ (vpc-host-nonprod-pu645-uh372)$ █
```

Figure 3-24. *Adding* editor *role to* joseph@dariokart.com *in project* frontend-devs

```
itsmedario@cloudshell:~ (vpc-host-nonprod-pu645-uh372)$ gcloud projects add-iam-policy-binding backend-devs-7736
--member='user:samuele@dariokart.com' --role='roles/editor'
Updated IAM policy for project [backend-devs-7736].
bindings:
- members:
  - serviceAccount:service-211670805257@compute-system.iam.gserviceaccount.com
  role: roles/compute.serviceAgent
- members:
  - serviceAccount:211670805257-compute@developer.gserviceaccount.com
  - serviceAccount:211670805257@cloudservices.gserviceaccount.com
  - user:samuele@dariokart.com
  role: roles/editor
- members:
  - user:itsmedario@dariokart.com
  role: roles/owner
etag: BwXhX66wgGI=
version: 1
itsmedario@cloudshell:~ (vpc-host-nonprod-pu645-uh372)$
```

Figure 3-25. *Adding editor role to samuele@dariokart.com in project backend-devs*

To scope IAM allow policies at the organization level, we need first to obtain the organization ID, as described in Figure 3-20.

Creating the Shared VPC

So far, we have assigned the necessary IAM roles to the three principals. Next, we need to create the actual VPC and its two subnets (Figures 3-26 to 3-28).

```
itsmedario@cloudshell:~ (vpc-host-nonprod-pu645-uh372)$ gcloud compute networks create your-app-shared-vpc --subn
et-mode=custom
Created [https://www.googleapis.com/compute/v1/projects/vpc-host-nonprod-pu645-uh372/global/networks/your-app-sha
red-vpc].
NAME: your-app-shared-vpc
SUBNET_MODE: CUSTOM
BGP_ROUTING_MODE: REGIONAL
IPV4_RANGE:
GATEWAY_IPV4:

Instances on this network will not be reachable until firewall rules
are created. As an example, you can allow all internal traffic between
instances as well as SSH, RDP, and ICMP by running:

$ gcloud compute firewall-rules create <FIREWALL_NAME> --network your-app-shared-vpc --allow tcp,udp,icmp --sourc
e-ranges <IP_RANGE>
$ gcloud compute firewall-rules create <FIREWALL_NAME> --network your-app-shared-vpc --allow tcp:22,tcp:3389,icmp

itsmedario@cloudshell:~ (vpc-host-nonprod-pu645-uh372)$
```

Figure 3-26. *Creating the shared VPC*

```
itsmedario@cloudshell:~ (vpc-host-nonprod-pu645-uh372)$ gcloud compute networks subnets create subnet-frontend --
network=your-app-shared-vpc --range=192.168.0.0/27
Did you mean region [us-east1] for subnetwork: [subnet-frontend] (Y/n)? Y

Created [https://www.googleapis.com/compute/v1/projects/vpc-host-nonprod-pu645-uh372/regions/us-east1/subnetworks
/subnet-frontend].
NAME: subnet-frontend
REGION: us-east1
NETWORK: your-app-shared-vpc
RANGE: 192.168.0.0/27
STACK_TYPE: IPV4_ONLY
IPV6_ACCESS_TYPE:
INTERNAL_IPV6_PREFIX:
EXTERNAL_IPV6_PREFIX:
```

Figure 3-27. *Creating subnet-frontend in region us-east1*

```
itsmedario@cloudshell:~ (vpc-host-nonprod-pu645-uh372)$ gcloud compute networks subnets create subnet-backend --n
etwork=your-app-shared-vpc --range=192.168.1.0/27 --region=us-central1
Created [https://www.googleapis.com/compute/v1/projects/vpc-host-nonprod-pu645-uh372/regions/us-central1/subnetwo
rks/subnet-backend].
NAME: subnet-backend
REGION: us-central1
NETWORK: your-app-shared-vpc
RANGE: 192.168.1.0/27
STACK_TYPE: IPV4_ONLY
IPV6_ACCESS_TYPE:
INTERNAL_IPV6_PREFIX:
EXTERNAL_IPV6_PREFIX:
itsmedario@cloudshell:~ (vpc-host-nonprod-pu645-uh372)$
```

Figure 3-28. *Creating* subnet-backend *in region* us-central1

Last, in order to test connectivity from the subnets, we need to allow incoming traffic using the SSH, TCP, and ICMP protocols. Firewall rules are defined for the whole VPC. As a result, they apply to all its subnets. Figure 3-29 illustrates the creation of such firewall rule.

```
itsmedario@cloudshell:~ (vpc-host-nonprod-pu645-uh372)$ gcloud compute firewall-rules create allow-ssh-ping-share
d-vpc --network your-app-shared-vpc --allow tcp:22,tcp:3389,icmp
Creating firewall...working..Created [https://www.googleapis.com/compute/v1/projects/vpc-host-nonprod-pu645-uh372
/global/firewalls/allow-ssh-ping-shared-vpc].
Creating firewall...done.
NAME: allow-ssh-ping-shared-vpc
NETWORK: your-app-shared-vpc
DIRECTION: INGRESS
PRIORITY: 1000
ALLOW: tcp:22,tcp:3389,icmp
DENY:
DISABLED: False
itsmedario@cloudshell:~ (vpc-host-nonprod-pu645-uh372)$
```

Figure 3-29. *Enabling ingress* ssh, tcp, ICMP *into the shared VPC*

Creating the Service Projects

The next step is to create the two service projects (Figure 3-30).

```
itsmedario@cloudshell:~ (evocative-hour-351120)$ gcloud projects create frontend-devs-7734 --folder=47243179562 -
-name=frontend-devs
Create in progress for [https://cloudresourcemanager.googleapis.com/v1/projects/frontend-devs-7734].
Waiting for [operations/cp.6620130166879488424] to finish...done.
Enabling service [cloudapis.googleapis.com] on project [frontend-devs-7734]...
Operation "operations/acat.p2-239408874101-37c53d14-a288-4652-aec8-12b8d68c1fa8" finished successfully.
itsmedario@cloudshell:~ (evocative-hour-351120)$ gcloud projects create backend-devs-7736 --folder=47243179562 --
name=backend-devs
Create in progress for [https://cloudresourcemanager.googleapis.com/v1/projects/backend-devs-7736].
Waiting for [operations/cp.4683443581822127223] to finish...done.
Enabling service [cloudapis.googleapis.com] on project [backend-devs-7736]...
Operation "operations/acat.p2-211670805257-ee3f0503-3afd-4439-9594-0489eba5c75e" finished successfully.
itsmedario@cloudshell:~ (evocative-hour-351120)$
```

Figure 3-30. *Creating the two service projects* frontend-devs *and* backend-devs

Make sure each of the two newly created projects is linked to a billing account. Remember that a project can only be linked to one billing account. Also, remember that a billing account pays for a project, which owns Google Cloud resources.

Figure 3-31 shows how to link the two newly created service projects to a billing account. Notice how the project IDs (frontend-devs-7734, backend-devs-7736) and not the project names (frontend-devs, backend-devs) are required.

```
itsmedario@cloudshell:~ (vpc-host-nonprod-pu645-uh372)$ gcloud alpha billing accounts projects link frontend-devs
-7734 --billing-account=
WARNING: The `gcloud <alpha|beta> billing accounts projects` groups have been moved to
`gcloud beta billing projects`. Please use the new, shorter commands instead.
billingAccountName: billingAccounts/
billingEnabled: true
name: projects/frontend-devs-7734/billingInfo
projectId: frontend-devs-7734
itsmedario@cloudshell:~ (vpc-host-nonprod-pu645-uh372)$ gcloud alpha billing accounts projects link backend-devs-
7736 --billing-account=
WARNING: The `gcloud <alpha|beta> billing accounts projects` groups have been moved to
`gcloud beta billing projects`. Please use the new, shorter commands instead.
billingAccountName: billingAccounts/
billingEnabled: true
name: projects/backend-devs-7736/billingInfo
projectId: backend-devs-7736
```

Figure 3-31. *Linking service projects to a billing account*

Also, the billing account ID has been redacted, given the sensitivity nature of this data.

For more information on this command, visit `https://cloud.google.com/sdk/gcloud/reference/alpha/billing/accounts/projects/link`.

Enabling Compute API for Service and Host Projects

In order to establish a shared VPC, host and service projects must have the compute API enabled. Figure 3-32 shows you how to enable it.

```
itsmedario@cloudshell:~ (vpc-host-nonprod-pu645-uh372)$ gcloud services enable compute.googleapis.com --project=f
rontend-devs-7734
Operation "operations/acf.p2-239408874101-6fb3d755-85cc-4fb5-ac5d-1cb7dec0e5ec" finished successfully.
itsmedario@cloudshell:~ (vpc-host-nonprod-pu645-uh372)$ gcloud services enable compute.googleapis.com --project=b
ackend-devs-7736
Operation "operations/acf.p2-211670805257-428921f2-80af-482b-8277-8592a22bfac1" finished successfully.
itsmedario@cloudshell:~ (vpc-host-nonprod-pu645-uh372)$ gcloud services enable compute.googleapis.com --project=v
pc-host-nonprod-pu645-uh372
itsmedario@cloudshell:~ (vpc-host-nonprod-pu645-uh372)$
```

Figure 3-32. *Enabling the compute API to service and host projects*

Enabling Host Project

Now log out of your organization admin account (`itsmedario@dariokart.com`) and log in to Cloud Shell as `gianni@dariokart.com`. This is because this principal has been granted the minimal set of roles necessary—in accordance with the least privilege principle—to enable a project to host a shared VPC.

The `gcloud compute shared-vpc enable` command is displayed in Figure 3-33. The only required argument is the project ID, where you want your shared VPC to live in.

```
gianni@cloudshell:~ (vpc-host-nonprod-pu645-uh372)$ gcloud compute shared-vpc enable vpc-host-nonprod-pu645-uh372
Updated [https://www.googleapis.com/compute/v1/projects/vpc-host-nonprod-pu645-uh372].
gianni@cloudshell:~ (vpc-host-nonprod-pu645-uh372)$
```

Figure 3-33. *Enabling host project*

As a result of this command, the project `vpc-host-nonprod`, whose ID is `vpc-host-nonprod-pu645-uh372`, is officially a host project.

Let's make sure the newly enabled host project is listed as such in our organization (Figure 3-34).

```
gianni@cloudshell:~ (vpc-host-nonprod-pu645-uh372)$ gcloud compute shared-vpc organizations list-host-projects 58
5269232696
NAME: vpc-host-nonprod-pu645-uh372
CREATION_TIMESTAMP:
XPN_PROJECT_STATUS:
gianni@cloudshell:~ (vpc-host-nonprod-pu645-uh372)$ ▮
```

Figure 3-34. *Listing host projects*

Attaching Service Projects

Now that you have enabled your host project, you will need to attach the two newly created service projects, frontend-devs sharing the subnet-frontend subnet and backend-devs sharing the subnet-backend subnet.

Figure 3-35 shows the dariokart.com organization hierarchy, where you can see the host project we just enabled and the two other projects we are about to associate to it.

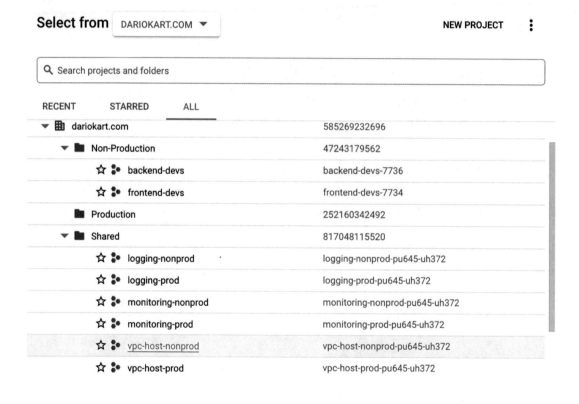

Figure 3-35. *Service projects in the resource hierarchy*

The intent of this use case is to show you how to configure a shared VPC with two subnets that are essentially mutually exclusive. As a result, principals who have permissions to create compute resources in the subnet-frontend subnet will not be able to create compute resources in the subnet-backend subnet and vice versa.

Likewise, all compute resources attached to `subnet-frontend` will be billed to the billing account associated to the `frontend-devs` project, and all compute resources attached to `subnet-backend` will be billed to the billing account associated to the `backend-devs` project. These two billing accounts may be the same, although this is not required.

To associate a project to a host project, use the `gcloud compute shared-vpc associated-projects` add command as illustrated in Figure 3-36.

```
gianni@cloudshell:~ (vpc-host-nonprod-pu645-uh372)$ gcloud compute shared-vpc associated-projects add frontend-de
vs-7734 --host-project vpc-host-nonprod-pu645-uh372
Updated [https://www.googleapis.com/compute/v1/projects/vpc-host-nonprod-pu645-uh372].
gianni@cloudshell:~ (vpc-host-nonprod-pu645-uh372)$ gcloud compute shared-vpc associated-projects add backend-dev
s-7736 --host-project vpc-host-nonprod-pu645-uh372
Updated [https://www.googleapis.com/compute/v1/projects/vpc-host-nonprod-pu645-uh372].
gianni@cloudshell:~ (vpc-host-nonprod-pu645-uh372)$ ▊
```

Figure 3-36. *Associating service projects to host project*

Upon completion of the preceding command, the two projects `frontend-devs` and `backend-devs` are officially service projects of a shared VPC.

Assigning Individual Subnet-Level Roles to Service Project Admins

As per the use case, we are going to configure two IAM allow policies for the two subnets as follows:

- Principal `joseph@dariokart.com` is an admin of `subnet-frontend`.

- Principal `samuele@dariokart.com` is an admin of `subnet-backend`.

Let's start from `subnet-frontend`.

First, we need to retrieve the current IAM allow policy for `subnet-frontend` as displayed in Figure 3-37.

```
gianni@cloudshell:~/iam (vpc-host-nonprod-pu645-uh372)$ gcloud beta compute networks subnets get-iam-policy subne
t-frontend    --region us-east1    --project vpc-host-nonprod-pu645-uh372    --format json > subnet-frontend-p
olicy.json
gianni@cloudshell:~/iam (vpc-host-nonprod-pu645-uh372)$
```

Figure 3-37. *Getting `subnet-frontend-policy.json` IAM policy*

As you can see by editing the JSON file (Figure 3-38), no role bindings are present in this IAM allow policy. This means access to the GCP resource `subnet-frontend` is implicitly denied for anyone.

```
{
    "etag": "BwXg5ykHUyQ=",
    "version": 1
▊
~
```

Figure 3-38. *Viewing `subnet-frontend-policy.json` IAM policy*

Therefore, we are going to add a new role binding that maps the principal `joseph@dariokart.com` to the IAM role `roles/compute.networkUser`. This role allows service owners to create VMs in a subnet of a shared VPC as you will see shortly.

■ **Note** You should have a basic understanding of Google Cloud IAM allow policies. For more details, visit https://cloud.google.com/iam/docs/policies.

Figure 3-39 shows the edited file.

```
{
  "bindings": [
    {
      "members": 
        "user:joseph@dariokart.com"
      ],
      "role": "roles/compute.networkUser"
    }
  ],
  "etag": "BwXg5ykHUyQ=",
  "version": 1
}
~
~
~
~
"subnet-frontend-policy.json" 12L, 172B
```

Figure 3-39. *Editing* subnet-frontend-policy.json *IAM policy*

Last, let's apply this IAM allow policy to our resource. This can be done by using the gcloud beta compute networks subnets set-iam-policy as illustrated in Figure 3-40.

```
gianni@cloudshell:~/iam (vpc-host-nonprod-pu645-uh372)$ gcloud beta compute networks subnets set-iam-policy subne
t-frontend subnet-frontend-policy.json    --region us-east1    --project vpc-host-nonprod-pu645-uh372
Updated IAM policy for subnetwork [subnet-frontend].
bindings:
- members:
  - user:joseph@dariokart.com
  role: roles/compute.networkUser
etag: BwXg57JJC6o=
version: 1
gianni@cloudshell:~/iam (vpc-host-nonprod-pu645-uh372)$ []
```

Figure 3-40. *Applying IAM allow policy to* subnet-frontend

■ **Note** While editing the file subnet-frontend-policy.json, make sure you don't use the tab character for indentation; otherwise, the YAML parser will throw an error.

Next, let's repeat the same procedure to ensure the principal samuele@dariokart.com is the only admin of subnet-backend (Figures 3-41 to 3-44).

```
gianni@cloudshell:~/iam (vpc-host-nonprod-pu645-uh372)$ gcloud beta compute networks subnets get-iam-policy subne
t-backend    --region us-central1    --project vpc-host-nonprod-pu645-uh372    --format json > subnet-backend-
policy.json
gianni@cloudshell:~/iam (vpc-host-nonprod-pu645-uh372)$ []
```

Figure 3-41. *Getting* subnet-backend-policy.json *IAM policy*

```
{
  "etag": "ACAB"

~
```

Figure 3-42. *Viewing* subnet-backend-policy.json *IAM policy*

```
{
  "bindings": [

    "members": [
      "user:samuele@dariokart.com"
    ],
    "role": "roles/compute.networkUser"

  ],
  "etag": "ACAB",
  "version": 1
}
~
~
~
~
~
~
"subnet-backend-policy.json" 12L, 165B
```

Figure 3-43. *Editing* subnet-backend-policy.json *IAM policy*

```
gianni@cloudshell:~/iam (vpc-host-nonprod-pu645-uh372)$ gcloud beta compute networks subnets set-iam-policy subne
t-backend subnet-backend-policy.json    --region us-central1    --project vpc-host-nonprod-pu645-uh372
Updated IAM policy for subnetwork [subnet-backend].
bindings:
- members:
  - user:samuele@dariokart.com
  role: roles/compute.networkUser
etag: BwXhDryGOCI=
version: 1
gianni@cloudshell:~/iam (vpc-host-nonprod-pu645-uh372)$
```

Figure 3-44. *Applying IAM allow policy to* subnet-backend

Using a Shared VPC

In this section, you will learn how the two principals joseph@dariokart.com and samuele@dariokart.com are allowed to use the shared VPC by creating compute resources limited to the subnets they have been granted access to, that is, subnet-frontend and subnet-backend, respectively. These compute resources include VMs, instance templates, managed instance groups, internal load balancers, and others.

For the sake of simplicity, we will first list the subnets each principal can use, and then we will create a VM in each subnet. Finally, we will demonstrate that the two VMs can effectively communicate with each other, even though they are managed and billed separately, that is, they are owned by two different (service) projects. The ability of the two VMs to communicate is provided by design because they belong to different subnets of the same VPC, and internal routing is provided by default.

Figure 3-45 shows the setup.

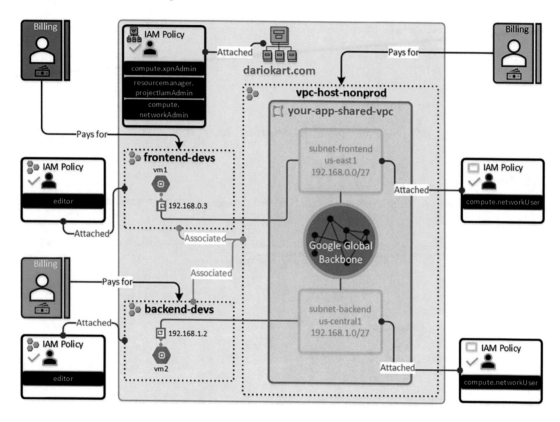

Figure 3-45. *Shared VPC separation of concerns*

Listing Usable Subnets

Let's log in to Cloud Shell as principal joseph@dariokart.com, which is a service administrator for project frontend-devs, and let's verify this principal can use subnet-frontend but not subnet-backend. Figure 3-46 shows how to use the gcloud compute networks subnets list-usable command to perform this verification.

```
joseph@cloudshell:~ (frontend-devs-7734)$ gcloud compute networks subnets list-usable --project vpc-host-nonprod-
pu645-uh372
PROJECT: vpc-host-nonprod-pu645-uh372
REGION: us-east1
NETWORK: your-app-shared-vpc
SUBNET: subnet-frontend
RANGE: 192.168.0.0/27
SECONDARY_RANGES:
joseph@cloudshell:~ (frontend-devs-7734)$ █
```

Figure 3-46. *Listing usable subnets for principal joseph@dariokart.com*

Similarly, let's log in to Cloud Shell as principal samuele@dariokart.com, which is a service administrator for project backend-devs, and let's verify this principal can use subnet-backend but not subnet-frontend. Figure 3-47 illustrates how to perform this verification.

```
samuele@cloudshell:~ (backend-devs-7736)$ gcloud compute networks subnets list-usable --project vpc-host-nonprod-
pu645-uh372
PROJECT: vpc-host-nonprod-pu645-uh372
REGION: us-central1
NETWORK: your-app-shared-vpc
SUBNET: subnet-backend
RANGE: 192.168.1.0/27
SECONDARY_RANGES:
samuele@cloudshell:~ (backend-devs-7736)$ █
```

Figure 3-47. *Listing usable subnets for principal samuele@dariokart.com*

Creating VMs

Next, let's create two VMs: the first in subnet-frontend and the second in subnet-backend. Figures 3-48 and 3-49 display the VM creation.

```
joseph@cloudshell:~ (frontend-devs-7734)$ gcloud compute instances create vm1 --project=frontend-devs-7734 --subnet=projects/vpc-
host-nonprod-pu645-uh372/regions/us-east1/subnetworks/subnet-frontend --zone=us-east1-c
Created [https://www.googleapis.com/compute/v1/projects/frontend-devs-7734/zones/us-east1-c/instances/vm1].
NAME: vm1
ZONE: us-east1-c
MACHINE_TYPE: n1-standard-1
PREEMPTIBLE:
INTERNAL_IP: 192.168.0.3
EXTERNAL_IP: 35.227.84.39
STATUS: RUNNING
joseph@cloudshell:~ (frontend-devs-7734)$
```

Figure 3-48. *Creating vm1 in subnet-frontend*

```
samuele@cloudshell:~ (backend-devs-7736)$ gcloud compute instances create vm2 --project=backend-devs-7736 --subnet=projects/vpc-h
ost-nonprod-pu645-uh372/regions/us-central1/subnetworks/subnet-backend --zone=us-central1-a
Created [https://www.googleapis.com/compute/v1/projects/backend-devs-7736/zones/us-central1-a/instances/vm2].
NAME: vm2
ZONE: us-central1-a
MACHINE_TYPE: n1-standard-1
PREEMPTIBLE:
INTERNAL_IP: 192.168.1.2
EXTERNAL_IP: 34.71.21.93
STATUS: RUNNING
samuele@cloudshell:~ (backend-devs-7736)$
```

Figure 3-49. *Creating vm2 in subnet-backend*

Given the existing project boundaries, principal joseph@dariokart.com has permissions to create a VM in subnet-frontend, but not in subnet-backend.

Likewise, principal samuele@dariokart.com has permissions to create a VM in subnet-backend, but not in subnet-frontend.

Verifying VM Connectivity

Finally, let's connect via the SSH protocol to each VM and verify the two VMs can connect to each other.

Figure 3-50 illustrates how to connect with SSH. Once connected, we use the hostname Linux command to determine the internal IP address of vm1.

```
joseph@cloudshell:~ (frontend-devs-7734)$ gcloud compute ssh vm1 --zone=us-east1-c
Enter passphrase for key '/home/joseph/.ssh/google_compute_engine':
Linux vm1 5.10.0-15-cloud-amd64 #1 SMP Debian 5.10.120-1 (2022-06-09) x86_64

The programs included with the Debian GNU/Linux system are free software;
the exact distribution terms for each program are described in the
individual files in /usr/share/doc/*/copyright.

Debian GNU/Linux comes with ABSOLUTELY NO WARRANTY, to the extent
permitted by applicable law.
Last login: Fri Jun 24 15:11:43 2022 from 35.231.59.42
joseph@vm1:~$ hostname -I
192.168.0.3
joseph@vm1:~$ ▮
```

Figure 3-50. *Determining internal IP address for* vm1 *in* subnet-frontend

Figure 3-51 shows the same process to determine the internal IP address of vm2.

```
samuele@cloudshell:~ (backend-devs-7736)$ gcloud compute ssh vm2 --zone=us-central1-a
Enter passphrase for key '/home/samuele/.ssh/google_compute_engine':
Linux vm2 5.10.0-15-cloud-amd64 #1 SMP Debian 5.10.120-1 (2022-06-09) x86_64

The programs included with the Debian GNU/Linux system are free software;
the exact distribution terms for each program are described in the
individual files in /usr/share/doc/*/copyright.

Debian GNU/Linux comes with ABSOLUTELY NO WARRANTY, to the extent
permitted by applicable law.
Last login: Fri Jun 24 15:17:28 2022 from 34.139.31.11
samuele@vm2:~$ hostname -I
192.168.1.2
samuele@vm2:~$
```

Figure 3-51. *Determining internal IP address for* vm2 *in* subnet-backend

Finally, let's test connectivity from vm1 to vm2 (Figure 3-52).

```
joseph@vm1:~$ ping 192.168.1.2
PING 192.168.1.2 (192.168.1.2) 56(84) bytes of data.
64 bytes from 192.168.1.2: icmp_seq=1 ttl=64 time=34.5 ms
64 bytes from 192.168.1.2: icmp_seq=2 ttl=64 time=33.2 ms
64 bytes from 192.168.1.2: icmp_seq=3 ttl=64 time=33.3 ms
64 bytes from 192.168.1.2: icmp_seq=4 ttl=64 time=33.2 ms
^C
--- 192.168.1.2 ping statistics ---
4 packets transmitted, 4 received, 0% packet loss, time 3005ms
rtt min/avg/max/mdev = 33.193/33.561/34.517/0.554 ms
joseph@vm1:~$
```

Figure 3-52. *Pinging vm2 from vm1*

As you can see, the connectivity is successful. Let's repeat the same test to validate connectivity from vm2 to vm1.

As shown in Figure 3-53, even though there are 20% packet loss, the test is still successful because the ping command was interrupted after just a few seconds.

```
samuele@vm2:~$ hostname -I
192.168.1.2
samuele@vm2:~$ ping 192.168.0.3
PING 192.168.0.3 (192.168.0.3) 56(84) bytes of data.
64 bytes from 192.168.0.3: icmp_seq=1 ttl=64 time=34.4 ms
64 bytes from 192.168.0.3: icmp_seq=2 ttl=64 time=33.2 ms
64 bytes from 192.168.0.3: icmp_seq=3 ttl=64 time=33.2 ms
64 bytes from 192.168.0.3: icmp_seq=4 ttl=64 time=33.2 ms
^C
--- 192.168.0.3 ping statistics ---
5 packets transmitted, 4 received, 20% packet loss, time 4006ms
rtt min/avg/max/mdev = 33.224/33.515/34.367/0.491 ms
samuele@vm2:~$ █
```

Figure 3-53. *Pinging vm1 from vm2*

Deleting VMs

In order to avoid incurring unnecessary costs, if you no longer need the two VMs we just created it is always a good idea to delete them. This will keep your cloud cost under control and will reinforce the concept that infrastructure in the cloud is ephemeral by nature.

Figures 3-54 and 3-55 display how to delete vm1 and vm2, respectively.

```
joseph@cloudshell:~ (frontend-devs-7734)$ gcloud compute instances delete vm1 --zone=us-east1-c
The following instances will be deleted. Any attached disks configured to be auto-deleted will be deleted unless they are
attached to any other instances or the `--keep-disks` flag is given and specifies them for keeping. Deleting a disk is
irreversible and any data on the disk will be lost.
 - [vm1] in [us-east1-c]

Do you want to continue (Y/n)?  Y

Deleted [https://www.googleapis.com/compute/v1/projects/frontend-devs-7734/zones/us-east1-c/instances/vm1].
joseph@cloudshell:~ (frontend-devs-7734)$ █
```

Figure 3-54. *Deleting vm1*

```
samuele@cloudshell:~ (backend-devs-7736)$ gcloud compute instances delete vm2 --zone=us-central1-a
The following instances will be deleted. Any attached disks configured to be auto-deleted will be deleted unless they are
attached to any other instances or the `--keep-disks` flag is given and specifies them for keeping. Deleting a disk is
irreversible and any data on the disk will be lost.
 - [vm2] in [us-central1-a]

Do you want to continue (Y/n)?  Y

Deleted [https://www.googleapis.com/compute/v1/projects/backend-devs-7736/zones/us-central1-a/instances/vm2].
samuele@cloudshell:~ (backend-devs-7736)$
```

Figure 3-55. *Deleting vm2*

■ **Exam tip**　Notice how `gcloud` asked in which zone the VMs are located. Remember, as you learned in Chapter 2, VMs are zonal resources.

Shared VPC Summary

An important point this exercise has demonstrated is how the construct of a shared VPC effectively enables separation of duties by letting a team administer the shared VPC network infrastructure (e.g., the network administrators team) while letting other teams (e.g., frontend developers and backend developers) manage their own compute infrastructure.

Each service project is linked to their own billing account, which pays for the resources consumed by each service project. This feature furthers the level of decoupling among resources.

It is not required that each service project shares the same billing account. In fact, it is best practice that each service project be linked to its own, separate billing account. This way—for example—cost incurred by frontend developers are separated from cost incurred by backend developers.

In summary, the shared VPC construct enables separation of duties from security and cost standpoints while leveraging the built-in, internal routing capabilities between subnets of the shared VPC.

Sharing Subnets Using Folders

Projects are not the only way to administer a shared VPC. You can also administer a Shared VPC using folders.

For example, if you want to isolate your billing pipeline VPC from your web-app VPC, you can do so by creating two separate folders, each containing a host project.

A separate shared VPC administrator for each host project can then set up the respective Shared VPCs and associate service projects to each host project.

In this scenario, Google Cloud recommends to

- Group service projects consuming their Shared VPC in the same folder, so you can attach organization-level IAM policies to that folder at a later time

- Use subnet-level IAM policies so that you can specify which service project has access to create VMs in which subnet

The infographic in Figure 3-56 illustrates how to share subnets using folders. You can model your folder structure after your company's organizational structure. In the example, each business unit (BU) has its own GCP folder (BU1, BU2), which has its own shared VPC. The BU1 shared VPC admin cannot manage the shared VPC in the BU2 folder. Conversely, the BU2 shared VPC admin cannot manage the shared VPC in the BU1 folder.

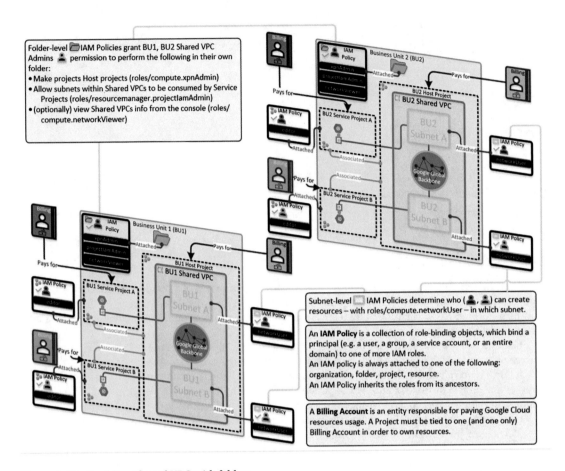

Figure 3-56. Enabling Shared VPC with folders

Configuring API Access to Google Services (e.g., Private Google Access, Public Interfaces)

So far, you learned that a VPC is a routing domain, which provides implicit connectivity between its subnets by using the Google Global Backbone. You created a custom-mode VPC, with subnets in different regions, and learned how to peer it with another VPC in order to extend internal RFC 1918 connectivity. Finally, you learned how a VPC can be shared across projects in order to separate network and security concerns from DevOps concerns. The shared VPC paradigm is powerful in that it allows an organization to scale its network infrastructure to a large number of teams while centralizing network and security operations.

A VPC as a standalone object is not very useful if it cannot access the ecosystem of products and services provided by Google Cloud or even by other cloud service providers. This interaction is expressed in the form of API consumption, where a service is made available to consumers by exposing its functionality in an API, typically built in accordance with the Representational State Transfer (REST). These APIs are exposed to the Internet for broader audience and come in two flavors or bundles:

1. The **all-apis** bundle provides access to the same APIs as `private.googleapis.com`.

2. The **vpc-sc** bundle provides access to the same APIs as `restricted.googleapis.com`.

The rationale about choosing between the two API bundles is based on the level of security needed to protect your workloads. If your security requirements mandate that you protect your workload from data exfiltration, then your workload will need to consume the vpc-sc bundle. In most of the remaining use cases, the all-apis bundle will suffice.

This section will teach you what you need to do to let compute resources in your VPC (e.g., VMs, GKE clusters, serverless functions, etc.) consume the Google APIs.

Configuring Private Google Access (PGA)

Private Google Access is a means to let VMs (or other compute resources) in your VPC consume the public endpoint of Google APIs *without requiring an external IP address*, that is, without traversing the Internet.

If your VM has an external IP address, then access to a public endpoint of a Google API, for example, https://redis.googleapis.com, is guaranteed by default. As a result, there is no need to enable PGA for the subnet where the VM's network interface is attached to.

■ **Exam tip**   Egress traffic is charged based on whether the traffic uses an internal or external IP address, whether the traffic crosses zone or region boundaries within Google Cloud, whether the traffic leaves or stays inside Google Cloud, and the network tier of traffic that leaves Google's network (premium or standard). For more information on network pricing, visit https://cloud.google.com/vpc/network-pricing.

Unlike routing and firewall rules which are scoped at the entire VPC level, Private Google Access operates on a per-subnet basis, that is, it can be toggled for a single subnet.

To enable GPA, make sure that the user updating the subnet has the permission compute.subnetworks. setPrivateIpGoogleAccess. In our dariokart.com organization, user Gianni needs this permission, and the role roles/compute.networkAdmin contains this permission. In Figure 3-57, we update the IAM allow policy attached to the organization, with a binding that maps the user Gianni to the roles/compute.networkAdmin.

```
itsmedario@cloudshell:~ (frontend-devs-7734)$ gcloud organizations add-iam-policy-binding 585269232696 --member='
user:gianni@dariokart.com' --role="roles/compute.networkAdmin"
Updated IAM policy for organization [585269232696].
```

Figure 3-57. *Adding compute.networkAdmin role to gianni@dariokart.com*

Next, as shown in Figure 3-58, we update the subnet that requires PGA and validate the change.

```
gianni@cloudshell:~ (vpc-host-nonprod-pu645-uh372)$ gcloud compute networks subnets update subnet-frontend --regi
on=us-east1 --enable-private-ip-google-access
Updated [https://www.googleapis.com/compute/v1/projects/vpc-host-nonprod-pu645-uh372/regions/us-east1/subnetworks
/subnet-frontend].
gianni@cloudshell:~ (vpc-host-nonprod-pu645-uh372)$ gcloud compute networks subnets describe subnet-frontend \
--region=us-east1 \
--format="get(privateIpGoogleAccess)"
True
gianni@cloudshell:~ (vpc-host-nonprod-pu645-uh372)$ ▊
```

Figure 3-58. *Enabling Private Google Access to subnet-frontend*

The flag --enable-private-ip-google-access is available also when you create a subnet with the gcloud compute networks subnets create.

Configuring Private Service Connect (PSC)

Private Service Connect is another way for VMs (or other compute resources) running in your VPC to consume Google APIs.

The idea is to allow your VMs to consume Google APIs using only RFC 1918 connectivity. This approach requires two design choices:

1. Avoid using the API public endpoint, for example, `https://storage.googleapis.com`.

2. Allow a direct, private link from an endpoint in your VPC and the target endpoint of the API your VM needs to consume.

■ **Exam tip**   The key difference between PSC and PGA is that Private Google Access still uses external IP addresses. It allows access to the external IP addresses used by App Engine and other eligible APIs and services. PSC lets you access Google APIs via internal IP addresses instead, always keeping traffic in the Google Global Backbone.

Let's configure a PSC endpoint in our shared VPC to provide VMs with access to the `all-apis` bundle. First and foremost, you need to make sure your network administrator has the following roles:

- `roles/servicedirectory.editor`

- `roles/dns.admin`

Similar to the role binding we added before, we update the organization IAM allow policy as shown in Figures 3-59 and 3-60.

```
itsmedario@cloudshell:~ (frontend-devs-7734)$ gcloud organizations add-iam-policy-binding 585269232696 --member='
user:gianni@dariokart.com' --role="roles/servicedirectory.editor"
Updated IAM policy for organization [585269232696].
```

Figure 3-59. *Adding* servicedirectory.editor *role to gianni@dariokart.com*

```
itsmedario@cloudshell:~ (frontend-devs-7734)$ gcloud organizations add-iam-policy-binding 585269232696 --member='
user:gianni@dariokart.com' --role="roles/dns.admin"
Updated IAM policy for organization [585269232696].
```

Figure 3-60. *Adding* dns.admin *role to gianni@dariokart.com*

Correspondingly, in the project whose PSC endpoint will be created, you need to enable the Service Directory API and the Cloud DNS API. The project we will be using is our host project vpc-host-nonprod, whose ID is vpc-host-nonprod-pu645-uh372. The compute.googleapis.com is also required, but we already enabled it as a prerequisite to create our shared VPC in the host project.

To discover the exact name of the Service Directory API and the Cloud DNS API, use the gcloud command in Figure 3-61.

```
itsmedario@cloudshell:~ (vpc-host-nonprod-pu645-uh372)$ gcloud services list --available | grep -E "(directory|dns)"
NAME: active-directory-dc-2016-cloud-infrastructure-services.cloudpartnerservices.goog
NAME: bind-dns-ubuntu-18-04-cloud-infrastructure-services.cloudpartnerservices.goog
NAME: bind-dns-ubuntu-20-04-cloud-infrastructure-services.cloudpartnerservices.goog
NAME: bluecat-dns-edge-proxy-service-bluecat-networks.cloudpartnerservices.goog
NAME: bluecatdns-bluecat-networks.cloudpartnerservices.goog
NAME: dns-server-windows-2016-cloud-infrastructure-services.cloudpartnerservices.goog
NAME: dns-server-windows-2019-cloud-infrastructure-services.cloudpartnerservices.goog
NAME: dns.googleapis.com
NAME: servicedirectory.googleapis.com
itsmedario@cloudshell:~ (vpc-host-nonprod-pu645-uh372)$ █
```

Figure 3-61. *Resolving Service Directory API and the Cloud DNS API names*

Now, we are ready to enable the two required APIs in the project (Figure 3-62).

```
itsmedario@cloudshell:~ (vpc-host-nonprod-pu645-uh372)$ gcloud services enable servicedirectory.googleapis.com --project=vpc-
host-nonprod-pu645-uh372
Operation "operations/acat.p2-755396457069-8d1a6ff8-3053-4524-a594-c05253761a9a" finished successfully.
itsmedario@cloudshell:~ (vpc-host-nonprod-pu645-uh372)$ gcloud services enable dns.googleapis.com --project=vpc-host-nonprod-
pu645-uh372
Operation "operations/acat.p2-755396457069-8bc7f7ce-ba24-4303-bca2-04fa0e915ac8" finished successfully.
itsmedario@cloudshell:~ (vpc-host-nonprod-pu645-uh372)$ █
```

Figure 3-62. *Enabling the Service Directory API and the Cloud DNS API*

Another prerequisite to enable PSC is that the subnet from which the VMs will consume the `all-apis` bundle must have PGA enabled. We already enabled PGA for subnet-frontend in the previous section.

Now, log in as the Shared VPC administrator, and follow the steps to create a private IP address (Figure 3-63) and a PSC endpoint (Figure 3-64).

```
gianni@cloudshell:~ (vpc-host-nonprod-pu645-uh372)$ gcloud compute addresses create psc-internal-ip-to-all-apis \
    --global \
    --purpose=PRIVATE_SERVICE_CONNECT \
    --addresses=192.168.3.14 \
    --network=your-app-shared-vpc
Created [https://www.googleapis.com/compute/v1/projects/vpc-host-nonprod-pu645-uh372/global/addresses/psc-internal-ip-to-all-
apis].
gianni@cloudshell:~ (vpc-host-nonprod-pu645-uh372)$ █
```

Figure 3-63. *Creating reserved IP for PSC endpoint*

```
gianni@cloudshell:~ (vpc-host-nonprod-pu645-uh372)$ gcloud compute forwarding-rules create psc2allapis --global --network=you
r-app-shared-vpc --address=psc-internal-ip-to-all-apis --target-google-apis-bundle=all-apis
Created [https://www.googleapis.com/compute/v1/projects/vpc-host-nonprod-pu645-uh372/global/forwardingRules/psc2allapis].
gianni@cloudshell:~ (vpc-host-nonprod-pu645-uh372)$
```

Figure 3-64. *Creating PSC endpoint with a forwarding rule*

In order to validate the newly created PSC endpoint, we are going to create a VM in subnet-backend (Figure 3-65) and a bucket in the project backend-devs (Figure 3-66). We will show that the VM can list the objects in the bucket.

```
samuele@cloudshell:~ (backend-devs-7736)$ gcloud compute instances create vm2 --project=backend-devs-7736 --subnet=projects/v
pc-host-nonprod-pu645-uh372/regions/us-central1/subnetworks/subnet-backend --zone=us-central1-a
Created [https://www.googleapis.com/compute/v1/projects/backend-devs-7736/zones/us-central1-a/instances/vm2].
NAME: vm2
ZONE: us-central1-a
MACHINE_TYPE: n1-standard-1
PREEMPTIBLE:
INTERNAL_IP: 192.168.1.3
EXTERNAL_IP: 35.193.61.230
STATUS: RUNNING
samuele@cloudshell:~ (backend-devs-7736)$ gcloud compute ssh vm2 --zone=us-central1-a
Warning: Permanently added 'compute.848186757702912721' (ECDSA) to the list of known hosts.
Enter passphrase for key '/home/samuele/.ssh/google_compute_engine':
Linux vm2 5.10.0-15-cloud-amd64 #1 SMP Debian 5.10.120-1 (2022-06-09) x86_64

The programs included with the Debian GNU/Linux system are free software;
the exact distribution terms for each program are described in the
individual files in /usr/share/doc/*/copyright.

Debian GNU/Linux comes with ABSOLUTELY NO WARRANTY, to the extent
permitted by applicable law.
samuele@vm2:~$
```

Figure 3-65. *Creating a VM in subnet-backend*

```
samuele@cloudshell:~ (backend-devs-7736)$ gsutil mb -c nearline -p backend-devs-7736 gs://dariokart-backend-bucket
Creating gs://dariokart-backend-bucket/...
samuele@cloudshell:~ (backend-devs-7736)$ touch a.txt
samuele@cloudshell:~ (backend-devs-7736)$ gsutil cp a.txt gs://dariokart-backend-bucket
Copying file://a.txt [Content-Type=text/plain]...
/ [1 files][    0.0 B/    0.0 B]
Operation completed over 1 objects.
samuele@cloudshell:~ (backend-devs-7736)$ █
```

Figure 3-66. *Creating a bucket with an object in project backend-devs*

In Figure 3-67, we want to test HTTP connectivity from our VM to our PSC endpoint, which is mapped to our reserved internal IP address.

```
samuele@vm2:~$ curl -v 192.168.3.14/generate_204
*   Trying 192.168.3.14:80...
* Connected to 192.168.3.14 (192.168.3.14) port 80 (#0)
> GET /generate_204 HTTP/1.1
> Host: 192.168.3.14
> User-Agent: curl/7.74.0
> Accept: */*
>
* Mark bundle as not supporting multiuse
< HTTP/1.1 204 No Content
< Content-Length: 0
< Date: Fri, 01 Jul 2022 19:12:45 GMT
<
* Connection #0 to host 192.168.3.14 left intact
samuele@vm2:~$ █
```

Figure 3-67. *Verifying accessibility to PSC*

We also want to make sure—always from the VM in subnet-backend—that we can call the GCP storage API, which can be accessed internally (using RFC 1918 IP space) by prefixing the name of the PSC forwarding rule psc2allapis as shown in Figure 3-68.

```
samuele@vm2:~$ nslookup storage-psc2allapis.p.googleapis.com
Server:        169.254.169.254
Address:       169.254.169.254#53

Non-authoritative answer:
Name:     storage-psc2allapis.p.googleapis.com
Address: 192.168.3.14  PSC reserved IP address

samuele@vm2:~$
```

Figure 3-68. *Resolving storage API hostname*

Next, in Figure 3-69, we list the content of our bucket using the gsutil command from vm2.

```
samuele@vm2:~$ gsutil ls gs://dariokart-backend-bucket
gs://dariokart-backend-bucket/a.txt
samuele@vm2:~$
```

Figure 3-69. *Listing content of gs://dariokart-backend-bucket from vm2*

As you can see, the command returned the newly created file a.txt. This confirms that the VM can consume the GCP storage API internally by using a Private Service Connect endpoint.

Finally, to avoid incurring unnecessary charges, let's clean up the resources we just created for this exercise, namely, the VM (Figure 3-70), the bucket (Figure 3-71), and the PSC endpoint (Figure 3-72).

```
samuele@cloudshell:~ (backend-devs-7736)$ gcloud compute instances delete vm2 --zone=us-central1-a
The following instances will be deleted. Any attached disks configured to be auto-deleted will be deleted unless they are
attached to any other instances or the `--keep-disks` flag is given and specifies them for keeping. Deleting a disk is
irreversible and any data on the disk will be lost.
 - [vm2] in [us-central1-a]

Do you want to continue (Y/n)?  Y

Deleted [https://www.googleapis.com/compute/v1/projects/backend-devs-7736/zones/us-central1-a/instances/vm2].
samuele@cloudshell:~ (backend-devs-7736)$
```

Figure 3-70. *Deleting vm2*

```
samuele@cloudshell:~ (backend-devs-7736)$ gsutil rm -r gs://dariokart-backend-bucket
Removing gs://dariokart-backend-bucket/a.txt#1656701201724459...
/ [1 objects]
Operation completed over 1 objects.
Removing gs://dariokart-backend-bucket/...
samuele@cloudshell:~ (backend-devs-7736)$
```

Figure 3-71. *Removing gs://dariokart-backend-bucket*

```
gianni@cloudshell:~ (vpc-host-nonprod-pu645-uh372)$ gcloud compute forwarding-rules delete psc2allapis --global
The following global forwarding rules will be deleted:
 - [psc2allapis]

Do you want to continue (Y/n)? Y

Deleted [https://www.googleapis.com/compute/v1/projects/vpc-host-nonprod-pu645-uh372/global/forwardingRules/psc2allapis].
gianni@cloudshell:~ (vpc-host-nonprod-pu645-uh372)$
```

Figure 3-72. *Deleting* psc2allapis *PSC endpoint*

Expanding VPC Subnet Ranges After Creation

VPCs are designed for extensibility. When you design the overall network architecture for your workloads, you have to make a number of choices, one of them being how many IP addresses are needed for each component of your workload. Obviously, this number is an estimate, yet this figure has to take into consideration the rate of scale for each architectural component of your workload, for example, frontend web servers, backend servers, database servers, and others.

The good news is that you can expand the subnets of your VPC if you discover that the mask you used for your subnet IP ranges is too small.

However, there are a few caveats you need to be aware of in these scenarios.

First, you can only expand the *primary* IP range of a subnet, and this operation cannot be undone, that is, you cannot shrink the subnet primary IP range once it's been defined.

Second, the primary IP range of a subnet that is used exclusively for load balancer proxies cannot be expanded. You will learn more about this constraint in Chapter 5.

Last, if your VPC is auto-mode, there is a limit of /16 for the mask you are allowed to use as the broadest prefix.

To expand the IP range of subnet-backend from /27 to /26, follow the step as indicated in Figure 3-73.

```
gianni@cloudshell:~ (vpc-host-nonprod-pu645-uh372)$ gcloud compute networks subnets expand-ip-range subnet-backend \
  --region=us-central1 \
  --prefix-length=26
The IP range of subnetwork [subnet-backend] will be expanded from 192.168.1.0/27 to 192.168.1.0/26. This operation may take
several minutes to complete and cannot be undone.

Do you want to continue (Y/n)? Y

Updated [https://www.googleapis.com/compute/v1/projects/vpc-host-nonprod-pu645-uh372/regions/us-central1/subnetworks/subnet-back
end].
gianni@cloudshell:~ (vpc-host-nonprod-pu645-uh372)$ █
```

Figure 3-73. *Expanding* subnet-backend

With this change, subnet-backend has been expanded from 32 to 64 IP addresses.

Configuring Routing

Every VPC comes with a distributed, scalable, virtual routing system.

Routes define the *paths* network traffic takes from a VM to other destinations. Network traffic is composed of packets, each characterized by a source and a destination, which can be inside your VPC network—for example, in another VM in the same or a different subnet—or outside of it.

Each VM has a controller that is kept informed of all applicable routes from the VPC's routing table. Each packet leaving a VM is delivered to the appropriate next hop of an applicable route based on a routing order. When you add or delete a route, the set of changes is propagated to the VM controllers by using an eventually consistent design.

Routes are defined as a network-wide configuration. Let's see the routes defined in our shared VPC (Figure 3-74).

```
gianni@cloudshell:~ (vpc-host-nonprod-pu645-uh372)$ gcloud compute routes list
NAME: default-route-193dd7b81a01d42b
NETWORK: your-app-shared-vpc
DEST_RANGE: 192.168.1.0/26
NEXT_HOP: your-app-shared-vpc
PRIORITY: 0

NAME: default-route-4b85d8f51a29229f
NETWORK: your-app-shared-vpc
DEST_RANGE: 192.168.0.0/27
NEXT_HOP: your-app-shared-vpc
PRIORITY: 0

NAME: default-route-6687972f3751cf18
NETWORK: your-app-shared-vpc
DEST_RANGE: 0.0.0.0/0
NEXT_HOP: default-internet-gateway
PRIORITY: 1000
gianni@cloudshell:~ (vpc-host-nonprod-pu645-uh372)$ ▯
```

Figure 3-74. *Listing your-app-shared-vpc static routes*

As you can see, each route is identified by the combination of the following elements:

```
route = <name, network, destination_range, next_hop, priority>
```

name: Every route in your project must have a unique name.

network: Every route in your project must belong to *one, and one only, VPC.*

destination_range: A single IPv4 CIDR block, which denotes the destination to which packets are being sent. Google Cloud does not support IPv6 destination ranges. Destinations must be expressed in CIDR notation, and the broadest destination possible is the entire Internet, that is, 0.0.0.0/0.

next_hop: 0.0.0.0/0 (default Internet gateway)

next_hop: A Cloud VPN tunnel

next_hop: A VM IP address

priority: Determines which route should be used if multiple routes have identical or overlapping destinations. Lower numbers indicate higher priorities; for example, a route with a priority value of 100 has higher priority than one with a priority value of 200.

network_tags: Optionally, a list of *network tags* so that the route will only apply to VMs that have at least one of the listed tags. If you don't specify network tags, Google Cloud applies the route to all VMs in the network.

Before learning route concepts and behavior, let's introduce a summary of route types (Figure 3-75).

System-generated Routes

Type	Destination	Next Hop	Removable?	Applicability
Default Route	`0.0.0.0/0` – Broadest IPv4 `::/0` – Broadest IPv6	Default-internet-gateway	Yes, to completely isolate your VPC from the Internet	Entire VPC
Subnet Route 1 per Subnet IP Range	Primary and Secondary subnet IP ranges, which are always the most specific → are always chosen before priority in route selection	VPC, which forwards packets to VMs or ILBs in its subnets	• Primary: No, unless you delete the entire subnet • Secondary: Yes, if you delete the Secondary IP range	Entire VPC • Always priority 0 • Cannot be overridden by other routes

Custom Routes

Type	Destination	Next Hop	Removable?	Applicability
Static Route	• IP range that does not overlap with any subnet IP range • IP range mask `/x` broader than any subnet IP range `/s`: `x < s`	• VM by name and zone • VM by IP address • Default-internet-gateway, PGA external IPs • Cloud VPN tunnel and its region • Internal Load Balancer (ILB) and its region	Yes	Entire VPC
Dynamic Route Always managed by a VPC Cloud Router	• IP range that does not overlap with any subnet IP range • Ignored if destination mask `/x` fits-in or equal-to a subnet IP range `/s`: `x ≥ s`	Cloud Router's BGP peer IP address	Yes, only by a Cloud Router if it stops receiving the route from its BGP peer	• Entire VPC if VPC's `bgp-routing-mode = global` • All VMs in the same region as the Cloud Router, otherwise

Peering Routes (Routes imported by Peer VPC)

Type	Destination	Next Hop	Removable?	Applicability
Peering Subnet Route	Primary and Secondary Peer VPC's subnet IP ranges	Peer VPC	• Primary: No, unless you delete the entire Peer VPC's subnet • Secondary: Yes, if you delete the Peer VPC's Secondary IP range	Entire Peer VPC
Peering Custom Route	Destinations of Custom Routes defined in the Peer VPC	Peer VPC	• Static: Yes • Dynamic: Yes, only by a Cloud Router if it stops receiving the route from its BGP peer	• Static: routes whose next hop is an ILB in Peer VPC are imported based on ILB's `allow-global-access` • Dynamic: routes imported based on VPC's `bgp-routing-mode`

Figure 3-75. Route types

Static vs. Dynamic Routing

Custom routes are either static routes you manually create and maintain or dynamic routes maintained and advertised automatically by one or more Cloud Routers.

Static Routes

Static routes can be created using the `gcloud compute routes create` command. An easy way to learn how to use this command is the `gcloud help` command (Figure 3-76, and its output in Figure 3-77).

```
gianni@cloudshell:~ (vpc-host-nonprod-pu645-uh372)$ gcloud help compute routes create
```

Figure 3-76. Using the `gcloud help` command

```
NAME
    gcloud compute routes create - create a new route

SYNOPSIS
    gcloud compute routes create NAME --destination-range=DESTINATION_RANGE
        (--next-hop-address=NEXT_HOP_ADDRESS
          | --next-hop-gateway=NEXT_HOP_GATEWAY | --next-hop-ilb=NEXT_HOP_ILB
          | --next-hop-instance=NEXT_HOP_INSTANCE
          | --next-hop-vpn-tunnel=NEXT_HOP_VPN_TUNNEL)
        [--description=DESCRIPTION] [--network=NETWORK; default="default"]
        [--next-hop-ilb-region=NEXT_HOP_ILB_REGION]
        [--next-hop-instance-zone=NEXT_HOP_INSTANCE_ZONE]
        [--next-hop-vpn-tunnel-region=NEXT_HOP_VPN_TUNNEL_REGION]
        [--priority=PRIORITY; default=1000] [--tags=TAG,[TAG,...]]
        [GCLOUD_WIDE_FLAG ...]
```

Figure 3-77. gcloud compute routes create synopsis

In addition to the route NAME, you must provide a destination range of outgoing packets the route will apply to, which is denoted by the flag --destination-range=DESTINATION_RANGE. The broadest destination range is 0.0.0.0/0.

Another required flag is the next hop, which can be one, *and one only*, of the following flags:

- **Next hop gateway** (--next-hop-gateway=default-internet-gateway): It denotes a path to the Internet (0.0.0.0/0) through the default Internet gateway, which routes packets to external IP addresses or Google API endpoints (Private Google Access).

- **Next hop instance by name** (--next-hop-instance=VM_HOSTNAME): You can denote the next hop of a route by using an existing VM's hostname and its zone *only* if the VM and the route are in the same project. In shared VPC setups, where a VM is in a service project and the route is in its associated host project, you need to use the VM's internal IP address instead. The VM must already exist, and its hostname must match VM_HOSTNAME when creating or updating the route. Also, the VM must have at least one network interface in the route's VPC. This flag requires that you specify the zone of the VM as well by setting the flag --next-hop-instance-zone.

- **Next hop instance by address** (--next-hop-address=VM_IPV4_ADDRESS): It denotes the internal IPv4 address of a VM (from the VM's primary IP or alias IP ranges) that should handle matching packets. The VM must have at least one network interface in the route's VPC, whose internal IP address must match VM_IPV4_ADDRESS. The VM must also be configured with IP forwarding enabled (e.g., by setting the flag --can-ip-forward when creating the VM with the gcloud compute instances create command).

- **Next hop internal TCP/UDP load balancer** (--next-hop-ilb=FORWARDING_RULE_NAME): It denotes the name or the IP address of an internal network TCP/UDP load balancer forwarding rule. When configuring the forwarding rule, the flag --load-balancing-scheme must be INTERNAL. When configuring the custom static route with an ILB as next hop, you cannot assign values to the --destination-range flag that match or are more specific than the IP range of a subnet route destination in the route's VPC. This is because the former would "eclipse" the latter, and subnet routes cannot be deleted or overridden, as indicated in Figure 3-75.

- **Next hop VPN tunnel** (`--next-hop-vpn-tunnel=VPN_TUNNEL_NAME`): It denotes the name of a Classic VPN tunnel that will receive forwarded traffic. This flag requires that you specify the region where the VPN tunnel has been created. Consider egress costs and network latency when routing traffic to a VPN tunnel in another region. You will learn more about VPN tunnels and their types (Classic or HA) in Chapter 7.

The relevant optional flags you need to know for the exam are

- **Network** (`--network=NETWORK`): It denotes the VPC the route applies to. Remember that a route is defined on a VPC basis.

- **Next hop ILB region** (`--next-hop-ilb-region=REGION`): It denotes the region of the next hop forwarding rule.

- **Next hop instance zone** (`--next-hop-instance-zone=ZONE`): It denotes the zone of the VM and is required when the VM's hostname is used as the next hop.

- **Next hop VPN tunnel region** (`--next-hop-vpn-tunnel-region=REGION`): It denotes the region of the next hop VPN tunnel and is required when a VPN tunnel is used as the next hop.

- **Priority** (`--priority=PRIORITY`): It denotes the route priority, relative to other routes with the same specificity. The lower the value, the higher the priority. Its default value is 1000.

- **Tags** (`--tags=TAG,[TAG,...]`): It denotes the set of VMs the route will be applied to. It can be a single tag (e.g., `--tags=web-qa`) or a list of tags (e.g., `--tags=web-qa,app-qa,db-qa,mw-qa`). If not specified, it defaults to all VMs in the VPC.

Dynamic Routes

Custom dynamic routes are managed by one or more cloud routers in your VPC. You no longer have to create routes using the `gcloud` command because a cloud router does the job for you.

A cloud router is a regional, fully distributed and managed Google Cloud service that uses the Border Gateway Protocol (BGP) to advertise IP address ranges. It programs custom dynamic routes based on the BGP advertisements that it receives from a peer router in the same or in a different VPC.

A cloud router is used to provide dynamic routes for

- Dedicated Interconnect

- Partner Interconnect

- HA VPN

- Classic VPN with dynamic routing

You may be thinking that by using dynamic routing instead of static routing, we just moved the problem to the cloud router. After all, we still need to create a cloud router responsible for advertising newly defined routes to its peer. Conversely, we need to create a cloud router responsible for learning newly defined routes from its peer.

Put differently, whether you choose to create custom static routes or you choose to create a cloud router that does the job for you, you still need to create something manually, for example, using `gcloud`. So, what's the advantage of using dynamic routing vs. static routing?

The main advantage is that dynamic routes—unlike static routes—are *change-tolerant*, that is, when the routing infrastructure changes, you don't have to do anything because the cloud router has been programmed to learn the change and automatically readjust the routes for you.

A metaphor I often like to use is traveling from location A to location B using a physical map or using a modern GPS system, for example, a mobile phone with access to Google Maps.

For short distances, chances of high traffic, construction work, or inclement weather—which won't be detected in your physical map—are low. As a result, your "good old map" will work most of the times.

For large distances, a number of unpredictable factors will likely impact your travel itinerary, resulting in detours, unexpected delays, and other hurdles. This is when your GPS system comes in handy by detecting issues ahead of time and by dynamically recalculating routes for you in order to select an optimal path toward your destination (location B).

In conclusion, static routes are great for small networks, which are not often subject to change. For large enterprises, using static routes is simply not a sustainable solution. That's when a cloud router "shines." Let's see how you create a cloud router (Figures 3-78 and 3-79).

```
gianni@cloudshell:~ (vpc-host-nonprod-pu645-uh372)$ gcloud help compute routers create
```

Figure 3-78. *Using the* gcloud help *command*

```
gcloud compute routers create - create a Compute Engine router

SYNOPSIS
    gcloud compute routers create NAME --network=NETWORK
        [--advertisement-mode=MODE] [--asn=ASN] [--async]
        [--description=DESCRIPTION] [--keepalive-interval=KEEPALIVE_INTERVAL]
        [--region=REGION] [--set-advertisement-groups=[GROUP,...]]
        [--set-advertisement-ranges=[CIDR_RANGE=DESC,...]]
        [GCLOUD_WIDE_FLAG ...]

DESCRIPTION
    gcloud compute routers create is used to create a router to provide dynamic
    routing to VPN tunnels and interconnects.

POSITIONAL ARGUMENTS
    NAME
        Name of the router to create.

REQUIRED FLAGS
    --network=NETWORK
        The network for this router
```

Figure 3-79. gcloud compute routers create *synopsis*

At a minimum, you have to provide a name for your cloud router and a VPC network where the cloud router will operate.

The optional flags you need to know for the exam are

- **Advertisement mode** (--advertisement-mode=MODE): MODE can be one of the two—CUSTOM or DEFAULT. The former indicates that you will manually configure BGP route advertisement. The latter indicates that Google will automatically configure BGP route advertisement for you.

- **Autonomous system number** (--asn=ASN): It denotes the ASN for the router. It must be a 16-bit or 32-bit private ASN as defined in https://tools.ietf.org/html/rfc6996, for example, --asn=64512.

- **Async** (--async): It denotes that you want the router to return immediately, without waiting for the operation in progress to complete.

- **Keep alive** (`--keepalive-interval=KEEPALIVE_INTERVAL`): It denotes the interval in seconds between keepalive messages, which the router exchanges with its peer in a BGP session. It ranges from 20 (default) to 60 seconds. Keepalive messages are used by BGP routers to determine whether a link or a host is alive.

- **Region** (`--region=REGION`): It denotes the region where the cloud router will operate.

- **Advertisement groups** (`--set-advertisement-groups=[GROUP,...]`): It can be set only when advertisement mode is `CUSTOM` and denotes the list of predefined IP range names, which will be dynamically advertised by the router to its BGP peer. The only value currently supported is `ALL_SUBNETS`, to indicate all subnets in the cloud router's VPC will be automatically advertised.

- **Advertisement ranges** (`--set-advertisement-ranges=[CIDR_RANGE=DESC,...]`): Similarly to advertisement groups, advertisement ranges can be set only when advertisement mode is `CUSTOM` and denotes the list of CIDR ranges, which will be dynamically advertised by the router to its BGP peer. `CIDR_RANGE` can be denoted as IPv4 or IPv6, the latter requiring the BGP session to enable IPv6. Optionally, a description can be added to the CIDR range listed, for example, to let the router advertise only a subnet `subnet1` with CIDR range 192.168.3.0/27, use `--set-advertisement-ranges=192.168.3.0/27=subnet1`.

Routing Order

A route is a rule that specifies how certain packets should be handled by the VPC. Routes are associated with VMs by tag, and the set of routes for a particular VM is called its routing table. For each packet leaving a VM, the system searches that VM's routing table for a single best matching route. Routes match packets by destination IP address, preferring *smaller or more specific ranges* over larger ones (see `--destination-range`). If there is a tie, the system selects the route with the smallest priority value (see `--priority`). If there is still a tie, it uses the layer 3 and 4 packet headers to select just one of the remaining matching routes.

For static routes, the packet is then forwarded as specified by `--next-hop-address`, `--next-hop-instance`, `--next-hop-vpn-tunnel`, or `--next-hop-gateway` of the winning route.

For dynamic routes, the next hop will be determined by the cloud router route advertisement.

Packets that do not match any route in the sending virtual machine routing table will be dropped.

Global vs. Regional Dynamic Routing

The behavior of your cloud router depends on whether the VPC it's associated with has been created with regional (default) or global BGP routing mode.

Let's review this setting for our shared VPC (Figure 3-80).

```
gianni@cloudshell:~ (vpc-host-nonprod-pu645-uh372)$ gcloud compute networks describe your-app-shared-vpc
autoCreateSubnetworks: false
creationTimestamp: '2022-06-03T07:06:09.499-07:00'
id: '6942442671499094974'
kind: compute#network
name: your-app-shared-vpc
networkFirewallPolicyEnforcementOrder: AFTER_CLASSIC_FIREWALL
routingConfig:
  routingMode: REGIONAL
selfLink: https://www.googleapis.com/compute/v1/projects/vpc-host-nonprod-pu645-uh372/global/networks/your-app-shared-vpc
selfLinkWithId: https://www.googleapis.com/compute/v1/projects/vpc-host-nonprod-pu645-uh372/global/networks/6942442671499094974
subnetworks:
- https://www.googleapis.com/compute/v1/projects/vpc-host-nonprod-pu645-uh372/regions/us-central1/subnetworks/subnet-backend
- https://www.googleapis.com/compute/v1/projects/vpc-host-nonprod-pu645-uh372/regions/us-east1/subnetworks/subnet-frontend
x_gcloud_bgp_routing_mode: REGIONAL
x_gcloud_subnet_mode: CUSTOM
gianni@cloudshell:~ (vpc-host-nonprod-pu645-uh372)$ █
```

Figure 3-80. *BGP routing mode default assignment in* your-app-shared-vpc

As highlighted, our shared VPC uses the default value REGIONAL. This means that any cloud router associated with our shared VPC—remember, routing is a *network-wide* configuration—advertises subnets and propagates learned routes to all VMs in the same *region* where the router is configured.

For example, if we create a cloud router for your-app-shared-vpc in us-east1, then the routes it learned from other VPCs and the subnets it propagated are available only to VMs in subnet-frontend, because this subnet is in the us-east1 region. VMs in subnet-backend have no clue about "foreign" routes, that is, routes about other VPCs connected to our shared VPCs.

If you want your cloud router to advertise subnets and propagate learned routes to VMs in all subnets of your VPC—*regardless of which region they belong to*—then set the -bgp-routing mode flag to GLOBAL, as indicated in Figure 3-81.

```
gianni@cloudshell:~ (vpc-host-nonprod-pu645-uh372)$ gcloud compute networks update your-app-shared-vpc --bgp-routing-mode=GLOBAL
gianni@cloudshell:~ (vpc-host-nonprod-pu645-uh372)$ gcloud compute networks describe your-app-shared-vpc
autoCreateSubnetworks: false
creationTimestamp: '2022-06-03T07:06:09.499-07:00'
id: '6942442671499094974'
kind: compute#network
name: your-app-shared-vpc
networkFirewallPolicyEnforcementOrder: AFTER_CLASSIC_FIREWALL
routingConfig:
  routingMode: GLOBAL
selfLink: https://www.googleapis.com/compute/v1/projects/vpc-host-nonprod-pu645-uh372/global/networks/your-app-shared-vpc
selfLinkWithId: https://www.googleapis.com/compute/v1/projects/vpc-host-nonprod-pu645-uh372/global/networks/6942442671499094974
subnetworks:
- https://www.googleapis.com/compute/v1/projects/vpc-host-nonprod-pu645-uh372/regions/us-central1/subnetworks/subnet-backend
- https://www.googleapis.com/compute/v1/projects/vpc-host-nonprod-pu645-uh372/regions/us-east1/subnetworks/subnet-frontend
x_gcloud_bgp_routing_mode: GLOBAL
x_gcloud_subnet_mode: CUSTOM
gianni@cloudshell:~ (vpc-host-nonprod-pu645-uh372)$ █
```

Figure 3-81. *Updating BGP routing mode flag in* your-app-shared-vpc

Let's visually explain this concept with the diagram in Figure 3-82.

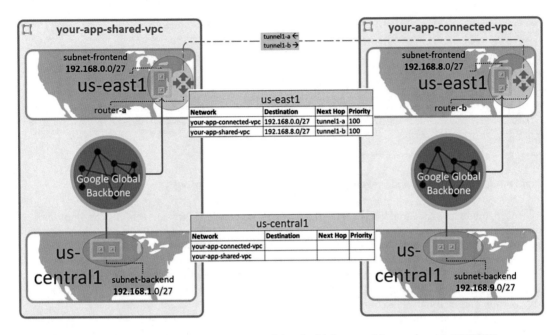

Figure 3-82. *Route exchange between two VPCs configured with* `bgp-routing-mode` *set to* `REGIONAL`

On the left side, we have our shared VPC `your-app-shared-vpc` you are familiar with, which was configured with the default BGP routing mode, that is, `REGIONAL`.

On the right side, we have another VPC `your-app-connected-vpc`, which is connected to the first VPC network using HA VPN—you will learn more about HA VPN in Chapter 7. For the sake of simplicity, we are showing in the diagram only the first two tunnels, `tunnel1-a` and `tunnel1-b`, even though there are two other tunnels to ensure fault tolerance. VPC `your-app-connected-vpc` is also configured with the default BGP routing mode, that is, `REGIONAL`.

Behind the scenes, there are two Cloud VPN gateways, one in each VPC network, which are responsible for enabling the secure IPsec channels. What is relevant to this diagram are the two cloud routers, which are regional resources—both in `us-east1`—and are responsible for establishing a BGP session in which subnet and custom routes are being exchanged.

Let's focus on the two regional route tables now: one for region `us-east1` and another for region `us-central1`. I intentionally chose to group routes by region because it's important that you relate the concept of a route to a physical region. After all, packets of data are being exchanged across a medium, which at the physical layer of the OSI model (layer 1) is implemented by interconnecting physical components, such as network interface controllers (NICs), Ethernet hubs, network switches, and many others.

As you can see, the first row in the `us-east1` regional table shows a subnet route advertised by `router-a` to `router-b`.

Symmetrically, the second row in the `us-east1` regional table shows a subnet route advertised by `router-b` to `router-a`.

In addition to the network, destination (prefix), and next hop, the cloud routers include the priority for the advertised route.

You control the advertised priority by defining a base priority for the prefixes. We will show you how to set up this value in the upcoming section "Updating the Base Priority for Advertised Routes." For the time being, we are using the base priority default value of 100.

■ **Note**   The region for both advertised subnet routes matches the region of the cloud routers, that is, us-east1.

On the other hand, the us-central1 regional table shows no routes for any of the two VPCs. This is because the BGP routing mode setting to REGIONAL in both VPCs has caused the two cloud routers to only exchange with each other's routes related to their own region, that is, us-east1. As a result, VMs in 192.168.9.0/27 cannot reach any VMs in 192.168.0.0/27 or 192.168.1.0/27. Likewise, VMs in 192.168.1.0/27 cannot reach any VMs in 192.168.8.0/27 or 192.168.9.0/27.

Now let's update both VPCs by setting the BGP routing mode to GLOBAL. With this simple change as illustrated in Figure 3-83, it's a very different story. Let's see why.

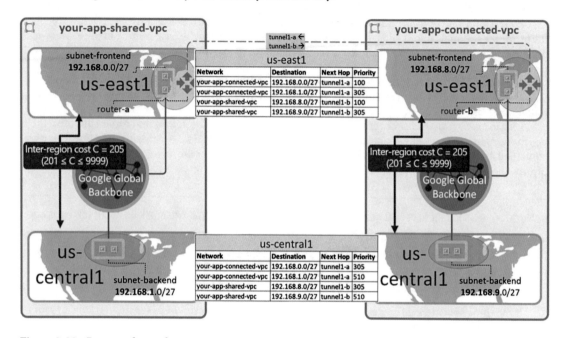

Figure 3-83. Route exchange between two VPCs configured with bgp-routing-mode set to GLOBAL

First, the two us-east1 regional routes we reviewed before are still there (rows 1 and 3), but this time router-a and router-b are no longer limited to advertising routes from their own region. Instead, a VPC configured to use bgp-routing-mode set to GLOBAL always tells its cloud routers to advertise routes (system-generated, custom, peering) from *any region spanned by the VPC.*

Consequently, router-a also advertised the subnet route for subnet-backend in your-app-shared-vpc. Likewise, router-b also advertised the subnet route for subnet-backend in your-app-connected-vpc. The effect of these two actions resulted in the addition of rows 2 and 4 to the regional table us-east1. We will explain the rationale about the priority set to 305 shortly. For the time being, just remember that the VPC BGP dynamic routing property set to GLOBAL has caused the cloud routers to advertise subnets located in a different region—that is, us-central1—from the one where they operate, that is, us-east1.

You'll probably wonder why even bother using the default value REGIONAL of bgp-routing-mode for a VPC if the number of routes advertised is limited to a single region.

Here is the caveat, and this is why I wanted to reiterate the fact that a cloud router is a regional resource to denote that it is always tied to a region. Inter-region routes add latency and egress charges to traffic leaving the region through the advertised route. As a result, an *inter-region cost* is added to the base priority of the route.

■ **Note** With reference to the well-architected framework, one of the pillars you need to consider when designing the network architecture for your workload is cost. By letting your VPC routing capability become global, you need to be aware of the effects of this choice. You get an enhanced connectivity across the components of your workload with a solid degree of automation by fully leveraging the BGP protocol and the scalability of the Google Global Backbone. However, this comes at the expense of higher cost and increased latency due to inter-region paths your workload traffic needs to cross.

The inter-region cost is a system-generated value, which is dynamically calculated by Google, and its value depends on a number of factors including distance between the regions, network performance, available bandwidth, and others. Its value ranges from 201 to 9999.

When cloud `router-a` advertises the prefix `192.168.1` to cloud `router-b` as illustrated in row 2 of the `us-east1` regional table, it adds the inter-region cost (e.g., C=205) to the base priority of the route (we used the default value 100). As a result, the advertised inter-regional route has a priority of 305. The same principle applies to row 4.

You learned so far that a cloud router associated with a VPC configured with BGP routing mode set to GLOBAL advertises routes in any regional table the VPC spans across—not just the region where the cloud router operates.

Let's focus now on the `us-central1` regional table. At a minimum, you wouldn't expect this table to be empty, right? Your assumption would be correct. In fact, this regional table contains the same rows contained in the regional table `us-east1`, but the priorities for all routes are lowered by adding to each route priority the extra inter-region cost (C=205).

■ **Note** One important thing you need to be aware of for the exam is that when talking about routes, lower numbers mean higher priorities. If you want to increase the priority of a route, you need to subtract something from the route priority. A route with priority 0 (zero) always wins because it has the highest possible priority a route can have.

If you think about it, it all makes sense because the path to connect a VM in `subnet-backend` of your-`app-connected-vpc` and another VM in `subnet-backend` of your-`app-shared-vpc` requires two inter-region costs in addition to the base priority, that is, 100 + 2*C.

Figure 3-83 illustrates this concept.

Viewing Inter-region Routes Programmed by a Cloud Router

Unlike custom static routes, which are created by Google in all regional tables with the *same* priority, custom dynamic routes automatically add into consideration the inter-region cost when they are advertised by a cloud router across regions.

One way to view these dynamic routes is by using the `gcloud compute routers get-status` command, as illustrated in Figures 3-84 and 3-85.

```
gianni@cloudshell:~ (vpc-host-nonprod-pu645-uh372)$ gcloud help compute routers get-status
```

Figure 3-84. *Using the gcloud help command*

```
NAME
    gcloud compute routers get-status - get status of a Compute Engine router

SYNOPSIS
    gcloud compute routers get-status NAME [--region=REGION]
        [GCLOUD_WIDE_FLAG ...]

DESCRIPTION
    gcloud compute routers get-status displays all runtime data associated with
    a Compute Engine router.

POSITIONAL ARGUMENTS
     NAME
        Name of the router to describe.
```

Figure 3-85. *gcloud compute routers get-status synopsis*

The only required argument is the name of your cloud router, that is, NAME. If you don't specify a region using the --region flag, Google will try to determine the region where the router you are inquiring about operates.

Assuming a cloud router in the specified region exists, the output of this command includes the following three sections:

- **Best routes** (Result -> bestRoutes): List of all routes programmed by the router NAME in the regional routing table REGION, filtered by the VPC network associated to the router

- **Best routes for router** (Result -> bestRoutesForRouter): List of all routes the router NAME has learned from routers in other regions

- **Advertised routes** (Result -> bgpPeerStatus -> advertisedRoutes): List of all advertised routes by the router NAME

Updating the Base Priority for Advertised Routes

In the previous example, you learned the effect of toggling the --bgp-routing-mode flag in a VPC. We mentioned that you control the value of the base priority assigned during a BGP session between a cloud router and its peer. Keep in mind that the value you choose applies to *all* routes advertised during a BGP session.

You need to be mindful on how to choose a suitable value for route base priority because this value has an impact on how dynamic routes are chosen during a conflict, for example, when multiple routes with the same destination are available.

Here are a few guidelines on what to consider when setting a value B for advertised route base priority:

- **Single region** (route advertisement between cloud routers in the same region): B<201, for example, B=100 (default) for BGP sessions between router-a and router-b in Figure 3-83—both routers operate in the same region us-east1, even though they are associated with different VPC networks. This guarantees that route prefixes in the same region always have higher priority than inter-region routes reaching the same destination. In fact, the highest priority inter-regional route has a value of 201, which is obtained by adding 201 (the lowest Inter-region cost) to 0 (the highest priority route).

- **Multiple region** (route advertisement between cloud routers in different regions): The general guidance is to use B ≥ 10200 for advertised inter-regional routes.

With this in mind, you can set the base priority for advertised routes with the gcloud compute routers update-bgp-peer command (Figures 3-86 and 3-87).

```
gianni@cloudshell:~ (vpc-host-nonprod-pu645-uh372)$ gcloud help compute routers update-bgp-peer
```

Figure 3-86. *Using the gcloud help command*

```
NAME
    gcloud compute routers update-bgp-peer - update a BGP peer on a Compute
        Engine router

SYNOPSIS
    gcloud compute routers update-bgp-peer NAME --peer-name=PEER_NAME
        [--advertised-route-priority=ADVERTISED ROUTE PRIORITY]
        [--advertisement-mode=MODE] [--async] [--[no-]enable-ipv6]
        [--[no-]enabled] [--interface=INTERFACE] [--ip-address=IP_ADDRESS]
        [--ipv6-nexthop-address=IPV6_NEXTHOP_ADDRESS] [--peer-asn=PEER_ASN]
        [--peer-ip-address=PEER_IP_ADDRESS]
        [--peer-ipv6-nexthop-address=PEER_IPV6_NEXTHOP_ADDRESS]
        [--region=REGION] [--set-advertisement-groups=[GROUP,...]]
        [--set-advertisement-ranges=[CIDR_RANGE=DESC,...]]
        [--add-advertisement-groups=[GROUP,...]
          | --add-advertisement-ranges=[CIDR_RANGE=DESC,...]
          | --remove-advertisement-groups=[GROUP,...]
          | --remove-advertisement-ranges=[CIDR_RANGE,...]]
        [--bfd-min-receive-interval=BFD_MIN_RECEIVE_INTERVAL
          --bfd-min-transmit-interval=BFD_MIN_TRANSMIT_INTERVAL
          --bfd-multiplier=BFD_MULTIPLIER
          --bfd-session-initialization-mode=BFD_SESSION_INITIALIZATION_MODE]
        [GCLOUD_WIDE_FLAG ...]

DESCRIPTION
    gcloud compute routers update-bgp-peer is used to update a BGP peer on a
    Compute Engine router.

POSITIONAL ARGUMENTS
    NAME
        Name of the router to operate on.

REQUIRED FLAGS
    --peer-name=PEER_NAME
        The name of the new BGP peer being updated.
```

Figure 3-87. *gcloud compute routers update-bgp-peer synopsis*

At a minimum, you need to specify the name of your cloud router NAME and the name of its BGP peer PEER_NAME and substitute the highlighted ADVERTISED_ROUTE_PRIORITY with the value B we just discussed.

Routing Policies Using Tags and Priorities

Routing policies are a means to establish path enforcements when multiple routes with the same destination are available.

One way to do it is by leveraging the route priority, which in the case of dynamic routes can be properly tweaked with a suitable value for a base priority. As we mentioned earlier, once determined a base priority for advertised routes, this value applies to all VMs in the same region of the cloud router if the `bgp-routing-mode` flag for the VPC is set to `REGIONAL` (default) or to all VMs in all regions spanned by the VPC if the flag is set to `GLOBAL`.

Another way to establish path enforcements is by restricting the VMs that can be reached by a route with the usage of network (or instance) tags. This way can be only achieved using static routes, because cloud routers are not expressive enough to advertise routes using a tag to limit the reachable VMs applicable to dynamic routes.

Let's see a couple of examples to better understand this concept.

First, let's start from the example in Figure 3-83 and connect the two VPC networks with another pair of HA VPN gateways (one gateway per VPC), this time between the two subnets `subnet-backend` in the `us-central1` region.

Each HA VPN gateway has a cloud router associated with it. Figure 3-88 illustrates the updated topology, where you can see `router-c` and `router-d` located in the region `us-central1` of `your-app-shared-vpc` and `your-app-connected-vpc`, respectively.

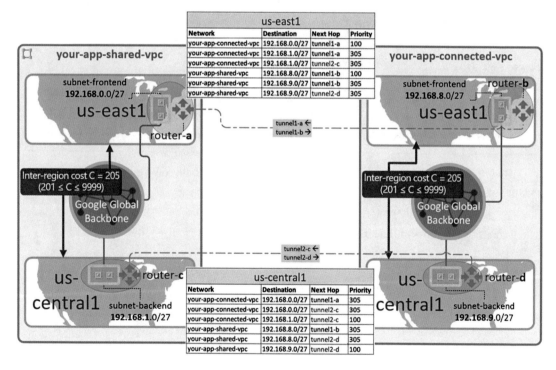

Figure 3-88. Adding another pair of HA VPN gateways between us-central1 subnets

The addition of this second pair of HA VPN gateways to the us-central1 region has caused the following changes to the regional routing tables:

- There are no more routes with priority 510 (lowest priority in the regional routing tables).

- Each subnet has *exactly* two routes with the same priority, that is, 305.

If multiple custom routes exist for the same destination and have the same priority and an active (IKE (Internet Key Exchange) SA (Security Association) established) next hop tunnel, Google Cloud uses equal-cost multipath (ECMP) routing to distribute packets among the tunnels.

This balancing method is based on a hash, so all packets from the same flow use the same tunnel as long as that tunnel is up.

Now, let's say the us-central1 HA VPN tunnels (tunnel2-c, tunnel2-d) are your *preferred* path to route traffic from VMs in subnet-frontend in your-app-connected-vpc (CIDR block 192.168.8.0/27) to VMs in subnet-backend in your-app-shared-vpc (CIDR block 192.168.1.0/27).

To achieve this, you need to update the base route priority for advertised routes that use the other HA VPN tunnels, that is, tunnel1-a and tunnel1-b. Remember, higher numbers mean lower priorities. You can update this value by using the gcloud compute routers update-bgp-peer command as illustrated in Figure 3-87. In our use case, by setting a value of 10200 (as shown in Figure 3-89), we are sure that any other path leading to the same destination has a higher priority, including the path that uses tunnel2-c—our preferred route.

```
gianni@cloudshell:~ (vpc-host-nonprod-pu645-uh372)$ gcloud compute routers update-bgp-peer router-a --peer-name=router-b --advertise
d-route-priority=10200
Did you mean region [us-east1] for router: [router-a] (Y/n)?  Y
```

Figure 3-89. *Updating advertised route base priority for* router-a

---

■ **Note**   The advertised route (base) priority B combined with the inter-region cost C is the overall route priority and is referred to as the Multi-exit Discriminator (MED). MED = B + C

This is because, in the worst possible scenario, an inter-regional route could have a MED of 10199, obtained as follows:

MED = 200 (lowest regional base priority) + 9999 (highest inter-region cost)

Figure 3-90 illustrates the effect of updating the base priority for advertised routes.

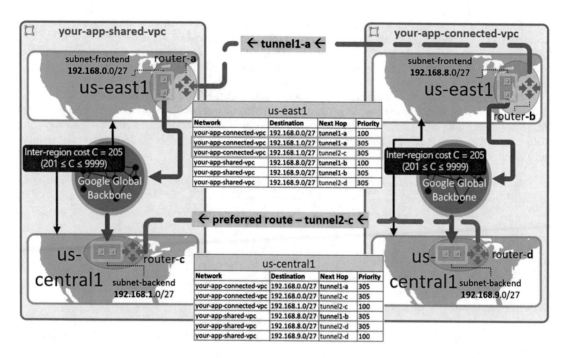

Figure 3-90. *Equal-cost multipath routing (ECMP) routes*

Keep in mind you don't have to take the advertised base route priority of the `tunnel1-a` route to this extreme (10200) in order to make it lower priority than the route that uses `tunnel2-c`. In fact, any number greater than 100 would have been sufficient to make the `tunnel1-a` route a less preferable path than `tunnel2-c`. However, since you don't have control over the inter-region costs (as of the writing of this book, its range is 201 ≤ C ≤ 9999), it is always a good idea to use a large number.

Another example of a routing policy is the use of network (or instance) *tags* to limit the VMs the route will be applied to. This type of routing policy is specific to static routes, because with static routes you manually create the route. As a result, you have direct access to the `--tags` flag as explained in the "Static Routes" section.

Instead, with dynamic routes a cloud router manages the routes for you, and the `--tags` flag is not available to limit the VMs that can use the advertised dynamic routes. In fact, the only way to limit the VMs is by using the `--set-advertisement-ranges` flag during creation or update of a cloud router. In other words, the selection of VMs the dynamic routes apply to is by CIDR block only, and not by instance tag.

To learn how a routing policy with tags works, let's say you are a member of the network administrators group for your company. You installed Network Address Translation (NAT) software in a VM you created in a subnet of your Google Cloud shared VPC.

■ **Note** From Wikipedia, *a Network Address Translation (NAT) is a technique of modifying the network address information in the IP packet headers while transferring the packet across a traffic routing device; such a technique remaps a given address space into another address space. This allows multiple computers to share a single public IP address, which has become necessary because there are not enough IP addresses for every computer in the world.*

You now have your NAT gateway ready for use. The next step is to create a static route to allow VMs in your company VPC networks access to the Internet so they can download OS and runtime updates. The question is, which VMs should use the NAT? Do you want any VMs, or do you want to use a more restrictive policy to only allow servers? Typically, enterprises control access to the Internet with egress policies targeting a specific set of users, and that's where tags come in handy.

The command in Figure 3-91 creates a static route nat-vm-internet-route in our shared VPC your-app-shared-vpc whose destination is the Internet (0.0.0.0/0) via our NAT gateway as the next hop. Notice that since we use a next hop instance by name (--next-hop-instance=nat-vm), we must specify a zone using the --next-hop-instance-zone=us-east1-a flag. Last, to select only VMs that host server software, we include the flag --tags=server.

```
gianni@cloudshell:~ (vpc-host-nonprod-pu645-uh372)$ gcloud compute routes create nat-vm-internet-route --destination-range=0.0.0.0/0
 --next-hop-instance=nat-vm --next-hop-instance-zone=us-east1-c --network=your-app-shared-vpc --tags=server
Created [https://www.googleapis.com/compute/v1/projects/vpc-host-nonprod-pu645-uh372/global/routes/nat-vm-internet-route].
WARNING: Some requests generated warnings:
 - Next hop instance 'https://www.googleapis.com/compute/v1/projects/vpc-host-nonprod-pu645-uh372/zones/us-east1-c/instances/nat-vm'
 does not exist.

NAME: nat-vm-internet-route
NETWORK: your-app-shared-vpc
DEST_RANGE: 0.0.0.0/0
NEXT_HOP: us-east1-c/instances/nat-vm
PRIORITY: 1000
gianni@cloudshell:~ (vpc-host-nonprod-pu645-uh372)$
```

Figure 3-91. *Creating a static route with tags*

Notice that the command created our static route even though the VM was not created yet. Also, since we did not specify a priority, the default route priority (1000) was chosen.

Finally, to let existing VMs in your-app-shared-vpc use this newly created route, all you have to do is to add the server tag as indicated in Figure 3-92.

```
gianni@cloudshell:~ (vpc-host-nonprod-pu645-uh372)$ gcloud compute instances add-tags your-app-server --tags=server
Did you mean zone [us-east1-c] for instance: [your-app-server] (Y/n)?  Y

ERROR: (gcloud.compute.instances.add-tags) Could not fetch resource:
 - The resource 'projects/vpc-host-nonprod-pu645-uh372/zones/us-east1-c/instances/your-app-server' was not found
```

Figure 3-92. *Adding tags to a VM*

As you can see, this time the gcloud CLI reported an error because it expected an existing VM in order to add to it the server tag.

Instead, for new VMs we should have used the gcloud compute instances create command with the --tags=server flag.

It is always good practice to clean up after you're done. To delete the newly created static route, use the gcloud compute routes delete command as indicated in Figure 3-93.

```
gianni@cloudshell:~ (vpc-host-nonprod-pu645-uh372)$ gcloud compute routes delete nat-vm-internet-route
The following routes will be deleted:
 - [nat-vm-internet-route]

Do you want to continue (Y/n)?  Y

Deleted [https://www.googleapis.com/compute/v1/projects/vpc-host-nonprod-pu645-uh372/global/routes/nat-vm-internet-route].
gianni@cloudshell:~ (vpc-host-nonprod-pu645-uh372)$ █
```

Figure 3-93. *Deleting a custom static route*

Internal Load Balancer As a Next Hop

A common use case for a custom static route with an internal load balancer (ILB) as a next hop is to implement a NAT service. The diagram in Figure 3-94 illustrates how an ILB is used to load-balance traffic from internal VMs to multiple NAT gateway instances that route traffic to the Internet.

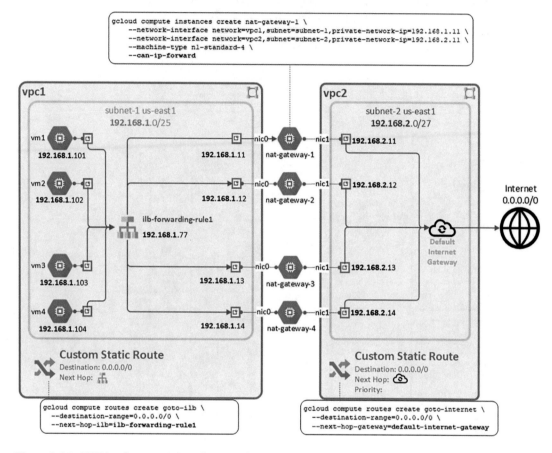

Figure 3-94. *NAT implementation with internal load balancer as a next hop*

There are a few design constraints you need to know when using an ILB as a next hop:

- Distinct network interface controllers (NICs) attached to the same VM cannot be in the same VPC.

- The VMs comprising the backend instances of your ILB must route traffic to a different VPC from the one where your ILB has been created. Put differently, your ILB cannot be used to route traffic between subnets in the same VPC. This is because subnet routes cannot be overridden.

- The ILB acts as a TCP/UDP pass-through load balancer, that is, it does not alter the packets' source and destination.

Custom Route Import/Export over VPC Peering

You learned in the beginning of this chapter the construct of VPC peering as a way to extend the internal routing capabilities of a VPC to another VPC.

When you establish a peering relation between two VPCs, the subnet routes of each VPC are automatically exchanged between the two. You don't have to worry about it—after all, the definition refers to extension of *internal routing*, which means subnet routes.

But what happens to the custom routes you or a Cloud Router might have created in each VPC?

To answer this question, let's walk you through an example of a hub and spoke topology (Figure 3-95).

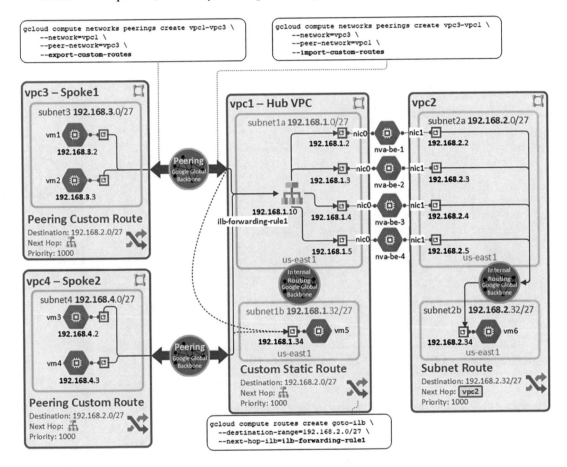

Figure 3-95. *Hub and spoke with internal load balancer as a next hop*

The network vpc1 is a hub network, which exposes shared capabilities to a number of consumers—or spokes.

The consumer networks vpc3 and vpc4 are peered to the hub and use these capabilities to fulfill the business and technical requirements for their workloads.

To allow for scalability, we created an ILB in the hub network, which will distribute incoming TCP/UDP traffic to the interface nic0 of four backends nva-be1, nva-be2, nva-be3, and nva-be4. Each of these backends is a network virtual appliance, which allows *IP forwarding* and uses another interface nic1 to route traffic to vpc2 following packet inspection.

Assuming firewall rules allow ingress/egress traffic through the ICMP protocol, since vpc1 and vpc3 are peered, vm1 and vm2 can ping vm5 and vice versa.

Likewise, since vpc1 and vpc4 are peered, vm3 and vm4 can also ping vm5 and vice versa.

This connectivity vpc1->vpc5, vpc2->vpc5, vpc3->vpc5, vpc4->vpc5 is denoted using dotted lines and is automatically provided to you when the peering relations vpc1-vpc3 and vpc1-vpc4 are established.

Also, since none of the VMs have an external IP, all traffic remains in RFC 1918 space and doesn't traverse the Internet.

For packets egressing the VMs in the spokes to reach VMs (vm6) in vpc2, you need to configure your peering relations in the hub network—vpc1-vpc3 and vpc1-vpc4—so that custom routes from the hub can be exported into the spokes.

You also need to allow the peering relation in the spokes—vpc3-vpc1 and vpc4-vpc1—to accept custom routes from the hub.

The diagram shows the gcloud commands you need to know in order to create peering relations with the ability to export or import custom routes.

In our example, the hub VPC has a custom static route goto-ilb, which routes traffic to an internal TCP/UDP load balancer, configured to distribute incoming traffic to four multi-NIC NVAs.

The top of the diagram also shows the creation of two hub peerings:

- vpc1-vpc3, which is configured to export custom routes—including goto-ilb

- vpc3-vpc1, which is configured to import custom routes—including goto-ilb

As a result, packets sent from VMs in the spoke vpc3, whose destination is the internal IP address of vm6, that is, 192.168.2.34, can be properly routed to their destination—provided the packet inspection performed by one of the four backend NVAs is successful.

The exact same setup can be performed for all other spokes, for example, vpc4, thereby allowing vm3 and vm4 to send packets to vm6.

Without explicitly configuring custom route export from the hub (or provider) network and custom route import from the spoke (or consumer) network, no packets sent from any VM in the spokes would have reached VMs in vpc2.

Configuring and Maintaining Google Kubernetes Engine Clusters

VPC-Native Clusters Using Alias IP Ranges

One of the ways to classify GKE clusters is based on how pods route traffic with each other. A cluster that uses alias IPs is called a *VPC-native* cluster. A cluster that uses Google Cloud routes is called a *route-based* cluster.

An alias IP range gives you the ability to leverage a subnet *secondary* IP range to allocate IP addresses for your cluster pods. As a bonus, GKE *automatically* manages the routing between pods for you, whether they are in the same node or in different nodes of your cluster.

Put differently, with alias IP ranges you don't have to create custom static routes to let pods communicate between each other or to reach resources outside of the cluster.

Figure 3-96 shows a multi-zonal VPC-native cluster your-gke-cluster with two nodes in us-central1-b and two nodes in us-central1-c. Each node has four pods, denoted in light blue.

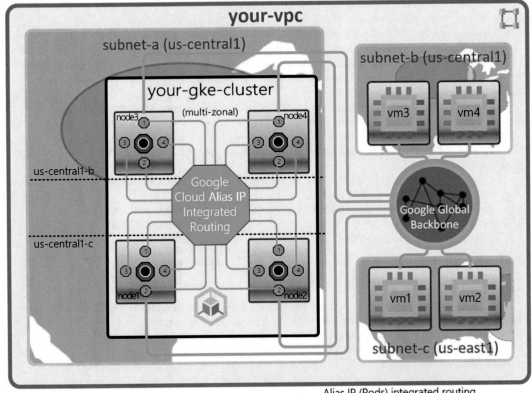

Figure 3-96. *Alias IP integrated routing in a VPC-native cluster*

Provided firewall rules and network policies allow traffic (we'll review these topics in the upcoming sections), since the cluster is VPC-native each pod can route traffic to and from any other pod in the cluster by leveraging subnet-a's alias IP range.

■ **Exam tip**   The inter-pod routes denoted in blue come free with VPC-native clusters and don't count against the project route quota.

Now that you learned what VPN-native clusters are and why you should use them, you may wonder how do you create one. The "secret" to create a VPC-native cluster is to leverage the --enable-ip-alias flag in the gcloud container clusters create command, as described in Figure 3-97.

```
samuele@cloudshell:~ (backend-devs-7736)$ gcloud container clusters create your-gke-cluster --project=backend-devs-7736
--zone=us-central1-b --num-nodes=2 --node-locations=us-central1-b,us-central1-c --enable-ip-alias --network=your-vpc --s
ubnetwork=subnet-a --cluster-secondary-range-name=backend-pods --services-secondary-range-name=backend-services
```

Figure 3-97. *Creating a VPC-native GKE cluster*

Keep in mind that when you use the `--enable-ip-alias` flag to create your VPC-native GKE cluster, you have the option to select your own CIDR ranges for the pods and services, or you can let Google do the job for you.

The former method is called *user-managed alias IP assignment*, and it requires that you create a subnet *before* creating your cluster.

The latter method is called *GKE-managed alias IP assignment*, and it allows you to let GKE create the subnet and the cluster *simultaneously*. This can be achieved by using the `--create-subnetwork` flag in the `gcloud container clusters create` command.

To summarize, with GKE and alias IP ranges, you get

- **Central IP management for GKE**: You can centrally manage your cluster RFC 1918 IP addresses because your node IP addresses, your pod IP addresses, and your service IP addresses are allocated respectively from the primary and the first and the second secondary ranges of your subnet.

- **Native networking capabilities**: You can scale your GKE cluster without worrying about exceeding your project route quota. This is because alias IP ranges provide native support for routing.

- **Pod direct connectivity**: You can create firewall rules that target pod IP addresses instead of node IP addresses. Also, pod connectivity is not limited to Google Cloud workloads. Your firewall rules can use source IP ranges located in your on-premises data center and targets defined by your cluster pod IP ranges.

Clusters with Shared VPC

The shared VPC network design is intended to promote separation of concerns by delegating network and security duties to a highly specialized network and security administration team, whereas app development and operations (DevOps) responsibilities are carried out by other teams.

This approach gives you all the tools and capabilities to allow for expansion of your DevOps teams while keeping the necessary level of isolation between apps.

Whether your company's DevOps teams are skilled to build apps running in VMs, or in containers, the shared VPC network design will still work.

However, when the target artifacts are containerized apps instead of apps running in VMs, there are a few caveats you need to be aware of.

First, if you intend to run your containerized apps in a shared VPC using GKE, your GKE clusters must be VPC-native. This means when you create your cluster—assuming you use the `gcloud` CLI—you must use the `--enable-ip-alias` flag.

■ **Exam tip** Once your route-based GKE cluster has been created, if you change your mind and decide to make it VPC-native, you cannot update the cluster. The `--enable-ip-alias` flag is only available at creation time. As a result, before spinning up your clusters, make sure you have a good understanding of the business and the technical requirements for your apps. Do you need a route-based or a VPC-native cluster? Will the cluster live in a standalone or a shared VPC network?

Second—as you will see in the upcoming example—a principal with the network admin role in the host project must create the subnet where your cluster will live as well as its secondary IP ranges for its pods and services. As you learned in the "Shared VPC Deep Dive" section, the service admin who will create the cluster must have subnet-level IAM permissions to create the cluster in the subnet being shared.

Third, each service project's GKE service account (generated by enabling the container API) must be granted the Host Service Agent User role in the host project.

To summarize, when you deploy a GKE cluster in a shared VPC, the cluster must be VPC-native, its *alias IP assignment* must be user-managed, and a special role needs to be granted in the host project to the each service project's GKE service account.

Let's now consolidate these concepts with a real example.

Clusters with Shared VPC Deep Dive

At the beginning of this chapter, you learned how to implement a shared VPC with two service projects frontend-devs and backend-devs, which we set up to let their developer team access their own subnet, that is, subnet-frontend and subnet-backend, respectively.

This time, the developers of each project want to deploy their artifacts using containerized apps instead of apps running on VMs.

In the upcoming sections, you will learn how to set up the necessary compute infrastructure for each developer team (frontend and backend) in the form of GKE clusters using our original shared VPC your-app-shared-vpc.

We will perform all the preliminary steps to enable a successful cluster creation in each project. We will create two GKE clusters frontend-cluster and backend-cluster in subnet-frontend and subnet-backend, which are owned by projects frontend-devs and backend-devs, respectively. We will create firewall rules to allow communication between the two clusters. We will validate the connectivity between the two clusters at the node and the pod level. Finally, we will delete the clusters and verify that the underlying managed infrastructure has been cleaned up as well.

Enabling Container API for Service and Host Projects

First and foremost, you need to enable the container API in the host project and in all the service projects whose shared subnets will be hosting the intended clusters (Figure 3-98).

```
itsmedario@cloudshell:~ (backend-devs-7736)$ gcloud services enable container.googleapis.com --project vpc-host-no
nprod-pu645-uh372
Operation "operations/acf.p2-755396457069-3cb6da1d-3cfa-43bc-9050-cb09ce8ef082" finished successfully.
itsmedario@cloudshell:~ (backend-devs-7736)$ gcloud services enable container.googleapis.com --project frontend-de
vs-7734
itsmedario@cloudshell:~ (backend-devs-7736)$ gcloud services enable container.googleapis.com --project backend-dev
s-7736
Operation "operations/acf.p2-211670805257-f6f290e3-f187-4f02-a2d3-ea5c498c8213" finished successfully.
```

Figure 3-98. *Enabling the container API to service and host projects*

As a result, a new service account—specific to GKE—is created in each project. For our example, we need to know the name of the GKE service account in each service project. This is because the GKE service account in each service project will need subnet-level permissions to create the GKE cluster in the shared subnet.

In order to get the name, we need to find out what the project number is (Figure 3-99).

```
itsmedario@cloudshell:~ (backend-devs-7736)$ gcloud projects list | grep -A1 frontend
PROJECT_ID: frontend-devs-7734
NAME: frontend-devs
PROJECT_NUMBER: 239408874101
itsmedario@cloudshell:~ (backend-devs-7736)$ gcloud projects list | grep -A1 backend
PROJECT_ID: backend-devs-7736
NAME: backend-devs
PROJECT_NUMBER: 211670805257
itsmedario@cloudshell:~ (backend-devs-7736)$
```

Figure 3-99. *Determining the service project number*

You will see in the next section how the project number relates to the GKE service account name.

Assigning Subnet-Level Roles to Service Accounts

Subnet-level IAM permissions are achieved with the `gcloud compute networks subnets set-iam-policy` command. Before using this command, we need to get the existing IAM policy attached to each subnet, add principal-role pairs to its `binding` section, and finally apply the new policy configuration to the subnet.

■ **Note** Each resource in Google Cloud has an IAM policy (also referred to as an IAM *allow* policy) attached to it, which clearly states who can access the resource and in what capacity. The core part of the policy is a list of bindings, which are nothing but a collection of members-role pairs. The "who" part is expressed in the `members` value of the binding by a list of principals, which can be users (prefixed by `user:`), service accounts (prefixed by `serviceAccount:`), Google groups (prefixed by `group:`), or even your entire organization's domain (prefixed by `domain:`). The "in what capacity" part is expressed in the `role` value of the binding, which is exactly *one* Google Cloud role per list of principals. If you need to add more than one role to the same list of principals, another binding is required. Think of an IAM policy as a private property sign "No trespassing: authorized personnel only." The sign is attached to any room of a private property, not just the external perimeter. The rules of inheritance apply to this metaphor as well, in that if the property is, for example, a military facility, where classified data is stored, an individual who wants to read the classified data will need access to the military facility first and also access to the room where the classified data is stored, that is, the union of roles to access the facility and access the room. A regular visitor won't be allowed access to the room.

Let's start from `subnet-frontend` in `us-east1` (Figure 3-100).

```
gianni@cloudshell:~ (vpc-host-nonprod-pu645-uh372)$ gcloud beta compute networks subnets get-iam-policy subnet-front
end    --region us-east1    --project vpc-host-nonprod-pu645-uh372    --format json > subnet-frontend-policy.json
gianni@cloudshell:~ (vpc-host-nonprod-pu645-uh372)$ █
```

Figure 3-100. *Getting `subnet-frontend-policy.json` IAM policy*

If you remember in the previous shared VPC deep dive example, we allowed the principal joseph@ dariokart.com to access the `subnet-frontend` with a role `roles/compute.networkUser`, which granted him a permission (among others in the role) to create VMs in its own subnet.

Notice the syntax of the policy file in JSON format with the sections I described in the previous note, including `bindings`, `members`, and `role` (Figure 3-101).

```
{
  "bindings": [
    {
      "members": [
        "user:joseph@dariokart.com"
      ],
      "role": "roles/compute.networkUser"
    }
  ],
  "etag": "BwXg57JJC6o=",
  "version": 1
}
~
~
~
~
~
~
"subnet-frontend-policy.json" 12L, 184B
```

Figure 3-101. *Viewing subnet-frontend-policy.json IAM policy*

Now we let the project built-in service accounts and the GKE service account do the same (Figure 3-102).

```
{
  "bindings": [
    {
      "members": [
        "user:joseph@dariokart.com",
        "serviceAccount:239408874101@cloudservices.gserviceaccount.com",
        "serviceAccount:service-239408874101@container-engine-robot.iam.gserviceaccount.com"
      ],
      "role": "roles/compute.networkUser"
    }
  ],
  "etag": "BwXg57JJC6o=",
  "version": 1
}
~
~
~
~
"subnet-frontend-policy.json" 14L, 351B
```

Figure 3-102. *Editing subnet-frontend-policy.json IAM policy*

Notice the project built-in service accounts and the GKE service account emails include the project number we determined in the previous section.

Now we can use the `gcloud beta compute networks subnets set-iam-policy` command to enforce this IAM allow policy to the subnet (Figure 3-103).

```
gianni@cloudshell:~ (vpc-host-nonprod-pu645-uh372)$ gcloud beta compute networks subnets set-iam-policy subnet-front
end subnet-frontend-policy.json --region=us-east1 --project=vpc-host-nonprod-pu645-uh372
Updated IAM policy for subnetwork [subnet-frontend].
bindings:
- members:
  - serviceAccount:239408874101@cloudservices.gserviceaccount.com
  - serviceAccount:service-239408874101@container-engine-robot.iam.gserviceaccount.com
  - user:joseph@dariokart.com
  role: roles/compute.networkUser
etag: BwXmDdLgurs=
version: 1
gianni@cloudshell:~ (vpc-host-nonprod-pu645-uh372)$ █
```

Figure 3-103. *Applying IAM policy to subnet-frontend*

Let's repeat the same steps for subnet-backend in us-central1 (Figures 3-104 to 3-107).

```
gianni@cloudshell:~ (vpc-host-nonprod-pu645-uh372)$ gcloud beta compute networks subnets get-iam-policy subnet-backe
nd    --region us-central1    --project vpc-host-nonprod-pu645-uh372    --format json > subnet-backend-policy.jso
n
gianni@cloudshell:~ (vpc-host-nonprod-pu645-uh372)$ vi subnet-backend-policy.json
```

Figure 3-104. *Getting subnet-backend-policy.json IAM policy*

```
{
  "bindings": [
    {
      "members": [
        "user:samuele@dariokart.com"
      ],
      "role": "roles/compute.networkUser"
    }
  ],
  "etag": "BwXhDryGOCI=",
  "version": 1
}
~
~
~
~
~
~
"subnet-backend-policy.json" 12L, 185B
```

Figure 3-105. *Viewing subnet-backend-policy.json IAM policy*

```
{
  "bindings": [
    {
      "members": [
        "user:samuele@dariokart.com",
        "serviceAccount:211670805257@cloudservices.gserviceaccount.com",
        "serviceAccount:service-211670805257@container-engine-robot.iam.gserviceaccount.com"
      ],
      "role": "roles/compute.networkUser"
    }
  ],
  "etag": "BwXhDryGOCI=",
  "version": 1
}
~
~
~
~
-- INSERT --
```

Figure 3-106. Editing subnet-backend-policy.json *IAM policy*

Finally, let's enforce the newly updated IAM policy to the subnet subnet-backend.

```
gianni@cloudshell:~ (vpc-host-nonprod-pu645-uh372)$ gcloud beta compute networks subnets set-iam-policy subnet-backe
nd subnet-backend-policy.json --region=us-central1 --project=vpc-host-nonprod-pu645-uh372
Updated IAM policy for subnetwork [subnet-backend].
bindings:
- members:
  - serviceAccount:211670805257@cloudservices.gserviceaccount.com
  - serviceAccount:service-211670805257@container-engine-robot.iam.gserviceaccount.com
  - user:samuele@dariokart.com
  role: roles/compute.networkUser
etag: BwXmFcU-RF0=
version: 1
gianni@cloudshell:~ (vpc-host-nonprod-pu645-uh372)$
```

Figure 3-107. Applying IAM policy to subnet-backend

Assigning Host Service Agent User Role to GKE Service Accounts

For the GKE service accounts service-239408874101@container-engine-robot.iam.gserviceaccount.com and service-211670805257@container-engine-robot.iam.gserviceaccount.com to be able to create clusters in their respective subnets—subnet-frontend and subnet-backend—another role binding needs to be added, this time not scoped to subnets but to the entire host project.

The gcloud projects add-iam-policy-binding command adds a binding to the IAM policy of a project. The command takes the project ID as a positional argument and the actual binding in the form of two required flags, that is, --member and --role. In this case, the member can be *one and one only* principal.

The required role is roles/container.hostServiceAgentUser and is only needed for cluster deployments in a shared VPC.

Figures 3-108 and 3-109 show how to add this role binding to the host project's IAM allow policy for the frontend-devs and backend-devs GKE service accounts, respectively.

```
gianni@cloudshell:~ (vpc-host-nonprod-pu645-uh372)$ gcloud projects add-iam-policy-binding vpc-host-nonprod-pu645-uh
372 \
    --member serviceAccount:service-239408874101@container-engine-robot.iam.gserviceaccount.com \
    --role roles/container.hostServiceAgentUser
Updated IAM policy for project [vpc-host-nonprod-pu645-uh372].
bindings:
- members:
  - serviceAccount:service-755396457069@compute-system.iam.gserviceaccount.com
  role: roles/compute.serviceAgent
- members:
  - serviceAccount:service-239408874101@container-engine-robot.iam.gserviceaccount.com
  role: roles/container.hostServiceAgentUser
- members:
  - serviceAccount:service-755396457069@container-engine-robot.iam.gserviceaccount.com
  role: roles/container.serviceAgent
- members:
  - serviceAccount:service-755396457069@containerregistry.iam.gserviceaccount.com
  role: roles/containerregistry.ServiceAgent
- members:
  - serviceAccount:755396457069-compute@developer.gserviceaccount.com
  - serviceAccount:755396457069@cloudservices.gserviceaccount.com
  role: roles/editor
- members:
  - group:gcp-network-admins@dariokart.com
  - serviceAccount:525148556512@cloudbuild.gserviceaccount.com
  role: roles/owner
- members:
  - serviceAccount:service-755396457069@gcp-sa-pubsub.iam.gserviceaccount.com
  role: roles/pubsub.serviceAgent
etag: BwXmFeuu6KY=
version: 1
gianni@cloudshell:~ (vpc-host-nonprod-pu645-uh372)$ █
```

Figure 3-108. *Updating host project IAM policy with binding for subnet-frontend*

```
gianni@cloudshell:~ (vpc-host-nonprod-pu645-uh372)$ gcloud projects add-iam-policy-binding vpc-host-nonprod-pu645-uh
372 \
    --member serviceAccount:service-211670805257@container-engine-robot.iam.gserviceaccount.com \
    --role roles/container.hostServiceAgentUser
Updated IAM policy for project [vpc-host-nonprod-pu645-uh372].
bindings:
- members:
  - serviceAccount:service-755396457069@compute-system.iam.gserviceaccount.com
  role: roles/compute.serviceAgent
- members:
  - serviceAccount:service-211670805257@container-engine-robot.iam.gserviceaccount.com
  - serviceAccount:service-239408874101@container-engine-robot.iam.gserviceaccount.com
  role: roles/container.hostServiceAgentUser
- members:
  - serviceAccount:service-755396457069@container-engine-robot.iam.gserviceaccount.com
  role: roles/container.serviceAgent
- members:
  - serviceAccount:service-755396457069@containerregistry.iam.gserviceaccount.com
  role: roles/containerregistry.ServiceAgent
- members:
  - serviceAccount:755396457069-compute@developer.gserviceaccount.com
  - serviceAccount:755396457069@cloudservices.gserviceaccount.com
  role: roles/editor
- members:
  - group:gcp-network-admins@dariokart.com
  - serviceAccount:525148556512@cloudbuild.gserviceaccount.com
  role: roles/owner
- members:
  - serviceAccount:service-755396457069@gcp-sa-pubsub.iam.gserviceaccount.com
  role: roles/pubsub.serviceAgent
etag: BwXmFfGDM7k=
version: 1
gianni@cloudshell:~ (vpc-host-nonprod-pu645-uh372)$
```

Figure 3-109. *Updating host project IAM policy with binding for subnet-backend*

Listing Usable Subnets

Before creating the clusters in our service projects, let's make sure the IAM permissions for our principals have been correctly set up. The principals we will be using are the two developers joseph@dariokart.com and samuele@dariokart.com, who have permissions to deploy compute infrastructure (GKE clusters) and build their apps in their own (service) projects, that is, frontend-devs and backend-devs, respectively.

Since GKE is fully managed by Google, the validation we are about to do relates to the each service project's GKE service account, which are the principals Google uses to spin up and maintain the clusters.

Therefore, let's verify in each service project what the usable subnets are for GKE to use along with IP ranges for nodes, pods, and services (Figure 3-110).

```
joseph@cloudshell:~ (frontend-devs-7734)$ gcloud container subnets list-usable \
    --project frontend-devs-7734 \
    --network-project vpc-host-nonprod-pu645-uh372
PROJECT: vpc-host-nonprod-pu645-uh372
REGION: us-east1
NETWORK: your-app-shared-vpc
SUBNET: subnet-frontend
RANGE: 192.168.0.0/26

SECONDARY_RANGE_NAME: service-cidr-frontend
IP_CIDR_RANGE: 192.168.130.0/25
STATUS: usable for pods or services

SECONDARY_RANGE_NAME: pod-cidr-frontend
IP_CIDR_RANGE: 192.168.13.0/24
STATUS: usable for pods or services

joseph@cloudshell:~ (frontend-devs-7734)$
```

Figure 3-110. *Listing usable subnets for GKE in* frontend-devs *project*

First, the primary IP range 192.168.0.0/26 will be used for cluster worker nodes. The /26 mask indicates there are $2^{(32-26)} = 2^6 = 64$ IP addresses available—actually, the effective number of available IP addresses is 60 because the first two and the last two IP addresses in the range are reserved by Google, as we learned in the section "Creating Subnets."

Notice the command is similar to the one we used in the shared VPC deep dive example at the beginning of this chapter, with the difference that the second keyword in gcloud is container instead of compute.

As highlighted in blue, the IP ranges for the pods and services look good as per our specification.

Let's repeat the validation for the backend-devs service project (Figure 3-111).

```
samuele@cloudshell:~ (backend-devs-7736)$ gcloud container subnets list-usable \
    --project backend-devs-7736 \
    --network-project vpc-host-nonprod-pu645-uh372
PROJECT: vpc-host-nonprod-pu645-uh372
REGION: us-central1
NETWORK: your-app-shared-vpc
SUBNET: subnet-backend
RANGE: 192.168.1.0/26

SECONDARY_RANGE_NAME: service-cidr-backend
IP_CIDR_RANGE: 192.168.150.0/25
STATUS: usable for pods or services

SECONDARY_RANGE_NAME: pod-cidr-backend
IP_CIDR_RANGE: 192.168.15.0/24
STATUS: usable for pods or services

samuele@cloudshell:~ (backend-devs-7736)$ ▮
```

Figure 3-111. *Listing usable subnets for GKE in backend-devs project*

As highlighted in green, the IP ranges for the pods and services look good as per our specification. At this point, all the preliminary steps to deploy our clusters in our shared VPC have been completed.

Creating GKE Clusters

Let's go ahead and create a cluster frontend-cluster in the subnet subnet-frontend (Figure 3-112).

```
joseph@cloudshell:~ (frontend-devs-7734)$ gcloud container clusters create frontend-cluster
 --project=frontend-devs-7734 --zone=us-east1-c --enable-ip-alias --network=projects/vpc-ho
st-nonprod-pu645-uh372/global/networks/your-app-shared-vpc --subnetwork=projects/vpc-host-n
onprod-pu645-uh372/regions/us-east1/subnetworks/subnet-frontend --cluster-secondary-range-n
ame=pod-cidr-frontend  --services-secondary-range-name=service-cidr-frontend --num-nodes=2
Default change: During creation of nodepools or autoscaling configuration changes for clust
er versions greater than 1.24.1-gke.800 a default location policy is applied. For Spot and
PVM it defaults to ANY, and for all other VM kinds a BALANCED policy is used. To change the
 default values use the `--location-policy` flag.
Note: The Pod address range limits the maximum size of the cluster. Please refer to https:/
/cloud.google.com/kubernetes-engine/docs/how-to/flexible-pod-cidr to learn how to optimize
IP address allocation.
Creating cluster frontend-cluster in us-east1-c... Cluster is being configured...working..
.
Creating cluster frontend-cluster in us-east1-c... Cluster is being configured...working..
.
Creating cluster frontend-cluster in us-east1-c... Cluster is being deployed...done.
ERROR: (gcloud.container.clusters.create) Operation [<Operation
 clusterConditions: [<StatusCondition
 canonicalCode: CanonicalCodeValueValuesEnum(RESOURCE_EXHAUSTED, 9)
 message: "[IP SPACE EXHAUSTED]: Instance 'gke-frontend-cluster-default-pool-d6f669fb-04fj'
 creation failed: IP space of 'projects/vpc-host-nonprod-pu645-uh372/regions/us-east1/subne
tworks/subnet-frontend-pod-cidr-fronte-9f83b686a82a340d' is exhausted. ">, <StatusCondition
```

Figure 3-112. *Failed attempt to create a cluster in subnet-frontend*

The command is quite long. Let's find out why the command failed.

With the default settings for standard clusters, GKE requires a /24 mask (256 IP addresses allocated for pods) for each node and three worker nodes per cluster. See the official Google Cloud documentation here.

Our `subnet-frontend` has allocated a /24 mask for pods (`pod-cidr-frontend` in Figure 3-110), that is, 256 IP addresses.

However, in the gcloud command, we have requested the number of nodes to be two *without* specifying a maximum number of pods per node, that is, the default /24 mask will be used for each of the two nodes.

As a result, the overall CIDR range for pods should have been at least `192.168.13.0/23` instead of the existing `192.168.13.0/24`. This miscalculation has caused the cluster creation to fail due to IP space exhaustion in the pod range.

Now you know how to fix the error! As you correctly guessed, let's try again, but this time by forcing a limit on the maximum number of pods per node. Instead of the default value of 256 (actually, to reduce address reuse, GKE uses 110 as the default maximum number of pods per node), let's use a maximum of 10 pods per node, as shown in Figure 3-113.

```
joseph@cloudshell:~ (frontend-devs-7734)$ gcloud container clusters create frontend-cluster
  --project=frontend-devs-7734 --zone=us-east1-c --enable-ip-alias --network=projects/vpc-ho
st-nonprod-pu645-uh372/global/networks/your-app-shared-vpc --subnetwork=projects/vpc-host-n
onprod-pu645-uh372/regions/us-east1/subnetworks/subnet-frontend --cluster-secondary-range-n
ame=pod-cidr-frontend  --services-secondary-range-name=service-cidr-frontend --num-nodes=2
--max-pods-per-node=10
Default change: During creation of nodepools or autoscaling configuration changes for clust
er versions greater than 1.24.1-gke.800 a default location policy is applied. For Spot andP
VM it defaults to ANY, and for all other VM kinds a BALANCED policy is used. To change the
default values use the `--location-policy` flag.
Note: The Pod address range limits the maximum size of the cluster. Please refer to https:/
/cloud.google.com/kubernetes-engine/docs/how-to/flexible-pod-cidr to learn how to optimizeI
P address allocation.
Creating cluster frontend-cluster in us-east1-c... Cluster is being configured...working..
.
Creating cluster frontend-cluster in us-east1-c... Cluster is being health-checked...worki
ng..
Creating cluster frontend-cluster in us-east1-c... Cluster is being health-checked (master
is healthy)...done.
Created [https://container.googleapis.com/v1/projects/frontend-devs-7734/zones/us-east1-c/c
lusters/frontend-cluster].
To inspect the contents of your cluster, go to: https://console.cloud.google.com/kubernetes
/workload_/gcloud/us-east1-c/frontend-cluster?project=frontend-devs-7734
kubeconfig entry generated for frontend-cluster.
NAME: frontend-cluster
LOCATION: us-east1-c
MASTER_VERSION: 1.22.10-gke.600
MASTER_IP: 34.74.141.216
MACHINE_TYPE: e2-medium
NODE_VERSION: 1.22.10-gke.600
NUM_NODES: 2
STATUS: RUNNING
joseph@cloudshell:~ (frontend-devs-7734)$ ▮
```

Figure 3-113. Successful attempt to create a cluster in subnet-frontend

The deployment will take a few minutes. Upon completion, make sure to review the summary of the deployment, which indicates, among others, the cluster name, the location, the master IP address (the control plane endpoint), the worker node's machine type, the number of worker nodes, and the status.

Let's make sure the worker nodes use the correct CIDR range 192.168.0.0/26 (Figure 3-114).

```
joseph@cloudshell:~ (frontend-devs-7734)$ gcloud compute instances list --project=frontend-
devs-7734
NAME: gke-frontend-cluster-default-pool-f6cf79d6-jtw1
ZONE: us-east1-c
MACHINE_TYPE: e2-medium
PREEMPTIBLE:
INTERNAL IP: 192.168.0.9
EXTERNAL_IP: 35.196.214.59
STATUS: RUNNING

NAME: gke-frontend-cluster-default-pool-f6cf79d6-nj8v
ZONE: us-east1-c
MACHINE_TYPE: e2-medium
PREEMPTIBLE:
INTERNAL IP: 192.168.0.10
EXTERNAL_IP: 34.74.20.3
STATUS: RUNNING
joseph@cloudshell:~ (frontend-devs-7734)$ ▮
```

Figure 3-114. *Listing GKE* frontend-cluster *worker nodes*

Next, let's create a second GKE cluster in subnet-backend (Figure 3-115).

```
samuele@cloudshell:~ (backend-devs-7736)$ gcloud container clusters create backend-cluster --project=backend-devs-7736 -
-zone=us-central1-c --enable-ip-alias --network=projects/vpc-host-nonprod-pu645-uh372/global/networks/your-app-shared-vp
c --subnetwork=projects/vpc-host-nonprod-pu645-uh372/regions/us-central1/subnetworks/subnet-backend --cluster-secondary-
range-name=pod-cidr-backend  --services-secondary-range-name=service-cidr-backend --num-nodes=2 --max-pods-per-node=10
Default change: During creation of nodepools or autoscaling configuration changes for cluster versions greater than 1.24
.1-gke.800 a default location policy is applied. For Spot and PVM it defaults to ANY, and for all other VM kinds a BALAN
CED policy is used. To change the default values use the `--location-policy` flag.
Note: The Pod address range limits the maximum size of the cluster. Please refer to https://cloud.google.com/kubernetes-
engine/docs/how-to/flexible-pod-cidr to learn how to optimize IP address allocation.
Creating cluster backend-cluster in us-central1-c... Cluster is being health-checked (master is healthy)...done.
Created [https://container.googleapis.com/v1/projects/backend-devs-7736/zones/us-central1-c/clusters/backend-cluster].
To inspect the contents of your cluster, go to: https://console.cloud.google.com/kubernetes/workload_/gcloud/us-central1
-c/backend-cluster?project=backend-devs-7736
kubeconfig entry generated for backend-cluster.
NAME: backend-cluster
LOCATION: us-central1-c
MASTER_VERSION: 1.22.10-gke.600
MASTER_IP: 104.154.69.64
MACHINE_TYPE: e2-medium
NODE_VERSION: 1.22.10-gke.600
NUM_NODES: 2
STATUS: RUNNING
samuele@cloudshell:~ (backend-devs-7736)$ ▮
```

Figure 3-115. *Successful attempt to create a cluster in* subnet-backend

Let's make sure the worker nodes use the correct CIDR range 192.168.1.0/26 (Figure 3-116).

```
samuele@cloudshell:~ (backend-devs-7736)$ gcloud compute instances list --project=backend-devs-7736
NAME: gke-backend-cluster-default-pool-5ca2b1de-t7hf
ZONE: us-central1-c
MACHINE_TYPE: e2-medium
PREEMPTIBLE:
INTERNAL_IP: 192.168.1.2
EXTERNAL_IP: 35.192.58.229
STATUS: RUNNING

NAME: gke-backend-cluster-default-pool-5ca2b1de-vtb8
ZONE: us-central1-c
MACHINE_TYPE: e2-medium
PREEMPTIBLE:
INTERNAL_IP: 192.168.1.3
EXTERNAL_IP: 35.202.38.217
STATUS: RUNNING
samuele@cloudshell:~ (backend-devs-7736)$ █
```

Figure 3-116. *Listing GKE* `backend-cluster` *worker nodes*

Figure 3-117 illustrates the resources we created so far and how they relate to each other from network, security, and cost points of view.

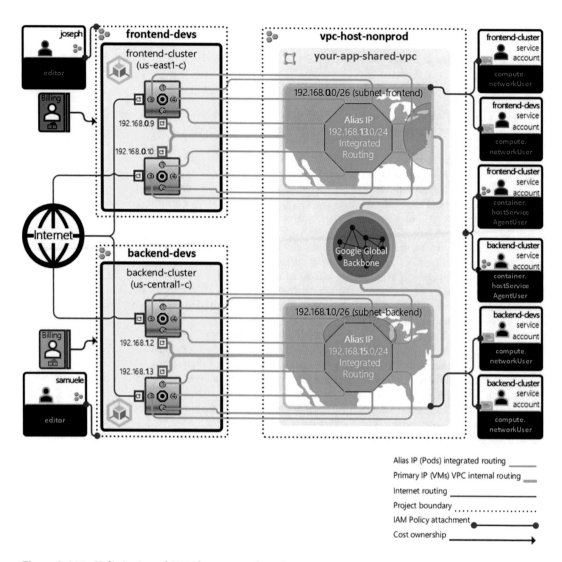

Figure 3-117. *Holistic view of GKE clusters in a shared VPC*

From a networking standpoint, the frontend-cluster and backend-cluster have built-in routes, which allow them to send and receive traffic to and from each other—provided firewall rules allow, as we will discuss in the next section. Green routes are defined at the worker node level (VMs), whereas blue routes are defined at the pod level. Notice the blue routes all collapse in the *Alias IP Integrated Routing* blue octagon, which resides in the first secondary IP range of each subnet. Also, for the sake of simplicity, we did not visualize the clusters' services VPC-native routing, which are implemented by the second secondary IP range for each cluster, that is, 192.168.130.0/25 for frontend-cluster (Figure 3-110) and 192.168.150.0/25 for backend-cluster (Figure 3-111).

■ **Note**   Since we did not create the clusters using the `--enable-private-nodes` flag, by default the clusters are public, that is, each worker node has an external IP (denoted in pink) in addition to its internal IP (denoted in green).

From a security standpoint, the frontend developer `joseph@dariokart.com` has the editor role in his own project `frontend-devs` and can *only* use `subnet-frontend` (Figure 3-110) for any container-related compute resources.

As an editor in the project `frontend-devs`, Joseph can create resources in his project, whose consumption is paid by the billing account linked to `frontend-devs`.

Let's focus on GKE now. Since GKE is a managed service, when Joseph requests the creation of a GKE cluster in `frontend-devs`, Google uses the `frontend-cluster` service account (created when we enabled the container API in the project), that is, `service-239408874101@container-engine-robot.iam.gserviceaccount.com`, to create its underlying infrastructure. Since this service account has the role `roles/compute.networkUser` bound to it at the subnet `subnet-frontend` level, the GKE cluster will be allowed to use `subnet-frontend` primary and secondary IP ranges.

As a result, `frontend-cluster`—along with its underlying compute infrastructure, for example, VMs for the worker nodes, pods, services, and others—is owned by the project `frontend-devs`, but its "territory" or more formally its *scope of concern* is `subnet-frontend`, which is located in the `us-east1` region, along with its primary and secondary ranges.

Symmetrically, `backend-cluster`—along with its underlying compute infrastructure, for example, VMs for the worker nodes, pods, services, and others—is owned by the project `backend-devs`, but its "territory" is `subnet-backend`, which is located in the `us-central1` region, along with its primary and secondary ranges.

Last, from a billing standpoint, the charges incurred by the `frontend-cluster` usage are paid by the billing account linked to the project `frontend-devs`, which is denoted in blue in Figure 3-117.

Likewise, the charges incurred by the `backend-cluster` usage are paid by the billing account linked to the project `backend-devs`, which is denoted in green in Figure 3-117.

This network design promotes separation of concerns from network, security, and cost standpoints while delivering the necessary *native* connectivity between workloads running in containerized applications.

Testing Connectivity

In this example, we will use the Secure Shell (SSH) protocol to connect into one of the two `frontend-cluster` worker nodes, and we will perform a few connectivity tests.

Even though routing connectivity is established, packet transmission cannot succeed until firewall rules allow traffic from origin to destination.

With our travel metaphor, there may be routes connecting location A with location B, but if a checkpoint in the middle won't allow traffic, you won't make it to location B.

In this example, the VPC `your-app-shared-vpc` was already configured to allow ingress SSH, TCP, and ICMP (Internet Control Message Protocol) traffic as illustrated in Figure 3-29.

Nevertheless, let's list all firewall rules for the VPC and double-check (Figure 3-118).

```
gianni@cloudshell:~ (vpc-host-nonprod-pu645-uh372)$ gcloud compute firewall-rules list
NAME: allow-ssh-ping-shared-vpc
NETWORK: your-app-shared-vpc
DIRECTION: INGRESS
PRIORITY: 1000
ALLOW: tcp:22,tcp:3389,icmp
DENY:
DISABLED: False

NAME: gke-backend-cluster-7bf21e51-all
NETWORK: your-app-shared-vpc
DIRECTION: INGRESS
PRIORITY: 1000
ALLOW: icmp,esp,ah,sctp,tcp,udp
DENY:
DISABLED: False

NAME: gke-backend-cluster-7bf21e51-ssh
NETWORK: your-app-shared-vpc
DIRECTION: INGRESS
PRIORITY: 1000
ALLOW: tcp:22
DENY:
DISABLED: False

NAME: gke-backend-cluster-7bf21e51-vms
NETWORK: your-app-shared-vpc
DIRECTION: INGRESS
PRIORITY: 1000
ALLOW: icmp,tcp:1-65535,udp:1-65535
DENY:
DISABLED: False

NAME: gke-frontend-cluster-3b621688-all
```

Figure 3-118. Listing your-app-shared-vpc firewall rules

Notice that behind the scenes GKE—as a fully managed Kubernetes engine—has already created ingress firewall rules to allow traffic into the VPC using a predefined group of protocols and ports.

Let's connect via SSH to one of the two frontend-cluster worker nodes (Figure 3-119).

```
joseph@cloudshell:~ (frontend-devs-7734)$ gcloud compute ssh gke-frontend-cluster-default-p
ool-f6cf79d6-jtw1 --project=frontend-devs-7734 --zone=us-east1-c
Warning: Permanently added 'compute.4361758387119761131' (ED25519) to the list of known hos
ts.
Enter passphrase for key '/home/joseph/.ssh/google_compute_engine':

Welcome to Kubernetes v1.22.10-gke.600!

You can find documentation for Kubernetes at:
  http://docs.kubernetes.io/

The source for this release can be found at:
  /home/kubernetes/kubernetes-src.tar.gz
Or you can download it at:
  https://storage.googleapis.com/kubernetes-release-gke/release/v1.22.10-gke.600/kubernetes
-src.tar.gz

It is based on the Kubernetes source at:
  https://github.com/kubernetes/kubernetes/tree/v1.22.10-gke.600

For Kubernetes copyright and licensing information, see:
  /home/kubernetes/LICENSES

joseph@gke-frontend-cluster-default-pool-f6cf79d6-jtw1 ~ $ █
```

Figure 3-119. *Connecting via SSH to a frontend-cluster worker node*

To test connectivity, we need to install toolbox, which is a set of tools on Container-Optimized OS to execute certain tasks, such as debugging (Figure 3-120).

```
joseph@gke-frontend-cluster-default-pool-f6cf79d6-jtw1 ~ $ /usr/bin/toolbox
gcr.io/cos-cloud/toolbox:v20210217:                                    resolved
      |++++++++++++++++++++++++++++++++++++++++|
index-sha256:a0d659686e8fe8da9609483148ef59c68d594500cc234d84d9425d40b7d1dafb:    done
  |++++++++++++++++++++++++++++++++++++++++|
manifest-sha256:d18e6a2837c23fbf02ba4fc445ccb8fb08fa37007e8c962ca25330561acead3d: done
  |++++++++++++++++++++++++++++++++++++++++|
layer-sha256:33fe2e595877d0690dc00f44042d43ea61152a01b258646b591756fec53d561e:    done
  |++++++++++++++++++++++++++++++++++++++++|
config-sha256:d3b3a9f35a87ecaa64292c09957a412c1027b5ef3df5c66ee18f54b8c54347e1:   done
  |++++++++++++++++++++++++++++++++++++++++|
layer-sha256:0ecb575e629cd60aa802266a3bc6847dcf4073aa2a6d7d43f717dd61e7b90e0b:    done
  |++++++++++++++++++++++++++++++++++++++++|
layer-sha256:ea88ecbad7fea841093973ceddeb3c935e472e69df64851cfb6ee708cf5f77a7:    done
  |++++++++++++++++++++++++++++++++++++++++|
layer-sha256:2588b2bf9c0542801eba6adee41567328a3af530918d51fa84b06bcbdf77d98a:    done
  |++++++++++++++++++++++++++++++++++++++++|
layer-sha256:c91803d107e91e50a9c3ac3498f40ce57e0c5e4ed14a5f0721b4dbb6ad5aa275:    done
  |++++++++++++++++++++++++++++++++++++++++|
layer-sha256:406504a0737f5af04b1be49c6d764e45eb7d3d9171e4a8731653928eeebe8a2b:    done
  |++++++++++++++++++++++++++++++++++++++++|
layer-sha256:cdacc2cc65e7bcab6751c0c9e5a867e3180c83c6191a30685bd0ae398a6869f3:    done
  |++++++++++++++++++++++++++++++++++++++++|
layer-sha256:ea04cb3a751810fe8770457011355518da2020034378fa2267eddf193b507035:    done
  |++++++++++++++++++++++++++++++++++++++++|
elapsed: 5.5 s                                                       total:   3
12.0  (56.7 MiB/s)
unpacking linux/amd64 sha256:a0d659686e8fe8da9609483148ef59c68d594500cc234d84d9425d40b7d1da
fb...
done: 22.529444961s

Please do not use --share-system anymore, use $SYSTEMD_NSPAWN_SHARE_* instead.
Spawning container joseph-gcr.iocos-cloudtoolbox-v20210217 on /var/lib/toolbox/joseph-gcr.i
o_cos-cloud_toolbox-v20210217.
Press ^] three times within 1s to kill container.

root@gke-frontend-cluster-default-pool-f6cf79d6-jtw1:~#
```

Figure 3-120. *Installing CoreOS toolbox*

Let's test connectivity to another worker node in the same cluster (Figure 3-121).

```
root@gke-frontend-cluster-default-pool-f6cf79d6-jtw1:~# ping 192.168.0.10
PING 192.168.0.10 (192.168.0.10) 56(84) bytes of data.
64 bytes from 192.168.0.10: icmp_seq=1 ttl=64 time=1.72 ms
64 bytes from 192.168.0.10: icmp_seq=2 ttl=64 time=0.496 ms
64 bytes from 192.168.0.10: icmp_seq=3 ttl=64 time=0.347 ms
64 bytes from 192.168.0.10: icmp_seq=4 ttl=64 time=0.299 ms
^C
--- 192.168.0.10 ping statistics ---
4 packets transmitted, 4 received, 0% packet loss, time 47ms
rtt min/avg/max/mdev = 0.299/0.715/1.719/0.584 ms
root@gke-frontend-cluster-default-pool-f6cf79d6-jtw1:~#
```

Figure 3-121. *Pinging another node in the* frontend-cluster

Let's test connectivity to another worker node in a different cluster (Figure 3-122).

```
root@gke-frontend-cluster-default-pool-f6cf79d6-jtw1:~# ping 192.168.1.3
PING 192.168.1.3 (192.168.1.3) 56(84) bytes of data.
64 bytes from 192.168.1.3: icmp_seq=1 ttl=64 time=33.1 ms
64 bytes from 192.168.1.3: icmp_seq=2 ttl=64 time=32.3 ms
64 bytes from 192.168.1.3: icmp_seq=3 ttl=64 time=32.2 ms
64 bytes from 192.168.1.3: icmp_seq=4 ttl=64 time=32.3 ms
64 bytes from 192.168.1.3: icmp_seq=5 ttl=64 time=32.2 ms
64 bytes from 192.168.1.3: icmp_seq=6 ttl=64 time=32.3 ms
64 bytes from 192.168.1.3: icmp_seq=7 ttl=64 time=32.3 ms
64 bytes from 192.168.1.3: icmp_seq=8 ttl=64 time=32.3 ms
64 bytes from 192.168.1.3: icmp_seq=9 ttl=64 time=32.3 ms
^C
--- 192.168.1.3 ping statistics ---
9 packets transmitted, 9 received, 0% packet loss, time 20ms
rtt min/avg/max/mdev = 32.228/32.374/33.098/0.296 ms
root@gke-frontend-cluster-default-pool-f6cf79d6-jtw1:~# █
```

Figure 3-122. *Pinging another node in the* backend-cluster

Let's test connectivity to a pod in backend-cluster (Figure 3-123).

```
root@gke-frontend-cluster-default-pool-f6cf79d6-jtw1:~# ping 192.168.15.1
PING 192.168.15.1 (192.168.15.1) 56(84) bytes of data.
64 bytes from 192.168.15.1: icmp_seq=1 ttl=64 time=32.8 ms
64 bytes from 192.168.15.1: icmp_seq=2 ttl=64 time=31.8 ms
64 bytes from 192.168.15.1: icmp_seq=3 ttl=64 time=31.7 ms
64 bytes from 192.168.15.1: icmp_seq=4 ttl=64 time=31.8 ms
^C
--- 192.168.15.1 ping statistics ---
4 packets transmitted, 4 received, 0% packet loss, time 7ms
rtt min/avg/max/mdev = 31.726/32.036/32.817/0.502 ms
root@gke-frontend-cluster-default-pool-f6cf79d6-jtw1:~# █
```

Figure 3-123. *Pinging a pod in the* backend-cluster

This connectivity test is important because it's telling us that components built in subnet-frontend (located in zone us-east1-c) can use containerized apps built in subnet-backend (located in zone us-central1-c).

When I say "can use" I mean they can *natively* consume containerized apps in subnet-backend. There is no intermediary between the two, which is good because latency is reduced and risks of packet losses or even data exfiltration are minimized.

This native connectivity is the product of Shared VPC and VPC-native clusters.

Now, let's test connectivity to another pod in backend-cluster (Figure 3-124).

```
root@gke-frontend-cluster-default-pool-f6cf79d6-jtw1:~# ping 192.168.15.2
PING 192.168.15.2 (192.168.15.2) 56(84) bytes of data.
^C
--- 192.168.15.2 ping statistics ---
10 packets transmitted, 0 received, 100% packet loss, time 242ms

root@gke-frontend-cluster-default-pool-f6cf79d6-jtw1:~#
```

Figure 3-124. *Failed attempt to ping a pod in the backend-cluster*

This time, the ping failed, why? The reason it failed is because we told GKE to create a cluster with a maximum of ten pods per node and an initial size of two nodes (see Figure 3-115). The available IP space we set up the backend-cluster with was /24 (see pod-cidr-backend in Figure 3-111) for a total of 256 IP addresses.

As a result, only 20 out of 256 IP addresses in the 192.168.15.0/24 CIDR range are being used.

Deleting GKE Clusters

As always, upon completion of our work let's clean up our resources to avoid incurring unnecessary costs.

Let's delete frontend-cluster and make sure the underlying VMs comprising the cluster worker nodes have also been deleted (Figure 3-125).

```
joseph@cloudshell:~ (frontend-devs-7734)$ gcloud container clusters delete frontend-cluster
  --zone=us-east1-c
The following clusters will be deleted.
 - [frontend-cluster] in [us-east1-c]

Do you want to continue (Y/n)?  Y

Deleting cluster frontend-cluster...done.
Deleted [https://container.googleapis.com/v1/projects/frontend-devs-7734/zones/us-east1-c/c
lusters/frontend-cluster].
joseph@cloudshell:~ (frontend-devs-7734)$ gcloud compute instances list --project=frontend-
devs-7734
Listed 0 items.
joseph@cloudshell:~ (frontend-devs-7734)$ █
```

Figure 3-125. *Deleting frontend-cluster*

Finally, let's delete backend-cluster (Figure 3-126).

```
samuele@cloudshell:~ (backend-devs-7736)$ gcloud container clusters delete backend-cluster --zone=us-central1-c
The following clusters will be deleted.
 - [backend-cluster] in [us-central1-c]

Do you want to continue (Y/n)?  Y

Deleting cluster backend-cluster...done.
Deleted [https://container.googleapis.com/v1/projects/backend-devs-7736/zones/us-central1-c/clusters/backend-cluster].
samuele@cloudshell:~ (backend-devs-7736)$ gcloud compute instances list --project=backend-devs-7736
Listed 0 items.
samuele@cloudshell:~ (backend-devs-7736)$ █
```

Figure 3-126. *Deleting backend-cluster*

Creating Cluster Network Policies

Cluster network policies are a fine-grained way to control access to the pods of your GKE cluster.

By *access* we mean ingress and egress traffic directed to and from the pods of your GKE cluster. By *control* we mean validation at the IP address, protocol (TCP, UDP, SCTP), and port level (OSI layer 3 or 4).

Network policies are coded in the form of a file—this approach is also called *policy-as-code*. This file tells the GKE API server what entities are allowed to communicate with your pods.

Entities can be one or a combination of these three:

- Other pods

- Namespaces

- CIDR blocks

You specify which pods or namespaces you are allowing ingress or egress traffic by using a *selector*. Allowed entities (pods, namespaces) are the ones that match the expression in the selector. Selectors are not used to specify CIDR blocks.

The best way to explain how network policies work is with an example.

Let's say you want a containerized web server app labeled app=hello to only receive incoming requests from another containerized app labeled app=foo. This will be our first use case.

Conversely, you want the containerized app labeled app=foo to only send traffic to the containerized web app labeled app=hello, and nothing else. This will be our second use case.

Here is how to implement these two use cases.

Cloning the GKE Sample Apps from GitHub

The GKE sample apps provide great examples on how to use GKE. We will use this repo to explain how network policies work.

The gcloud CLI, which is available with Google Cloud Shell, is all you need to go through this example because it comes with the kubect utility (among many other developer runtimes), which is the official Kubernetes command-line tool.

Go ahead and clone the repo in a suitable directory (Figure 3-127).

```
joseph@cloudshell:~ (frontend-devs-7734)$ mkdir code
joseph@cloudshell:~ (frontend-devs-7734)$ cd code
joseph@cloudshell:~/code (frontend-devs-7734)$ git clone https://github.com/GoogleCloudPlatform/kubernetes-engine-samples
Cloning into 'kubernetes-engine-samples'...
remote: Enumerating objects: 1725, done.
remote: Counting objects: 100% (54/54), done.
remote: Compressing objects: 100% (30/30), done.
remote: Total 1725 (delta 25), reused 42 (delta 19), pack-reused 1671
Receiving objects: 100% (1725/1725), 1.48 MiB | 13.50 MiB/s, done.
Resolving deltas: 100% (940/940), done.
joseph@cloudshell:~/code (frontend-devs-7734)$ cd kubernetes-engine-samples/network-policies
joseph@cloudshell:~/code/kubernetes-engine-samples/network-policies (frontend-devs-7734)$ █
```

Figure 3-127. Cloning the GKE sample app repo from GitHub

Creating a Network Policy–Enabled GKE Cluster

First, we need to tell the GKE API server that the GKE cluster where the two containerized apps will live will enforce network policies.

Let's use the frontend-devs project and start by enabling the container.googleapis.com service (Figure 3-128).

```
joseph@cloudshell:~/code/kubernetes-engine-samples/network-policies (frontend-devs-7734)$ gcloud services enable
  container.googleapis.com --project=frontend-devs-7734
Operation "operations/acf.p2-239408874101-56493cd8-806d-42c2-b338-a75d7d8bdb6f" finished successfully.
joseph@cloudshell:~/code/kubernetes-engine-samples/network-policies (frontend-devs-7734)$
```

Figure 3-128. *Enabling the container API to frontend-devs project*

Enabling the container API is the first prerequisite to create and use a GKE cluster. Without this action, you won't be able to create your GKE cluster.

■ **Note** If you performed the cluster with Shared VPC deep dive example, the container API has already been enabled for the project frontend-devs, so you won't need to perform this step. Also, in this example, we will use the default VPC, and not your-app-shared-vpc. The default VPC is an auto-mode network that has one subnet in each region. On the other hand, our shared VPC is a *custom-mode* network with only two subnets subnet-frontend in us-east1 and subnet-backend in us-central1.

Next, let's create our GKE cluster (Figure 3-129). Notice that a region or a zone must be specified to denote respectively a regional or a zonal cluster.

```
joseph@cloudshell:~/code/kubernetes-engine-samples/network-policies (frontend-devs-7734)$ gcloud container clusters
  create test --zone=us-east1-c --enable-network-policy
Default change: VPC-native is the default mode during cluster creation for versions greater than 1.21.0-gke.1500. T
o create advanced routes based clusters, please pass the `--no-enable-ip-alias` flag
Default change: During creation of nodepools or autoscaling configuration changes for cluster versions greater than
  1.24.1-gke.800 a default location policy is applied. For Spot and PVM it defaults to ANY, and for all other VM kin
ds a BALANCED policy is used. To change the default values use the `--location-policy` flag.
Note: Your Pod address range (`--cluster-ipv4-cidr`) can accommodate at most 1008 node(s).
Creating cluster test in us-east1-c... Cluster is being health-checked (master is healthy)...done.
Created [https://container.googleapis.com/v1/projects/frontend-devs-7734/zones/us-east1-c/clusters/test].
To inspect the contents of your cluster, go to: https://console.cloud.google.com/kubernetes/workload_/gcloud/us-eas
t1-c/test?project=frontend-devs-7734
kubeconfig entry generated for test.
NAME: test
LOCATION: us-east1-c
MASTER_VERSION: 1.22.10-gke.600
MASTER_IP: 35.196.202.251
MACHINE_TYPE: e2-medium
NODE_VERSION: 1.22.10-gke.600
NUM_NODES: 3
STATUS: RUNNING
joseph@cloudshell:~/code/kubernetes-engine-samples/network-policies (frontend-devs-7734)$ []
```

Figure 3-129. *Creating a GKE cluster test with --enable-network-policy flag*

Regional clusters have multiple control planes across multiple compute zones in a region, while zonal clusters have one control plane in a single compute zone.

Restricting Ingress Traffic

Now, with a running GKE cluster, which is enabled to enforce network policies, we can apply an ingress policy to a containerized web application labeled app=hello. In Kubernetes, labels are key/value pairs that are attached to objects, such as pods. In our example, app is the key; hello is its value.

Let's run the containerized web app first (Figure 3-130). The web app will expose the endpoint http://hello-web:8080.

```
joseph@cloudshell:~/code/kubernetes-engine-samples/network-policies (frontend-devs-7734)$ kubectl run hello-web
  --labels app=hello \
    --image=us-docker.pkg.dev/google-samples/containers/gke/hello-app:1.0 --port 8080 --expose
service/hello-web created
pod/hello-web created
joseph@cloudshell:~/code/kubernetes-engine-samples/network-policies (frontend-devs-7734)$ ▌
```

Figure 3-130. *Running containerized web app labeled* app=hello

The network policy in the first use case is intended to limit incoming traffic to only requests originating from another containerized application labeled app=foo. Let's review how this rule is expressed in the form of policy-as-code by viewing the hello-allow-from-foo.yaml file (Figure 3-131).

```
joseph@cloudshell:~/code/kubernetes-engine-samples/network-policies (frontend-devs-7734)$ vim hello-allow-from-
foo.yaml
```

Figure 3-131. *Viewing cluster* test *ingress network policy*

The network policy is a YAML file (Figure 3-132), and there are a few things to mention:

- The network policy is a Kubernetes API resource: kind: NetworkPolicy

- The network policy is scoped at the entire GKE cluster level.

- The network policy type is *ingress*. Other available types are *egress*, or both.

- The network policy subject entity is a pod. Other entities can be namespace(s) or CIDR block(s).

- Since the entity this ingress network policy applies to is a pod, a pod selector construct is included in the spec section to match the desired pod, that is, a pod whose label's key app matches the value hello.

- Likewise, since the target of this ingress policy is another pod, a pod selector is also included in the ingress definition to match the desired pod, that is, a pod whose label's key app matches the value foo.

```
# Copyright 2021 Google LLC
#
# Licensed under the Apache License, Version 2.0 (the "License");
# you may not use this file except in compliance with the License.
# You may obtain a copy of the License at
#
#       http://www.apache.org/licenses/LICENSE-2.0
#
# Unless required by applicable law or agreed to in writing, software
# distributed under the License is distributed on an "AS IS" BASIS,
# WITHOUT WARRANTIES OR CONDITIONS OF ANY KIND, either express or implied.
# See the License for the specific language governing permissions and
# limitations under the License.

# [START gke_network_policies_hello_allow_from_foo_networkpolicy_hello_allow_from_foo]
kind: NetworkPolicy
apiVersion: networking.k8s.io/v1
metadata:
  name: hello-allow-from-foo
spec:
  policyTypes:
  - Ingress
  podSelector:
    matchLabels:
      app: hello
  ingress:
  - from:
    - podSelector:
        matchLabels:
          app: foo
# [END gke_network_policies_hello_allow_from_foo_networkpolicy_hello_allow_from_foo]
---
```

Figure 3-132. *Sections of cluster* test *ingress network policy*

Let's now apply this ingress network policy to the cluster (Figure 3-133).

```
joseph@cloudshell:~/code/kubernetes-engine-samples/network-policies (frontend-devs-7734)$ kubectl apply -f
  hello-allow-from-foo.yaml
networkpolicy.networking.k8s.io/hello-allow-from-foo created
joseph@cloudshell:~/code/kubernetes-engine-samples/network-policies (frontend-devs-7734)$
```

Figure 3-133. *Enforcing cluster* test *ingress network policy*

Validating Ingress Network Policy

To validate the ingress network policy, let's run a temporary pod with a containerized app labeled app=foo, and from the pod, let's make a request to the endpoint http://hello-web:8080.

Conversely, let's run another temporary pod with a containerized app labeled app=other, and from the pod, let's make another request to the endpoint http://hello-web:8080.

Figure 3-134 illustrates the aforementioned actions.

```
joseph@cloudshell:~/code/kubernetes-engine-samples/network-policies (frontend-devs-7734)$ kubectl run -l
app=foo --image=alpine --restart=Never --rm -i -t test-1
If you don't see a command prompt, try pressing enter.
/ # wget -qO- --timeout=2 http://hello-web:8080
Hello, world!
Version: 1.0.0
Hostname: hello-web
/ # exit
pod "test-1" deleted
joseph@cloudshell:~/code/kubernetes-engine-samples/network-policies (frontend-devs-7734)$ kubectl run -l
app=other --image=alpine --restart=Never --rm -i -t test-1
If you don't see a command prompt, try pressing enter.
/ # wget -qO- --timeout=2 http://hello-web:8080
wget: download timed out
/ # exit
pod "test-1" deleted
pod default/test-1 terminated (Error)
joseph@cloudshell:~/code/kubernetes-engine-samples/network-policies (frontend-devs-7734)$ ▉
```

Figure 3-134. *Validating cluster* test *ingress network policy*

With the ingress network policy in effect, the former request succeeded, whereas the latter timed out.

Restricting Egress Traffic

Similarly to ingress network policies, egress traffic can be controlled with *egress network policies*.

However, to be able to query internal hostnames such as hello-web or external hostnames such as www. example.com, you must allow DNS (Domain Name System) resolution in your egress network policies. DNS traffic occurs on port 53 using TCP and UDP protocols.

Let's run another containerized web app labeled app=hello-2 in a temporary pod named pod/hello-web-2 (Figure 3-135). The web app consumes a service Kubernetes resource service/hello-web-2 to expose an endpoint http://hello-web-2:8080.

```
joseph@cloudshell:~/code/kubernetes-engine-samples/network-policies (frontend-devs-7734)$ kubectl run
hello-web-2 --labels app=hello-2 \
  --image=us-docker.pkg.dev/google-samples/containers/gke/hello-app:1.0 --port 8080 --expose
service/hello-web-2 created
pod/hello-web-2 created
joseph@cloudshell:~/code/kubernetes-engine-samples/network-policies (frontend-devs-7734)$ ▉
```

Figure 3-135. *Running containerized web app labeled* app=hello-2

We will use this containerized web app labeled app=hello-2 to validate the network policy in the second use case, which is intended to limit outgoing traffic originating from the app labeled app=foo to only the following two destinations:

- Pods in the same namespace with the label app=hello

- Cluster pods or external endpoints on port 53 (UDP and TCP)

Let's view the manifest for this egress network policy (Figures 3-136 and 3-137).

```
joseph@cloudshell:~/code/kubernetes-engine-samples/network-policies (frontend-devs-7734)$ vim foo-allow-
to-hello.yaml ▉
```

Figure 3-136. *Viewing cluster* test *egress network policy*

```
#
#       http://www.apache.org/licenses/LICENSE-2.0
#
# Unless required by applicable law or agreed to in writing, software
# distributed under the License is distributed on an "AS IS" BASIS,
# WITHOUT WARRANTIES OR CONDITIONS OF ANY KIND, either express or implied.
# See the License for the specific language governing permissions and
# limitations under the License.

# [START gke_network_policies_foo_allow_to_hello_networkpolicy_foo_allow_to_hello]
kind: NetworkPolicy
apiVersion: networking.k8s.io/v1
metadata:
  name: foo-allow-to-hello
spec:
  policyTypes:
  - Egress
  podSelector:
    matchLabels:
      app: foo
  egress:
  - to:
    - podSelector:
        matchLabels:
          app: hello
  - ports:
    - port: 53
      protocol: TCP
    - port: 53
      protocol: UDP
# [END gke_network_policies_foo_allow_to_hello_networkpolicy_foo_allow_to_hello]
---
```

Figure 3-137. *Sections of cluster* test *egress network policy*

The manifest declares the policy type as egress, and it applies to pods in the test cluster whose label's key app matches the value foo.

Notice the egress section denotes two targets, that is, pods whose label's key app matches the value hello and the set of protocol-ports pairs {(TCP, 53), (UDP,53)}.

Let's now apply this egress network policy to the cluster (Figure 3-138).

```
joseph@cloudshell:~/code/kubernetes-engine-samples/network-policies (frontend-devs-7734)$ kubectl apply
-f foo-allow-to-hello.yaml
networkpolicy.networking.k8s.io/foo-allow-to-hello created
joseph@cloudshell:~/code/kubernetes-engine-samples/network-policies (frontend-devs-7734)$
```

Figure 3-138. *Enforcing cluster* test *egress network policy*

Validating Egress Network Policy

As you can see in Figure 3-139, to validate the egress network policy all we have to do is to run a temporary pod with a containerized app labeled app=foo and from the pod make requests to

- The endpoint http://hello-web:8080

- Another internal endpoint http://hello-web-2:8080

- An external endpoint http://www.example.com

```
joseph@cloudshell:~/code/kubernetes-engine-samples/network-policies (frontend-devs-7734)$ kubectl run
-l app=foo --image=alpine --rm -i -t --restart=Never test-3
If you don't see a command prompt, try pressing enter.
/ # wget -qO- --timeout=2 http://hello-web:8080
Hello, world!
Version: 1.0.0
Hostname: hello-web
/ # wget -qO- --timeout=2 http://hello-web-2:8080
wget: download timed out
/ # wget -qO- --timeout=2 http://www.example.com
wget: download timed out
/ # exit
pod "test-3" deleted
pod default/test-3 terminated (Error)
joseph@cloudshell:~/code/kubernetes-engine-samples/network-policies (frontend-devs-7734)$ ▊
```

Figure 3-139. *Validating cluster* test *egress network policy*

With the egress network policy in effect, the only allowed outbound connection from the containerized app labeled app=foo is the endpoint http://hello-web:8080. This is because this endpoint is exposed by a service that lives in a pod labeled app=hello, which is an allowed connection as shown in the egress section of Figure 3-137.

Since there is no entry denoted by app=hello-2 in the egress section of the manifest YAML file, the containerized app labeled app=foo is not allowed to connect to the endpoint http://hello-web-2:8080.

Deleting the Cluster

As a good practice to avoid incurring charges, let's now delete our test GKE cluster, which is still up and running along with its three e2-medium nodes all located in us-east1-c (Figure 3-140).

```
joseph@cloudshell:~/code/kubernetes-engine-samples/network-policies (frontend-devs-7734)$ gcloud container
clusters list
NAME: test
LOCATION: us-east1-c
MASTER_VERSION: 1.22.10-gke.600
MASTER_IP: 35.196.202.251
MACHINE_TYPE: e2-medium
NODE_VERSION: 1.22.10-gke.600
NUM_NODES: 3
STATUS: RUNNING
joseph@cloudshell:~/code/kubernetes-engine-samples/network-policies (frontend-devs-7734)$
```

Figure 3-140. *Listing GKE clusters*

We will use the gcloud container clusters delete command as indicated in Figure 3-141. Notice the zone is required because our GKE cluster test is zonal.

```
joseph@cloudshell:~/code/kubernetes-engine-samples/network-policies (frontend-devs-7734)$ gcloud container
clusters delete test --zone=us-east1-c
The following clusters will be deleted.
 - [test] in [us-east1-c]

Do you want to continue (Y/n)?  Y

Deleting cluster test...done.
Deleted [https://container.googleapis.com/v1/projects/frontend-devs-7734/zones/us-east1-c/clusters/test].
joseph@cloudshell:~/code/kubernetes-engine-samples/network-policies (frontend-devs-7734)$
```

Figure 3-141. *Deleting GKE* test *cluster*

Upon deleting the cluster, the list is now empty (Figure 3-142).

```
joseph@cloudshell:~/code/kubernetes-engine-samples/network-policies (frontend-devs-7734)$ gcloud container
clusters list
joseph@cloudshell:~/code/kubernetes-engine-samples/network-policies (frontend-devs-7734)$ █
```

Figure 3-142. *Effect of GKE cluster* test *deletion*

Additional Guidelines

There are a couple of things to remember about cluster network policies, which are important for the exam.

First, in a cluster network policy, you define only the *allowed* connections between pods. There is no action allowed/denied like in firewall rules (you will learn more about firewall rules in the following section). If you need to enable connectivity between pods, you must explicitly define it in a network policy.

Second, if you don't specify any network policies in your GKE cluster namespace, the default behavior is to *allow any connection* (ingress and egress) among all pods in the same namespace.

In other words, all pods in your cluster that have the same namespace can communicate with each other by default.

Let's view a couple of examples on how to override this behavior.

The extreme opposite of the default behavior is by isolating all pods in a namespace from ingress and egress traffic. The network policy in Figure 3-143 shows you how to achieve just that.

```
---
apiVersion: networking.k8s.io/v1
kind: NetworkPolicy
metadata:
  name: default-deny-all
spec:
  podSelector: {}          {} means ALL pods
  policyTypes:
  - Ingress
  - Egress

~                        No "ingress" node means ingress traffic denied
~                        No "egress" node means egress traffic denied
"network-policy-default-deny-all.yaml" 11L, 155B
```

Figure 3-143. *Deny all network policy*

If you want to *deny* only ingress traffic to your pods, but allow egress traffic, just remove the Egress item from the list in the policyTypes node as shown in Figure 3-144.

```
---
apiVersion: networking.k8s.io/v1
kind: NetworkPolicy
metadata:
  name: default-deny-ingress
spec:
  podSelector: {}
  policyTypes:
  - Ingress

"network-policy-default-deny-ingress.yaml" 10L, 148B
```

Figure 3-144. *Deny all ingress network policy*

Conversely, if you want to *allow* incoming traffic for all your pods, just add the ingress node and indicate all pods {} as the first item in the list as illustrated in Figure 3-145.

```
---
apiVersion: networking.k8s.io/v1
kind: NetworkPolicy
metadata:
  name: default-allow-ingress
spec:
  podSelector: {}
  policyTypes:
  - Ingress
  ingress:
  - {}

"network-policy-default-allow-ingress.yaml" 12L, 167B
```

Figure 3-145. *Allow all ingress network policy*

Private Clusters and Private Control Plane Endpoints

Before we start this section, let's refresh our knowledge on how GKE works.

A GKE cluster is comprised of the following infrastructure:

1. **Control plane(s)**: A group of VMs in a *google-owned-project*, which hosts the Kubernetes API server, the Kubernetes scheduler, the Kubernetes key-value store (named *etcd*), the Google Cloud controller manager, and the core controller manager. Zonal clusters (e.g., --zone=us-central1-c) have a single control plane. Regional clusters (e.g., --region=us-central1) have replicas of the control plane in different zones of the same region where the cluster lives.

2. **Worker nodes**: Another group of VMs in *your-project*, where each VM hosts the container runtime, an agent named *kubelet*—responsible for ensuring containers are running healthy in a pod—and a network proxy named *kube-proxy*, responsible for the interaction with other worker nodes in the cluster and the interaction with the control plane.

A review of Figures 2-52 to 2-54 in Chapter 2 is recommended to visualize these concepts and prepare for this section.

The control plane is the single pane of glass for your GKE cluster, and the Kubernetes API server is the *hub* for all interactions with the cluster. The control plane exposes a public endpoint by default and a private endpoint. Both endpoints can be directly accessed via the HTTPS or gRPC (gRPC Remote Procedure Call) protocols.

The VPC network where the control plane Google-managed VMs live is peered with the VPC where your cluster worker nodes live. The worker nodes and the control plane VMs interact with each other using the Kubernetes API server.

In the previous example (Figure 3-117), each worker node had an internal IP address denoted in green and an external IP address denoted in pink.

You learned that the internal IP address is used to route RFC 1918 traffic between VMs in the same VPC network. It doesn't matter if the two VMs are located in the same subnet or in different subnets. The only two constraints for the traffic to flow are that the subnets are part of the same VPC network and the VPC firewall rules allow traffic to flow between the two VMs.

Conversely, the external IP address of a VM is used to route traffic to the Internet or to Google public APIs and services.

What we just described is the default GKE cluster configuration as it relates to worker node IP addressing.

> *By default, GKE clusters are created with external IP addresses for master (control plane) and worker nodes.*

There are scenarios where your workload security requirements constrain your design to exclude external IP addresses for any of your cluster's worker nodes. When you use this network design, the cluster is called a *private cluster* because all worker nodes are isolated from the Internet, that is, zero worker nodes have an external IP address.

This network design can be accomplished by creating your cluster with the `--enable-private-nodes` flag.

■ **Exam tip**   Even though a cluster is private—that is, none of its worker nodes use an external IP address—its control plane can still be accessed from the Internet. If you want to completely isolate your private cluster's control plane from the Internet, you must use the `--enable-private-endpoint` flag at cluster creation, which essentially tells GKE that the cluster is managed *exclusively* using the private IP address of the master API endpoint. This is the most secure configuration for GKE clusters in that none of its worker nodes have external IP addresses, and the control plane public endpoint has been disabled. See Figure 2-52 in Chapter 2.

The `--enable-private-nodes` flag requires that you also specify an RFC 1918 CIDR block for your cluster control plane (also known as master) nodes unless your cluster is Autopilot (see more info here). This makes sense because you don't want any of your cluster nodes—whether they be master nodes (i.e., Google-managed VMs in a `google-owned-project`) or worker nodes (i.e., Google-managed VMs in `your-project`)—to have an external IP address. You already specified the CIDR block for the worker nodes when you "told" gcloud which subnet in `your-project` to use, and now you need to "tell" gcloud where your master nodes will live. How do you do that?

You accomplish this by setting the `--master-ipv4-cidr` flag to a CIDR block with a /28 mask.

Adding Authorized Networks for Cluster Control Plane Endpoints

Whether your cluster is public or private, it is best practice to add an extra layer of security by limiting the access to your cluster control plane.

Google Cloud allows you to specify a list of CIDR blocks, which are authorized to access via HTTPS your cluster control plane endpoints, which can be

- One enabled endpoint only, which is *private* and is activated when the `--enable-private-endpoint` flag is used at creation time—with this configuration, the control plane public endpoint is automatically disabled.

- Two enabled endpoints, one private and one public.

Figure 3-146 illustrates how the control plane can be accessed from authorized CIDR blocks.

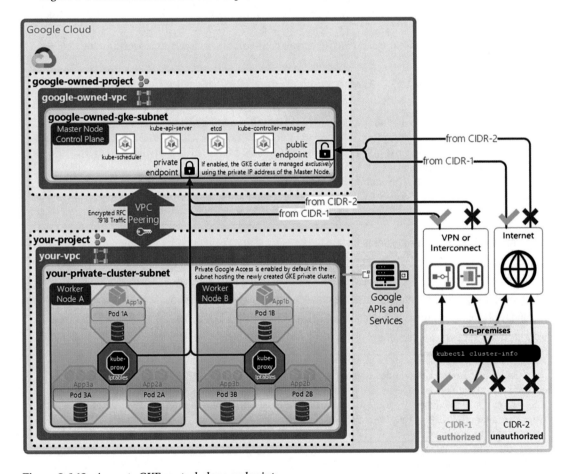

Figure 3-146. *Access to GKE control plane endpoints*

If your cluster has been created *with* the `--enable-private-endpoint` flag, then the only way to access the control plane is by using its private endpoint. This can be achieved from an on-premises client connected with VPN or Interconnect (Dedicated or Partner), provided the client NIC is associated with an IP address in an authorized CIDR block.

If the cluster has been created *without* the `--enable-private-endpoint` flag, then the control plane can be accessed by using its public endpoint from on-premises authorized clients connected to the Internet or by using its private endpoint either from requestors in the VPC where the worker nodes live or from on-premises authorized client connected with VPN or Interconnect.

Now, how do you tell GKE which CIDR block is authorized to access the cluster control plane?

This can be achieved by using the `--enable-master-authorized-networks` flag when you create your cluster. This flag requires that you specify the list of CIDR blocks by using the `--master-authorized-networks` flag. You can specify up to 100 CIDR blocks for private clusters and up to 50 CIDR blocks for public clusters.

There are several flags in the command `gcloud container clusters create` you need to know for the exam. Each flag has a specific purpose, and a proper use of a single or a combination of them allows you to define the optimal configuration for your GKE cluster, in accordance with your workload security and network requirements.

Figure 3-147 summarizes what we just learned in the form of a decision tree.

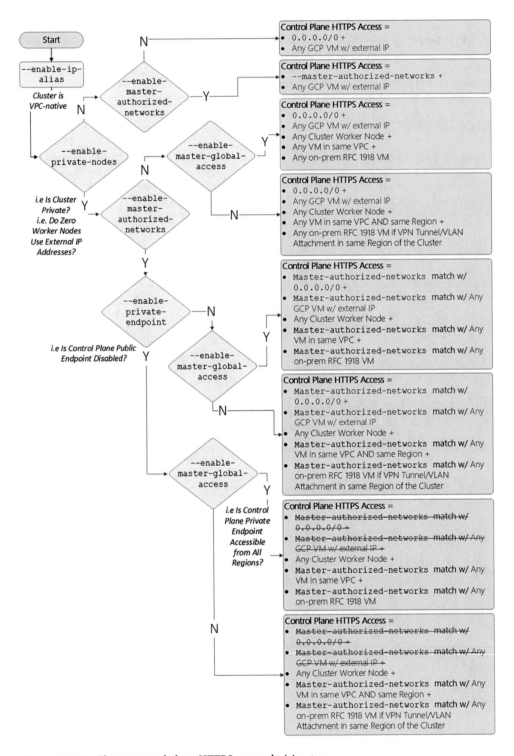

Figure 3-147. *Cluster control plane HTTPS access decision tree*

The top-right box indicates the least restrictive access to your GKE cluster's master endpoint, that is, a public cluster with no restrictions to its public endpoint.

The bottom-right box indicates the most restrictive—and recommended for workloads managing sensitive data—access to your GKE cluster's master endpoint, that is, a private cluster with public endpoint disabled.

Going from the top-right box down, more access restrictions are added, resulting in a reduction of the attack surface of your cluster's control plane.

Last, your cluster's control plane private endpoint is exposed using an internal network TCP/UDP load balancer (ILB) in the `google-owned-vpc`. By default, clients consuming the Kubernetes API with the private endpoint must be located in the same region where the ILB lives (the ILB is a regional resource). These can be VMs hosted in Google Cloud or on-premises VM connected through Cloud VPN tunnels or VLAN attachments.

By adding the `--enable-master-global-access` flag, you are allowing clients in any region to consume your cluster Kubernetes API using its private endpoint.

Configuring and Managing Firewall Rules

Similar to your data center's DMZ, each VPC network has a firewall that blocks by default all incoming traffic from outside a VPC network to all the instances in your VPC. You can protect the perimeter of your VPC network by configuring firewall rules, which are a means to unambiguously control what traffic is allowed to enter (ingress) your VPC network and what traffic is allowed to exit (egress) your VPC network.

Unlike traditional DMZs, however, Google Cloud firewalls are *globally* distributed to help avoid problems related to scaling with traffic. As a result, since Google Cloud firewalls are globally distributed, there are no single choke points (as you learned in Chapter 2, i.e., Figure 2-24). Here are the main differentiating features of Google Cloud firewall rules, when compared to traditional firewall rules:

- **VPC scope**: By default, firewall rules are applied to the *whole* VPC network, not its partitions, that is, its subnets.

- **Network tag target**: However, you can restrict the scope of a firewall rule to a specific group of VMs in your VPC. This is where the concept of a *target* comes into play. You can configure the firewall rule to only target a set of VMs in your VPC by adding a **network tag** (also referred to as *instance tag*) to a specific group of VMs and then by applying the firewall rule to the VMs with that tag.

- **Service account target**: You can also configure a firewall rule to only target specific VMs by selecting their associated service account. To do so, choose the specified service account, indicate whether the service account is in the current project or another one under **Service account scope**, and set the service account name in the **Source/Target service account** field.

- **VM-to-VM traffic control**: You can also use firewall rules to control internal traffic between VMs by defining a set of permitted source machines in the rule.

Firewall rules are flexible in allowing ingress/egress directions and allow/deny actions using priorities (0 highest priority, 65535 lowest priority).

Figure 3-148 shows the global, distributed nature of two firewall rules for our `vpc-host-nonprod` VPC. As you can see, the firewall protection spans the whole perimeter of the VPC, which includes subnets in two different regions.

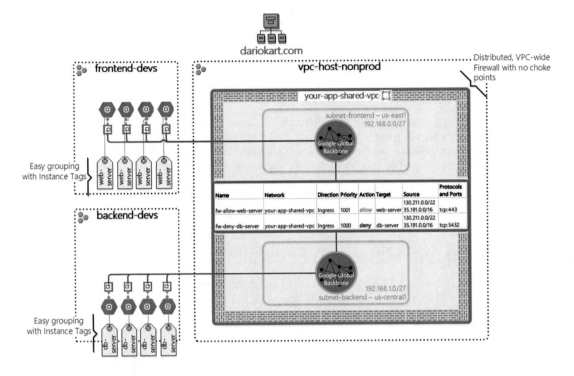

Figure 3-148. *Distributed firewall in a VPC*

The first firewall rule allows only incoming traffic over the TCP protocol and port 443 targeting the VMs denoted by the web-server network tag.

The second firewall rule denies incoming traffic over the TCP protocol and port 5432 targeting the VMs denoted by the db-server network tag.

■ **Note** The Source CIDR blocks in Figure 3-148 refer to Google Front Ends (GFEs), which are located in the Google Edge Network and are meant to protect your workload infrastructure from DDoS (Distributed Denial-of-Service) attacks. You will learn more about GFEs in Chapter 5.

Target Network Tags and Service Accounts

You can use network tags or service accounts (one of the two, not both) to selectively target the VMs in your VPC you want to apply firewall rules on. Keep in mind that when you add a *network tag* to a VM, and subsequently use the network tag as the target in a firewall rule, there is no additional access-control check that happens by default. *Nobody keeps one from creating a network tag whose instance can anonymously expose sensitive data (e.g., PII (Personally Identifiable Information), PHI (Protected Health information), PCI (Payment Card Industry) data). To prevent this security risk, GCP has introduced the ability to create firewall rules that target instances associated to service accounts.*

You can create *a service account and use it as a source or a target of a firewall rule,* and you can rest assured that when you associate a service account to a VM, then there is an access-control check that happens behind the scenes, that is, you must have IAM permissions to use the service account, because a service account is an identity and a resource at the same time.

■ **Exam tip** Service accounts and network tags are mutually exclusive and can't be combined in the same firewall rule. However, they are often used in complementary rules to reduce the attack surface of your workloads.

The target of a firewall rule indicates a group of VMs in your VPC network, which are selected by network tags or by associated service accounts. The definition of a target varies based on the rule direction, that is, ingress or egress.

If the direction is ingress, the target of your firewall rule denotes a group of destination VMs in your VPC, whose traffic from a specified source outside of your VPC is allowed or denied. For this reason, ingress firewall rules cannot use the destination parameter.

Conversely, if the direction is egress, the target of your firewall rule denotes a group of source VMs in your VPC, whose traffic to a specified destination outside of your VPC is allowed or denied. For this reason, egress firewall rules cannot use the source parameter.

Let's review the syntax to create a firewall rule.

Syntax for Creating Firewall Rules

Similarly to routes, firewall rules are defined on a per-VPC basis. You don't associate a firewall rule to a single subnet or a single VM. As shown in Figure 3-149, with the `gcloud compute firewall-rules create` command, you specify the VPC the firewall rules is associated to by setting the flag `--network` to the name of the VPC you want to protect.

```
NAME
    gcloud compute firewall-rules create - create a Compute Engine firewall
        rule

SYNOPSIS
    gcloud compute firewall-rules create NAME
        (--action=ACTION | --allow=PROTOCOL[:PORT[-PORT]],[...])
        [--description=DESCRIPTION]
        [--destination-ranges=CIDR_RANGE,[CIDR_RANGE,...]]
        [--direction=DIRECTION] [--disabled] [--[no-]enable-logging]
        [--logging-metadata=LOGGING_METADATA]
        [--network=NETWORK; default="default"] [--priority=PRIORITY]
        [--rules=PROTOCOL[:PORT[-PORT]],[...]]
        [--source-ranges=CIDR_RANGE,[CIDR_RANGE,...]]
        [--source-service-accounts=EMAIL,[EMAIL,...]]
        [--source-tags=TAG,[TAG,...]]
        [--target-service-accounts=EMAIL,[EMAIL,...]]
        [--target-tags=TAG,[TAG,...]] [GCLOUD_WIDE_FLAG ...]

DESCRIPTION
    gcloud compute firewall-rules create is used to create firewall rules to
    allow/deny incoming/outgoing traffic.
```

Figure 3-149. `gcloud compute firewall-rules create` syntax

Use the parameters as follows. More details about each parameter are available in the SDK reference documentation.

- `--network`: The network where the rule will be created. If omitted, the rule will be created in the default network. If you don't have a default network or want to create the rule in a specific network, you must use this field.

- `--priority`: An integer between 0 and 65535(both inclusive) that indicates the priority for the rule. The lower the number, the higher the priority. Priority is helpful when you want to override the behavior of the two implied firewall rules automatically configured for any VPC, that is, an implied rule that permits outgoing connections and an implied rule that blocks incoming connections.

- `--direction`: The direction of traffic, which must be one of INGRESS, IN, EGRESS, OUT.

- `--action`: Denotes the action on match, either ALLOW or DENY. Must be used with the `--rules` flag.

- Specify a target in one of three ways:

  - Omit `--target-tags` and `--target-service-accounts` if the rule should apply to all targets in the network.

  - `--target-tags`: Use this flag to define targets by network tags.

  - `--target-service-accounts`: Use this flag to define targets by associated service accounts.

- For an ingress rule, specify a source:

  - Omit `--source-ranges`, `source-tags`, and `--source-service-accounts` if the ingress source should be anywhere, that is, 0.0.0.0/0.

  - `--source-ranges`: Use this flag to specify ranges of source IP addresses in CIDR format.

  - `--source-tags`: Use this flag to specify source instances by network tags. Filtering by source tag is only available if the target is *not* specified by service account. For more information, see filtering by service account vs. network tag.

  - `--source-ranges` and `--source-tags` can be used *together*. If both are specified, the effective source set is the *union* of the source range IP addresses and the instances identified by network tags, even if the tagged instances do not have IPs in the source ranges.

  - `--source-service-accounts`: Use this flag to specify instances by the service accounts they use. Filtering by source service account is only available if the target is *not* specified by network tag. For more information, see filtering by service account vs. network tag.

- For an egress rule, specify a destination:

  - Omit `--destination-ranges` if the egress destination should be anywhere, that is, 0.0.0.0/0.

  - `--destination-ranges`: Use this flag to specify ranges of destination IP addresses in CIDR format.

- `--rules`: A list of protocols and ports to which the rule will apply. Use `all` to make the rule applicable to all protocols and all ports. Requires the `--action` flag.

- By default, firewall rules are created and enforced automatically; however, you can change this behavior.

  - If both `--disabled` and `--no-disabled` are omitted, the firewall rule is created and enforced.

  - `--disabled`: Add this flag to create the firewall rule but not enforce it. The firewall rule will remain in a disabled state until you update the firewall rule to enable it.

  - `--no-disabled`: Add this flag to ensure the firewall rule is enforced.

- You can enable Firewall Rules Logging for a rule when you create or update it. *Firewall Rules Logging* allows you to audit, verify, and analyze the effects of your firewall rules. Firewall Rules Logging will be reviewed in detail in Chapter 8.

■ **Exam tip** You cannot change the direction (i.e., ingress, egress) of an *existing* firewall rule. For example, an existing ingress firewall rule cannot be updated to become an egress rule. You have to create a new rule with the correct parameters, then delete the old one. Similarly, you cannot change the action (i.e., deny, allow) of an existing firewall rule.

Priority

The firewall rule priority is an integer from 0 to 65535, inclusive. Lower integers indicate higher priorities. If you do not specify a priority when creating a rule, it is assigned a default priority of 1000.

The relative priority of a firewall rule determines if the rule is applicable when evaluated against others. The evaluation logic works as follows:

A rule with a *deny* action overrides another with an allow action *only if the two rules have the same priority*. Using relative priorities, it is possible to build allow rules that override deny rules, and vice versa.

Example

Consider the following example where two firewall rules exist:

- An ingress rule from sources `0.0.0.0/0` (anywhere) applicable to *all* targets, all protocols, and all ports, having a deny action and a priority of 1000

- An ingress rule from sources `0.0.0.0/0` (anywhere) applicable to *specific* targets with the network tag `webserver`, for traffic on TCP 80, with an `allow` action

The priority of the second rule determines whether TCP traffic on port 80 is allowed for the `webserver` network targets:

- If the priority of the second rule > 1000, it will have a lower priority, so the first rule denying all traffic will apply.

- If the priority of the second rule = 1000, the two rules will have identical priorities, so the first rule denying all traffic will apply.

- If the priority of the second rule < 1000, it will have a higher priority, thus allowing traffic on TCP 80 for the `webserver` targets. Absent other rules, the first rule would still deny other types of traffic to the webserver targets, and it would also deny all traffic, including TCP 80, to instances without the `webserver` network tag.

Protocols and Ports

You can narrow the scope of a firewall rule by specifying protocols or protocols and ports. You can specify a protocol or a combination of protocols and their ports. If you omit both protocols and ports, the firewall rule is applicable for all traffic on any protocol and any port. Table 3-1 shows examples of how protocols and ports can be combined when creating or updating a firewall rule. These combinations of protocols and ports can be assigned to the `--allow` or the `--rules` flags in the aforementioned gcloud compute firewall-rules create command (Figure 3-149).

Table 3-1. *Filtering traffic by protocols and ports*

Specification	Example	Explanation
No protocol and port	—	If you do not specify a protocol, the firewall rule applies to all protocols and their applicable ports
Protocol	tcp	If you specify a protocol without any port information, the firewall rule applies to that protocol and all of its applicable ports
Protocol and single port	tcp:80	If you specify a protocol and a single port, the firewall rule applies to just that port of the protocol
Protocol and port range	tcp:20-22	If you specify a protocol and a port range, the firewall rule applies to just the port range for the protocol
Combinations	icmp,tcp:80,tcp:443,udp:67-69	You can specify various combinations of protocols and ports to which the firewall rule applies. For more information, see creating firewall rules

Direction

The direction of a firewall rule can be either ingress or egress. The direction is always defined from the perspective of your VPC.

- The ingress direction describes traffic sent from a source to your VPC. Ingress rules apply to packets for new sessions where the destination of the packet is the target.

- The egress direction describes traffic sent from your VPC to a destination. Egress rules apply to packets for new sessions where the source of the packet is the target.

- If you omit a direction, GCP uses ingress as default.

Example

Consider an example connection between two VMs in the same network. Traffic from VM1 to VM2 can be controlled using either of these firewall rules:

- An ingress rule with a target of VM2 and a source of VM1

- An egress rule with a target of VM1 and a destination of VM2

Firewall Rule Logs

In the context of implementing VPCs, these are the important points you need to know for the exam:

- *Firewall Rules Logging* allows you to audit, verify, and analyze the effects of your firewall rules. For example, you can determine if a firewall rule designed to deny traffic is functioning as intended. Logging is also useful if you need to determine how many connections are affected by a given firewall rule.

- You enable Firewall Rules Logging *individually* for each firewall rule whose connections you need to log. Firewall Rules Logging is an option for any firewall rule, regardless of the action (allow or deny) or direction (ingress or egress) of the rule.

- When you enable logging for a firewall rule, Google Cloud Platform (GCP) creates an entry called a *connection record* each time the rule allows or denies traffic. You can export these connection records to Cloud Logging, Cloud Pub/Sub, or BigQuery for analysis.

- Each connection record contains the source and destination IP addresses, the protocol and ports, date and time, and a reference to the firewall rule that applied to the traffic.

Firewall Rule Summary

Tables 3-2 and 3-3 summarize the Google Cloud firewall rule syntax.

Table 3-2. *Ingress firewall rule description*

Ingress (Inbound) Rule

Priority	Action	Enforcement	Target (Defines the Destination)	Source	Protocols and Ports
Integer from 0 (highest) to 65535 (lowest), inclusive; default 1000	Either *allow* or *deny*	Either enabled (default) or disabled	The target parameter specifies the destination. It can be one of the following: • All instances in the VPC network • Instances by service account • Instances by network tag	One of the following: • Range of IPv4 addresses; the default is any (0.0.0.0/0) • Instances by service account • Instances by network tag	Specify a protocol or protocol and a port.If not set, the rule applies to all protocols

Table 3-3. *Egress firewall rule description*

Priority	Action	Enforcement	Target (Defines the Source)	Destination	Protocols and Ports
Integer from 0 (highest) to 65535 (lowest), inclusive; default 1000	Either *allow* or *deny*	Either enabled (default) or disabled	The target parameter specifies the source. It can be one of the following: • All instances in the VPC network • Instances by service account • Instances by network tag	Any network or a specific range of IPv4 addresses; the default is any (0.0.0.0/0)	Specify a protocol or protocol and a port.If not set, the rule applies to all protocols

Additionally, we included a few exam tips, which come in handy when trying to remember the parameters required by ingress (default) or egress firewall rules using gcloud.

■ **Exam tip**   For the exam, you will need to remember that destination ranges are not valid parameters for ingress firewall rules. Likewise, source ranges are not valid parameters for egress rules. A good way to remember this is by memorizing the timezone acronyms IST and EDT, respectively, for ingress rules and egress rules: in the former scenario (**I**ngress direction), you use **S**ource and **T**arget parameters, whereas in the latter (**E**gress direction), you use **D**estination and **T**arget parameters only.

Exam Questions
Question 3.1 (Routing)

You need to configure a static route as a backup to an existing static route. You want to ensure that the new route is only used when the existing route is no longer available. What should you do?

- **A.** Create a network tag with a value of backup for the new static route.
- **B.** Set a lower priority value for the new static route than the existing static route.
- **C.** Set a higher priority value for the new static route than the existing static route.
- **D.** Configure the same priority value for the new static route as the existing static route.

Rationale

A is not correct because a route with a specific network tag is only applied to instances with the tag value.

B is not correct because static route priority uses lower values to indicate a higher priority.

C is CORRECT because the higher value will make the route take effect only when the lower value route is not available.

D is not correct because if you use the same value, GCP uses equal-cost multipath routing and would use the new route some of the time when the existing static route is still available.

Question 3.2 (Firewall Rules)

You create a VPC named Prod in custom mode with two subnets, as shown in Figure 3-150. You want to make sure that (1) only app VM can access the DB VM instance, (2) web VM can access app VM, and (3) users outside the VPC can send HTTPS requests to web VM only. Which two firewall rules should you create?

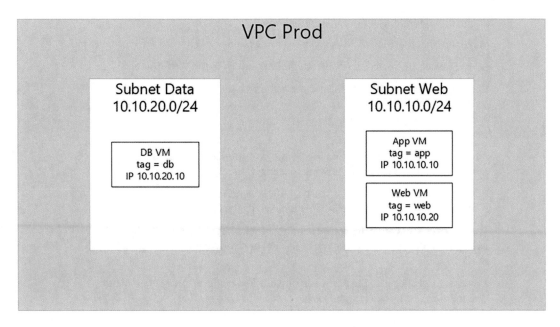

Figure 3-150. *VPC with two subnets*

- **A.** Block all traffic from source tag "web."
- **B.** Allow traffic from source tag "app" to port 80 only.
- **C.** Allow all traffic from source tag "app" to target tag "db."
- **D.** Allow ingress traffic from 0.0.0.0/0 on port 80 and 443 for target tag "web."
- **E.** Allow ingress traffic using source filter = IP ranges where source IP ranges = 10.10.10.0/24.

Rationale

A is not correct because web VM still needs to talk to app VM.

B is not correct because this is not required as per the requirements.

C is CORRECT because this rule will allow traffic from app VM to DB VM.

D is CORRECT because this will allow outside users to send request to web VM.

E is not correct because this will provide web VM access to DB VM.

Question 3.3 (Firewall Rules, VPC Flow Logs)

You created two subnets named Test and Web in the same VPC network. You enabled VPC Flow Logs for the Web subnet. You are trying to connect instances in the Test subnet to the web servers running in the Web subnet, but all of the connections are failing. You do not see any entries in the stackdriver logs. What should you do?

A. Enable VPC Flow Logs for the Test subnet also.

B. Make sure that there is a valid entry in the route table.

C. Add a firewall rule to allow traffic from the Test subnet to the Web subnet.

D. Create a subnet in another VPC, and move the web servers in the new subnet.

Rationale

A is not correct because enabling the flow logs in subnet "Test" will still not provide any data as the traffic is being blocked by the firewall rule.

B is not correct because subnets are part of the same VPC and do not need routing configured. The traffic is being blocked by the firewall rule.

C is CORRECT because the traffic is being blocked by the firewall rule. Once configured, the request will reach to the VM and the flow will be logged in the stackdriver.

D is not correct because the traffic is being blocked by the firewall rule and not due to subnet being in the same VPC.

Question 3.4 (Firewall Rules, Target Network Tags)

You want to allow access over ports 80 and 443 to servers with the tag "webservers" from external addresses. Currently, there is a firewall rule with priority of 1000 that denies all incoming traffic from an external address on all ports and protocols. You want to allow the desired traffic without deleting the existing rule. What should you do?

A. Add an ingress rule that allows traffic over ports 80 and 443 from any external address in the rules prior to the deny statement.

B. Add an ingress rule that allows traffic over ports 80 and 443 from any external address to the target network tag "webservers" with a priority value of 500.

C. Add an egress rule that allows traffic over ports 80 and 443 from any external address in the rules prior to the deny statement.

D. Add an egress rule that allows traffic over ports 80 and 443 from any external address to the target network tag "webservers" with a priority value of 1500.

Rationale

A is incorrect because the firewall denies traffic if both the permit and deny have the same priority regardless of rule order.

B is CORRECT because the firewall will allow traffic to pass with the proper allow ingress rule with a priority lower than the default value of 1000.

C is incorrect because the scenario described does not apply to egress traffic. By design, the firewall is stateful, and if the tunnel exists, traffic will pass.

D is incorrect because the scenario described does not apply to egress traffic. By design, the firewall is stateful, and if the tunnel exists, traffic will pass and the priority value is set higher than the default, meaning the rule would not be considered.

CHAPTER 4

■ ■ ■

Implementing Virtual Private Cloud Service Controls

In computer engineering, networking and security go hand in hand. There is no way to effectively design a network architecture without considering security. The opposite holds true as well.

In the cloud, this "symbiotic" relationship between networking and security is even more important than in traditional data centers.

So far, you were introduced to firewall rules as a means to secure the perimeter of your VPCs. VPC service controls were also briefly discussed in Chapter 2 as an approach to prevent exfiltration of sensitive data.

In this chapter, we will deep dive into VPC Service Controls, and you will understand how this GCP service is a lot more than a product to prevent data exfiltration. When effectively implemented, VPC Service Controls will strengthen your enterprise security posture by introducing context-aware safeguards into your workloads.

To get started, the concepts of an access policy and an access level will be formally defined, unambiguously. These are the building blocks of a service perimeter, which is the key GCP resource you use to protect services used by projects in your organization.

You will then learn how to selectively pick and choose what services consumed by your workloads need context-aware protection.

We will walk you through these constructs through a deep dive exercise on service perimeters, which will help you visualize and understand how all these pieces fit together.

You will then learn how to connect service perimeters by using *bridges*, and you will get familiar with Cloud Logging to detect perimeter violations and respond to them.

Finally, the different behaviors of a service perimeter will be presented through another deep dive exercise, which will help you understand the different behavior between an enforced perimeter and a perimeter in dry-run mode.

VPC Service Controls Introduction

You learned in Chapter 3 how firewall rules are an effective way to secure the perimeter of your VPC network. Firewall rules operate as a *distributed* firewall, which is scoped to the entire VPC. As a result, there are no "choke points," and your perimeter protection will scale elastically based on demand.

When compared to other public cloud providers, a key differentiating feature of GCP firewall rules is their ability to use a service account in the source or the target of your firewall rule (ingress or egress).

© Dario Cabianca 2023
D. Cabianca, *Google Cloud Platform (GCP) Professional Cloud Network Engineer Certification Companion*, Certification Study Companion Series, https://doi.org/10.1007/978-1-4842-9354-6_4

What if a malicious user were to compromise this service account and try to access data in some VM in a subnet of your "firewall-protected" VPC?

This is where VPC Service Control comes into play.

In the preceding scenario, your VPC firewall rule would not know that the service account has been compromised, resulting in an *allow* action to the VPC desired resources—let's say a VM storing sensitive data. Once access is allowed, VPC firewall rules are not expressive enough to determine access based on the *verb* the service account is going to perform on the resource. For example, if the malicious user wanted to copy sensitive data stored in the disk of a VM, the firewall rule would have no way to prevent this action.

VPC Service Controls and their "companions" *VPC service perimeters* are a means to further validate the authenticity of a request based on the API for the service being requested on a resource in the VPC.

Just like VPC firewall rules determine access to resources hosted in a VPC based on IP ranges, ports, protocols, network tags, or service accounts, VPC Service Controls determine access to resources based on the Google Cloud API that is needed to consume the resource.

In our scenario, a VPC Service Control limiting the use of the `compute.googleapis.com` to only a selected list of projects would have likely prevented the malicious user impersonating the service account from copying sensitive data from the targeted VM.

Let's see how VPC Service Controls work.

Creating and Configuring Access Levels and Service Perimeters

To implement VPC Service Controls, you need to establish a boundary to determine who has access to what and when. This concept of boundary is formalized with a service perimeter, or simply a perimeter.

The "who," "what," and "when" aspects of an access request are all captured by the components of the perimeter. The perimeter then will determine whether the access is granted or denied.

The outcome will be based on the mode the perimeter operates under: *enforced* or *dry-run*. In the former case, access will be simply denied or granted. In the latter case, any access violation will not result in a deny action. Instead, the violation will be tracked as an audit log.

Perimeters

So what are the components of a perimeter, and most importantly how does a service perimeter differ from a network perimeter (i.e., VPC firewall rules)?

The components of a perimeter are

- **Resources**: These are containers of resources the perimeter needs to protect from data exfiltration.

- **Restricted services**: These are the Google API endpoints (e.g., `storage,googleapis.com`) whose access is restricted to the resources within the perimeter.

- **VPC allowed services**: These are the Google API endpoints that can be accessed from network endpoints within the perimeter.

- **Access levels**: These are means to classify the context of a request based on device, geolocation, source CIDR range, and identity.

- **Ingress policy**: This is a set of rules that allow an API client outside the perimeter to access resources inside the perimeter.

- **Egress policy**: This is a set of rules that allow an API client inside the perimeter to access resources outside the perimeter.

Before learning each component, let's first review how to create a perimeter with the gcloud command. A *perimeter* is a GCP resource, which can be created with the gcloud CLI as shown in Figure 4-1.

```
NAME
    gcloud access-context-manager perimeters create - create a new service
        perimeter

SYNOPSIS
    gcloud access-context-manager perimeters create
        (PERIMETER : --policy=POLICY) --title=TITLE
        [--access-levels=[LEVEL,...]] [--async] [--description=DESCRIPTION]
        [--egress-policies=YAML_FILE] [--ingress-policies=YAML_FILE]
        [--perimeter-type=PERIMETER_TYPE; default="regular"]
        [--resources=[RESOURCES,...]] [--restricted-services=[SERVICE,...]]
        [--enable-vpc-accessible-services
           --vpc-allowed-services=[VPC_SERVICE,...]] [GCLOUD_WIDE_FLAG ...]
```

Figure 4-1. `gcloud access-context-manager perimeters create` *synopsis*

In addition to its perimeter ID (PERIMETER), you must provide an access policy by assigning the policy ID to the --policy flag—unless you have already set a default access policy for your project, folder, or your entire organization. You'll learn about access policies in the upcoming "Service Perimeter Deep Dive" section. For the time being, all you need to know is that an access policy is a Google Cloud resource where you store perimeter components.

The only required flag is the --title, which is a short, human-readable title for the service perimeter. The relevant, optional flags you need to know for the exam are

- **Access levels** (--access-levels=[LEVEL, …]): It denotes a comma-separated list of IDs for access levels (in the same policy) that an intra-perimeter request must satisfy to be allowed.

- **Resources** (--resources=[RESOURCE, …]): It's a list of projects you want to protect by including them in the perimeter and is denoted as a comma-separated list of project numbers, in the form projects/<projectnumber>.

- **Restricted services** (--restricted-services=[SERVICE, …]): It denotes a comma-separated list of Google API endpoints to which the perimeter boundary does apply (e.g., storage.googleapis.com).

- **VPC allowed services** (--vpc-allowed-services=[SERVICE, …]): It requires the flag --enable-vpc-accessible-services and denotes a comma-separated list of Google API endpoints accessible from network endpoints within the perimeter. In order to include all restricted services, use the keyword RESTRICTED-SERVICES.

- **Ingress policies** (--ingress-policies=YAML_FILE): It denotes a path to a file containing a list of ingress policies. This file contains a list of YAML-compliant objects representing ingress policies, as described in the API reference.

- **Egress policies** (--ingress-policies=YAML_FILE): It denotes a path to a file containing a list of egress policies. This file contains a list of YAML-compliant objects representing egress policies, as described in the API reference.

- **Perimeter type** (`--perimeter-type=PERIMETER_TYPE`): It must be either the keyword `regular` (default) or the keyword `bridge`. You will learn perimeter bridges in the upcoming "Perimeter Bridges" section.

Access Levels

An access level is a one-directional form of validation. *It only validates ingress requests* to access resources inside the perimeter.

Whether the request originates from the Internet, from your corporate network, or from network endpoints within the perimeter, an access level performs the validation you specify and determines whether the access to the requested resource is granted or denied.

The validation is based on your workload security requirements, which include endpoint verification (i.e., device attributes), identity verification (i.e., principal attributes), geolocation, and dependencies with other access levels.

When you create an access level, you need to decide whether you need a *basic access level* or a *custom access level*. For most use cases, a basic level of validation suffices, while a few ones require a higher degree of sophistication.

When you use the `gcloud` command to create or update an access level, both types (basic and custom) are expressed in the form of a YAML file, whose path is assigned to the `--basic-level-spec` or the `--custom-level-spec` flag, respectively. The two flags are mutually exclusive.

A basic access level YAML spec file is a list of conditions built using assignments to a combination of one or more of the five following attributes:

- `ipSubnetworks`: Validates the IPv4 or IPv6 CIDR block of the requestor. RFC 1918 blocks are not allowed.

- `regions`: Validates the region(s) of the requestor.

- `requiredAccessLevels`: Validates whether the request meets the criteria of one or more dependent access levels, which must be formatted as `<accessPolicies/policy-name/accessLevels/level-name>`.

- `members`: Validates whether the request originated from a specific user or service account.

- `devicePolicy`: Requires endpoint verification and validates whether the device of the requestor meets specific criteria, including

  - `requireScreenlock`: Boolean

  - `allowedEncryptionStatuses`: Predefined list of values

  - `requireCorpOwned`: Boolean

  - `osConstraints`

    - `osType`: Predefined list of values

    - `minimumVersion`: Requires `osType`

The reference guide to the complete list of basic access level attributes can be found at `https://cloud.google.com/access-context-manager/docs/access-level-attributes#ip-subnetworks`

An example of a YAML file can be found at `https://cloud.google.com/access-context-manager/docs/example-yaml-file`. Also, for basic access levels, you need to choose whether all conditions are to be met or just one. This is done using the `--combine-function` flag, whose allowed values are `AND` (default) and `OR`.

For more complex access patterns, use a custom access level. A custom access level YAML spec file contains a list of Common Expression Language (CEL) expressions formatted as a single key-value pair: `expression: CEL_EXPRESSION`.

Similarly to basic access levels, the spec file lets you create expressions based on attributes from the following four objects:

- `origin`: Contains attributes related to the origin of the request, for example, `(origin.ip == "203.0.113.24" && origin.region_code in ["US", "IT"])`

- `request.auth`: Contains attributes related to authentication and authorization aspects of the request, for example, `request.auth.principal == "accounts. google.com/1134924314572461055"`

- `levels`: Contains attributes related to dependencies on other access levels, for example, `level.allow_corporate_ips` where `allow_corporate_ips` is another access level

- `device`: Contains attributes related to devices the request originates from, for example, `device.is_corp_owned_device == true`

To learn how to build Common Expression Language (CEL) expressions for custom access levels, refer to the Custom Access Level Specification: `https://cloud.google.com/access-context-manager/docs/ custom-access-level-spec`.

The synopsis of the `gcloud` command to create an access level is displayed in Figure 4-2 for your reference.

```
NAME
    gcloud access-context-manager levels create - create a new access level

SYNOPSIS
    gcloud access-context-manager levels create (LEVEL : --policy=POLICY)
        --title=TITLE
        (--custom-level-spec=CUSTOM_LEVEL_SPEC
        | [--basic-level-spec=BASIC_LEVEL_SPEC
        : --combine-function=COMBINE_FUNCTION; default="and"]) [--async]
        [--description=DESCRIPTION] [GCLOUD_WIDE_FLAG ...]
```

Figure 4-2. `gcloud access-context-manager levels create` synopsis

In addition to `LEVEL`, that is, the fully qualified identifier for the level, and the access policy `POLICY` (required only if you haven't set a default access policy), you must specify a title for your access level.

As you learned before, the level type flags are mutually exclusive. With basic access level (as noted in Figure 4-2), you have to decide whether all or at least one condition must be true for the validation to pass or fail. This can be achieved by setting the `--combine-function` flag to the value `"and"` (default) or the value `"or"`.

In the next section, we will put these concepts to work by walking you through a simple example of a perimeter and an access level. With a real example, all these concepts will make sense, and you'll be ready to design perimeters and access levels in Google Cloud like a "pro."

Service Perimeter Deep Dive

In this section, we will build a perimeter to protect the service projects and the host project in our shared VPC. We will protect the storage API from unauthorized consumption in a way that only user `gianni@ dariokart.com` is authorized to perform storage API actions, for example, create a bucket, upload a file to the bucket, etc. Let's get started!

Enabling Access Context Manager and Cloud Resource Manager APIs

First, to create a perimeter and access levels, we need to enable the access context manager API. The cloud resource manager API is also needed in this exercise to update the metadata of some resource containers. Figure 4-3 shows you how to enable both APIs.

```
itsmedario@cloudshell:~ (vpc-host-nonprod-pu645-uh372)$ gcloud services enable accesscontextmanager.googleapis.com
Operation "operations/acat.p2-755396457069-994bf1e2-38b3-4a37-a6a9-183009185f57" finished successfully.
itsmedario@cloudshell:~ (vpc-host-nonprod-pu645-uh372)$ gcloud services enable cloudresourcemanager.googleapis.com
Operation "operations/acat.p2-755396457069-88ec2698-4d6b-4b42-949b-beecef25c064" finished successfully.
itsmedario@cloudshell:~ (vpc-host-nonprod-pu645-uh372)$
```

Figure 4-3. *Enabling the access context manager API*

Creating an Access Policy for the Organization

Next, we need to be able to group the security controls we described in the previous section, that is, perimeters and access levels. This is where the concept of an access context manager policy or—better yet—an *access policy* comes in handy.

Access policies are containers intended to logically group perimeters and access levels. They must always be associated to an organization—also known as the parent organization—and their scope is either the entire organization they are associated with (default), a folder, or a project within the organization. Notice that the scope of an access policy can only be *one of the three* resource "containers," that is, an organization, a folder, or a project. Put differently, you cannot have a scope resulting from a mix and match of organizations, folders, or projects when you create an access policy.

■ **Exam tip**   Do not confuse an IAM allow policy with an access policy. Both constructs use the term "access" after all—IAM stands for *Identity and Access Management*. However, an IAM policy, also known as an allow policy, is strictly related to what identities (or principals) are allowed to do on a given resource, whether it be a VM, a Pub/Sub topic, a subnet, a project, a folder, or an entire organization. Each of these resources (or containers of resources) has an IAM policy attached to them. Think of it as a sign that lists only the ones who are allowed to do something on the resource. The "something" is the list of verbs—permissions—and is expressed in the form of an IAM role, for example, `roles/networkUser` or `roles/securityAdmin`, which is indeed a set of permissions. Conversely, while access policies are also focused on access, they take into consideration a lot more than just identity and role bindings. Unlike IAM policies, access policies are applicable to resource containers only, that is, projects, folders, and organizations (one only), and they are used to enable conditional access to resources in the container based on the device, request origin (e.g., source CIDR blocks), request authentication/authorization, and dependencies with other access levels.

In our exercise, for the sake of simplicity we are going to create an access policy, whose scope is the entire dariokart.com organization, as displayed in Figure 4-4.

```
itsmedario@cloudshell:~ (vpc-host-nonprod-pu645-uh372)$ gcloud access-context-manager policies create --organization=585269232696
  --title=dariokart-default-access-policy
Create request issued
Created.
```

Figure 4-4. *Creating an organization-level access policy*

■ **Exam tip** The only required flags are the access policy title (`--title`) and its parent organization (`--organization`). You can also create an access policy scoped to a specific folder or a specific project in your organization. This can be achieved by setting the folder (or project) number as value to the `--scopes` flag. For more details, visit `https://cloud.google.com/sdk/gcloud/reference/access-context-manager/policies/create#--scopes`.

The name of the access policy is system generated. You only get to choose its title. It's also a good idea to set the policy as the default access policy for our organization, as illustrated in Figure 4-5.

```
itsmedario@cloudshell:~ (vpc-host-nonprod-pu645-uh372)$ gcloud access-context-manager policies list --organization=585269232696
NAME: 330593771297
ORGANIZATION: 585269232696
SCOPES:
TITLE: dariokart-default-access-policy
ETAG: 76e5ee48d303e099
itsmedario@cloudshell:~ (vpc-host-nonprod-pu645-uh372)$ gcloud access-context-manager policies describe accessPolicies/330593771297
etag: 76e5ee48d303e099
name: accessPolicies/330593771297
parent: organizations/585269232696
title: dariokart-default-access-policy
itsmedario@cloudshell:~ (vpc-host-nonprod-pu645-uh372)$ gcloud config set access_context_manager/policy 330593771297
Updated property [access_context_manager/policy].
itsmedario@cloudshell:~ (vpc-host-nonprod-pu645-uh372)$
```

Figure 4-5. *Setting the default organization access policy*

Creating an Access Level

With our access policy in place, we can now create a basic access level `dariokart_level`, which will be associated to the perimeter for the service projects `frontend-devs` and `backend-devs` and their associated host project `vpc-host-nonprod`.

To get started, we need first to create a YAML file (Figure 4-6), which declaratively specifies the conditions that determine who is authorized to access the service perimeter.

```
itsmedario@cloudshell:~ (vpc-host-nonprod-pu645-uh372)$ mkdir perimeters
itsmedario@cloudshell:~ (vpc-host-nonprod-pu645-uh372)$ cd perimeters/
itsmedario@cloudshell:~/perimeters (vpc-host-nonprod-pu645-uh372)$ vi your-app-shared-vpc-access-level.yaml
```

Figure 4-6. *Creating access level YAML for `your-app-shared-vpc` perimeter*

Since the access level is basic, the YAML file is a simple list of conditions. The conditions apply to the attributes of any of these four objects:

- origin, for example, `origin.ip`, `origin.region.code`
- request.auth, for example, `request.auth.principal`, `origin.region.code`
- levels, for example, `levels <access_level_name>`
- device, for example, `device.os_type`, `device.encryption_status`

The complete list of objects and their attributes can be referenced at `https://cloud.google.com/access-context-manager/docs/custom-access-level-spec#objects`.

The syntax of the YAML file uses the Common Expression Language. See `https://github.com/google/cel-spec/blob/master/doc/langdef.md` for more details.

Our YAML file is very simple. We want to enforce a basic access level stating that only user `gianni@dariokart.com` is authorized to perform storage API actions.

The first constraint—that is, only a selected user is authorized to do something—is expressed by the condition in the YAML file, as shown in Figure 4-7.

```
▌ members:
    - user:gianni@dariokart.com
~
~
~
~
~
~
~
~
~
~
~
~
~
~
~
~
~
~
~
~
~
"your-app-shared-vpc-access-level.yaml" 2L, 43B
```

Figure 4-7. Allowing user gianni@dariokart.com perimeter access

The second constraint, that is, preventing any user other than `gianni@dariokart.com` from consuming `storage.googleapis.com`, will be enforced when we create the perimeter in the next section.

With the YAML file saved, we can now create our access level (Figure 4-8).

```
itsmedario@cloudshell:~/perimeters (vpc-host-nonprod-pu645-uh372)$ gcloud access-context-manager levels create dariokart_level --bas
ic-level-spec=your-app-shared-vpc-access-level.yaml --title=your-app-shared-vpc-access-level --combine-function=AND
Create request issued for: [dariokart_level]
Created level [dariokart_level].
itsmedario@cloudshell:~/perimeters (vpc-host-nonprod-pu645-uh372)$
```

Figure 4-8. Creating dariokart_level

Creating a Perimeter

Because the user `gianni@dariokart.com` is the shared VPC administrator, it makes sense that he creates the perimeter for our shared VPC. The perimeter will encompass the two service projects and the host project.

In order for `gianni@dariokart.com` to be able to create a perimeter, we are going to grant him the `roles/accesscontextmanager.policyAdmin` role at the organization level, as shown in Figure 4-9.

```
itsmedario@cloudshell:~/perimeters (vpc-host-nonprod-pu645-uh372)$ gcloud organizations add-iam-policy-binding 585269232696
--member user:gianni@dariokart.com --role roles/accesscontextmanager.policyAdmin
Updated IAM policy for organization [585269232696].
bindings:
- members:
  - user:gianni@dariokart.com
  role: roles/accesscontextmanager.policyAdmin
```

Figure 4-9. *Granting gianni@dariokart.com policyAdmin role at org level*

■ **Note**   You should always use the least privilege principle when designing the security architecture for your workloads. However, this exercise is solely intended to explain how access levels and perimeters work together to enforce access control over the Google Cloud Storage API, and for the sake of simplicity, we haven't strictly used the principle.

With all permissions in place, we can finally create the perimeter `dariokart_perimeter` and associate it to our newly created access level `dariokart_level`. Figure 4-10 shows you how to create the perimeter.

```
gianni@cloudshell:~ (vpc-host-nonprod-pu645-uh372)$ gcloud access-context-manager perimeters create dariokart_perimeter --ti
tle=your-app-shared-vpc-perimeter --resources=projects/755396457069,projects/239408874101,projects/211670805257 --restricted
-services=storage.googleapis.com --access-levels=dariokart_level --policy=330593771297
Create request issued for: [dariokart_perimeter]
Created perimeter [dariokart_perimeter].
gianni@cloudshell:~ (vpc-host-nonprod-pu645-uh372)$ ▮
```

Figure 4-10. *Creating dariokart_perimeter*

There are a few observations:

- The enforcement of the first constraint (only a selected user is authorized to do something within the perimeter) is effectuated by the flag `--access-level=dariokart_level`.

- The enforcement of the second constraint (to limit the usage of the storage API from requestors within the perimeter) is effectuated by the flag `--restricted-services=storage.googleapis.com`.

- The `--resources` flag is set to a comma-delimited list of projects denoted as `projects/<project-number>`. This is where we specify the projects we want to protect within the perimeter. At the time of writing this book, only projects are supported in this list.

- The `--title` flag is required just like the access level create command.

Testing the Perimeter

This is the fun part!

Users `samuele@dariokart.com` and `joseph@dariokart.com` have `roles/editor` roles in their projects, `backend-devs` and `frontend-devs`, respectively.

As a result, without perimeters and access levels they should be able to modify the state of resources in their respective project, such as creating new VMs and changing or deleting existing VMs or other GCP resources.

Let's check if `samuele@dariokart.com` can create a bucket in his project (Figure 4-11).

```
samuele@cloudshell:~ (backend-devs-7736)$ gsutil mb -c nearline -p backend-devs-7736 gs://dariokart-backend-bucket
Creating gs://dariokart-backend-bucket/...
AccessDeniedException: 403 Request is prohibited by organization's policy. vpcServiceControlsUniqueIdentifier: 00xXA6d98ydTN
kUjLk1_0jlW-K6mugh_y3egVFA4YeLDx5pwF3mPfg
samuele@cloudshell:~ (backend-devs-7736)$
```

Figure 4-11. *`samuele@dariokart.com` forbidden from creating a bucket*

As you can see, the response returned an HTTP status code 403, which clearly explained the reason why the request failed, namely, the perimeter blocked the request after checking the organization access policy.

The same response is returned after `joseph@dariokart.com` attempted to create a bucket in his project, as shown in Figure 4-12.

```
joseph@cloudshell:~ (frontend-devs-7734)$ gsutil mb -c nearline -p frontend-devs-7734 gs://dariokart-frontend-bucket
Creating gs://dariokart-frontend-bucket/...
AccessDeniedException: 403 Request is prohibited by organization's policy. vpcServiceControlsUniqueIdentifier: JZGVxjijEOZw9
O81x6J113iJixOR62dEW56spvBBy-6f-N2HjNltGw
joseph@cloudshell:~ (frontend-devs-7734)$
```

Figure 4-12. *`joseph@dariokart.com` forbidden from creating a bucket*

This is what we expected, right? Since the YAML file in Figure 4-7 did not include `samuele@dariokart.com` nor `joseph@dariokart.com` as authorized members of the access level, the result is that none of them can perform any actions invoking the storage API, even though both principals have editor roles in their respective project.

Now, let's check whether the authorized user `gianni@dariokart.com` is allowed to create a bucket in both `backend-devs` and `frontend-devs` projects.

Before we do that, we need to grant `gianni@dariokart.com` permissions to create storage objects in both projects.

This can be achieved by binding the role `roles/storage.admin` to the principal `gianni@dariokart.com` at the project level scope for each project as illustrated in Figures 4-13 and 4-14.

```
itsmedario@cloudshell:~/perimeters (vpc-host-nonprod-pu645-uh372)$ gcloud projects add-iam-policy-binding backend-devs-7736
--member user:gianni@dariokart.com --role roles/storage.admin
Updated IAM policy for project [backend-devs-7736].
```

Figure 4-13. *Granting `gianni@dariokart.com` `storage.admin` role in backend-devs project*

```
itsmedario@cloudshell:~/perimeters (vpc-host-nonprod-pu645-uh372)$ gcloud projects add-iam-policy-binding frontend-devs-7734
--member user:gianni@dariokart.com --role roles/storage.admin
Updated IAM policy for project [frontend-devs-7734].
```

Figure 4-14. *Granting `gianni@dariokart.com` `storage.admin` role in frontend-devs project*

With these two role bindings, user `gianni@dariokart.com` has the same storage permissions, user `samuele@dariokart.com` has in project `backend-devs`, and user `joseph@dariokart.com` has in project `frontend-devs`.

As a result, we can rest assured the accessibility test we are about to perform with `gianni@dariokart.com` is an "apple-to-apple" comparison among the three principals.

Finally, let's check whether `gianni@dariokart.com` can effectively create a bucket in either project (Figures 4-15 and 4-16).

```
gianni@cloudshell:~ (vpc-host-nonprod-pu645-uh372)$ gsutil mb -c nearline -p backend-devs-7736 gs://dariokart-backend-bucket
Creating gs://dariokart-backend-bucket/...
gianni@cloudshell:~ (vpc-host-nonprod-pu645-uh372)$
```

Figure 4-15. *Verifying gianni@dariokart.com's bucket creation in backend-devs*

```
gianni@cloudshell:~ (vpc-host-nonprod-pu645-uh372)$ gsutil mb -c nearline -p frontend-devs-7734 gs://dariokart-frontend-bucket
Creating gs://dariokart-frontend-bucket/..
gianni@cloudshell:~ (vpc-host-nonprod-pu645-uh372)$
```

Figure 4-16. *Verifying gianni@dariokart.com's bucket creation in frontend-devs*

As expected, user gianni@dariokart.com is allowed to create a bucket in each project in which he had proper permissions.

This time, the basic access level dariokart_level associated to the perimeter dariokart_perimeter has authorized gianni@dariokart.com to perform any storage API operation, resulting in the successful creation of a bucket in each service project within the perimeter.

A picture is worth a thousand words! Figure 4-17 provides a holistic view of what we just accomplished in this exercise.

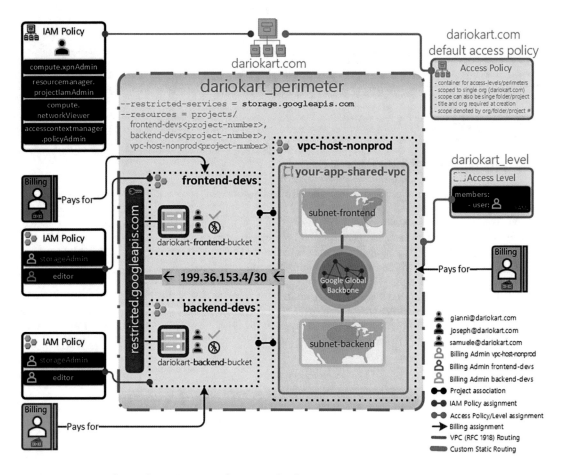

Figure 4-17. *Visualizing the perimeter and its access level*

■ **Exam tip**   A project can belong to only one service perimeter.

You may wonder, what's the custom static route whose destination is the CIDR block 199.36.153.4/30?

To answer this question, we need to mention that not every Google API can be protected by VPC Service Controls. However, the many Google APIs supported—including storage.googleapis.com—are only accessible with routes whose destination is the CIDR block 199.36.153.4/30 and whose next hop is the default-internet-gateway.

The fully qualified domain name restricted.googleapis.com resolves to the CIDR block 199.36.153.4/30, and this block is not routable from the Internet.

Instead, this block can only be routed from within the Google Global Backbone.

In other words, if you try to ping this CIDR block from a terminal in a computer connected to your Internet Service Provider (ISP), you will get a request timeout. However, if you try from a VM in a subnet of your VPC, you will get a response.

Deleting the Buckets

As always, to avoid incurring unexpected charges, it is a good idea to delete the buckets we just created (Figure 4-18).

```
gianni@cloudshell:~ (vpc-host-nonprod-pu645-uh372)$ gsutil rm -r gs://dariokart-backend-bucket
Removing gs://dariokart-backend-bucket/...
gianni@cloudshell:~ (vpc-host-nonprod-pu645-uh372)$ gsutil rm -r gs://dariokart-frontend-bucket
Removing gs://dariokart-frontend-bucket/...
gianni@cloudshell:~ (vpc-host-nonprod-pu645-uh372)$ █
```

Figure 4-18.   *Deleting the buckets*

VPC Accessible Services

Perimeters are not just about protecting your data from unauthorized Google API access that originates outside your perimeter.

When you create or update a perimeter, you can also limit the Google APIs that can be accessed using Private Google Access *from network endpoints within the perimeter.*

As you learned in the "Configuring API Access to Google Services" section of Chapter 3, with Private Google Access your workloads don't need the Internet to consume Google APIs and services. All traffic stays in the Google Cloud backbone.

The Google APIs supported by VPC service controls are exposed using the domain name restricted. googleapis.com, which resolves to the *restricted VIP* (Virtual IP address range) 199.36.153.4/30. These four public IP addresses 199.36.153.4, 199.36.153.5, 199.36.153.6, 199.36.153.7 are not routable on the Internet, as you can see from my attempt using my Internet Service Provider (Figure 4-19).

```
[DariosMacStudio:~ dariocabianca$ ping restricted.googleapis.com
PING restricted.googleapis.com (199.36.153.4): 56 data bytes
Request timeout for icmp_seq 0
Request timeout for icmp_seq 1
Request timeout for icmp_seq 2
Request timeout for icmp_seq 3
Request timeout for icmp_seq 4
Request timeout for icmp_seq 5
Request timeout for icmp_seq 6
Request timeout for icmp_seq 7
Request timeout for icmp_seq 8
Request timeout for icmp_seq 9
Request timeout for icmp_seq 10
^C
—— restricted.googleapis.com ping statistics ——
12 packets transmitted, 0 packets received, 100.0% packet loss
DariosMacStudio:~ dariocabianca$ ▊
```

Figure 4-19. *Restricted VIP is not routable on the Internet*

So how do you limit access to the Google APIs exposed by the *restricted VIP* from network endpoints within the perimeter?

The answer depends on whether you are creating a new perimeter or you are updating an existing perimeter.

If you are creating a new perimeter with the gcloud access-context-manager perimeters create command, then use both flags:

- --enable-vpc-accessible-services

- --vpc-allowed-services=[API_ENDPOINT,...]

Keep in mind that the perimeter boundary is only enforced on the list of API endpoints assigned to the --restricted-services flag, regardless of whether they are on the list assigned to the --vpc-allowed-services flag.

The list of API endpoints assigned to the --vpc-allowed-services flag has a default value of all services, that is, all services on the configured restricted VIP are accessible using Private Google Access by default. If you want to be more selective, provide a comma-delimited list as follows:

- **Empty comma-delimited list ("")**: None of the services on the configured restricted VIP are accessible using Private Google Access.

- **All restricted services** (RESTRICTED-SERVICES): Use the keyword RESTRICTED-SERVICES to denote the list of all restricted services, as specified by the value of the --restricted-services flag. All these restricted API endpoints will be accessible using Private Google Access.

- **Selected services (e.g.,** "bigquery.googleapis.com"**)**: Only services explicitly selected by you will be accessible using Private Google Access.

If you are updating an existing perimeter with the command gcloud access-context-manager perimeters update, then use

- --enable-vpc-accessible-services if the list of VPC allowed services is empty and you are going to add services

- --add-vpc-allowed-services=[API_ENDPOINT,...] to add new services

- --remove-vpc-allowed-services=[API_ENDPOINT,...] to remove existing services

193

If you want to disable the ability to restrict access to services from network endpoints within the perimeter, use both

- `--no-enable-vpc-accessible-services`
- `--clear-vpc-allowed-services`

Perimeter Bridges

A perimeter comes in two "flavors": a regular perimeter (default option) or a perimeter *bridge*. From now on, when we use the term *perimeter* we will always refer to a regular perimeter, which protects a group of projects (even one single project) by controlling the use of selected Google APIs—that you get to choose when you create the perimeter—to only the projects inside the perimeter.

While perimeters are an effective means to prevent data exfiltration, there are scenarios where projects in different perimeters need to interact with each other and share data.

This is when perimeter bridges come in handy. A perimeter bridge allows *inter-perimeter* communication **between two projects** in two different perimeters. Perimeter bridges are symmetrical, allowing projects from each perimeter bidirectional and equal access within the scope of the bridge. However, the access levels and service restrictions of the project are controlled solely by the perimeter the project belongs to.

In fact, when you choose to create a perimeter bridge, you should not attach an access level to it, nor should you specify which APIs are to be restricted. I'll explain in a minute why I said "should not" instead of "cannot."

■ **Exam tip**   A project may have multiple perimeter bridges connecting it to other projects. However, for this to happen, the project must already belong to a regular perimeter. Also, all "bridged" projects must be part of the same organization.

To create a perimeter bridge, use the gcloud `access-context-manager perimeters create` command with the flag `--perimeter-type=bridge`.

If you try to update an existing regular perimeter to a perimeter bridge, the gcloud `access-context-manager perimeters update` does not return an error status code as displayed in Figure 4-20.

```
gianni@cloudshell:~ (vpc-host-nonprod-pu645-uh372)$ gcloud access-context-manager perimeters update dariokart_peri
meter --type=bridge --policy=330593771297
Waiting for PATCH operation [accessPolicies/330593771297/servicePerimeters/dariokart_perimeter/update/16638107915
39897]...done.
gianni@cloudshell:~ (vpc-host-nonprod-pu645-uh372)$ gcloud access-context-manager perimeters list
NAME: dariokart_perimeter
TITLE: your-app-shared-vpc-perimeter
gianni@cloudshell:~ (vpc-host-nonprod-pu645-uh372)$ gcloud access-context-manager perimeters describe  dariokart_p
erimeter
name: accessPolicies/330593771297/servicePerimeters/dariokart_perimeter
status:
  accessLevels:
  - accessPolicies/330593771297/accessLevels/dariokart_level
  resources:
  - projects/755396457069
  - projects/239408874101
  - projects/211670805257
  restrictedServices:
  - storage.googleapis.com
title: your-app-shared-vpc-perimeter
gianni@cloudshell:~ (vpc-host-nonprod-pu645-uh372)$ █
```

Figure 4-20. *Updating dariokart_perimeter*

You would think that the operation succeeded, right? However, as you can see from the console in Figure 4-21—in this exceptional case, we use the console because the console reveals more details (the perimeter type) than gcloud—the perimeter type has not changed!

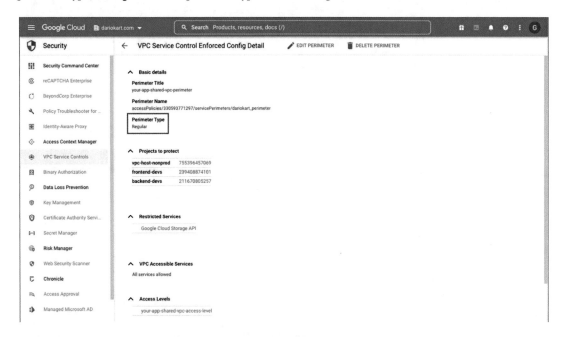

Figure 4-21. Editing dariokart_perimeter with the console

If you think about it, this makes sense because unlike regular perimeters, which are essentially groups of one, two, three, or more projects, *a perimeter bridge connects only two projects that belong to different perimeters*. As a result, which one of the two access levels should be used? And which one of the two lists of restricted (or unrestricted) APIs should be used?

Probably, the gcloud access-context-manager perimeters update command should prohibit a patch operation when the --type=bridge if the existing regular perimeter has an access level or a list of restricted services predefined.

In fact, if we try to change dariokart_perimeter's type from regular to bridge using the console, this option is grayed out, as you can see in Figure 4-22.

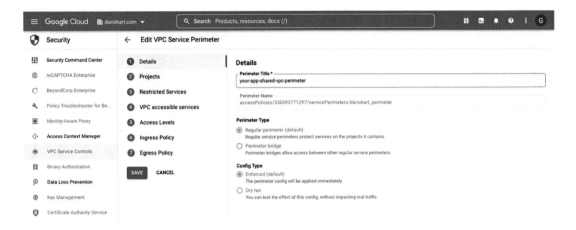

Figure 4-22. *Trying to change* dariokart_perimeter's *type with the console*

Figure 4-23 shows what we just learned and visualizes the key characteristics of perimeter bridges.

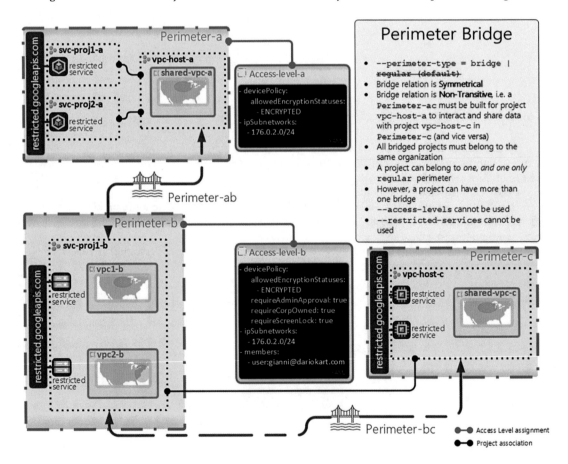

Figure 4-23. *Perimeter bridge overview*

Audit Logging

By default, VPC Service Controls write to Cloud Logging all requests that are denied because of security policy violations. More information about Cloud Logging—as it pertains to network operations and optimization—will be provided in Chapter 8.

The most useful fields to check in the logs to better understand a violation are

- `timestamp`: The date and time when violation happened.

- `protopayload_auditlog.requestMetadata.callerIp`: The client IP address.

- `protopayload_auditlog.methodName`: The API and method invoked.

- `protopayload_auditlog.authenticationInfo.principalEmail`: The user email or service account that invoked the API.

- `protopayload_auditlog.metadataJson`: This field contains interesting information in JSON format, for example, name of violated perimeter, direction (ingress/egress), source project, target project, and unique ID.

Dry-Run Mode

You can think of VPC service controls as a firewall that controls which Google APIs the components of your workload are authorized to consume.

The VPC service perimeter construct was introduced to establish the boundary around these accessible APIs.

In order to further verify the identity of each request, you may attach one or more access levels to a VPC service perimeter.

When used in conjunction with other network controls (e.g., firewall rules and other network services you will learn in the next chapter), VPC service controls are an effective way to prevent data exfiltration.

However, you need to use caution when configuring VPC service controls for your workload. A misconfiguration may be overly permissive by allowing requests to access some Google APIs they shouldn't be allowed to consume. Conversely, a misconfiguration may also be too restrictive to the point that even authorized requests are mistakenly denied access to one or more accessible Google APIs.

You may wonder, why not test a VPC service control in a non-production environment first, and then if it works and it passes all forms of test, "promote" this configuration to production?

This is a feasible approach, but it's not practical because a VPC service control configuration takes into consideration a large number of "moving parts," which include a combination of identity data, contextual data (e.g., geolocation, origination CIDR block, device type, device OS, etc.), and infrastructure data.

Moreover, your non-production VPC service control configuration may work in your non-production cloud environment, but it may fail in production because, for example, your request didn't originate from the expected CIDR block using the expected principal and a trusted device.

Wouldn't it be nice to be able to test your VPC service control configuration *directly in the targeted environment* without creating adverse effects on the environment itself?

This is exactly what a dry-run mode configuration does. A VPC service control dry-run configuration will not prevent unauthorized requests from accessing the targeted Google APIs. Instead, it will simply report a *perimeter dry-run violation* in the audit logs.

For this reason, it is best practice to leverage dry-run mode perimeter configurations with increasing level of restrictions. Put differently, a VPC service perimeter dry-run configuration should always be more restrictive than the perimeter enforced configuration.

Upon enforcement (or "promotion") of the dry-run configuration, unauthorized requests will be denied access to the targeted Google APIs, and a *VPC service control violation* will be reported in the audit logs.

Dry-Run Concepts

A VPC service perimeter dry-run configuration can be in one of these four states:

1. **Inherited from enforced**: By default, the dry-run configuration is identical to the enforced configuration. This happens, for example, if you create a perimeter in enforced mode from scratch, as we did in the service perimeter deep dive before.

2. **Updated**: The dry-run configuration is different from the enforced configuration. This happens when you want to apply additional restrictions to the perimeter, and you choose to test them in the dry-run configuration instead of the enforced configuration. The upcoming perimeter dry-run deep dive exercise will show you exactly this approach.

3. **New**: The perimeter has a dry-run configuration only. No enforced configurations exist for the perimeter. The status persists as *new* until an enforced configuration is created for the perimeter.

4. **Deleted**: The perimeter dry-run configuration was deleted. The status persists as *deleted* until a dry-run configuration is created.

Perimeter Dry-Run

In this exercise, you will learn how to use a dry-run mode perimeter configuration to test your workload security posture.

First, we will configure `subnet-frontend` with private connectivity to Google APIs and services.

Then, we will update `dariokart_perimeter` to allow the two principals `joseph@dariokart.com` and `samuele@dariokart.com` to use the restricted service, that is, the storage API.

Last, we will limit the access of Google APIs from network endpoints within the perimeter *to only the storage API*. This change constrains even more the actions an authorized principal can do—whether these actions originated from inside or outside of the perimeter. Put differently, the only action allowed will be consumption of the storage API from authorized requestors within the perimeter.

Now—and this is the important part—instead of applying this change immediately (as we did in the previous deep dive exercise), you will learn how to test this change by creating a perimeter *dry-run* configuration.

You will test the perimeter dry-run configuration, and if this works as expected, then you will enforce it. At the end of this exercise, you will have learned

- How to create and to enforce a dry-run mode perimeter configuration

- How to find perimeter violations in the audit logs

- How VPC accessible services work

- How to fully set up private connectivity to Google APIs and services

Let's get started!

Setting Up Private Connectivity to Google APIs

Unlike routes and firewall rules which are scoped for the entire VPC network, private connectivity is defined on a per-subnetwork basis.

We will set up private connectivity for subnet-frontend and make sure that any request for the compute Google API, which originates from this subnet, gets routed to the restricted VIP, that is, the CIDR block 199.36.153.4/30.

We chose the compute Google API, that is, compute.googleapis.com, as an example just to prove that when the VPC allowed services are set for a perimeter, only these services can be accessed from network endpoints within the perimeter.

There are a number of steps you need to complete in order to establish private connectivity for a subnet.

First, you need to make sure the subnet is configured to use Private Google Access.

This is achieved by using the --enable-private-ip-google-access flag when you create or update a subnet. We already enabled Private Google Access for subnet-frontend in the "Private Google Access" section of Chapter 3 (Figure 3-58). Let's check to make sure this flag is still enabled (Figure 4-24).

```
gianni@cloudshell:~ (vpc-host-nonprod-pu645-uh372)$ gcloud compute networks subnets describe subnet-f
rontend --region=us-east1 --format="get(privateIpGoogleAccess)"
True
gianni@cloudshell:~ (vpc-host-nonprod-pu645-uh372)$ gcloud compute networks subnets describe subnet-b
ackend --region=us-central1 --format="get(privateIpGoogleAccess)"
False
gianni@cloudshell:~ (vpc-host-nonprod-pu645-uh372)$ █
```

Figure 4-24. *Checking Private Google Access enablement*

As you can see in Figure 4-24, Private Google Access is enabled for subnet-frontend but is disabled for subnet-backend.

Second, we need to make sure there are routes whose next step is the default-internet-gateway and whose destination is the restricted VIP.

To ensure the highest level of network isolation, I deleted the default Internet route (Figure 4-25), and I created a custom static route whose next step is the default-internet-gateway and whose destination is the restricted VIP (Figure 4-26).

```
gianni@cloudshell:~ (vpc-host-nonprod-pu645-uh372)$ gcloud compute routes delete default-route-668797
2f3751cf18
```

Figure 4-25. *Deleting the default Internet route*

```
gianni@cloudshell:~ (vpc-host-nonprod-pu645-uh372)$ gcloud compute routes create goto-restricted-apis --netw
ork=your-app-shared-vpc --destination-range=199.36.153.4/30 --next-hop-gateway=default-internet-gateway
Created [https://www.googleapis.com/compute/v1/projects/vpc-host-nonprod-pu645-uh372/global/routes/goto-rest
ricted-apis].
NAME: goto-restricted-apis
NETWORK: your-app-shared-vpc
DEST_RANGE: 199.36.153.4/30
NEXT_HOP: default-internet-gateway
PRIORITY: 1000
```

Figure 4-26. *Creating a custom static route to the restricted VIP*

■ **Note** While you cannot delete VPC routes, you *can* delete the default Internet route. To do so, run the gcloud compute routes list command and find out the name of the route whose destination range is 0.0.0.0/0. Then run the gcloud compute routes delete command as shown in Figure 4-25.

■ **Exam tip**   One of the effects of deleting the default Internet route is that you won't be able to `ssh` into any VM with an external IP.

Since I didn't want to lose the ability to `ssh` into VMs with an external IP, I chose to recreate a default Internet route, but this time with lower priority (1500) than the newly created custom static route (defaulted to 1000).

Figure 4-27 shows how to create the new default Internet route.

```
gianni@cloudshell:~ (vpc-host-nonprod-pu645-uh372)$ gcloud compute routes create goto-internet --netw
ork=your-app-shared-vpc --destination-range=0.0.0.0/0 --next-hop-gateway=default-internet-gateway --p
riority=1500
```

Figure 4-27.   *Creating a new Internet route*

So, just to make sure I have the routes I need, in Figure 4-28 I listed all the routes that use the default Internet gateway in our shared VPC.

```
gianni@cloudshell:~ (vpc-host-nonprod-pu645-uh372)$ gcloud compute routes list      --filter="default-
internet-gateway"
NAME: goto-internet
NETWORK: your-app-shared-vpc
DEST_RANGE: 0.0.0.0/0
NEXT_HOP: default-internet-gateway
PRIORITY: 1500

NAME: goto-restricted-apis
NETWORK: your-app-shared-vpc
DEST_RANGE: 199.36.153.4/30
NEXT_HOP: default-internet-gateway
PRIORITY: 1000
gianni@cloudshell:~ (vpc-host-nonprod-pu645-uh372)$
```

Figure 4-28.   *Listing routes that use the default-internet-gateway as next-hop*

The first route will allow egress traffic to the Internet, which will allow me (among many things) to `ssh` to VMs with external IPs I created in any of my subnets.

The second route will allow egress traffic to the restricted VIP.

■ **Exam tip**   In order for your workloads to privately consume Google APIs, you need to allow egress traffic with protocol and port `tcp` and `443`, respectively, to reach the restricted VIP.

Third, with Private Google Access enabled and a route to the restricted VIP, we need to make sure firewall rules won't block any outbound `tcp:443` traffic whose destination is the restricted VIP.

As a result, in Figure 4-29 I created a firewall rule `allow-restricted-apis`.

```
gianni@cloudshell:~ (vpc-host-nonprod-pu645-uh372)$ gcloud compute firewall-rules create allow-restri
ced-apis --network=your-app-shared-vpc --direction=egress --allow=tcp:443 --destination-ranges=199.36
.153.4/30
```

Figure 4-29.   *Creating* `allow-restricted-apis` *egress firewall rule*

Fourth, we need to set up a DNS resource record set to resolve the fully qualified domain name compute.googleapis.com.—yes, the trailing dot is required!—to one of the four IPv4 addresses in the restricted VIP.

An easy way to do it is by leveraging the newly developed Cloud DNS feature *Cloud DNS response policies*, which was introduced exactly to simplify access to Google APIs, as illustrated in Figure 4-30.

```
gianni@cloudshell:~ (vpc-host-nonprod-pu645-uh372)$ gcloud dns response-policies create dariokart-dns-respon
se-policy    --networks=your-app-shared-vpc    --description="This is a Cloud DNS private zone concept tha
t contains rules instead of records for our shared VPC name resolution"
Created ResponsePolicy [https://dns.googleapis.com/dns/v1/projects/vpc-host-nonprod-pu645-uh372/responsePoli
cies/dariokart-dns-response-policy].
{
  "description": "This is a Cloud DNS private zone concept that contains rules instead of records for our sh
ared VPC name resolution",
  "id": "6150852549575710475",
  "kind": "dns#responsePolicy",
  "networks": [
    {
      "kind": "dns#responsePolicyNetwork",
      "networkUrl": "https://compute.googleapis.com/compute/v1/projects/vpc-host-nonprod-pu645-uh372/global/
networks/your-app-shared-vpc"
    }
  ],
  "responsePolicyName": "dariokart-dns-response-policy"
}
gianni@cloudshell:~ (vpc-host-nonprod-pu645-uh372)$ █
```

Figure 4-30. *Creating dariokart-dns-response-policy for the shared VPC*

A Cloud DNS response policy is a Cloud DNS private zone concept that contains rules instead of records for our shared VPC name resolution.

Last, in Figure 4-31 we need to add a rule that lets the fully qualified domain name compute.googleapis.com. resolve to one of the four IPv4 addresses in the restricted VIP CIDR block 199.36.153.4/30.

```
gianni@cloudshell:~ (vpc-host-nonprod-pu645-uh372)$ gcloud dns response-policies rules create compute-google
apis-com-rule \
    --response-policy=dariokart-dns-response-policy \
    --dns-name=compute.googleapis.com. \
    --local-data=name="compute.googleapis.com.",type="A",ttl=300,rrdatas="199.36.153.4|199.36.153.5|199.36.1
53.6|199.36.153.7"
Created ResponsePolicyRule [https://dns.googleapis.com/dns/v1/projects/vpc-host-nonprod-pu645-uh372/response
Policies/dariokart-dns-response-policy/rules/compute-googleapis-com-rule].
{
  "dnsName": "compute.googleapis.com."        Fully-qualified Domain Name
                                              The trailing dot is required
  "kind": "dns#responsePolicyRule",
  "localData": {
    "localDatas": [
      {
        "kind": "dns#resourceRecordSet",
        "name": "compute.googleapis.com.",
        "rrdatas": [
          "199.36.153.4",
          "199.36.153.5",        Restricted VIP
          "199.36.153.6",
          "199.36.153.7"
        ],
        "ttl": 300,
        "type": "A"
      }
    ]
  },
  "ruleName": "compute-googleapis-com-rule"
}
gianni@cloudshell:~ (vpc-host-nonprod-pu645-uh372)$
```

Figure 4-31. *Creating compute-googleapis-com-rule for the shared VPC*

With these five steps successfully completed, you can rest assured that `tcp:443` egress traffic from `subnet-frontend`, whose destination is the compute Google API, will reach its destination without using the Internet.

Updating the Access Level

Next, we need to update our access level to allow also the two principals joseph@dariokart.com and samuele@dariokart.com to use the restricted service, that is, the storage API.

All we need to do is to add them to the basic access level spec YAML file (Figure 4-32), save the file, and update `dariokart_level` access level (Figure 4-33).

```
- members:
    - user:gianni@dariokart.com
    - user:joseph@dariokart.com
    - user:samuele@dariokart.com█
~
~
~
~
~
~
~
~
~
~
~
~
-- INSERT --
```

Figure 4-32. *Editing basic access level spec YAML file*

```
itsmedario@cloudshell:~/perimeters (vpc-host-nonprod-pu645-uh372)$ gcloud access-context-manager levels update dariokart_lev
el --basic-level-spec=your-app-shared-vpc-access-level.yaml --title=your-app-shared-vpc-access-level --combine-function=AND
--policy=330593771297
Waiting for PATCH operation [accessPolicies/330593771297/accessLevels/dariokart_level/update/1663859388615256]...done.
itsmedario@cloudshell:~/perimeters (vpc-host-nonprod-pu645-uh372)$ █
```

Figure 4-33. *Updating* `dariokart_level`

Updating the Perimeter

Now we need to make sure the updated access level is reassigned to the perimeter. This is accomplished by leveraging the `--set-access-levels` flag in the gcloud `access-context-manager perimeters update` command (Figure 4-34).

```
gianni@cloudshell:~ (vpc-host-nonprod-pu645-uh372)$ gcloud access-context-manager perimeters update
dariokart_perimeter --set-access-levels=dariokart_level --policy=330593771297
Waiting for PATCH operation [accessPolicies/330593771297/servicePerimeters/dariokart_perimeter/upda
te/1664546674896941]...done.
gianni@cloudshell:~ (vpc-host-nonprod-pu645-uh372)$
```

Figure 4-34. *Updating* `dariokart_perimeter`

Testing the Perimeter

In this section, we will test the perimeter by showing that the principal joseph@dariokart.com is allowed to create a GET request targeting the compute Google API endpoint in order to list the VMs (instances) in its project.

Let's first look at the perimeter description (Figure 4-35) to check whether the perimeter actually allows requestors from a project inside the perimeter, matching one of the three principals in the abovementioned access level—joseph@dariokart.com being one of the three—to consume the https://compute.googleapis.com endpoint.

```
Welcome to Cloud Shell! Type "help" to get started.
To set your Cloud Platform project in this session use "gcloud config set project [PROJECT_ID]"
gianni@cloudshell:~$ gcloud config set project  vpc-host-nonprod-pu645-uh372
gianni@cloudshell:~ (vpc-host-nonprod-pu645-uh372)$ gcloud access-context-manager perimeters describe dariokart_perimeter
name: accessPolicies/330593771297/servicePerimeters/dariokart_perimeter
status:
  accessLevels:
  - accessPolicies/330593771297/accessLevels/dariokart_level
  resources:
  - projects/755396457069
  - projects/239408874101
  - projects/211670805257
  restrictedServices:
  - storage.googleapis.com
  vpcAccessibleServices: {}  ──────  {} indicates all VPC accessible APIs can be consumed from requests inside the perimeter
title: your-app-shared-vpc-perimeter
gianni@cloudshell:~ (vpc-host-nonprod-pu645-uh372)$ █
```

Figure 4-35. *Viewing dariokart_perimeter description*

Remember, when we originally created dariokart_perimeter in Figure 4-10, we did not use the --vpc-allowed-services flag. Also, when we updated it (Figure 4-34), we did not use any of the --add-vpc-allowed-services or --remove-vpc-allowed-services flags to modify the VPC accessible and allowed services.

As a result, *all* the VPC accessible and allowed services are available to consumers within the perimeter, as noted with {} in Figure 4-35.

Since *all* VPC accessible APIs can be consumed from requestors inside the perimeter, we expect a request from joseph@dariokart.com originated from a VM in subnet-frontend to succeed.

■ **Note**   For the request to hit the restricted VIP, we need to make sure the VM has no external IP address.

Let's try exactly this scenario.

With the gcloud compute instances create command, you tell the CLI you want a VM *without an external IP address* by setting the --network-interface flag to the value no-address along with the subnet where the VM will live in as displayed in Figure 4-36.

```
joseph@cloudshell:~ (frontend-devs-7734)$ gcloud compute instances create vm1 --project=frontend-devs-7734 --zone=us-east1-c
  --network-interface=no-address,subnet=projects/vpc-host-nonprod-pu645-uh372/regions/us-east1/subnetworks/subnet-frontend
Created [https://www.googleapis.com/compute/v1/projects/frontend-devs-7734/zones/us-east1-c/instances/vm1].
NAME: vm1
ZONE: us-east1-c
MACHINE_TYPE: n1-standard-1
PREEMPTIBLE:
INTERNAL_IP: 192.168.0.5 ─────────────RFC 1918 IPv4 address from subnet-frontend CIDR
EXTERNAL_IP: ───────────────── No external IP to allow for Private Google Access subnet connectivity
STATUS: RUNNING
joseph@cloudshell:~ (frontend-devs-7734)$
```

Figure 4-36. *Creating a VM with no external IP address*

Even though our shared VPC has an Internet route, since the VM has no external IP address we cannot ssh to the VM from Cloud Shell by default—the default option is to ssh into the VM using its external IP address and the default Internet route.

In order to SSH to our "private" VM, we need to leverage the Identity-Aware Proxy (IAP) tunnel.

As always, we start by enabling its corresponding API in the project (Figure 4-37).

```
joseph@cloudshell:~ (frontend-devs-7734)$ gcloud services enable iap.googleapis.com
Operation "operations/acat.p2-239408874101-8b59b605-83e8-4075-8221-3623df67e75f" finished successfully
```

Figure 4-37. *Enabling the Identity-Aware Proxy API in frontend-devs*

Then the principal joseph@dariokart.com needs to be granted the tunnel resource accessor role. In accordance with the least privilege principle, we will bind this role to this principal in his own project as scope.

Figure 4-38 shows how to update the project frontend-devs IAM allow policy accordingly.

```
itsmedario@cloudshell:~ (vpc-host-nonprod-pu645-uh372)$ gcloud projects add-iam-policy-binding frontend-devs-7734
--member=user:joseph@dariokart.com --role=roles/iap.tunnelResourceAccessor
Updated IAM policy for project [frontend-devs-7734].
```

Figure 4-38. *Granting joseph@dariokart.com iap.tunnelResourceAccessor role in frontend-devs project*

With these preliminary steps completed, we can SSH into vm1, as shown in Figure 4-39.

```
joseph@cloudshell:~ (frontend-devs-7734)$ gcloud compute ssh vm1 --project=frontend-devs-7734
Did you mean zone [us-east1-b] for instance: [vm1] (Y/n)? n

No zone specified. Using zone [us-east1-c] for instance: [vm1].
External IP address was not found; defaulting to using IAP tunneling.
WARNING:

To increase the performance of the tunnel, consider installing NumPy. For instructions,
please see https://cloud.google.com/iap/docs/using-tcp-forwarding#increasing_the_tcp_upload_bandwidth

Warning: Permanently added 'compute.2170652143589607956' (ECDSA) to the list of known hosts.
Enter passphrase for key '/home/joseph/.ssh/google_compute_engine':
Linux vm1 5.10.0-18-cloud-amd64 #1 SMP Debian 5.10.140-1 (2022-09-02) x86_64

The programs included with the Debian GNU/Linux system are free software;
the exact distribution terms for each program are described in the
individual files in /usr/share/doc/*/copyright.

Debian GNU/Linux comes with ABSOLUTELY NO WARRANTY, to the extent
permitted by applicable law.
joseph@vm1:~$
```

Figure 4-39. *Connecting to vm1 using an IAP tunnel over ssh*

Now that we are securely logged into vm1, let's test dariokart_perimeter.

In this test, we will create an HTTP GET request, whose target is the compute Google API endpoint, with a URI constructed to invoke the instances.list method.

See https://cloud.google.com/compute/docs/reference/rest/v1/instances/list for more details.

The request will be authenticated using joseph@dariokart.com's access token, which is redacted in Figure 4-40.

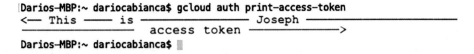

Figure 4-40. *Printing joseph@dariokart.com's access token (redacted)*

■ **Note** An access token is a temporary form of authentication, and by default it expires after one hour. In Figure 4-40, I used the `gcloud auth print-access-token` command from a gcloud session on my personal machine authenticated as principal joseph@dariokart.com. I could have used the same command from Cloud Shell—provided I was authenticated as joseph@dariokart.com.

Finally, we execute the HTTP GET request using the `curl` command in Figure 4-41.

```
joseph@vm1:~$ curl -H "Authorization: Bearer   <— Joseph
                       access token                 goes
 — here ————————> " --request GET https://compute.googleapis.com/compute/v1/projects/frontend-devs-7734/zones/us-east1-c/inst
ances
{
  "kind": "compute#instanceList",
  "id": "projects/frontend-devs-7734/zones/us-east1-c/instances",
  "items": [
    {
      "kind": "compute#instance",
      "id": "2170652143589607956",
      "creationTimestamp": "2022-09-28T18:29:32.850-07:00",
      "name": "vm1",  ————This is our VM with no external IP
      "tags": {
        "fingerprint": "42WmSpB8rSM="
      },
      "machineType": "https://www.googleapis.com/compute/v1/projects/frontend-devs-7734/zones/us-east1-c/machineTypes/n1-sta
ndard-1",
      "status": "RUNNING",
      "zone": "https://www.googleapis.com/compute/v1/projects/frontend-devs-7734/zones/us-east1-c",
      "canIpForward": false,
      "networkInterfaces": [
        {
          "kind": "compute#networkInterface",
          "network": "https://www.googleapis.com/compute/v1/projects/vpc-host-nonprod-pu645-uh372/global/networks/your-app-s
hared-vpc",
          "subnetwork": "https://www.googleapis.com/compute/v1/projects/vpc-host-nonprod-pu645-uh372/regions/us-east1/subnet
works/subnet-frontend",
          "networkIP": "192.168.0.5",  ————vm1 internal IP
          "name": "nic0",
          "fingerprint": "GHrCo2DmfrM=",
          "stackType": "IPV4_ONLY"
        }
      ],
      "disks": [
        {
```

Figure 4-41. *Executing HTTP GET request to* `compute.googleapis.com`

I copied the access token, and I pasted it as the value of the Bearer key in the HTTP header section.

As expected, the request was successful and the Google compute API returned a response listing the details of vm1—the only instance in the project frontend-devs.

In Figure 4-41, you can see the detailed response in JSON format. The access token was redacted.

Creating a Perimeter Dry-Run by Limiting VPC Allowed Services

We are now going to impose a higher level of protection to dariokart_perimeter by limiting the access of Google APIs from network endpoints within the perimeter *to only the storage API*.

Since we don't want to enforce this new configuration just yet, we are going to leverage the dry-run feature of service perimeters in order to thoroughly test this configuration and to make sure it provides the expected level of protection.

When you use a dry-run configuration for the first time, it is by default inherited from the perimeter enforced configuration.

The enforced configuration allows all VPC accessible APIs to be consumed by authorized requestors inside the perimeter (Figure 4-35).

As a result, we want to first remove all VPC allowed services from the inherited dry-run configuration—step 1.

This is achieved by using the `--remove-vpc-allowed-services` flag (set to the `ALL` keyword), in conjunction with the `--enable-vpc-accessible-services` flag, as displayed in Figure 4-42.

```
gianni@cloudshell:~ (vpc-host-nonprod-pu645-uh372)$ gcloud access-context-manager perimeters dry-run update
dariokart_perimeter --enable-vpc-accessible-services --remove-vpc-allowed-services=ALL --policy=330593771297
Waiting for PATCH operation [accessPolicies/330593771297/servicePerimeters/dariokart_perimeter/update/16643
81984956278]...done.
```

Figure 4-42. *Updating dariokart_perimeter dry-run configuration—step 1*

Subsequently, we want to add the restricted services, that is, `storage.googleapis.com`, to the list of VPC allowed services—step 2.

This is achieved by using the `--add-vpc-allowed-services` flag (set to the `RESTRICTED-SERVICES` keyword), also in conjunction with the `--enable-vpc-accessible-services` flag, as shown in Figure 4-43.

```
gianni@cloudshell:~ (vpc-host-nonprod-pu645-uh372)$ gcloud access-context-manager perimeters dry-run update
dariokart_perimeter --enable-vpc-accessible-services --add-vpc-allowed-services=RESTRICTED-SERVICES --policy
=330593771297
Waiting for PATCH operation [accessPolicies/330593771297/servicePerimeters/dariokart_perimeter/update/16643
82269944169]...done.
```

Figure 4-43. *Updating dariokart_perimeter dry-run configuration—step 2*

After completing these two steps, `dariokart_perimeter`'s dry-run configuration (surrounded by the green rectangle) has drifted from the enforced configuration (surrounded by the yellow rectangle), as illustrated in Figure 4-44.

```
gianni@cloudshell:~ (vpc-host-nonprod-pu645-uh372)$ gcloud access-context-manager perimeters describe dario
kart_perimeter --policy=330593771297
name: accessPolicies/330593771297/servicePerimeters/dariokart_perimeter
spec:                                              Dry-run Configuration
  accessLevels:
  - accessPolicies/330593771297/accessLevels/dariokart_level
  resources:
  - projects/755396457069
  - projects/239408874101
  - projects/211670805257
  restrictedServices:
  - storage.googleapis.com
  vpcAccessibleServices:
    allowedServices:
    - RESTRICTED-SERVICES ──── Only storage API is accessible from VPC in dry-run mode
    enableRestriction: true
status:                                            Enforced Configuration
  accessLevels:
  - accessPolicies/330593771297/accessLevels/dariokart_level
  resources:
  - projects/755396457069
  - projects/239408874101
  - projects/211670805257
  restrictedServices:
  - storage.googleapis.com
  vpcAccessibleServices: {}────── All services are accessible from VPC in enforced mode
title: your-app-shared-vpc-perimeter
useExplicitDryRunSpec: true
gianni@cloudshell:~ (vpc-host-nonprod-pu645-uh372)$
```

Figure 4-44. *Describing* dariokart_perimeter *enforced configuration*

An easier way to see the differences between the two configurations is by using the gcloud access-context-manager perimeters **dry-run describe** command, as shown in Figure 4-45.

```
gianni@cloudshell:~ (vpc-host-nonprod-pu645-uh372)$ gcloud access-context-manager perimeters dry-run describe
 dariokart_perimeter --policy=330593771297
  name: dariokart_perimeter
  title: your-app-shared-vpc-perimeter
  type: PERIMETER_TYPE_REGULAR
  accessLevels:
    accessPolicies/330593771297/accessLevels/dariokart_level
  resources:
    projects/755396457069
    projects/239408874101
    projects/211670805257
  restrictedServices:
    storage.googleapis.com
- vpcAccessibleServices: {}
+ vpcAccessibleServices:
+   allowedServices:
+     RESTRICTED-SERVICES
+   enableRestriction: true
```

Figure 4-45. *Describing* dariokart_perimeter *dry-run configuration*

The "+" sign denotes a row that is present in the perimeter dry-run configuration, but is absent from the perimeter enforced configuration.

Conversely, the "-" sign denotes a row that is present in the perimeter enforced configuration, but is absent from the perimeter dry-run configuration.

Now that you learned the difference between dariokart_perimeter's enforced and dry-run configurations, we are ready to test the perimeter dry-run configuration.

Testing the Perimeter Dry-Run

Since the dry-run configuration has not been enforced (yet!), the expected behavior is that the exact GET request in Figure 4-41 will succeed, but a perimeter violation will be appended to the audit logs.

This is because the dry-run configuration allows *only the restricted services*, that is, `storage.googleapis.com`, to be consumed from network endpoints inside the perimeter, whereas the GET request attempts to consume `compute.googleapis.com`.

Figure 4-46 shows the successful request to obtain the list of VMs in the `frontend-devs` project initiated by the principal `joseph@dariokart.com` we saw before.

```
joseph@vm1:~$ curl -H "Authorization: Bearer   <— Joseph ──────────────────────────────
                 ── access token ──────── goes ──
— here ────────> " --request GET https://compute.googleapis.com/compute/v1/projects/frontend-devs-7734/zones/us-east1-c/inst
ances
{
  "kind": "compute#instanceList",
  "id": "projects/frontend-devs-7734/zones/us-east1-c/instances",
  "items": [
    {
      "kind": "compute#instance",
      "id": "2170652143589607956",
      "creationTimestamp": "2022-09-28T18:29:32.850-07:00",
      "name": "vm1",     ────This is our VM with no external IP
      "tags": {
        "fingerprint": "42WmSpB8rSM="
      },
      "machineType": "https://www.googleapis.com/compute/v1/projects/frontend-devs-7734/zones/us-east1-c/machineTypes/n1-sta
ndard-1",
      "status": "RUNNING",
      "zone": "https://www.googleapis.com/compute/v1/projects/frontend-devs-7734/zones/us-east1-c",
      "canIpForward": false,
      "networkInterfaces": [
        {
          "kind": "compute#networkInterface",
          "network": "https://www.googleapis.com/compute/v1/projects/vpc-host-nonprod-pu645-uh372/global/networks/your-app-s
hared-vpc",
          "subnetwork": "https://www.googleapis.com/compute/v1/projects/vpc-host-nonprod-pu645-uh372/regions/us-east1/subnet
works/subnet-frontend",
          "networkIP": "192.168.0.5",   ────vm1 internal IP
          "name": "nic0",
          "fingerprint": "GHrCo2DmfrM=",
          "stackType": "IPV4_ONLY"
        }
      ],
      "disks": [
        {
```

Figure 4-46. *Executing HTTP GET request to* `compute.googleapis.com`

Even though the request succeeded, the audit logs tell a different story.

Figure 4-47 illustrates how to retrieve from Cloud Logging the past ten minutes (`--freshness=600s`) of logs that are reported by VPC Service Controls (read `'protoPayload.metadata.@type:"type.googleapis.com/google.cloud.audit.VpcServiceControlAuditMetadata"'`).

```
itsmedario@cloudshell:~ (vpc-host-nonprod-pu645-uh372)$ gcloud logging read 'protoPayload.metadata.@type:"type.goo
gleapis.com/google.cloud.audit.VpcServiceControlAuditMetadata"' --freshness=600s | more
```

Figure 4-47. *Reading VPC Service Control audit logs in the past ten minutes*

A perimeter violation was reported, as illustrated in Figure 4-48.

```
gleapis.com/google.cloud.audit.VpcServiceControlAuditMetadata"' --freshness=600s | more
---
insertId: 1h0a6yodegcj
logName: projects/vpc-host-nonprod-pu645-uh372/logs/cloudaudit.googleapis.com%2Fpolicy
protoPayload:
  '@type': type.googleapis.com/google.cloud.audit.AuditLog
  authenticationInfo:
    principalEmail: jo...h@da...m  ────── request originated by joseph@dariokart.com
  metadata:
    '@type': type.googleapis.com/google.cloud.audit.VpcServiceControlAuditMetadata
    accessLevels:
    - accessPolicies/330593771297/accessLevels/dariokart_level
    dryRun: true  ────── request is not denied by dariokart_perimeter's enforced configuration AND
    resourceNames:          request violates dariokart_perimeter's dry-run (spec) configuration
    - frontend-devs-7734
    securityPolicyInfo:
      organizationId: '585269232696'
      servicePerimeterName: accessPolicies/330593771297/servicePerimeters/dariokart_perimeter
    violationReason: SERVICE_NOT_ALLOWED_FROM_VPC
    vpcServiceControlsUniqueId: fAhWX_e6gnR9dXHptx17-KTi77T3YTOlv6vClbw7bB3D6kqcSDVV8w
  methodName: compute.v1.InstancesService.List
  requestMetadata:
    callerIp: 192.168.0.5  ────── vm1 internal IP
    callerNetwork: //compute.googleapis.com/projects/vpc-host-nonprod-pu645-uh372/global/networks/__unknown__
    destinationAttributes: {}
    requestAttributes: {}
  resourceName: projects/755396457069
  serviceName: compute.googleapis.com  ────── resolves to one of four restricted VIP, i.e. 199.36.153.4/30
  status:
    code: 7
    details:
    - '@type': type.googleapis.com/google.rpc.PreconditionFailure
      violations:
      - description: fAhWX_e6gnR9dXHptx17-KTi77T3YTOlv6vClbw7bB3D6kqcSDVV8w
        type: VPC_SERVICE_CONTROLS
    message: "(Dry Run Mode) Request is prohibited by organization's policy. vpcServiceControlsUniqueIdentifier:\
```

Figure 4-48. *Detecting a perimeter violation in the audit logs*

Notice the dryRun: true key-value pair (surrounded by the dark blue rectangle) to denote the audit log was generated by a perimeter dry-run configuration.

Enforcing the Perimeter Dry-Run

Now that we are satisfied with the level of protection provided by the perimeter dry-run configuration, we are all set to enforce the configuration. To do so, use the gcloud access-context-manager perimeters dry-run enforce command, as illustrated in Figure 4-49.

```
gianni@cloudshell:~ (vpc-host-nonprod-pu645-uh372)$ gcloud access-context-manager perimeters dry-run
enforce dariokart_perimeter --policy=330593771297
Waiting for PATCH operation [accessPolicies/330593771297/servicePerimeters/dariokart_perimeter/updat
e/1664421236654681]...done.
gianni@cloudshell:~ (vpc-host-nonprod-pu645-uh372)$ gcloud access-context-manager perimeters describe
 dariokart_perimeter --policy=330593771297
name: accessPolicies/330593771297/servicePerimeters/dariokart_perimeter
status:
  accessLevels:
  - accessPolicies/330593771297/accessLevels/dariokart_level
  resources:
  - projects/755396457069
  - projects/239408874101
  - projects/211670805257
  restrictedServices:
  - storage.googleapis.com
  vpcAccessibleServices:
    allowedServices:
    - RESTRICTED-SERVICES
    enableRestriction: true
title: your-app-shared-vpc-perimeter
gianni@cloudshell:~ (vpc-host-nonprod-pu645-uh372)$
```

Figure 4-49. *Enforcing perimeter dry-run configuration*

As you can see in Figure 4-49, the perimeter's newly enforced configuration matches exactly the spec section in Figure 4-44.

Put differently, the dry-run configuration was promoted to enforce mode, and the new dry-run configuration now matches the enforced one because it inherited from it.

Testing the Enforced Perimeter

Let's now test the perimeter with its newly enforced configuration, which was derived from the validated dry-run one.

Figure 4-50 demonstrates that the same test we tried before (Figure 4-46) this time fails with an HTTP status code 403 ("PERMISSION_DENIED").

```
joseph@vm1:~$ curl -H "Authorization: Bearer   <— Joseph ————————————————————————
———————— access token ———— goes ——————————————————————————————————————————
—— here ————> " --request GET https://compute.googleapis.com/compute/v1/projects/frontend-devs-7734/zones/us-east1-c/inst
ances
{
  "error": {
    "code": 403,
    "message": "Request is prohibited by organization's policy. vpcServiceControlsUniqueIdentifier: -XReoRkFyWFQ44sRdJy5tS1k
DVlQjMTVyR3wv5k0e1ZcE2IEf9wa3w",
    "errors": [
      {
        "message": "Request is prohibited by organization's policy. vpcServiceControlsUniqueIdentifier: -XReoRkFyWFQ44sRdJy5
tS1kDVlQjMTVyR3wv5k0e1ZcE2IEf9wa3w",
        "domain": "global",
        "reason": "forbidden"
      }
    ],
    "status": "PERMISSION_DENIED",
    "details": [
      {
        "@type": "type.googleapis.com/google.rpc.PreconditionFailure",
        "violations": [
          {
            "type": "VPC_SERVICE_CONTROLS",
            "description": "-XReoRkFyWFQ44sRdJy5tS1kDVlQjMTVyR3wv5k0e1ZcE2IEf9wa3w"
          }
        ]
      },
      {
        "@type": "type.googleapis.com/google.rpc.ErrorInfo",
        "reason": "SECURITY_POLICY_VIOLATED",
        "domain": "googleapis.com",
        "metadatas": {
          "uid": "-XReoRkFyWFQ44sRdJy5tS1kDVlQjMTVyR3wv5k0e1ZcE2IEf9wa3w",
          "consumer": "projects/frontend-devs-7734",   ————Project is not allowed to consume compute.googleapis.com
          "service": "compute.googleapis.com"
        }
      }
```

Figure 4-50. *Executing HTTP GET request to* compute.googleapis.com

In this exercise, you learned about the powerful dry-run feature available to GCP perimeter resources. When you design your service perimeters, it is best practice to thoroughly test their configurations before enforcing them to your production workloads.

A perimeter dry-run configuration is perfect for that. Depending on how mission-critical your workload is, the dry-run phase may last a few days, a few weeks, or even longer if you want to perform cybersecurity threat hunting in an effort to reduce your workload attack surface.

Cleaning Up

Before deleting vm1, let's check whether compute.googleapis.com resolves to one of the four IP addresses in the restricted VIP range (Figure 4-51).

```
joseph@vm1:~$ ping compute.googleapis.com
PING compute.googleapis.com (199.36.153.4) 56(84) bytes of data.
^C
--- compute.googleapis.com ping statistics ---
19 packets transmitted, 0 received, 100% packet loss, time 18427ms
```

Figure 4-51. *Pinging* compute.googleapis.com

Two things are important to emphasize.

First, the domain name compute.googleapis.com **did** resolve to one of the four restricted VIP IPv4 addresses, exactly as we wanted. This means that the compute-googleapis-com-rule we created in Figure 4-31 worked as expected.

Second, the ping command failed. This is because by design any restricted VIP can only be reached by TCP traffic on port 443. Instead, the ping command operates using the ICMP protocol.

Now, we are all set to delete vm1 (Figure 4-52).

```
joseph@cloudshell:~ (frontend-devs-7734)$ gcloud compute instances delete vm1 --zone=us-east1-c
The following instances will be deleted. Any attached disks configured to be auto-deleted will be deleted unless they are
attached to any other instances or the `--keep-disks` flag is given and specifies them for keeping. Deleting a disk is
irreversible and any data on the disk will be lost.
 - [vm1] in [us-east1-c]

Do you want to continue (Y/n)?  Y

Deleted [https://www.googleapis.com/compute/v1/projects/frontend-devs-7734/zones/us-east1-c/instances/vm1].
joseph@cloudshell:~ (frontend-devs-7734)$ gcloud compute instances list
Listed 0 items.
joseph@cloudshell:~ (frontend-devs-7734)$
```

Figure 4-52. Deleting vm1

Final Considerations

There are a few "gotchas" you need to be aware of for the exam. They relate to scenarios that include the combination of VPC Service Controls and VPCs connected in a number of ways. The main two common scenarios are briefly explained in the upcoming sections.

Shared VPC with VPC Service Controls

When using Shared VPC, treat the whole Shared VPC (i.e., host and all service projects) as *one* service perimeter. This way, when an operation involves resources distributed between the host and service projects, you don't incur a VPC Service Controls violation.

VPC Peering with VPC Service Controls

VPC peering allows peering VPC networks between two separate organizations. Because a service perimeter is limited to projects within one organization only, service perimeters do not affect peering VPCs.

Exam Questions
Question 4.1 (Perimeter with Shared VPC)

You are troubleshooting access denied errors between Compute Engine instances connected to a Shared VPC and BigQuery datasets. The datasets reside in a project protected by a VPC Service Controls perimeter. What should you do?

A. Add the host project containing the Shared VPC to the service perimeter.

B. Add the service project where the Compute Engine instances reside to the service perimeter.

C. Create a service perimeter between the service project where the Compute Engine instances reside and the host project that contains the Shared VPC.

D. Create a perimeter bridge between the service project where the Compute Engine instances reside and the perimeter that contains the protected BigQuery datasets.

Rationale

A is CORRECT because if you're using Shared VPC, you must always include the host project in a service perimeter along with any service project that consumes the Shared VPC.

B is not correct because the entire Shared VPC (host and all service projects) must be treated as one service perimeter.

C is not correct because a service perimeter already exists.

D is not correct because there is no need to create a perimeter bridge.

Question 4.2 (Dry-Run)

You need to enable VPC Service Controls and allow changes to perimeters in existing environments without preventing access to resources. Which VPC Service Controls mode should you use?

A. Cloud Run

B. Native

C. Enforced

D. Dry-run

Rationale

A is not correct because Cloud Run has nothing to do with VPC Service Controls.

B is not correct because the "native" perimeter mode does not exist.

C is not correct because the "enforced" mode achieves the opposite of what the requirement is.

D is CORRECT because the "dry-run" mode is intended to test the perimeter configuration and to monitor usage of services without preventing access to resources. This is exactly what the requirement is.

CHAPTER 5

■ ■ ■

Configuring Load Balancing

Enterprise applications are architected, designed, and built for elasticity, performance, security, cost-effectiveness, and resilience. These are the five pillars of the *well-architected framework*.

■ **Note** The well-architected framework is an organized and curated collection of best practices, which are intended to help you architect your workloads by taking full advantage of the cloud. Even though each public cloud provider has created its own framework, all these frameworks have in common the aforementioned five pillars, as key tenets. If you want to learn more, I recommend starting from the Google Cloud Architecture framework: `https://cloud.google.com/architecture/framework`.

In this chapter, you will learn how to choose the most appropriate combination of Google Cloud load balancing services that will help you architect, design, and build your workloads to be elastic, performant, secure, cost-effective, and resilient.

By *elasticity* we mean the ability of a workload to scale horizontally (*scale in* or *scale out*) based on the number of incoming requests it receives. If the workload receives low traffic, then the workload should only consume a small set of compute, network, and storage resources. As the number of incoming requests increases, the workload should be able to gradually increase the number of compute, network, and storage resources to be able to serve the increasing load while maintaining its SLOs.

Performance is typically measured in terms of requests per second (RPS) and request latency, that is, how many requests per second the workload can process in order to meet its SLOs and what is the average time (usually expressed in milliseconds—ms) for the workload to serve a request. More metrics may be added, but for the scope of this chapter, we will be mainly focused on RPS and latency as SLIs for performance.

The focus areas of *security* are identity protection, network protection, data protection, and application protection. Data protection includes encryption at rest, in transit, and in use.

Cost is another important pillar that has to be considered when designing the architecture for your workloads. Remember, in the cloud you pay for what you use, but ultimately your workloads need a network to operate. You will learn in this chapter that all the load balancing services available in Google Cloud come in different "flavors" based on the network tier you choose, that is, premium tier or standard tier—we introduced the two network service tiers in Chapter 2. The former is more expensive than the latter, but has the key benefit of leveraging the highly reliable, highly optimized, low-latency Google Global Backbone network instead of the Internet to connect the parts of your load balancing service. Some load balancing services are only available in a network tier (premium) rather than the other (standard). For more information, visit `https://cloud.google.com/network-tiers#tab1`.

© Dario Cabianca 2023
D. Cabianca, *Google Cloud Platform (GCP) Professional Cloud Network Engineer Certification Companion*, Certification Study Companion Series, https://doi.org/10.1007/978-1-4842-9354-6_5

Last, *resilience* indicates the ability of the workload to recover from failures, whether they be in its frontend, in its backends, or any other component of its architecture.

Google Cloud Load Balancer Family

Load balancing is concerned with elasticity, performance, and resilience.

Google Cloud offers a number of load balancing services that are meant to help you take full advantage of its globally distributed, performant, and secure network infrastructure. This is the same infrastructure that powers billion-user services you probably use every day, for example, Google Search, Gmail, Google Maps, YouTube, Google Workspace, and others.

Figure 5-1 provides an overview of the Google Cloud load balancing services.

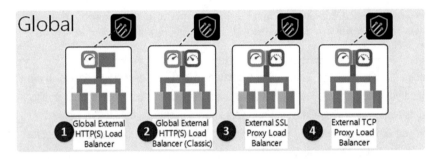

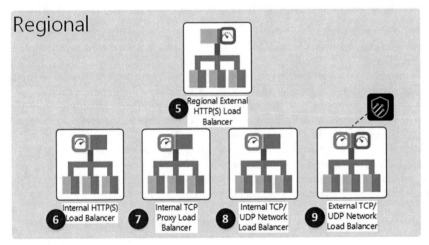

Figure 5-1. *Overview of Google Cloud load balancers*

As of the writing of this book, there are nine types of load balancers, which are grouped in Figure 5-1 by scope, that is, *global* or *regional*—the former to denote a load balancer with components (backends) in multiple regions and the latter with all components in a single region.

■ **Note**   Do not confuse the scope of a load balancer (global vs. regional) with its "client exposure," that is, external vs. internal. An *external* load balancer denotes a load balancer that accepts Internet traffic, whereas an *internal* load balancer only accepts RFC 1918 traffic.

In addition to the nine load balancer types, each type—not all—may come in the two network tiers you learned in Chapter 2.

To avoid confusion, from now on I will denote each load balancer type with a specific number as indicated in Figure 5-1.

For the exam, you are required to know which load balancer type is best suited for a specific use case. You will need to determine the most appropriate type of load balancer, as well as a combination of Google Cloud services that meet the requirements in the question. These are typically requirements related to the pillars of the well-architected framework, that is, operational efficiency, performance, resilience, security, and cost-effectiveness.

I have included in Figure 5-1 Cloud Armor's compatibility, which is a key service that goes hand in hand with global external load balancers. You will learn Cloud Armor in detail at the end of this chapter. For the time being, think of Cloud Armor—as the name suggests—as a GCP network service intended to provide an extra layer of protection for your workloads.

When an HTTPS load balancer combines "forces" with two other network services, that is, Cloud Armor and Identity-Aware Proxy, your workload is also more secure because it is protected from Distributed Denial-of-Service (DDoS) and other layer 7 attacks, for example, the Open Web Application Security Project (OWASP) top ten vulnerabilities.

You will learn first the common components of a load balancer, regardless of its type. Once you have acquired a good understanding of the parts that make up a load balancer, you will learn the differentiating capabilities each load balancer has.

Backend Services and Network Endpoint Groups (NEGs)

Backend services are the means a load balancer uses to send incoming traffic to compute resources responsible for serving requests. The compute resources are also known as *backends*, while a *backend service* is the Google Cloud resource that mediates between the load balancer frontend and the backends.

A backend service is configured by setting the protocol it uses to connect to the backends, along with distribution and session settings, health checks, and timeouts. These settings determine how your load balancer behaves.

If your workload serves *static* content using the HTTP(S) protocol, then there is really no compute resource needed. This is because the response is not the result of a computation performed by a system as an effect of the incoming HTTP(S) request and its metadata (e.g., HTTP headers). Instead, for the same HTTP(S) requests, identical HTML pages are returned in the HTTP(S) responses. As a result, the easiest way to manage static content is to use a Cloud Storage bucket to store the static content and let the HTTP(S) load balancer return the HTML page to the requestor.

Conversely, if your workload serves *dynamic* content, then backends are required to compute the data from the request and create a response to be sent back to the requestor.

A number of backend options are available, and you—as a network engineer—will need to make the right choice based on the business, technical, and security requirements for your workload.

If the preceding requirements drive you toward an IaaS (Infrastructure as a Service) approach, then managed instance groups (MIGs) are an excellent option for your workload backends.

On the other hand, if your workload's architecture was designed to be cloud-native, then the good news is that you can take full advantage of container-native or serverless services provided by Google Cloud (e.g., GKE, Cloud Run, Cloud Functions, App Engine). These services are nicely integrated with your Google Cloud load balancer as we will see in the next paragraph.

Google Cloud has generalized the "network endpoint group" construct (referred in the upcoming sections as NEG) from container-native only to a number of different "flavors" in order to meet the nonfunctional requirements presented by hybrid and multi-cloud topologies.

Figure 5-2 shows a summary of these "flavors" in the form of an infographic.

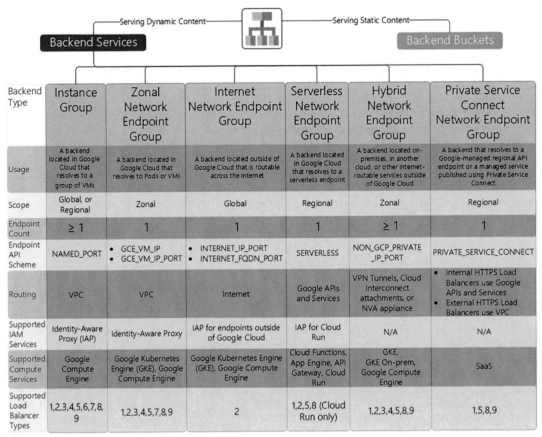

Backend Type	Instance Group	Zonal Network Endpoint Group	Internet Network Endpoint Group	Serverless Network Endpoint Group	Hybrid Network Endpoint Group	Private Service Connect Network Endpoint Group
Usage	A backend located in Google Cloud that resolves to a group of VMs	A backend located in Google Cloud that resolves to Pods or VMs	A backend located outside of Google Cloud that is routable across the internet	A backend located in Google Cloud that resolves to a serverless endpoint	A backend located on-premises, in another cloud, or other internet-routable services outside of Google Cloud	A backend that resolves to a Google-managed regional API endpoint or a managed service published using Private Service Connect
Scope	Global, or Regional	Zonal	Global	Regional	Zonal	Regional
Endpoint Count	≥ 1	1	1	1	≥ 1	1
Endpoint API Scheme	NAMED_PORT	• GCE_VM_IP • GCE_VM_IP_PORT	• INTERNET_IP_PORT • INTERNET_FQDN_PORT	SERVERLESS	NON_GCP_PRIVATE_IP_PORT	PRIVATE_SERVICE_CONNECT
Routing	VPC	VPC	Internet	Google APIs and Services	VPN Tunnels, Cloud Interconnect attachments, or NVA appliance	• Internal HTTPS Load Balancers use Google APIs and Services • External HTTPS Load Balancers use VPC
Supported IAM Services	Identity-Aware Proxy (IAP)	Identity-Aware Proxy	IAP for endpoints outside of Google Cloud	IAP for Cloud Run	N/A	N/A
Supported Compute Services	Google Compute Engine	Google Kubernetes Engine (GKE), Google Compute Engine	Google Kubernetes Engine (GKE), Google Compute Engine	Cloud Functions, App Engine, API Gateway, Cloud Run	GKE, GKE On-prem, Google Compute Engine	SaaS
Supported Load Balancer Types	1,2,3,4,5,6,7,8,9	1,2,3,4,5,7,8,9	2	1,2,5,8 (Cloud Run only)	1,2,3,4,5,8,9	1,5,8,9

Figure 5-2. *Overview of load balancer backends*

More information will be provided in the upcoming sections.

The exam will not require deep knowledge on each of the five different NEG types—the last five columns from the right in Figure 5-2. As a result, in this chapter we will just focus on how to configure managed instance groups and zonal network endpoint groups.

Configuring Managed Instance Groups (MIGs)

A managed instance group treats a group of identically configured VMs as one item. These VMs are all modeled after an *instance template*, which uses a custom image (selected to keep the boot time relatively short), and do not need an external IP address. This is because the load balancer backend services implement a mechanism to interact with each VM's internal IP address.

For proxy-based, external load balancers (1, 2, 3, 4, 5 in Figure 5-1), backends are connected to the load balancer Google Front End (GFE) with a named-port.

The value of the backend service attribute --port-name (e.g., port1) must match a value in the --named-ports list of key-value pairs for the instance group (e.g., port1:443,port2:80,port3:8080):

```
gcloud compute backend-services create your-backend-service \
    --port-name=port1 \
    --protocol=https
```

In this case, the backend service uses the value 443 as the port to use for communication with the instance group's VMs over the https protocol.

This is because port1 matches the key-value pair port1:443 in the --named-ports instance group list, thereby resolving port1 to https:443:

```
gcloud compute instance-groups managed set-named-ports your-managed-ig \
    --named-ports= port1:443,port2:80,port3:8080
```

Configuring a Zonal Network Endpoint Group (NEG)

A network endpoint group (NEG) abstracts the backends by letting the load balancer communicate directly with a group of backend endpoints or services.

Zonal NEGs are collections of either IP addresses or IP address/port pairs—see endpoint API scheme for zonal NEGs in Figure 5-2—for Google Cloud resources within a single subnet.

NEGs are useful because they allow you to create logical groupings of IP addresses and ports representing software services instead of entire VMs.

The following example creates an HTTP load balancing NEG and attaches four zonal network endpoints to the NEG. The zonal network endpoints will act as backends to the load balancer. It assumes you already have a VPC network network-a.

1. Create a subnet with alias IP addresses:

    ```
    gcloud compute networks subnets create subnet-a \
        --network network-a \
        --range 10.128.0.0/16 \
        --secondary-range container-range=192.168.0.0/16
    ```

2. Create two VMs:

    ```
    gcloud compute instances create vm1 \
        --zone us-central1-c \
        --network-interface \
          "subnet=subnet-a,aliases=r1:192.168.0.0/24"
    gcloud compute instances create vm2 \
        --zone us-central1-c \
        --network-interface \
            "subnet=subnet-a,aliases=r1:192.168.2.0/24"
    ```

3. Create the NEG:

    ```
    gcloud compute network-endpoint-groups create neg1 \
        --zone=us-central1-c \
        --network=network-a --subnet=subnet-a \
    ```

```
        --default-port=80
Created [https://www.googleapis.com/compute/beta/projects/project/zones/us-
central1-c/networkEndpointGroups/neg1].
     NAME      LOCATION       TYPE         ENDPOINT_TYPE    DEFAULT_PORT ENDPOINTS
     neg1  us-central1-c  LOAD_BALANCING  GCE_VM_IP_PORT         80          0
```

4. Update NEG with endpoints:

```
gcloud compute network-endpoint-groups update neg1 \
    --zone=us-central1-c \
    --add-endpoint 'instance=vm1,ip=192.168.0.1,port=8080' \
    --add-endpoint 'instance=vm1,ip=192.168.0.2,port=8080' \
    --add-endpoint 'instance=vm2,ip=192.168.2.1,port=8088' \
    --add-endpoint 'instance=vm2,ip=192.168.2.2,port=8080'
```

5. Create a health check:

```
gcloud compute health-checks create http healthcheck1 \
    --use-serving-port
```

6. Create the backend service:

```
gcloud compute backend-services create backendservice1 \
    --global --health-checks healthcheck1
```

7. Add the NEG neg1 backend to the backend service:

```
gcloud compute backend-services add-backend backendService1 \
    --global \
    --network-endpoint-group=neg1 \
    --network-endpoint-group-zone=us-central1-c \
    --balancing-mode=RATE --max-rate-per-endpoint=5
```

8. Create a URL map using the backend service backendservice1:

```
gcloud compute url-maps create urlmap1 --default-service \ backendservice1
```

9. Create the target http proxy using the url-map urlmap1:

```
gcloud compute target-http-proxies create httpproxy1 --url-map \ urlmap1
```

10. Create the forwarding rule, that is, the key component of a frontend load balancer's configuration, and attach it to the newly created target-http-proxy httpproxy1:

```
gcloud compute forwarding-rules create forwardingrule1 \
    --ip-protocol TCP \
    --ports=80 \
    --global \
    --target-http-proxy httpproxy1
```

Firewall Rules to Allow Traffic and Health Checks to Backend Services

When you configure a load balancer's backend services, you are required to specify one or more health checks for its backends.

As its name suggests, a *health check* is a Google Cloud resource, whose only job is to determine whether the backend instances of the load balancer they are associated with are healthy. This determination is based on the ability of the backend to respond to incoming traffic. But what type of traffic do the backends need to respond to in order to be deemed as healthy? The answer depends on the load balancer type. For HTTPS load balancers, the response must use the HTTPS protocol (layer 7); for TCP/UDP load balancers, the response must use the TCP/UDP protocol (layer 4).

This is why when you create a health check, you need to specify a protocol, optionally a port, and a scope, as shown in Figure 5-3.

```
NAME
    gcloud compute health-checks create - create (non-legacy) health checks for
        load balanced instances

SYNOPSIS
    gcloud compute health-checks create COMMAND [GCLOUD_WIDE_FLAG ...]

DESCRIPTION
    Create (non-legacy) health checks for load balanced instances.

GCLOUD WIDE FLAGS
    These flags are available to all commands: --help.

    Run $ gcloud help for details.

COMMANDS
    COMMAND is one of the following:

    grpc
        Create a gRPC health check to monitor load balanced instances.

    http
        Create a HTTP health check to monitor load balanced instances.

    http2
        Create a HTTP2 health check to monitor load balanced instances.

    https
        Create a HTTPS health check to monitor load balanced instances.

    ssl
        Create a SSL health check to monitor load balanced instances.

    tcp
        Create a TCP health check to monitor load balanced instances.
```

Figure 5-3. gcloud compute health-checks create synopsis

At the time of writing this book, the protocol can be one of the following options: grpc, http, https, http2, ssl, tcp. Legacy health checks only support http and https.

The scope indicates whether the backends are located in a single region or in multiple regions.

Keep in mind that health checks must be compatible with the type of load balancer and the backend types. For example, some load balancers only support legacy health checks—that is, they only support `http` and `https` protocols—while others support `grpc`, `http`, `https`, `http2`, `ssl`, and `tcp`.

In addition to compatibility, for the health check to work effectively, an *ingress allow firewall rule* that allows traffic to reach your load balancer backends must be created in the VPC where the backends live.

Figure 5-4 summarizes the minimum required firewall rules for each load balancer.

#	Load Balancer Type	Backends VPC Firewall Rule	When ALL Backends are Unhealthy Returns
1	Global External HTTP(S)	`gcloud compute firewall-rules create`	HTTP 503
2	Global External HTTP(S) (Classic)	**`fw-allow-proxy-lb-health-checks`**	HTTP 502
3	Global External SSL Proxy	`--network=`*`BACKENDS_VPC`*	Time out
4	Global External TCP Proxy	`--action=ALLOW`	Time out
5	Regional External HTTP(S)* * Envoy-based Load Balancer	`--direction=INGRESS` `--source-ranges=`	HTTP 503
6	Regional Internal HTTP(S)* * Envoy-based Load Balancer	`    `**`35.191.0.0/16,`** ◄ Google Front End (GFE) `    `**`130.211.0.0/22`**	HTTP 503
7	Regional Internal TCP Proxy* * Envoy-based Load Balancer	`--target-tags=allow-health-checks` `--rules=tcp:`*`PORT`*	Terminate Client Connections
8	Regional Internal TCP/UDP Network	`gcloud compute firewall-rules create` **`fw-allow-network-lb-health-checks`**	Last resort

9	Regional External TCP/UDP Network	`--network=`*`BACKENDS_VPC`*
		`--action=ALLOW`
		`--direction=INGRESS`
		`--source-ranges=`
		`    `**`35.191.0.0/16,`**
		`    `**`209.85.152.0/22,`**
		`    `**`209.85.204.0/22`**
		`--target-tags=allow-health-checks`
		`--rules=tcp`
			Last resort

Minimum Required Ingress Allow Firewall Rules

Figure 5-4. *Load balancer health check firewall rules*

The two TCP/UDP network load balancers (denoted by 8 and 9 in Figure 5-4) are the only nonproxy-based load balancers. Put differently, these load balancers preserve the original client IP address because the connection is not terminated until all packets reach their destination in one of the backends. Due to this behavior, the source ranges for their compatible health checks are different from the ones applicable to proxy-based load balancers (1–7 in Figure 5-4).

Also, regional load balancers that use the open source Envoy proxy (load balancers 5, 6, 7 in Figure 5-4) require an additional *ingress allow firewall rule* that accepts traffic from a specific subnet referred to as the *proxy-only* subnet.

These load balancers terminate incoming connections at the load balancer frontend. Traffic is then sent to the backends from IP addresses located on the proxy-only subnet.

As a result, in the region where your Envoy-based load balancer operates, you must first create the proxy-only subnet.

A key requirement is to set the `--purpose` flag to the value **REGIONAL_MANAGED_PROXY**, as shown in the following code snippet, where we assume the VPC network `lb-network` already exists:

```
gcloud compute networks subnets create proxy-only-subnet \
  --purpose=REGIONAL_MANAGED_PROXY \
  --role=ACTIVE \
  --region=us-central1 \
  --network=lb-network \
  --range=10.129.0.0/23
```

■ **Exam tip**   There can only be *one active* proxy-only subnet per region at a given time. All Envoy-based load balancers will use backend services configured to share the same proxy-only subnet to test the health of their backends. This is why it is recommended to use a CIDR block with a mask of /23 for the proxy-only subnet.

Upon creation of the proxy-only subnet, you must add another firewall rule to the load balancer VPC—`lb-network` in our preceding example. This firewall rule allows proxy-only subnet traffic flow in the subnet where the backends live—the two subnets are different, even though they reside in the load balancer VPC. This means adding one rule that allows TCP port 80, 443, and 8080 traffic from the range of the proxy-only subnet, that is, `10.129.0.0/23`.

```
gcloud compute firewall-rules create fw-allow-proxies \
  --network=lb-network \
  --action=allow \
  --direction=ingress \
  --source-ranges=10.129.0.0/23 \
  --target-tags=allow-health-checks \
  --rules=tcp:80,tcp:443,tcp:8080
```

In the preceding example, the firewall rule targets all VMs that are associated with the network tag `allow-health-checks`.

Configuring External HTTP(S) Load Balancers Including Backends and Backend Services with Balancing Method, Session Affinity, and Capacity Scaling/Scaler

External HTTP(S) load balancers (load balancers 1, 2, 5 in Figure 5-1) are proxy-based, layer 7 load balancers, which enable you to run and scale your workloads behind a single external IP address, that is, a virtual IP (VIP).

Proxy-based means that the end-to-end HTTP(S) connection between the client and the backend serving the client is broken in two connections:

- The first connection originates from the client and is terminated at the target-proxy component of the load balancer.

- The second connection starts at the target proxy and ends at the backend, which is responsible for serving the client request.

Layer 7 means that these load balancers are "smart" enough to exhibit load balancing behavior based on the OSI layer 7, application-specific characteristics. The OSI layer 7 is the *application* layer and is the closest layer to the end-user experience. As a result, this type of load balancers can route traffic based on—for example—HTTP headers, session affinity, specific URL patterns, and many other layer 7 features. None of these traffic routing and distribution capabilities are available to layer 4 load balancers.

External HTTP(S) load balancers distribute HTTP and HTTPS traffic to backend services hosted on a number of Google Cloud compute services (such as Compute Engine, Google Kubernetes Engine (GKE), Cloud Run, and many others), as well as backend buckets hosted on Google Cloud Storage. External backends can also be connected over the Internet or via hybrid connectivity.

Before delving into more details, it is important to emphasize the *scope* of the load balancer, that is, global vs. regional.

A regional (external HTTP(S)) load balancer is intended to serve content from a specific region, whereas a global (external HTTP(S)) load balancer is intended to serve content from multiple regions around the world. A typical use case for a regional (external HTTP(S)) load balancer is compliance due to sovereignty laws requiring backends to operate in a specific geolocation.

Because of that, global external HTTP(S) load balancers leverage a specific Google infrastructure, which is distributed globally in the Google Edge Network and operates using Google's global backbone network and Google's control plane. This infrastructure is called the Google Front End (GFE) and uses the CIDR blocks 130.211.0.0/22, 35.191.0.0/16.

■ **Exam tip**   There are a few IP ranges you need to remember for the exam. The GFE ones, that is, 130.211.0.0/22, 35.191.0.0/16, are definitely in the list to be remembered.

Modes of Operation

An external HTTP(S) load balancer comes in three "flavors":

- **Global external HTTP(S) load balancer**: This is the load balancer type 1 in Figure 5-1 and is implemented as a managed service on Google Front Ends (GFEs). It uses the open source Envoy proxy to support advanced traffic management capabilities such as traffic mirroring, weight-based traffic splitting, request/response-based header transformations, and more.

- **Global external HTTP(S) load balancer (classic)**: This is the load balancer type 2 in Figure 5-1 and is global in premium tier, but can be configured to be regional in standard tier. This load balancer is also implemented on Google Front Ends (GFEs).

- **Regional external HTTP(S) load balancer**: This is the load balancer type 5 in Figure 5-1 and is implemented as a managed service on the open source Envoy proxy. It includes advanced traffic management capabilities such as traffic mirroring, weight-based traffic splitting, request/response-based header transformations, and more.

Architecture

The architecture of all external HTTP(S) load balancers (global and regional) shows common components, such as forwarding rules, target proxies, URL maps, backend services, and backends.

Yet, there are a few differences among the three types (1, 2, 5 in Figure 5-1) we just described.

Instead of listing each common component of the architecture, and explaining what its intended purpose is, and how it differs across the three types, I like to visualize them in a picture and go from there.

Figure 5-5 illustrates the architecture of the two global external HTTP(S) load balancers ("regular" and classic, respectively, types 1 and 2), whereas the bottom part shows the regional external HTTP(S) load balancer (type 5) architecture. Let's start from the client, located in the very left part of the figure.

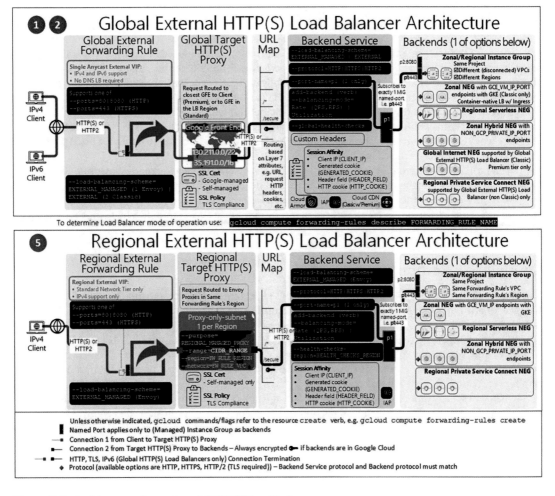

Figure 5-5. *Architecture of an external HTTP(S) load balancer*

Forwarding Rule

An external forwarding rule specifies an external IP address, port, and target HTTP(S) proxy. Clients use the IP address and port to connect to the load balancer from the Internet.

■ **Exam tip** Type 1, 2, 5 load balancers only support HTTP and HTTPS traffic on TCP ports 80 (or 8080) and TCP port 443, respectively. If your clients require access to your workload backend services using different TCP (or UDP) ports, consider using load balancer types 3, 4, 6, 7, 8, 9 instead (Figure 5-1). More information will be provided in the upcoming sections.

Global forwarding rules support external IP addresses in IPv4 and IPv6 format, whereas regional forwarding rules only support external IP addresses in IPv4 format.

Target HTTP(S) Proxy

A target HTTP(S) proxy receives a request from the client and terminates the HTTP connection or the TLS connection—if the protocol of the request is HTTPS. This behavior is denoted in Figure 5-5 by splitting the black line from the client to one of the backends into two lines. The split happens in the GFE in the case of global external HTTP(S) load balancers and in a specially designated subnet—hosted in the same region of the load balancer—in the case of regional external HTTP(S) load balancers.

As an effect of terminating the connection, the original client IP is no longer accessible in the second connection, that is, the connection that starts at the target HTTP(S) proxy and ends in one of the backends. For these types of load balancer, responses from the backend VMs go back to the target HTTP(S) proxy, instead of reaching directly the client.

Upon terminating the connection, the target HTTP(S) proxy evaluates the request by using the URL map (and other layer 7 attributes) to make traffic routing decisions.

For HTTPS requests, the target HTTP(S) proxy can also leverage SSL certificates to identify itself to clients and SSL policies to enforce TLS compliance, for example, to accept only TLS handshakes if the TLS version is greater than or equal to 1.2.

Multiple SSL Certificates

You attach the SSL certificate to the load balancer's HTTP(S) target proxy either while creating the load balancer or any time after. Any changes made to SSL certificates don't alter or interrupt existing load balancer connections.

You can configure up to the maximum number of SSL certificates per target HTTP(S) proxy (there is a quota to limit the number of certificates). Use multiple SSL certificates when your workload is serving content from multiple domains using the same load balancer VIP address and port, and you want to use a different SSL certificate for each domain.

When you specify more than one SSL certificate, the first certificate in the list of SSL certificates is considered the primary SSL certificate associated with the target proxy, as illustrated in Figure 5-6.

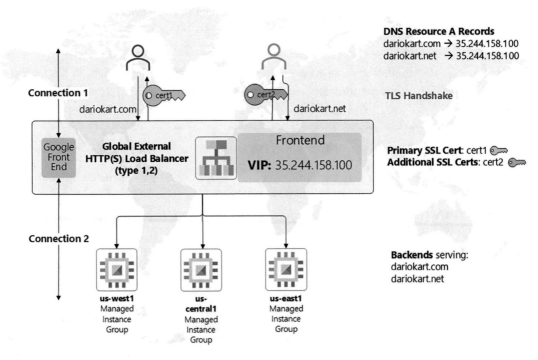

Figure 5-6. *Multiple SSL certificates feature of global HTTP(S) load balancer*

Self-Managed and Google-Managed SSL Certificates

Self-managed SSL certificates are certificates that you obtain, provision, and renew yourself. This type can be any of

- Domain Validation (DV)
- Organization Validation (OV)
- Extended Validation (EV) certificates

Google-managed SSL certificates are certificates that Google Cloud obtains and manages for your domains, renewing them automatically. Google-managed certificates are Domain Validation (DV) certificates. They don't demonstrate the identity of an organization or individual associated with the certificate, and they don't support wildcard common names.

All global external HTTP(S) load balancers support Google-managed and self-managed SSL certificates, whereas regional external HTTP(S) load balancers only support self-managed SSL certificates.

SSL Policies

From now on, the term SSL refers to both the SSL (Secure Sockets Layer) and TLS (Transport Layer Security) protocols.

SSL policies define the set of TLS features that external HTTP(S) load balancers use when negotiating SSL with clients.

For example, you can use an SSL policy to configure the minimum TLS version and features that every client should comply with in order to send traffic to your external HTTP(S) load balancer.

■ **Exam tip**   SSL policies affect only connections between clients and the target HTTP(S) proxy (Connection 1 in Figure 5-5). SSL policies do not affect the connections between the target HTTP(S) proxy and the backends (Connection 2).

To define an SSL policy, you specify a minimum TLS version and a profile. The profile selects a set of SSL features to enable in the load balancer.

Three preconfigured Google-managed profiles let you specify the level of compatibility appropriate for your application. The three preconfigured profiles are as follows:

- **COMPATIBLE**: Allows the broadest set of clients, including clients that support only out-of-date SSL features, to negotiate SSL with the load balancer

- **MODERN**: Supports a wide set of SSL features, allowing modern clients to negotiate SSL

- **RESTRICTED**: Supports a reduced set of SSL features, intended to meet stricter compliance requirements

A fourth CUSTOM profile lets you select SSL features individually.

The SSL policy also specifies the minimum version of the TLS protocol that clients can use to establish a connection. A profile can also restrict the versions of TLS that the load balancer can negotiate. For example, ciphers enabled in the RESTRICTED profile are only supported by TLS 1.2. Choosing the RESTRICTED profile effectively requires clients to use TLS 1.2 regardless of the chosen minimum TLS version.

If you do not choose one of the three preconfigured profiles or create a custom SSL policy, your load balancer uses the default SSL policy. The default SSL policy is equivalent to an SSL policy that uses the COMPATIBLE profile with a minimum TLS version of TLS 1.0.

Use the `gcloud compute target-https-proxies create` or `update` commands to attach an SSL policy (`--ssl-policy`) to your target HTTP(S) proxy.

■ **Exam tip**   You can attach an SSL policy to more than one target HTTP(S) proxy. However, you cannot configure more than one SSL policy for a particular target proxy. Any changes made to SSL policies don't alter or interrupt existing load balancer connections.

URL Map

The target HTTP(S) proxy uses a URL map to decide where to route the new request (Connection 2 in Figure 5-5)—remember the first request, which carried the original client IP, has been terminated.

Since the HTTP(S) load balancer operates at layer 7, it is fully capable of determining where to route the request based on HTTP attributes (i.e., the request path, cookies, or headers). When I say "where to route the request," I really mean to which backend service or backend bucket the target HTTP(S) proxy should route the request to.

In fact, the target HTTP(S) proxy forwards client requests to specific backend services or backend buckets. The URL map can also specify additional actions, such as sending redirects to clients.

Backend Service

A backend service distributes requests to healthy backends. Unlike regional global external HTTP(S) load balancers, the two global external HTTP(S) load balancers also support backend buckets. The key components of a backend service are

- **Scope** defined by one of the two flags:

  - **Global** (`--global`) to indicate the backend service operates with backends located in multiple regions

  - **Regional** (`--region=REGION`) to indicate the backend service operates with backends located in the specified region

- **Load balancing scheme** specifies the load balancer type. Set the scheme to `EXTERNAL_MANAGED` for types 1 and 5 load balancers because they both use the Envoy open source. Set the scheme to `EXTERNAL` for type 2, that is, global external HTTP(S) load balancer (classic).

- **Protocol** is the protocol the backend service uses to communicate to the backends (MIGs, various types of NEGs, buckets). The only available options are HTTP, HTTPS, and HTTP/2. This selection is "unforgiving" in that the load balancer does not fall back to one of the other protocols if it is unable to negotiate a connection to the backend with the specified protocol. HTTP/2 requires TLS.

- **Port name** is only applicable to backends whose type is instance groups. Each instance group backend exports a list including one or more named ports (see the `gcloud compute instance-groups get-named-ports` command), which map a user-configurable name to a port number. The backend service's port name subscribes to exactly one named port on each instance group. The resolved port number is used by the backend service to send traffic to the backend.

- **Health check** is the resource used by a backend service to ensure incoming requests are sent to healthy backends. For global external HTTP(S) load balancer health check probes, you must create in the load balancer VPC an ingress allow firewall rule that allows traffic to reach your backends from the GFE CIDR blocks, that is, `130.211.0.0/22` and `35.191.0.0/16`. For regional external HTTP(S) load balancers, you must create in the load balancer VPC an ingress allow firewall rule that allows traffic to reach your backends from the CIDR block of the *proxy-only* subnet. Although it is not required, it is a best practice to use a health check whose protocol matches the protocol of the backend service.

- **Timeout** is the amount of time (in seconds) that the backend service waits for a backend to return a full response to a request. If the backend does not reply at all, the load balancer returns a 502 Bad Gateway error to the client.

- **Enable Cloud CDN (Content Delivery Network)** is used to enable Cloud CDN for the backend service. Cloud CDN caches HTTP responses at the edge of Google's network. Cloud CDN is disabled by default. Use `--enable-cdn` to enable and `--no-enable-cdn` to disable.

- **Identity-Aware Proxy (IAP)**: If enabled, you can provide values for `oauth2-client-id` and `oauth2-client-secret`. For example, `--iap=enabled,oauth2-client-id=foo,oauth2-client-secret=bar` turns IAP on, and `--iap=disabled` turns it off.

- **Connection draining timeout** is used during removal of VMs from instance groups. This guarantees that for the specified time all existing connections to a VM will remain untouched, but no new connections will be accepted. This defaults to zero seconds, that is, connection draining is disabled.

- **Session affinity** must be one of

  - CLIENT_IP, that is, routes requests to instances based on the hash of the client's IP address.

  - GENERATED_COOKIE, that is, routes requests to backend VMs or endpoints in a NEG based on the contents of the cookie set by the load balancer.

  - HEADER_FIELD, that is, routes requests to backend VMs or endpoints in a NEG based on the value of the HTTP header named in the `--custom-request-header` flag.

  - HTTP_COOKIE, that is, routes requests to backend VMs or endpoints in a NEG based on an HTTP cookie named in the HTTP_COOKIE flag (with the optional `--affinity-cookie-ttl` flag). If the client has not provided the cookie, the target HTTP(S) proxy generates the cookie and returns it to the client in a `Set-Cookie` header.

  - NONE, that is, session affinity is disabled.

Backends

Backends are the ultimate destination of your load balancer incoming traffic.

Upon receiving a packet, they perform computation on its payload, and they send a response back to the client.

As shown in Figure 5-5, the type of backend depends on the scope of the external HTTP(S) load balancer, as well as its network tier.

In gcloud, you can add a backend to a backend service using the `gcloud compute backend-services add-backend` command.

When you add an instance group or a NEG to a backend service, you specify a balancing mode, which defines a method measuring backend load and a target capacity. External HTTP(S) load balancing supports two balancing modes:

- RATE, for instance groups or NEGs, is the target maximum number of requests (queries) per second (RPS, QPS). The target maximum RPS/QPS can be exceeded if all backends are at or above capacity.

- UTILIZATION is the backend utilization of VMs in an instance group.

How traffic is distributed among backends depends on the mode of the load balancer.

Container-Native Global HTTP(S) Load Balancing Deep Dive

In this exercise, you will learn how to configure container-native load balancing using a global external HTTP(S) load balancer.

As we mentioned in Chapter 2, when a load balancer—the target HTTP(S) proxy of the load balancer to be precise—can use containers as backends (instead of VMs or other endpoints), this type of load balancing is called *container-native load balancing*. Container-native load balancing allows load balancers to target Kubernetes pods directly and to evenly distribute traffic to pods.

There are several ways to create the networking infrastructure required for the load balancer to operate in container-native mode. You will learn two ways to accomplish this.

The first way is called *container-native load balancing through ingress*, and its main advantage is that all you have to code is the GKE cluster that will host your containers, a deployment for your workload, a service to mediate access to the pods hosting your containers, and a Kubernetes ingress resource to allow requests to be properly distributed among your pods. The deployment, the service, and the Kubernetes ingress can all be coded declaratively using YAML files, as we'll see shortly.

Upon creating these four components, Google Cloud does the job for you by creating the global external HTTP(S) load balancer (classic), along with all the components you learned so far. These are the backend service, the NEG, the backends, the health checks, the firewall rules, the target HTTP(S) proxy, and the forwarding rule. Not bad, right?

In the second way, we let Google Cloud create only the NEG for you. In addition to the GKE cluster, your workload deployment, and the Kubernetes service, you will have to create all the load balancing infrastructure earlier. This approach is called *container-native load balancing through standalone zonal NEGs*.

While this approach sounds like more Infrastructure as a Service oriented, it will help you consolidate the knowledge you need in order to master the configuration of a global external HTTP(S) load balancer that operates in container-native load balancing mode. Let's get started!

Container-Native Load Balancing Through Ingress

As shown in Figure 5-7, we start by creating a GKE VPC-native, zonal cluster, whose worker nodes are hosted in the service project frontend-devs of our shared VPC.

```
Welcome to Cloud Shell! Type "help" to get started.
Your Cloud Platform project in this session is set to frontend-devs-7734.
Use "gcloud config set project [PROJECT_ID]" to change to a different project.
joseph@cloudshell:~ (frontend-devs-7734)$ gcloud container clusters create frontend-cluster --project=frontend-devs-7734 --zone=us-east1-d --enable
-ip-alias --network=projects/vpc-host-nonprod-pu645-uh372/global/networks/your-app-shared-vpc --subnetwork=projects/vpc-host-nonprod-pu645-uh372/re
gions/us-east1/subnetworks/subnet-frontend --cluster-secondary-range-name=pod-cidr-frontend  --services-secondary-range-name=service-cidr-frontend
--num-nodes=2 --max-pods-per-node=10
Default change: During creation of nodepools or autoscaling configuration changes for cluster versions greater than 1.24.1-gke.800 a default locati
on policy is applied. For Spot and PVM it defaults to ANY, and for all other VM kinds a BALANCED policy is used. To change the default values use t
he `--location-policy` flag.
Note: The Pod address range limits the maximum size of the cluster. Please refer to https://cloud.google.com/kubernetes-engine/docs/how-to/flexible
-pod-cidr to learn how to optimize IP address allocation.
Creating cluster frontend-cluster in us-east1-d... Cluster is being health-checked (master is healthy)...done.
Created [https://container.googleapis.com/v1/projects/frontend-devs-7734/zones/us-east1-d/clusters/frontend-cluster].
To inspect the contents of your cluster, go to: https://console.cloud.google.com/kubernetes/workload_/gcloud/us-east1-d/frontend-cluster?project=fr
ontend-devs-7734
kubeconfig entry generated for frontend-cluster.
NAME: frontend-cluster
LOCATION: us-east1-d
MASTER_VERSION: 1.23.12-gke.100
MASTER_IP: 35.243.139.198
MACHINE_TYPE: e2-medium
NODE_VERSION: 1.23.12-gke.100
NUM_NODES: 2
STATUS: RUNNING
joseph@cloudshell:~ (frontend-devs-7734)$ []
```

Figure 5-7. *Creating a GKE zonal cluster in* subnet-frontend

Figures 5-8, 5-9, and 5-10 display the YAML manifests for the workload deployment, the service, and the ingress Kubernetes resources, respectively.

```
apiVersion: apps/v1
kind: Deployment
metadata:
  labels:
    run: neg-demo-app # Label for the Deployment
  name: neg-demo-app # Name of Deployment
spec:
  selector:
    matchLabels:
      run: neg-demo-app
  template: # Pod template
    metadata:
      labels:
        run: neg-demo-app # Labels Pods from this Deployment
    spec: # Pod specification; each Pod created by this Deployment has this specification
      containers:
      - image: k8s.gcr.io/serve_hostname:v1.4 # Application to run in Deployment's Pods
        name: hostname # Container name
        ports:
        - containerPort: 9376
          protocol: TCP


~
~
~
~
~
~
-- INSERT --
```

Figure 5-8. *Kubernetes deployment manifest*

```
apiVersion: v1
kind: Service
metadata:
  name: neg-demo-svc # Name of Service
  annotations:
    cloud.google.com/neg: '{"ingress": true}' # Creates a NEG after an Ingress is created
spec: # Service's specification
  type: ClusterIP
  selector:
    run: neg-demo-app # Selects Pods labelled run: neg-demo-app
  ports:
  - name: http
    port: 80 # Service's port
    protocol: TCP
    targetPort: 9376
~
~
~
~
~
~
~
~
~
~
~
~
~
~
-- INSERT --
```

Figure 5-9. *Kubernetes service manifest*

```
apiVersion: networking.k8s.io/v1
kind: Ingress
metadata:
  name: neg-demo-ing
spec:
  defaultBackend:
    service:
      name: neg-demo-svc # Name of the Service targeted by the Ingress
      port:
        number: 80 # Should match the port used by the Service█
~
~
~
~
~
~
~
~
~
~
~
~
~
~
~
~
~
~
-- INSERT --
```

Figure 5-10. *Kubernetes ingress manifest*

As shown in Figure 5-9, the service targets the sample deployment.

■ **Note** The Service's annotation, `cloud.google.com/neg: '{"ingress": true}'`, enables container-native load balancing. However, the load balancer is not created until you create an Ingress for the Service.

Next, we use the manifests to create a deployment (Figure 5-11), a service (Figure 5-12), and an ingress (Figure 5-13) Kubernetes resource.

```
joseph@cloudshell:~/neg-demo (frontend-devs-7734)$ kubectl apply -f neg-demo-app.yaml
deployment.apps/neg-demo-app created
```

Figure 5-11. *Creating a Kubernetes deployment*

```
joseph@cloudshell:~/neg-demo (frontend-devs-7734)$ kubectl apply -f neg-demo-svc.yaml
service/neg-demo-svc created
joseph@cloudshell:~/neg-demo (frontend-devs-7734)$
```

Figure 5-12. *Creating a Kubernetes service*

233

```
joseph@cloudshell:~/neg-demo (frontend-devs-7734)$ kubectl apply -f neg-demo-ing.yaml
ingress.networking.k8s.io/neg-demo-ing created
joseph@cloudshell:~/neg-demo (frontend-devs-7734)$
```

Figure 5-13. *Creating a Kubernetes ingress*

The creation of a Kubernetes ingress had the effect of triggering a number of actions behind the scenes. These included the creation of the following resources in the project frontend-devs:

1. A global external HTTP(S) load balancer (classic).

2. A target HTTP(S) proxy.

3. A backend service in each zone—in our case, since the cluster is a single zone, we have only a backend service in us-east1-d.

4. A global health check attached to the backend service.

5. A NEG in us-east1-d. The endpoints in the NEG and the endpoints of the Service are kept in sync.

Figure 5-14 displays the description of the newly created Kubernetes ingress resource.

```
joseph@cloudshell:~/neg-demo (frontend-devs-7734)$ kubectl apply -f neg-demo-ing.yaml
ingress.networking.k8s.io/neg-demo-ing created
joseph@cloudshell:~/neg-demo (frontend-devs-7734)$ kubectl describe ingress neg-demo-ing
Name:             neg-demo-ing
Labels:           <none>
Namespace:        default
Address:          34.95.111.178
Ingress Class:    <none>
Default backend:  neg-demo-svc:80 (<none>)
Rules:
  Host        Path  Backends
  ----        ----  --------
  *           *     neg-demo-svc:80 (<none>)
Annotations:  ingress.kubernetes.io/backends: {"k8s1-79c41ca3-default-neg-demo-svc-80-21c90b65":"Unknown"}
              ingress.kubernetes.io/forwarding-rule: k8s2-fr-ra6yx58t-default-neg-demo-ing-8x5gfz84
              ingress.kubernetes.io/target-proxy: k8s2-tp-ra6yx58t-default-neg-demo-ing-8x5gfz84
              ingress.kubernetes.io/url-map: k8s2-um-ra6yx58t-default-neg-demo-ing-8x5gfz84
Events:
  Type    Reason      Age                From                    Message
  ----    ------      ----               ----                    -------
  Normal  Sync        35s                loadbalancer-controller  UrlMap "k8s2-um-ra6yx58t-default-neg-demo-ing-8x5gfz84" created
  Normal  Sync        33s                loadbalancer-controller  TargetProxy "k8s2-tp-ra6yx58t-default-neg-demo-ing-8x5gfz84" created
  Normal  Sync        23s (x4 over 71s)  loadbalancer-controller  Scheduled for sync
  Normal  Sync        23s                loadbalancer-controller  ForwardingRule "k8s2-fr-ra6yx58t-default-neg-demo-ing-8x5gfz84" created
  Normal  IPChanged   23s                loadbalancer-controller  IP is now 34.95.111.178
  Normal  XPN         22s (x4 over 70s)  loadbalancer-controller  Firewall change required by security admin: `gcloud compute firewall-rules create
k8s-fw-l7--79c41ca3a2d4ec1f --network your-app-shared-vpc --description "GCE L7 firewall rule" --allow tcp:9376 --source-ranges 130.211.0.0/22,35.1
91.0.0/16 --target-tags gke-frontend-cluster-58d11162-node --project vpc-host-nonprod-pu645-uh372`
joseph@cloudshell:~/neg-demo (frontend-devs-7734)$
```

Figure 5-14. *Describing Kubernetes ingress*

■ **Note**   Since we deployed the GKE cluster in a shared VPC network, the kubectl command notified us that a firewall rule in the shared VPC your-app-shared-vpc is required to allow ingress traffic from the GFE CIDR blocks to the GKE cluster worker nodes using the deployment port and protocol tcp:9376.

User joseph@dariokart.com doesn't have the permission to add the required firewall rule, but itsmedario@dariokart.com does, as you can see in Figure 5-15.

```
itsmedario@cloudshell:~ (vpc-host-nonprod-pu645-uh372)$ gcloud compute firewall-rules create k8s-fw-17--79c41ca3a2d4ec1f --network your-app-shared-
vpc --description "GCE L7 firewall rule" --allow tcp:9376 --source-ranges 130.211.0.0/22,35.191.0.0/16 --target-tags gke-frontend-cluster-58d11162-
node --project vpc-host-nonprod-pu645-uh372
Creating firewall...working..Created [https://www.googleapis.com/compute/v1/projects/vpc-host-nonprod-pu645-uh372/global/firewalls/k8s-fw-17--79c41
ca3a2d4ec1f].
Creating firewall...done.
NAME: k8s-fw-17--79c41ca3a2d4ec1f
NETWORK: your-app-shared-vpc
DIRECTION: INGRESS
PRIORITY: 1000
ALLOW: tcp:9376
DENY:
DISABLED: False
itsmedario@cloudshell:~ (vpc-host-nonprod-pu645-uh372)$
```

Figure 5-15. *Creating a firewall rule to allow health checks to access backends*

In our example, when we tested the load balancer, we received a 502 status code "Bad Gateway" (Figure 5-16).

```
joseph@cloudshell:~/neg-demo (frontend-devs-7734)$ curl -s -I http://34.95.111.178/
HTTP/1.1 502 Bad Gateway
Transfer-Encoding: chunked
Date: Wed, 30 Nov 2022 03:37:17 GMT

joseph@cloudshell:~/neg-demo (frontend-devs-7734)$
```

Figure 5-16. *Testing the load balancer*

There are a number of reasons why the test returned a 502 error. For more information on how to troubleshoot 502 errors, see `https://cloud.google.com/load-balancing/docs/https/troubleshooting-ext-https-lbs`.

This exercise was intended to show you the automatic creation of the load balancer and all its components from the declarative configuration of the ingress manifest and the annotation in the Kubernetes service manifest.

If you are curious to learn more, I pulled the logs and I discovered that the target HTTP(S) proxy was unable to pick the backends (Figure 5-17). Can you discover the root cause?

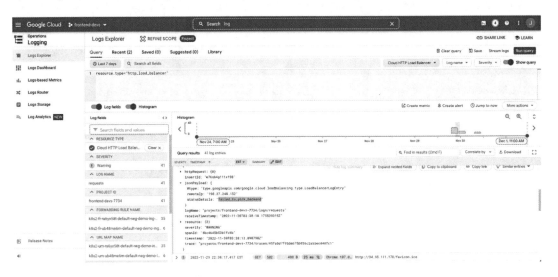

Figure 5-17. *Failed to pick backend 502 error*

```
cpu                           263m (27%)        0 (0%)
memory                        467179136 (15%)   1125Mi (39%)
ephemeral-storage             0 (0%)            0 (0%)
hugepages-1Gi                 0 (0%)            0 (0%)
hugepages-2Mi                 0 (0%)            0 (0%)
attachable-volumes-gce-pd     0                 0
Events:
  Type     Reason                   Age               From              Message
  ----     ------                   ----              ----              -------
  Normal   Starting                 40m               kubelet           Starting kubelet.
  Warning  InvalidDiskCapacity      40m               kubelet           invalid capacity 0 on image filesystem
  Normal   NodeAllocatableEnforced  40m               kubelet           Updated Node Allocatable limit across pods
  Normal   NodeHasNoDiskPressure    40m (x7 over 40m) kubelet           Node gke-frontend-cluster-default-pool-9641aa2d-r73g status is now: NodeHas
NoDiskPressure
  Normal   NodeHasSufficientPID     40m (x7 over 40m) kubelet           Node gke-frontend-cluster-default-pool-9641aa2d-r73g status is now: NodeHas
SufficientPID
  Normal   NodeHasSufficientMemory  39m (x8 over 40m) kubelet           Node gke-frontend-cluster-default-pool-9641aa2d-r73g status is now: NodeHas
SufficientMemory
  Normal   RegisteredNode           37m               node-controller   Node gke-frontend-cluster-default-pool-9641aa2d-r73g event: Registered Node
gke-frontend-cluster-default-pool-9641aa2d-r73g in Controller
  Warning  ContainerdStart          37m (x2 over 37m) systemd-monitor   Starting containerd container runtime...
  Warning  DockerStart              37m (x3 over 37m) systemd-monitor   Starting Docker Application Container Engine...
  Warning  KubeletStart             37m               systemd-monitor   Started Kubernetes kubelet.
joseph@cloudshell:~/neg-demo (frontend-devs-7734)$ gcloud container clusters delete frontend-cluster --zone=us-east1-d
The following clusters will be deleted.
 - [frontend-cluster] in [us-east1-d]

Do you want to continue (Y/n)?  Y

Deleting cluster frontend-cluster...done.
Deleted [https://container.googleapis.com/v1/projects/frontend-devs-7734/zones/us-east1-d/clusters/frontend-cluster].
joseph@cloudshell:~/neg-demo (frontend-devs-7734)$ █
```

Figure 5-18. *Deleting* frontend-cluster

Last, let's clean up the resources we just created in order to avoid incurring unexpected charges (Figure 5-18). Notice how the --zone flag is provided because the nodes of the cluster are VMs, and VMs are zonal resources.

It's worth to mention that by deleting the cluster, Google Cloud takes care of automatically deleting the load balancer and all its components except the NEG (this is a known issue) and the firewall rule we had to create in the shared VPC (this is because we deployed the cluster in a shared VPC).

You will have to manually delete these two resources.

Container-Native Load Balancing Through Standalone Zonal NEGs

Another approach to configuring container-native load balancing is to use standalone, zonal NEGs instead of an ingress Kubernetes resource.

This approach requires more work at the expense of higher flexibility.

To make it simpler, as we will be typing a number of gcloud commands, let's set some environment variables (Figure 5-19).

```
samuele@cloudshell:~/neg-demo (backend-devs-7736)$ PROJECT_ID=$(gcloud config list project --format='value(core.project)')
samuele@cloudshell:~/neg-demo (backend-devs-7736)$ ZONE=us-central1-a
samuele@cloudshell:~/neg-demo (backend-devs-7736)$ CLUSTER_NAME=neg-demo-cluster
```

Figure 5-19. *Setting environment variables*

Next, let's create another GKE VPC-native, zonal cluster, this time in the subnet-backend, which is also hosted in your-app-shared-vpc and is located in the region us-central1 (Figure 5-20).

```
samuele@cloudshell:~ (backend-devs-7736)$ PROJECT_ID=$(gcloud config list project --format='value(core.project)')
samuele@cloudshell:~ (backend-devs-7736)$ ZONE=us-central1-a
samuele@cloudshell:~ (backend-devs-7736)$ CLUSTER_NAME=neg-demo-cluster
samuele@cloudshell:~ (backend-devs-7736)$ gcloud container clusters create $CLUSTER_NAME --project=$PROJECT_ID --zone=$ZONE --enable-ip-alias --net
work=projects/vpc-host-nonprod-pu645-uh372/global/networks/your-app-shared-vpc --subnetwork=projects/vpc-host-nonprod-pu645-uh372/regions/us-centra
l1/subnetworks/subnet-backend --cluster-secondary-range-name=pod-cidr-backend  --services-secondary-range-name=service-cidr-backend --num-nodes=2 -
-max-pods-per-node=10 --preemptible
Default change: During creation of nodepools or autoscaling configuration changes for cluster versions greater than 1.24.1-gke.800 a default locati
on policy is applied. For Spot and PVM it defaults to ANY, and for all other VM kinds a BALANCED policy is used. To change the default values use t
he `--location-policy` flag.
Note: The Pod address range limits the maximum size of the cluster. Please refer to https://cloud.google.com/kubernetes-engine/docs/how-to/flexible
-pod-cidr to learn how to optimize IP address allocation.
Creating cluster neg-demo-cluster in us-central1-a... Cluster is being health-checked (master is healthy)...done.
Created [https://container.googleapis.com/v1/projects/backend-devs-7736/zones/us-central1-a/clusters/neg-demo-cluster].
To inspect the contents of your cluster, go to: https://console.cloud.google.com/kubernetes/workload_/gcloud/us-central1-a/neg-demo-cluster?project
=backend-devs-7736
kubeconfig entry generated for neg-demo-cluster.
NAME: neg-demo-cluster
LOCATION: us-central1-a
MASTER_VERSION: 1.23.12-gke.100
MASTER_IP: 104.154.236.218
MACHINE_TYPE: e2-medium
NODE_VERSION: 1.23.12-gke.100
NUM_NODES: 2
STATUS: RUNNING
samuele@cloudshell:~ (backend-devs-7736)$
```

Figure 5-20. *Creating* `neg-demo-cluster`

Unlike before, in this exercise we just create two Kubernetes resources (instead of three), that is, a deployment and a service, which targets the deployment. There is no ingress Kubernetes resource created this time.

The manifest YAML files for the deployment and the service are displayed in Figures 5-21 and 5-22, respectively.

```
apiVersion: apps/v1
kind: Deployment
metadata:
  name: nginx
spec:
  replicas: 3
  selector:
    matchLabels:
      app: nginx
  template:
    metadata:
      labels:
        app: nginx
    spec:
      containers:
      - name: nginx
        image: nginx:latest
        ports:
        - containerPort: 80
~
~
~
~
~
~
~
~
~
~
~
~
"app-deployment.yaml" 19L, 305B
```

Figure 5-21. *Kubernetes deployment manifest*

```
 1 apiVersion: v1
 2 kind: Service
 3 metadata:
 4   name: app-service
 5   annotations:
 6     cloud.google.com/neg: '{"exposed_ports": {"80":{"name": "app-service-80-neg"}}}'
 7     #cloud.google.com/neg: '{"ingress": true}' # Creates a NEG after an Ingress is created
 8 spec:
 9   type: ClusterIP
10   ports:
11   - port: 80
12     targetPort: 80
13   selector:
14     app: nginx
~
~
~
~
~
~
~
~
~
~
~
~
~
~
~
~
:se nu
```

Figure 5-22. *Kubernetes service manifest*

Notice the difference between the two in the metadata.annotation section of the manifest (Figure 5-22, lines 5–7).

During the creation of the service, the Kubernetes-GKE system integrator reads the annotation section, and—this time—it doesn't tell Google Cloud to create the load balancer and all its components anymore (line 7 in Figure 5-22 is commented).

Let's see what happens after creating the deployment and the service (Figure 5-23).

```
samuele@cloudshell:~/neg-demo (backend-devs-7736)$ kubectl apply -f app-deployment.yaml
deployment.apps/nginx created
samuele@cloudshell:~/neg-demo (backend-devs-7736)$ kubectl apply -f app-service.yaml
service/app-service created
```

Figure 5-23. *Creating a Kubernetes deployment and a service*

As you can see from line 6 of Figure 5-22, we are telling the Kubernetes-GKE system integrator to create a new NEG named app-service-80-neg. In accordance with the declarative statement in line 6, we are telling that this NEG should listen to TCP port 80 in order to distribute incoming HTTP requests to the pods hosting our app deployment. With container-native load balancing, the pods hosting our deployment are the backends serving incoming HTTP traffic.

To validate what we just described, let's list the NEGs in our project (Figure 5-24).

```
samuele@cloudshell:~/neg-demo (backend-devs-7736)$ gcloud compute network-endpoint-groups list
NAME: app-service-80-neg
LOCATION: us-central1-a
ENDPOINT_TYPE: GCE_VM_IP_PORT
SIZE: 0
samuele@cloudshell:~/neg-demo (backend-devs-7736)$ ▌
```

Figure 5-24. *Listing network endpoint groups*

Indeed, here it is! Our newly created NEG uses a `GCE_VM_IP_PORT` endpoint type to indicate that incoming HTTP(S) requests resolve to either the primary internal IP address of a Google Cloud VM's NIC (one of the GKE worker nodes, i.e., `192.168.1.0/26`) or an alias IP address on a NIC, for example, pod IP addresses in our VPC-native clusters `neg-demo-cluster`, that is, `192.168.15.0/24`.

See Figure 3-11 as a reminder of the list of usable subnets for containers in our shared VPC setup in Chapter 3.

So, now that you have your NEG ready, what's next? With *container-native load balancing through standalone zonal NEGs*, all you have automatically created is your NEG, nothing else. To put this NEG to work—literally, so the endpoints (pods) in the NEG can start serving HTTP(S) requests—you are responsible for creating all required load balancing infrastructure to use the NEG.

I'll quickly walk you through this process to get you familiarized with each component of an external global HTTP(S) load balancer as well as the related `gcloud` commands.

First, we need an ingress firewall rule to allow health check probes and incoming HTTP(S) traffic to reach the NEG. Incoming traffic originates at the start point of Connection 2 in Figure 5-5, which in our case is the GFE because our external HTTP(S) load balancer is global. The target of the ingress firewall rule is the GKE worker nodes, whose network tags are assigned at creation time by GKE, as shown in Figure 5-25.

```
samuele@cloudshell:~/neg-demo (backend-devs-7736)$ # find the network tags used by our cluster
NETWORK_TAGS=$(gcloud compute instances describe \
    $(kubectl get nodes -o jsonpath='{.items[0].metadata.name}') \
    --zone=$ZONE --format="value(tags.items[0])")
samuele@cloudshell:~/neg-demo (backend-devs-7736)$ echo $NETWORK_TAGS
gke-neg-demo-cluster-5aa1851a-node
samuele@cloudshell:~/neg-demo (backend-devs-7736)$
```

Figure 5-25. *Determining GKE worker nodes' network tags*

Since our network setup uses a shared VPC, the principal `samule@dariokart.com` is not responsible for managing the network.

Let's set the `CLUSTER_NAME` and `NETWORK_TAGS` environment variables for a principal who has permissions to create the firewall rule, for example, `itsmedario@dariokart.com` (Figure 5-26).

```
itsmedario@cloudshell:~ (vpc-host-nonprod-pu645-uh372)$ CLUSTER_NAME=neg-demo-cluster
itsmedario@cloudshell:~ (vpc-host-nonprod-pu645-uh372)$ NETWORK_TAGS=gke-neg-demo-cluster-5aa1851a-node
```

Figure 5-26. *Setting environment variables for itsmedario@dariokart.com*

Now, we can create the ingress firewall rule (Figure 5-27).

```
itsmedario@cloudshell:~ (vpc-host-nonprod-pu645-uh372)$ gcloud compute firewall-rules create $CLUSTER_NAME-lb-fw --network your-app-shared-vpc --pr
oject vpc-host-nonprod-pu645-uh372   --allow tcp:80   --source-ranges 130.211.0.0/22,35.191.0.0/16   --target-tags $NETWORK_TAGS
Creating firewall...working..Created [https://www.googleapis.com/compute/v1/projects/vpc-host-nonprod-pu645-uh372/global/firewalls/neg-demo-cluster
-lb-fw].
Creating firewall...done.
NAME: neg-demo-cluster-lb-fw
NETWORK: your-app-shared-vpc
DIRECTION: INGRESS
PRIORITY: 1000
ALLOW: tcp:80
DENY:
DISABLED: False
itsmedario@cloudshell:~ (vpc-host-nonprod-pu645-uh372)$
```

Figure 5-27. *Creating ingress firewall rule*

Next, we switch back to principal samuele@dariokart.com because he is a backend developer in charge of owning all compute resources to build and run his workload, including the load balancer infrastructure.

We need to create the backend components, beginning from a health check, which will be attached to a new backend service. Upon creating the backend service, we need to add a backend, which is our newly created NEG in Figure 5-24.

Figure 5-28 describes the creation of the backend components of the HTTP(S) load balancer.

```
samuele@cloudshell:~/neg-demo (backend-devs-7736)$ gcloud compute health-checks create http app-service-80-health-check \
  --request-path / \
  --port 80 \                                              1. Create a health check
  --check-interval 60 \
  --unhealthy-threshold 3 \
  --healthy-threshold 1 \
  --timeout 5
Created [https://www.googleapis.com/compute/v1/projects/backend-devs-7736/global/healthChecks/app-service-80-health-check].
NAME: app-service-80-health-check
PROTOCOL: HTTP
samuele@cloudshell:~/neg-demo (backend-devs-7736)$ gcloud compute backend-services create $CLUSTER_NAME-lb-backend \
  --health-checks app-service-80-health-check \
  --port-name http \                                       2. Create a backend service
  --global \                                                  and attach the health check to it
  --enable-cdn \
  --connection-draining-timeout 300
Created [https://www.googleapis.com/compute/v1/projects/backend-devs-7736/global/backendServices/neg-demo-cluster-lb-backend]
NAME: neg-demo-cluster-lb-backend   This backend service will be the default service of the URL map used by the frontend
BACKENDS:
PROTOCOL: HTTP
samuele@cloudshell:~/neg-demo (backend-devs-7736)$ gcloud compute backend-services add-backend $CLUSTER_NAME-lb-backend \
  --network-endpoint-group=app-service-80-neg \
  --network-endpoint-group-zone=$ZONE \
  --balancing-mode=RATE \                                  3. Add a backend (NEG or MIG) to it
  --capacity-scaler=1.0 \
  --max-rate-per-endpoint=1.0 \
  --global
Updated [https://www.googleapis.com/compute/v1/projects/backend-devs-7736/global/backendServices/neg-demo-cluster-lb-backend]
samuele@cloudshell:~/neg-demo (backend-devs-7736)$ ▮
```

Figure 5-28. *Creating backend resources*

Last, we need to create the frontend components, that is, the URL map, which will be attached to a new target HTTP(S) proxy, which will be attached to a global forwarding rule.

Figure 5-29 describes the creation of the aforementioned frontend components of the HTTP(S) load balancer.

```
samuele@cloudshell:~/neg-demo (backend-devs-7736)$ gcloud compute url-maps create $CLUSTER_NAME-url-map \
  --default-service $CLUSTER_NAME-lb-backend   This is how your load balancer frontend and backend "talk" to each together
Created [https://www.googleapis.com/compute/v1/projects/backend-devs-7736/global/urlMaps/neg-demo-cluster-url-map].
NAME: neg-demo-cluster-url-map
DEFAULT_SERVICE: backendServices/neg-demo-cluster-lb-backend
samuele@cloudshell:~/neg-demo (backend-devs-7736)$ gcloud compute target-http-proxies create $CLUSTER_NAME-http-proxy \
  --url-map $CLUSTER_NAME-url-map
Created [https://www.googleapis.com/compute/v1/projects/backend-devs-7736/global/targetHttpProxies/neg-demo-cluster-http-proxy].
NAME: neg-demo-cluster-http-proxy
URL_MAP: neg-demo-cluster-url-map
samuele@cloudshell:~/neg-demo (backend-devs-7736)$ gcloud compute forwarding-rules create $CLUSTER_NAME-forwarding-rule \
  --global \
  --ports 80 \
  --target-http-proxy $CLUSTER_NAME-http-proxy
Created [https://www.googleapis.com/compute/v1/projects/backend-devs-7736/global/forwardingRules/neg-demo-cluster-forwarding-rule]
```

Figure 5-29. *Creating frontend resources*

Notice how the URL map uses the newly created backend service neg-demo-cluster-lb-backend to bridge the load balancer frontend and backend resources.

This is also visually represented in the URL map boxes in Figure 5-5.

As you can see, container-native load balancing through standalone zonal NEGs requires extra work on your end. However, you get more control and flexibility than using container-native load balancing through ingress because you create your own load balancing infrastructure and you configure it to your liking.

Last, remember to delete the load balancer components and the cluster to avoid incurring unexpected charges (Figure 5-30).

```
samuele@cloudshell:~/neg-demo (backend-devs-7736)$ curl -s -I http://$IP_ADDRESS/
HTTP/1.1 502 Bad Gateway
Transfer-Encoding: chunked
Date: Tue, 29 Nov 2022 03:05:50 GMT

samuele@cloudshell:~/neg-demo (backend-devs-7736)$ gcloud -q compute forwarding-rules delete $CLUSTER_NAME-forwarding-rule --global
Deleted [https://www.googleapis.com/compute/v1/projects/backend-devs-7736/global/forwardingRules/neg-demo-cluster-forwarding-rule].
samuele@cloudshell:~/neg-demo (backend-devs-7736)$ gcloud -q compute target-http-proxies delete $CLUSTER_NAME-http-proxy
Deleted [https://www.googleapis.com/compute/v1/projects/backend-devs-7736/global/targetHttpProxies/neg-demo-cluster-http-proxy].
samuele@cloudshell:~/neg-demo (backend-devs-7736)$ gcloud -q compute url-maps delete $CLUSTER_NAME-url-map
Deleted [https://www.googleapis.com/compute/v1/projects/backend-devs-7736/global/urlMaps/neg-demo-cluster-url-map].
samuele@cloudshell:~/neg-demo (backend-devs-7736)$ gcloud -q compute backend-services delete $CLUSTER_NAME-lb-backend --global
Deleted [https://www.googleapis.com/compute/v1/projects/backend-devs-7736/global/backendServices/neg-demo-cluster-lb-backend].
samuele@cloudshell:~/neg-demo (backend-devs-7736)$ gcloud -q compute health-checks delete app-service-80-health-check
Deleted [https://www.googleapis.com/compute/v1/projects/backend-devs-7736/global/healthChecks/app-service-80-health-check].
samuele@cloudshell:~/neg-demo (backend-devs-7736)$ gcloud -q container clusters delete $CLUSTER_NAME --zone=$ZONE
Deleting cluster neg-demo-cluster...done.
Deleted [https://container.googleapis.com/v1/projects/backend-devs-7736/zones/us-central1-a/clusters/neg-demo-cluster].
samuele@cloudshell:~/neg-demo (backend-devs-7736)$ ▊
```

Figure 5-30. *Deleting load balancer infrastructure and the GKE cluster*

Global HTTP(S) Load Balancing with Managed Instance Groups

As you saw in the previous examples, a cloud load balancer is not a single Google Cloud resource. Instead, it's a group of resources, which need each other for the load balancer to work.

In Figure 5-5, we visualized all the resources, which are parts of an external HTTP(S) load balancer.

In this exercise, you will learn how to set up a global external HTTPS load balancer (classic)—load balancer 2 in Figure 5-1—with all its underlying resources.

This time, we will be using a management instance group (MIG) as backend, and the setup will be hosted in the service project backend-devs of our shared VPC.

■ **Exam tip**   There are multiple ways to set up an HTTPS load balancer in a shared VPC. One way is to use a service project with ID `backend-devs-7736` to host *all* the load balancer resources. Another way is to distribute the frontend resources (i.e., the reserved external IP address, the forwarding rule, the target proxy, the SSL certificate(s), the URL map) in a project (it can be the host or one of the service projects) and the backend resources (i.e., the backend service, the health check, the backend) in another service project. This latter approach is also called *cross-project backend service referencing*.

Figure 5-31 gives you an idea of what our setup will look like upon completion.

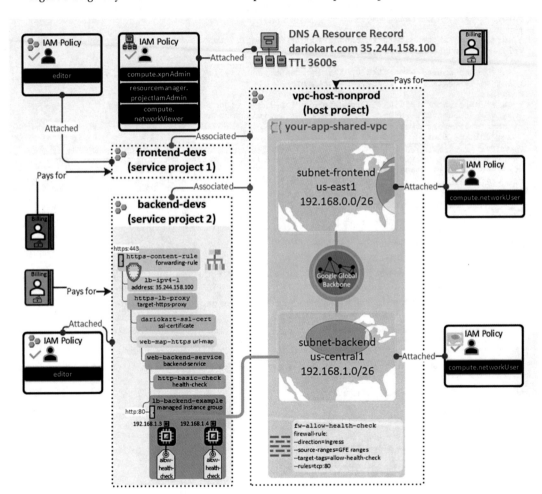

Figure 5-31. *Deploying a global HTTPS load balancer in a shared VPC*

Notice the setup will be using the HTTPS protocol, which requires the creation of an SSL certificate in use by the target HTTPS proxy.

For global external HTTPS load balancers, the SSL certificate is used for domain validation, and it can be a self-managed or a Google-managed SSL certificate.

■ **Exam tip**   Regional external HTTPS load balancers can only use self-managed SSL certificates.

First and foremost, let's refresh our memory on who can do what in the service project backend-devs. This is done by viewing the project's IAM allow policy as illustrated in Figure 5-32.

```
samuele@cloudshell:~ (backend-devs-7736)$ gcloud projects get-iam-policy backend-devs-7736 | more
bindings:
- members:
  - serviceAccount:211670805257-compute@developer.gserviceaccount.com
  role: roles/artifactregistry.reader
- members:
  - serviceAccount:service-211670805257@compute-system.iam.gserviceaccount.com
  role: roles/compute.serviceAgent
- members:
  - serviceAccount:service-211670805257@container-engine-robot.iam.gserviceaccount.com
  role: roles/container.serviceAgent
- members:
  - serviceAccount:service-211670805257@containerregistry.iam.gserviceaccount.com
  role: roles/containerregistry.ServiceAgent
- members:
  - serviceAccount:211670805257-compute@developer.gserviceaccount.com
  - serviceAccount:211670805257@cloudservices.gserviceaccount.com
  - user:samuele@dariokart.com
  role: roles/editor
- members:
  - serviceAccount:service-211670805257@gcp-sa-networkmanagement.iam.gserviceaccount.com
  role: roles/networkmanagement.serviceAgent
- members:
  - user:itsmedario@dariokart.com
  role: roles/owner
--More--
```

Figure 5-32. *Project backend-devs allow policies manifest*

The two principals itsmedario@dariokart.com and samuele@dariokart.com hold the owner and the editor roles, respectively.

As per Google recommendation, we will create a Google-managed SSL certificate (Figure 5-33).

```
itsmedario@cloudshell:~ (backend-devs-7736)$ gcloud compute ssl-certificates create dariokart-ssl-cert \
    --description="SSL dariokart.com Domain Validation" \
    --domains=dariokart.com \
    --global
Created [https://www.googleapis.com/compute/v1/projects/backend-devs-7736/global/sslCertificates/dariokart-ssl-cert]
NAME: dariokart-ssl-cert
TYPE: MANAGED
CREATION_TIMESTAMP: 2022-12-05T05:50:41.715-08:00
EXPIRE_TIME:
MANAGED_STATUS: PROVISIONING

dariokart.com: PROVISIONING

itsmedario@cloudshell:~ (backend-devs-7736)$ gcloud compute ssl-certificates describe dariokart-ssl-cert \
    --global \
    --format="get(name,managed.status, managed.domainStatus)"
dariokart-ssl-cert      PROVISIONING     dariokart.com=PROVISIONING
itsmedario@cloudshell:~ (backend-devs-7736)$
```

Figure 5-33. *Google-managed SSL certificate creation*

Notice the --domains flag, which requires a comma-delimited list of domains. Google Cloud will validate each domain in the list. For the load balancer to work, we will need to wait until both the managed. status and the managed.domainStatus properties are ACTIVE. This process is lengthy and may take one or more hours, depending on how quickly your domain provider can provide evidence that you own the domain. In my case, the validation took about an hour because I bought my domain `dariokart.com` from Google workspace. Nevertheless, while we are waiting for the SSL certificate to become active, we can move forward with the remaining steps.

Next, we need to create an instance template, which will be used by the managed instance group to create new instances (VMs) as incoming traffic increases above the thresholds we will set up in the backend service.

Since our global external HTTPS load balancer is intended to serve HTTPS requests, we need to make sure our instances come with an HTTP server preinstalled. As a result, our instance template will make sure Apache2 will be installed on the VM upon startup.

Also, the startup script is configured to show the hostname of the VM, which will be used by the backend service to serve the incoming HTTPS request, as illustrated in Figure 5-34.

```
samuele@cloudshell:~ (backend-devs-7736)$ gcloud compute instance-templates create your-app-template   --region=us-central1   --network=projects/
vpc-host-nonprod-pu645-uh372/global/networks/your-app-shared-vpc   --subnet=projects/vpc-host-nonprod-pu645-uh372/regions/us-central1/subnetworks/
subnet-backend   --tags=allow-health-check   --image-family=debian-10   --image-project=debian-cloud   --metadata=startup-script='#! /bin/bash
     sudo apt-get update
     sudo apt-get install apache2 -y
     sudo a2ensite default-ssl
     sudo a2enmod ssl
     vm_hostname="$(curl -H "Metadata-Flavor:Google" \
   http://metadata.google.internal/computeMetadata/v1/instance/name)"
     sudo echo "Page served from: $vm_hostname" | \
     tee /var/www/html/index.html
     sudo systemctl restart apache2'
Created [https://www.googleapis.com/compute/v1/projects/backend-devs-7736/global/instanceTemplates/your-app-template].
NAME: your-app-template
MACHINE_TYPE: n1-standard-1
PREEMPTIBLE:
CREATION_TIMESTAMP: 2022-12-05T07:31:23.827-08:00
samuele@cloudshell:~ (backend-devs-7736)$ █
```

Figure 5-34. *Instance template creation*

■ **Note**   The VMs will be using a network tag `allow-health-check` to be allowed to be health-checked from the CIDRs of Google Front End (GFE). We will use this network tag when we configure the load balancer frontend.

With the instance template ready, we can create our managed instance group (MIG). The MIG will start with two `n1-standard-1` size VMs in `us-central1-a`, as shown in Figure 5-35.

```
samuele@cloudshell:~ (backend-devs-7736)$ gcloud compute instance-groups managed create lb-backend-example \
--template=your-app-template --size=2 --zone=us-central1-a
Created [https://www.googleapis.com/compute/v1/projects/backend-devs-7736/zones/us-central1-a/instanceGroupManagers/lb-backend-example].
NAME: lb-backend-example
LOCATION: us-central1-a
SCOPE: zone
BASE_INSTANCE_NAME: lb-backend-example
SIZE: 0
TARGET_SIZE: 2
INSTANCE_TEMPLATE: your-app-template
AUTOSCALED: no
samuele@cloudshell:~ (backend-devs-7736)$ █
```

Figure 5-35. *Managed instance group creation*

■ **Note**   With a shared VPC setup, you need to make sure the zone (`us-central1-a`) you are using to host your MIG's VMs is part of the region (`us-central1`) where the instance template operates, which in turn needs to match the region of the subnet where your backend service will run (`us-central1`).

Once the MIG is ready, we need to tell it which named port its VMs will be listening to in order to serve incoming HTTPS traffic. Guess what named port we will use for HTTPS traffic? HTTPS, right 😊? No, it's going to be HTTP actually!

This is because our backends will be running in Google Cloud, and *when backends run in Google Cloud, traffic from the Google Front End (GFE) destined to the backends is automatically encrypted by Google.* As a result, there is no need to use an HTTPS named port.

Figure 5-36 illustrates how to set the list of key-value pairs for the desired MIG's protocol and port. In our case, the list contains only one key-value pair, that is, `http:80`.

```
samuele@cloudshell:~ (backend-devs-7736)$ gcloud compute instance-groups set-named-ports lb-backend-example \
    --named-ports http:80 \
    --zone us-central1-a
Updated [https://www.googleapis.com/compute/v1/projects/backend-devs-7736/zones/us-central1-a/instanceGroups/lb-backend-example]
samuele@cloudshell:~ (backend-devs-7736)$
```

Figure 5-36. *Configuring named port list for the MIG*

■ **Exam tip** An instance group can use multiple named ports, provided each named port uses a different name. As a result, the value of the `--named-ports` flag is a comma-delimited list of `named-port:port` key:value pairs.

With our managed instance group properly created and configured, we need to make sure health probes can access the two backend VMs using the named port `http` (see previous command in Figure 5-36), which is mapped to the port 80 in the MIG.

As a result, the ingress firewall rule (IST type, i.e., Ingress Source and Target) in Figure 5-37 must be created in our shared VPC—as you learned in Chapter 3, firewall rules are defined on a per-VPC network basis—to allow incoming HTTP traffic (`tcp:80`) originating from the GFE CIDR blocks (`130.211.0.0/22`, `35.191.0.0/16`) to reach the two backend VMs, which are tagged with the network tag `allow-health-check`.

```
itsmedario@cloudshell:~ (vpc-host-nonprod-pu645-uh372)$ gcloud compute firewall-rules create fw-allow-health-check    --network=projects/vpc-host-
nonprod-pu645-uh372/global/networks/your-app-shared-vpc    --action=allow    --direction=ingress    --source-ranges=130.211.0.0/22,35.191.0.0/16
    --target-tags=allow-health-check    --rules=tcp:80
Creating firewall...working..Created [https://www.googleapis.com/compute/v1/projects/vpc-host-nonprod-pu645-uh372/global/firewalls/fw-allow-health-
check].
Creating firewall...done.
NAME: fw-allow-health-check
NETWORK: your-app-shared-vpc
DIRECTION: INGRESS
PRIORITY: 1000
ALLOW: tcp:80
DENY:
DISABLED: False
itsmedario@cloudshell:~ (vpc-host-nonprod-pu645-uh372)$ ▊
```

Figure 5-37. *GFE to backend VM ingress firewall rule creation*

This traffic flow is visually represented in Connection 2 in Figure 5-5.

Next, we need to reserve a static external IP address with global scope. To make it simple, we use an IPv4 version (Figure 5-38).

```
samuele@cloudshell:~ (backend-devs-7736)$ gcloud compute addresses create lb-ipv4-1 \
    --ip-version=IPV4 \
    --network-tier=PREMIUM \
    --global
Created [https://www.googleapis.com/compute/v1/projects/backend-devs-7736/global/addresses/lb-ipv4-1]
samuele@cloudshell:~ (backend-devs-7736)$ gcloud compute addresses describe lb-ipv4-1 \
    --format="get(address)" \
    --global
35.244.158.100
samuele@cloudshell:~ (backend-devs-7736)$
```

Figure 5-38. *Global static external IP address creation*

As of the writing of this book, global external HTTP(S) load balancers support IPv4 and IPv6 IP addresses, whereas regional external HTTP(S) load balancers only support IPv4 IP addresses.

To make sure our backend VMs are continuously checked for health, we need to create a health check.

■ **Exam tip** As previously mentioned, just because you are using HTTPS—like in this exercise—on your forwarding rule (Connection 1 in Figure 5-5), you don't have to use HTTPS in your backend service and backends (Connection 2). Instead, you can use HTTP for your backend service and backends. This is because traffic between Google Front Ends (GFEs) and your backends is automatically encrypted by Google for backends that reside in a Google Cloud VPC network.

In Figure 5-39, we will create a health check to monitor the health status of our backend VMs. Then, we will use the newly created health check to create a backend service. Finally, we will add our newly created managed instance group (the MIG we created in Figure 5-35) to the backend service.

```
samuele@cloudshell:~ (backend-devs-7736)$   gcloud compute health-checks create http http-basic-check \
    --port 80
                                  Command can be one of "http", "https", "http2", "tcp", "ssl", "grpc"
Created [https://www.googleapis.com/compute/v1/projects/backend-devs-7736/global/healthChecks/http-basic-check].
NAME: http-basic-check
PROTOCOL: HTTP
samuele@cloudshell:~ (backend-devs-7736)$   gcloud compute backend-services create web-backend-service \
    --load-balancing-scheme=EXTERNAL \     Must match the <key> ("http") of one of the <key:value> pairs in the
    --protocol=HTTP \                       comma-delimited list ("http:80") assigned to the MIG "--named-ports" flag
    --port-name=http \                      using the "gcloud compute instance-groups set-named-ports" statement
    --health-checks=http-basic-check \
    --global

Created [https://www.googleapis.com/compute/v1/projects/backend-devs-7736/global/backendServices/web-backend-service]
NAME: web-backend-service
BACKENDS:
PROTOCOL: HTTP
samuele@cloudshell:~ (backend-devs-7736)$   gcloud compute backend-services add-backend web-backend-service \
    --instance-group=lb-backend-example \       Our Managed Instance Group (MIG)
    --instance-group-zone=us-central1-a \
    --global

Updated [https://www.googleapis.com/compute/v1/projects/backend-devs-7736/global/backendServices/web-backend-service]
samuele@cloudshell:~ (backend-devs-7736)$
```

Figure 5-39. *Health check, backend service, and backend creation*

With the backend service ready, we can create the remaining frontend resources, that is, the URL map, which is required along with our SSL certificate to create the target HTTPS proxy, and the globally scoped forwarding rule.

Figure 5-40 displays the creation of the aforementioned frontend GCP resources.

```
samuele@cloudshell:~ (backend-devs-7736)$   gcloud compute url-maps create web-map-https \
    --default-service web-backend-service ◄──────── Our backend service

Created [https://www.googleapis.com/compute/v1/projects/backend-devs-7736/global/urlMaps/web-map-https].
NAME: web-map-https
DEFAULT_SERVICE: backendServices/web-backend-service
samuele@cloudshell:~ (backend-devs-7736)$   gcloud compute target-https-proxies create https-lb-proxy \
    --url-map=web-map-https \
    --ssl-certificates=dariokart-ssl-cert ◄──────── Our Google-managed ssl certificate

Created [https://www.googleapis.com/compute/v1/projects/backend-devs-7736/global/targetHttpsProxies/https-lb-proxy].
NAME: https-lb-proxy
SSL_CERTIFICATES: dariokart-ssl-cert
URL_MAP: web-map-https
CERTIFICATE_MAP:
samuele@cloudshell:~ (backend-devs-7736)$   gcloud compute forwarding-rules create https-content-rule \
    --load-balancing-scheme=EXTERNAL \ ◄── Global external HTTPS Load balancer (Classic) uses the "EXTERNAL" scheme
    --network-tier=PREMIUM \
    --address=lb-ipv4-1 \ ◄──────────────── Our static, external IPv4 IP address
    --global \
    --target-https-proxy=https-lb-proxy \
    --ports=443 ◄────────────────────────── Clients can only connect using tcp port 443 (HTTPS)

Created [https://www.googleapis.com/compute/v1/projects/backend-devs-7736/global/forwardingRules/https-content-rule].
samuele@cloudshell:~ (backend-devs-7736)$ ▊
```

Figure 5-40. *URL map, target HTTPS proxy, and forwarding rule creation*

The last step in this setup is to add a DNS A record, which is required to point our domain dariokart.com to our load balancer.

Our load balancer global external IP address is 35.244.158.100 (Figure 5-38).

Since I bought my domain from Google Workspace, I will use the Google Workspace Admin Console and Google Domains to create two DNS A records. Figure 5-41 shows the newly created DNS A records.

| ✓ These DNS settings are active. Changes are published immediately, but may take time to propagate |

Resource records   ⊕ Export DNS records

Resource records point to the services your domain uses, including web and email services. Learn more about resource records

Custom records   ⌃
dariokart.com/A and play.dariokart.com/A

                                                                            Manage custom records

Host name	Type	TTL	Data
dariokart.com	A	1 hour	35.244.158.100
play.dariokart.com	A	1 hour	35.244.158.100

Figure 5-41. *Adding DNS A records to resolve domain names to the VIP*

When you save the changes, you get a notification that it may take some time to propagate the DNS changes over the Internet, but in most cases, the propagation happens within an hour or less, depending on how fast your domain registration service operates.

Now it's a matter to wait for the SSL certificate to become active so that an SSL handshake can be established between the clients and the target HTTPS proxy.

After about an hour, the SSL certificate became active, as you can see in Figure 5-42.

```
samuele@cloudshell:~ (backend-devs-7736)$ gcloud compute ssl-certificates describe dariokart-ssl-cert   --global   --format="get(name,managed.sta
tus, managed.domainStatus)"
dariokart-ssl-cert       PROVISIONING   dariokart.com=FAILED_NOT_VISIBLE
samuele@cloudshell:~ (backend-devs-7736)$ gcloud compute ssl-certificates describe dariokart-ssl-cert   --global   --format="get(name,managed.sta
tus, managed.domainStatus)"
dariokart-ssl-cert       ACTIVE   dariokart.com=ACTIVE
samuele@cloudshell:~ (backend-devs-7736)$
```

Figure 5-42. *The SSL certificate's managed domain status becomes active*

Figure 5-43 confirms all tests "hitting" the domain with HTTPS were successful!

```
samuele@cloudshell:~ (backend-devs-7736)$ curl https://dariokart.com
Page served from: lb-backend-example-t0vc
samuele@cloudshell:~ (backend-devs-7736)$ gcloud compute instances list
NAME: lb-backend-example-1dbf
ZONE: us-central1-a
MACHINE_TYPE: n1-standard-1
PREEMPTIBLE:
INTERNAL_IP: 192.168.1.4
EXTERNAL_IP: 34.27.196.55
STATUS: RUNNING

NAME: lb-backend-example-t0vc
ZONE: us-central1-a
MACHINE_TYPE: n1-standard-1
PREEMPTIBLE:
INTERNAL_IP: 192.168.1.3
EXTERNAL_IP: 35.239.154.231
STATUS: RUNNING
samuele@cloudshell:~ (backend-devs-7736)$ curl https://dariokart.com
Page served from: lb-backend-example-1dbf
samuele@cloudshell:~ (backend-devs-7736)$
```

Figure 5-43. *Testing the HTTPS load balancer from Cloud Shell*

More specifically, the first HTTPS request was served by the VM lb-backend-example-t0vc, and the second request was served by the VM lb-backend-example-1dbf.

To further validate that the HTTPS load balancer can serve traffic from the Internet, I tried https://dariokart.com from my phone. The result was also successful (Figure 5-44).

Page served from: lb-backend-example-t0vc

Figure 5-44. *Testing the HTTPS load balancer from a mobile device*

Now it's time to clean up—each resource we just created is billable—not to mention that the HTTPS load balancer is exposed to the public Internet.

Figures 5-45 and 5-46 show you how to delete the load balancer's resources.

```
samuele@cloudshell:~ (backend-devs-7736)$ gcloud -q compute forwarding-rules delete https-content-rule --global
Deleted [https://www.googleapis.com/compute/v1/projects/backend-devs-7736/global/forwardingRules/https-content-rule].
samuele@cloudshell:~ (backend-devs-7736)$ gcloud -q compute target-https-proxies delete https-lb-proxy
Deleted [https://www.googleapis.com/compute/v1/projects/backend-devs-7736/global/targetHttpsProxies/https-lb-proxy].
samuele@cloudshell:~ (backend-devs-7736)$ gcloud -q compute url-maps delete web-map-https
Deleted [https://www.googleapis.com/compute/v1/projects/backend-devs-7736/global/urlMaps/web-map-https].
samuele@cloudshell:~ (backend-devs-7736)$ gcloud -q compute backend-services delete web-backend-service --global
Deleted [https://www.googleapis.com/compute/v1/projects/backend-devs-7736/global/backendServices/web-backend-service].
samuele@cloudshell:~ (backend-devs-7736)$
samuele@cloudshell:~ (backend-devs-7736)$ gcloud compute instance-groups managed delete lb-backend-example --zone=us-central1-a
The following instance group managers will be deleted:
 - [lb-backend-example] in [us-central1-a]

Do you want to continue (Y/n)?  Y

Deleting Managed Instance Group...working..Deleted [https://www.googleapis.com/compute/v1/projects/backend-devs-7736/zones/us-central1-a/instanceGr
oupManagers/lb-backend-example].
Deleting Managed Instance Group...done.
samuele@cloudshell:~ (backend-devs-7736)$ gcloud -q compute health-checks delete http-basic-check
Deleted [https://www.googleapis.com/compute/v1/projects/backend-devs-7736/global/healthChecks/http-basic-check].
samuele@cloudshell:~ (backend-devs-7736)$ gcloud compute instances list
Listed 0 items.
samuele@cloudshell:~ (backend-devs-7736)$ █
```

Figure 5-45. *Deleting load balancer resources*

```
samuele@cloudshell:~ (backend-devs-7736)$ gcloud compute addresses delete lb-ipv4-1 --global
The following global addresses will be deleted:
 - [lb-ipv4-1]

Do you want to continue (Y/n)?  Y

Deleted [https://www.googleapis.com/compute/v1/projects/backend-devs-7736/global/addresses/lb-ipv4-1].
samuele@cloudshell:~ (backend-devs-7736)$ gcloud compute addresses list
Listed 0 items.
samuele@cloudshell:~ (backend-devs-7736)$ gcloud compute instance-templates delete your-app-template
The following instance templates will be deleted:
 - [your-app-template]

Do you want to continue (Y/n)?  Y

Deleted [https://www.googleapis.com/compute/v1/projects/backend-devs-7736/global/instanceTemplates/your-app-template].
samuele@cloudshell:~ (backend-devs-7736)$ █
```

Figure 5-46. *Deleting IP address and instance template*

Next, we delete the firewall rule (Figure 5-47).

```
itsmedario@cloudshell:~ (vpc-host-nonprod-pu645-uh372)$ gcloud compute firewall-rules delete fw-allow-health-check
The following firewalls will be deleted:
 - [fw-allow-health-check]

Do you want to continue (Y/n)?  Y

Deleted [https://www.googleapis.com/compute/v1/projects/vpc-host-nonprod-pu645-uh372/global/firewalls/fw-allow-health-check].
itsmedario@cloudshell:~ (vpc-host-nonprod-pu645-uh372)$
```

Figure 5-47. *Deleting fw-allow-health-check firewall rule*

Last, we delete the DNS A records (Figure 5-48).

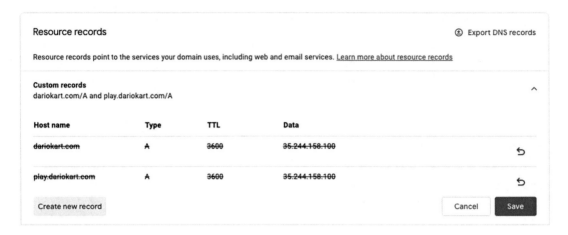

Figure 5-48. *Deleting DNS A resource records*

After saving the changes, the two A records are gone (Figure 5-49).

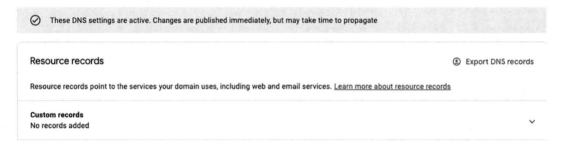

Figure 5-49. *Custom records list is empty.*

External TCP and SSL Proxy Load Balancers

You learned when to use and how to configure external HTTP(S) load balancers in different flavors (types 1, 2, and 5).

These types of load balancer operate at layer 7 of the OSI model, resulting in advanced routing and session-level capabilities, which are not available to load balancers that operate at lower layers of the OSI model.

For example, URL mapping is a feature only available to HTTP(S) load balancers, which makes sense because the URL construct is specific to the HTTP protocol. Likewise, session affinity based on HTTP headers is another feature unique to HTTP(S) load balancers.

> *What if your workload requires a solution to load-balance traffic other than HTTP(S) instead?*

To answer this question, you need to find out where the clients of your workload are located and whether you want the load balancer to remember the client IP address.

If your workload requires access from the Internet (i.e., if your load balancer forwarding rule is external), and its compute backends need to be distributed in more than one region—for example, because of reliability requirements—then Google Cloud offers the global external SSL proxy load balancer (type 3) and the global external TCP proxy load balancer (type 4).

Figure 5-50 illustrates the architecture for these types of load balancer.

As noted in the Global Target (SSL or TCP) Proxy column in Figure 5-50, these global load balancers are offered in the premium or in the standard tier. The difference is that with the premium tier, latency is significantly reduced (compared to the standard tier) because ingress traffic enters the Google Global Backbone from the closest Point of Presence (PoP) to the client—PoPs are geographically distributed around the globe. In contrast, with standard tier ingress traffic stays in the Internet for a longer period of time and enters the Google Global Backbone in the GCP region where the global forwarding rule lives.

Moreover, because these load balancers use a target proxy as an intermediary, they "break" the connection from the client in two connections. As a result, the second connection has no clue of the client IP address where the request originated.

■ **Exam tip**   Even though SSL proxy and TCP proxy load balancers don't preserve the client IP address by default, there are workarounds on how to let them "remember" the client IP address. One of these workarounds is by configuring the target (SSL or TCP) proxy to prepend a PROXY protocol version 1 header to retain the original connection information as illustrated in the following: `gcloud compute target-ssl-proxies update my-ssl-lb-target-proxy \`

`--proxy-header=[NONE | PROXY_V1]`

The architecture of these types of load balancer is shown in Figure 5-50.

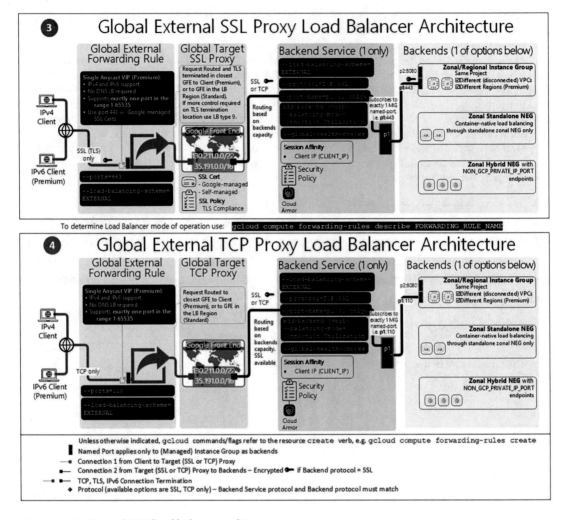

Figure 5-50. *SSL and TCP load balancer architecture*

These types of load balancers have a few commonalities:

1. They support IPv4 and IPv6 clients.

2. They terminate the connection from the client in a Google Front End.

3. The connection from the target proxy to the backends supports the TCP or the SSL (TLS) protocols.

4. They support the following backends:

    a. Instance groups

    b. Zonal standalone NEGs

    c. Zonal hybrid NEGs

External SSL Proxy Load Balancer

With an SSL (TLS) proxy load balancer, SSL sessions are terminated in one of the Google Front Ends (GFEs), then the load balancer creates a new connection and sends traffic to your workload backends using SSL (recommended) or TCP.

It is best practice to use end-to-end encryption for your SSL proxy deployment. To do this, you must configure your backend service to accept traffic over SSL. This ensures that client traffic decrypted in a GFE is encrypted again before being sent to the backends for processing.

End-to-end encryption requires you to provision certificates and keys on your backends so they can perform SSL processing.

The benefits of an SSL proxy load balancer are listed as follows:

- **IPv6 support** (with premium network tier): SSL proxy load balancing supports both IPv4 and IPv6 addresses for client traffic. Client IPv6 requests are terminated by a target SSL proxy located in one of the worldwide GFEs, then proxied over IPv4 to your backends.

- **Capacity-based routing**: The load balancer can route requests to backend locations where there is capacity. In contrast, a layer 3 or 4 load balancer must route traffic to regional backends without paying attention to capacity.

- **Efficient backend utilization**: SSL processing can be very CPU intensive if the ciphers used are not CPU efficient. To maximize CPU performance, use ECDSA SSL certs and TLS 1.2 and prefer the ECDHE-ECDSA-AES128-GCM-SHA256 cipher suite for SSL between the load balancer and your backends.

- **Certificate management**: Your customer-facing SSL certificates can be either certificates that you obtain and manage yourself (self-managed certificates) or certificates that Google obtains and manages for you (Google-managed certificates). You only need to provision certificates on the load balancer. On your backends, you can simplify SSL certificate management by using self-signed certificates.

- **Security patching**: If vulnerabilities arise in the SSL or TCP stack, Google Cloud will apply patches at the load balancer automatically in order to keep your instances safe.

- **Any port supported**: SSL proxy load balancing supports exactly one port in the range 1–65535. When you use Google-managed SSL certificates with SSL proxy load balancing, the frontend port for traffic must be 443 to enable the Google-managed SSL certificates to be provisioned and renewed.

- **SSL policies**: SSL policies give you the ability to control the features of SSL that your external SSL proxy load balancer negotiates with clients.

- **Cloud Armor support**: You can use Google Cloud Armor security policies to protect your infrastructure from Distributed Denial-of-Service (DDoS) attacks and other targeted attacks.

External TCP Proxy Load Balancer

As you can see from the architecture in Figure 5-50, an external TCP proxy load balancer shares many of the SSL proxy load balancer features.

However, since the only supported protocol from client requests is TCP, its target TCP proxies (located in the worldwide GFEs) do not need to perform SSL authentication. As a result, no SSL certificates nor SSL policies are supported.

■ **Exam tip**   External TCP proxy load balancers do not support end-to-end (client to backend) encryption. However, connection 2 (proxy to backend) *does* support SSL if needed.

Network Load Balancers

A Google Cloud network load balancer is a layer 4 (transport layer) load balancer with respect to the OSI reference model.

As a result, a network load balancer doesn't have layer 7 (application layer) advanced routing and session-level capabilities like the HTTP(S) load balancers (types 1, 2, and 5 and their internal companion type 6), which is why there are no URL map boxes in the architecture represented in Figure 5-51.

A key differentiating feature of a Google Cloud network load balancer is that it preserves the source client IP address by default.

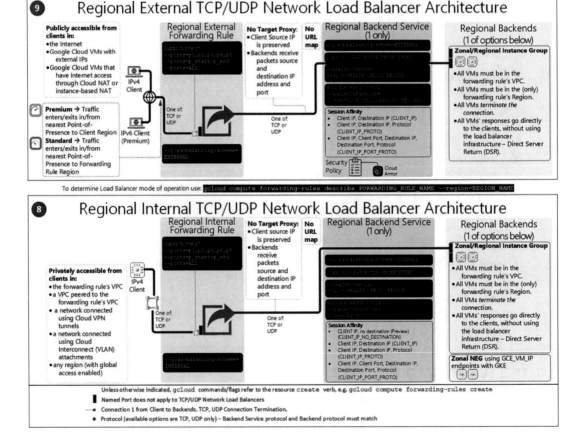

Figure 5-51. *Network load balancer architecture*

This is because there are no proxies to terminate the client connection and start a new connection to direct incoming traffic to the backends.

As you can see in Figure 5-51, there is no target proxy between the forwarding rule and the backend service, and there is only one connection from the clients to the backends. For this reason, a network load balancer is also referred to as a *pass-through load* balancer to indicate that the source client IP address is passed to the backends intact.

A network load balancer comes in two flavors based on whether the IP address of the forwarding rule is external (type 9) or internal (type 8). The former allows client IP addresses to be denoted in IPv6 format, but this feature requires the premium network tier. The latter doesn't allow clients in IPv6 format because the IP space is RFC 1918, and there is no concern about IP space saturation. For this reason, clients for type 8 network load balancers are denoted with the Google Cloud Compute Engine icon (VM) to indicate that they are either VMs in Google Cloud or VMs on-premises.

■ **Exam tip**   Network load balancers are regionally scoped to indicate that backends can only be located in a single region.

The way session affinity is handled is another differentiating factor that makes a network load balancer unique when compared to others in Google Cloud.

While HTTP(S)-based load balancers leverage HTTP-specific constructs (e.g., cookies, headers, etc.), a network load balancer—by virtue of being a layer 4 load balancer—can leverage any combination of source, destination, port, and protocols to determine session affinity semantics.

The following are some of the common use cases when a network load balancer is a good fit:

- Your workload requires to load-balance non-TCP traffic (e.g., UDP, ICMP, ESP) or an unsupported TCP port by other load balancers.

- It is acceptable to have SSL traffic decrypted by your backends instead of by the load balancer. The network load balancer cannot perform this task. When the backends decrypt SSL traffic, there is a greater CPU burden on the backends.

- It is acceptable to have SSL traffic decrypted by your backends using self-managed certificates. Google-managed SSL certificates are only available for HTTP(S) load balancers (types 1, 2, 5, and 6) and external SSL proxy load balancers (type 3).

- Your workload is required to forward the original client packets *unproxied*.

- Your workload is required to migrate an existing pass-through-based workload without changes.

- Your workload requires advanced network DDoS protection, which necessitates the use of Google Cloud Armor.

Examples

A simple example of a type 8 load balancer is a shopping cart application as illustrated in Figure 5-52. The load balancer operates in us-central1, but its internal regional forwarding rule is configured with the -allow-global-access flag set to true.

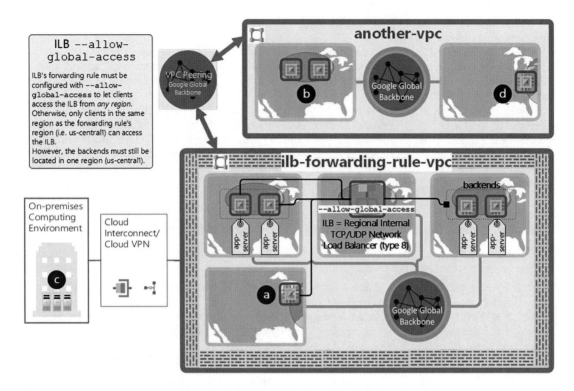

Figure 5-52. *Example of a regional internal network TCP/UDP load balancer*

As a result, clients in a different region (scenario "a") of the same VPC can use the shopping cart application. Also, clients in a VPC peered to the ILB's VPC can use the application (scenarios "b" and "d"). Even on-premises clients can use the shopping cart application (scenario "c").

Figure 5-53 illustrates another example of a type 8 load balancer, which is used to distribute TCP/UDP traffic between separate (RFC 1918) tiers of a three-tier web application.

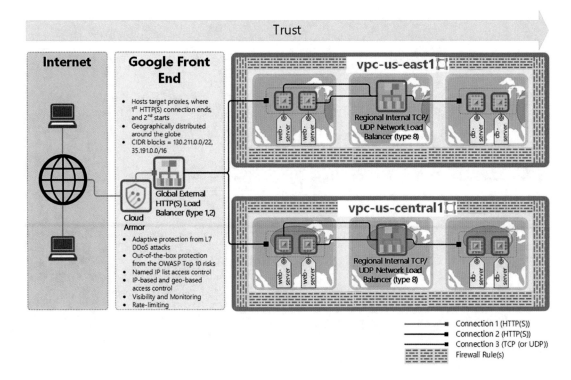

Figure 5-53. *Three-tier application with a regional internal network TCP/UDP load balancer*

Implementation

Let's see now how a regional internal network TCP/UDP load balancer works.

As illustrated in Figure 5-54, a type 8 load balancer is a software-defined load balancer, which leverages the Google Cloud software-defined network virtualization stack *Andromeda*. Andromeda acts as the middle proxy, thereby eliminating the risk of choke points and helping clients select the optimal backend ready to serve requests.

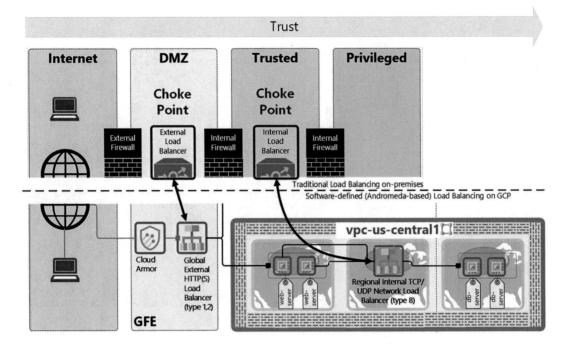

Figure 5-54. *Regional internal network TCP/UDP load balancer features*

In comparing traditional internal load balancing with software-defined load balancing on GCP, Figure 5-54 also highlights the distributed nature of software-defined components, that is, network load balancing, but also GCP firewall rules. The latter are also software-defined, distributed resources, which result in the elimination of choke points—when compared to traditional firewalls, as you learned in Chapters 2 and 3.

Internal HTTP(S) and TCP Proxy Load Balancers

Not every workload requires access from the Internet. That's a suitable use case for an internal load balancer (ILB), where all components (i.e., client, forwarding rule, proxy, URL map, backend services, and backends) operate in an RFC 1918 IP address space.

You have already learned an example of an internal load balancer in the previous section, that is, the regional internal TCP/UDP network load balancer (type 8). This load balancer is internal, but it operates at layer 4 of the OSI model.

> *What if your workload requires a solution to load-balance internal HTTP(S) traffic without burdening the backends with SSL offload instead?*

You definitely need an HTTPS proxy solution, which terminates the connection from the clients and takes the burden of decrypting the incoming packets.

The Google Cloud internal HTTP(S) load balancer (type 6) does just that!

The top part of Figure 5-55 illustrates the architecture of this type of load balancer.

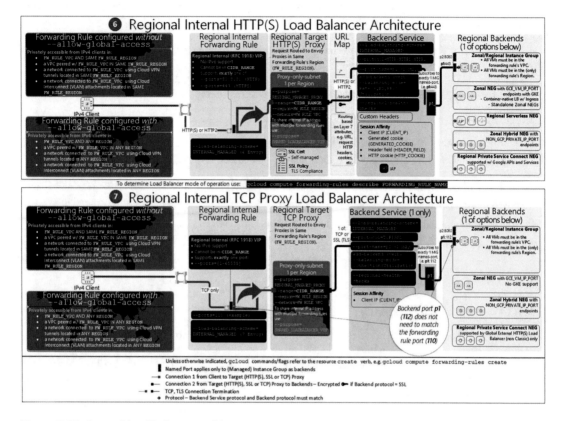

Figure 5-55. *Internal load balancer architecture*

This load balancer type is regional and proxy-based, operates at layer 7 in the OSI model, and enables you to run and scale your services behind an internal IP address.

These services operate in the form of backends hosted on one of the following:

- Zonal/regional instance groups

- Zonal NEGs

- Regional serverless NEGs

- Zonal hybrid NEGs

- Regional Private Service Connect NEGs

By default, the Google Cloud internal HTTP(S) load balancer (type 6) is accessible only from IPv4 clients in the same region of the internal regional forwarding rule's region.

If your workload requires access from clients located in a region other than the internal forwarding rule's region, then you must configure the load balancer internal forwarding rule to *allow global access* as indicated in Figure 5-55.

Last, an internal HTTP(S) load balancer is a managed service based on the open source Envoy proxy. This enables rich traffic control capabilities based on HTTP(S) parameters. After the load balancer has been configured, Google Cloud automatically allocates Envoy proxies in your designated *proxy-only* subnet to meet your traffic needs.

Another "flavor" of Google Cloud internal, proxy-based load balancers is the Google Cloud internal TCP proxy load balancer (type 7). See the bottom part of Figure 5-55.

This type of load balancer is essentially the internal version of the Google Cloud external TCP proxy load balancer (type 4), with a couple of caveats you need to remember for the exam.

■ **Exam tip**   The type 7 load balancer's target proxy is an Envoy proxy managed by Google Cloud. As a result, this proxy is located in your designated proxy-only subnet instead of a GFE location.

Unlike the case of type 4 load balancers, Regional Private Service Connect NEGs are a valid backend option for this type of load balancer. This makes sense because the load balancer is internal, and by operating in RFC 1918 IP address space, it has full access to Google APIs and services with a proper subnet configuration (`gcloud compute networks subnets update --enable-private-ip-google-access`).

Load Balancer Summary

Whether your workload needs to serve requests from the Internet or from your corporate network (external or internal access, respectively), using L7 or L4 OSI layers (i.e., application layer or transport layer, respectively), requiring SSL termination in the load balancer itself or its backends, Google Cloud has your load balancing needs covered.

As you learned so far, Google Cloud offers a wide range of load balancing services. Each service is available—in most cases—in the premium network tier or standard network tier, resulting in a significant number of load balancing available options.

You, as a professional Google Cloud network engineer, need to decide the best option for your workload load balancing requirements. This decision is based on the five pillars of the well-architected framework we introduced at the beginning of this chapter, that is, elasticity, performance, security, cost-effectiveness, and resilience (or reliability).

Figure 5-56 summarizes some of the decision criteria you need to consider in the decision process.

Frontend IP Address	#	Load Balancer Type	Scope	Network Tier	SSL Offload	Proxy or Passthrough	Traffic Type	Frontend Ports
External	1	Global External HTTP(S) Load Balancer	Global	Premium	Yes	Proxy	HTTP, HTTPS	80, 8080 (HTTP) 443 (HTTPS)
	2	Global External HTTP(S) Load Balancer (classic)	Global	Premium, Standard	Yes	Proxy	HTTP, HTTPS	80, 8080 (HTTP) 443 (HTTPS)
	3	Global External SSL Proxy Load Balancer	Global	Premium, Standard	Yes	Proxy	SSL	Exactly one of 1-65535
	4	Global External TCP Proxy Load Balancer	Global	Premium, Standard	No	Proxy	TCP	Exactly one of 1-65535
	9	Regional External TCP/UDP Network Load Balancer	Regional	Premium, Standard	No	Passthrough	TCP, UDP	• port_1, port_2, port_3, port_4, port_5 • p_start-p_end • All
	5	Regional External HTTP(S) Load Balancer	Regional	Standard	Yes	Proxy	HTTP, HTTPS	80, 8080 (HTTP) 443 (HTTPS)
Internal	6	Regional Internal HTTP(S) Load Balancer	Regional	Premium	Yes	Proxy	HTTP, HTTPS	80, 8080 (HTTP) 443 (HTTPS)
	7	Regional Internal TCP Proxy Load Balancer	Regional	Premium	Yes	Proxy	TCP	Exactly one of 1-65535
	8	Regional Internal TCP/UDP Network Load Balancer	Regional	Premium	No	Passthrough	TCP, UDP	• port_1, port_2, port_3, port_4, port_5 • p_start-p_end • All

Figure 5-56. *Google Cloud load balancer comparison*

Additionally, the decision tree in Figure 5-57 is also provided to help you choose what load balancer best suits your workload load balancing requirements.

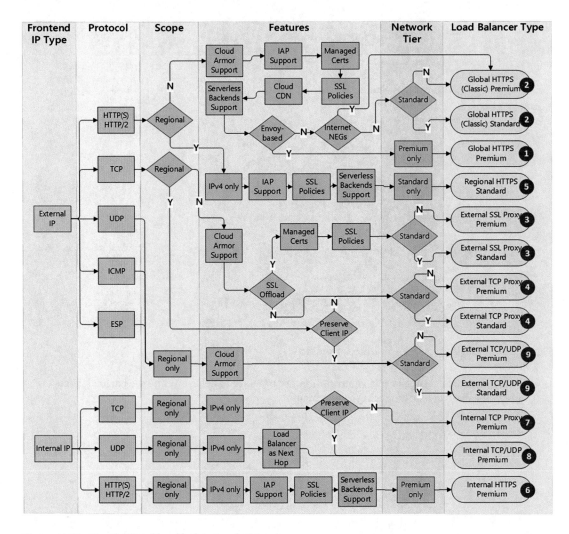

Figure 5-57. *Google Cloud load balancing decision tree*

There are many criteria that drive a decision on the best-suited load balancer. These can be grouped in categories that map to the five pillars of the well-architected framework, as outlined in the following:

- **Protocol from client to frontend**: Performance, technical requirements

- **Protocol from frontend to backends**: Performance

- **Backends**: Performance, operational efficiency

- **IP addresses**: Technical requirements

- **Network topology**: Resilience, operational efficiency

- **Failover**: Resilience

- **Session affinity**: Business requirements

- **Routing**: Performance

- **Autoscaling and self-healing**: Elasticity, resilience

- **Security**: Security

The decision tree in Figure 5-57 is not exhaustive, but highlights the right mix of criteria (in the features column) you need to consider for your load balancer, for example, backends and security.

■ **Exam tip**   Cloud Armor is supported for all external load balancer types but the regional external HTTP(S) load balancer (type 5). Identity-Aware Proxy (IAP) is supported by all HTTP(S) load balancer types (types 1, 2, 5, and 6). SSL offload is supported by all external proxy-based load balancer types but the global external TCP proxy load balancer (type 4).

Protocol Forwarding

Protocol forwarding is a Compute Engine feature that lets you create forwarding rule objects that can send packets to a single target Compute Engine instance (VM) instead of a target proxy.

A target instance contains a single VM that receives and handles traffic from the corresponding forwarding rule.

To create a target instance, you can use the gcloud command:

```
gcloud compute target-instances create your-target-instance
    --instance=your-vm
```

■ **Note**   The preceding command assumes you already have a VM your-vm, and it creates a target instance Google Cloud resource, which is different from the actual VM resource.

You then use the newly created target instance resource to create the forwarding rule with protocol forwarding:

```
gcloud compute forwarding-rules create your-pf-rule \
    --ip-protocol=TCP \
    --load-balancing-scheme=EXTERNAL \
    --network-tier=PREMIUM \
    --ports=80 \
    --target-instance=your-target-instance
```

Protocol forwarding can be used in a number of scenarios, including

- External protocol forwarding

- Virtual private networks (VPNs)

- Internal protocol forwarding

For external protocol forwarding and virtual private networks (VPNs), Google Cloud supports protocol forwarding for the AH (Authentication Header), ESP (Encapsulating Security Payload), ICMP (Internet Control Message Protocol), SCTP (Stream Control Transmission Protocol), TCP (Transmission Control Protocol), and UDP (User Datagram Protocol) protocols.

For internal protocol forwarding, only TCP and UDP are supported.

Accommodating Workload Increases Using Autoscaling vs. Manual Scaling

Google Cloud Compute Engine offers autoscaling to *automatically* add or remove VM instances to or from a managed instance group (MIG) based on increases or decreases in load. Autoscaling lets your apps gracefully handle increases in traffic, and it reduces cost when the need for resources decreases. You can autoscale a MIG based on its CPU utilization, Cloud Monitoring metrics, schedules, or load balancing serving capacity.

When you set up an autoscaler to scale based on load balancing serving capacity, the autoscaler watches the serving capacity of an instance group and *scales in* or *scales out* when the VM instances are under or over capacity, respectively.

■ **Exam tip**   The serving capacity of a load balancer is *always* defined in the load balancer's backend service. When you configure autoscaling for a MIG that serves requests from an HTTP(S) load balancer (types 1, 2, 5, and 6), the serving capacity of your load balancer is based on either utilization or rate (requests per second, i.e., RPS, or queries per second, i.e., QPS) as shown in Figure 5-5.

The values of the following fields in the backend services resource determine the backend's behavior:

- A *balancing mode*, which defines how the load balancer measures backend readiness for new requests or connections.

- A *target capacity*, which defines a target maximum number of connections, a target maximum rate, or target maximum CPU utilization.

- A *capacity scaler*, which adjusts overall available capacity without modifying the target capacity. Its value can be either 0.0 (preventing any new connections) or a value between 0.1 (10%) and 1.0 (100% default).

These fields can be set using the `gcloud compute backend-services add-backend` command, whose synopsis is displayed in Figure 5-58.

SYNOPSIS

```
gcloud compute backend-services add-backend BACKEND_SERVICE_NAME
    ([ --instance-group = INSTANCE_GROUP : --instance-group-region = INSTANCE_GROUP_REGION |
    --instance-group-zone = INSTANCE_GROUP_ZONE] |
    [ --network-endpoint-group = NETWORK_ENDPOINT_GROUP : --global-network-endpoint-group |
    --network-endpoint-group-region = NETWORK_ENDPOINT_GROUP_REGION |
    --network-endpoint-group-zone = NETWORK_ENDPOINT_GROUP_ZONE])
    [ --balancing-mode = BALANCING_MODE] [ --capacity-scaler = CAPACITY_SCALER]
    [ --description = DESCRIPTION] [ --failover] [ --max-utilization = MAX_UTILIZATION] [ --global  |
    --region = REGION] [ --max-connections = MAX_CONNECTIONS  |
    --max-connections-per-endpoint = MAX_CONNECTIONS_PER_ENDPOINT  |
    --max-connections-per-instance = MAX_CONNECTIONS_PER_INSTANCE  | --max-rate = MAX_RATE  |
    --max-rate-per-endpoint = MAX_RATE_PER_ENDPOINT  |
    --max-rate-per-instance = MAX_RATE_PER_INSTANCE] [ GCLOUD_WIDE_FLAG _]
```

Figure 5-58. *Syntax to set a load balancer target capacity*

Each load balancer type supports different balancing modes, and the balancing mode is based on what backend type is associated to the backend service.

Google Cloud has three balancing modes:

- CONNECTION: Determines how the load is spread based on the number of concurrent connections that the backend can handle.

- RATE: The target maximum number of requests (queries) per second (RPS, QPS). The target maximum RPS/QPS can be exceeded if all backends are at or above capacity.

- UTILIZATION: Determines how the load is spread based on the utilization of instances in an instance group.

Figure 5-59 shows which balancing mode is supported for each of the nine load balancer types based on backends.

Load Balancer Type	Backends	Balancing Modes
• Global External HTTP(S) (1) • Global External HTTP(S) (classic) (2) • Regional External HTTP(S) (5) • Regional Internal HTTP(S) (6)	Instance Groups	RATE or UTILIZATION
	Zonal NEGs (GCE_VM_IP_PORT endpoints)	RATE
	Hybrid NEGs (NON_GCP_PRIVATE_IP_PORT endpoints)	RATE
• Global External SSL Proxy (3) • Global External TCP Proxy (4) • Regional Internal TCP Proxy (7)	Instance Groups	CONNECTION or UTILIZATION
	Zonal NEGs (GCE_VM_IP_PORT endpoints)	CONNECTION
	Hybrid NEGs (NON_GCP_PRIVATE_IP_PORT endpoints) (supported by 7 only)	CONNECTION
Regional External TCP/UDP Network (9)	Instance Groups	CONNECTION
Regional Internal TCP/UDP Network (8)	Instance Groups	CONNECTION
	Zonal NEGs (GCE_VM_IP endpoints)	CONNECTION

Figure 5-59. *Load balancing mode matrix*

Configuring Cloud Armor Policies

You heard about Cloud Armor at the beginning of the chapter when we listed the load balancer types that support advanced DDoS (Distributed Denial-of-Service) protection—since this is a hot topic for the exam, let's repeat one more time; these are all external load balancer types except the regional external HTTP(S), that is, types 1, 2, 3, 4, and 9.

In this section, you will learn about Cloud Armor and how it can be used to better protect your workloads whether they operate in Google Cloud, in a hybrid, or a multi-cloud environment.

Security Policies

Google Cloud Armor uses *security policies* to protect your application from common web attacks. This is achieved by providing layer 7 filtering and by parsing incoming requests in a way to potentially block traffic before it reaches your load balancer's backend services or backend buckets.

Each security policy is comprised of a set of rules that filter traffic based on conditions such as an incoming request's IP address, IP range, region code, or request headers.

Google Cloud Armor security policies are available only for backend services of global external HTTP(S) load balancers (type 1), global external HTTP(S) load balancers (classic) (type 2), global external SSL proxy load balancers (type 3), or global external TCP proxy load balancers (type 4). The load balancer can be in a premium or standard tier.

The backends associated to the backend service can be any of the following:

- Instance groups

- Zonal network endpoint groups (NEGs)

- Serverless NEGs: One or more App Engine, Cloud Run, or Cloud Functions services

- Internet NEGs for external backends

- Buckets in Cloud Storage

■ **Exam tip** When you use Google Cloud Armor to protect a hybrid or a multi-cloud deployment, the backends must be *Internet NEGs*. Google Cloud Armor also protects serverless NEGs when traffic is routed through a load balancer. To ensure that only traffic that has been routed through your load balancer reaches your serverless NEG, see Ingress controls.

Google Cloud Armor also provides advanced network DDoS protection for regional external TCP/UDP network load balancers (type 9), protocol forwarding, and VMs with public IP addresses. For more information about advanced DDoS protection, see Configure advanced network DDoS protection.

Adaptive Protection

Google Cloud Armor Adaptive Protection helps you protect your Google Cloud applications, websites, and services against L7 DDoS attacks such as HTTP floods and other high-frequency layer 7 (application-level) malicious activity. Adaptive Protection builds machine learning models that do the following:

- Detect and alert on anomalous activity

- Generate a signature describing the potential attack

- Generate a custom Google Cloud Armor WAF (web application firewall) rule to block the signature

You enable or disable Adaptive Protection on a per–security policy basis.

Full Adaptive Protection alerts are available only if you subscribe to *Google Cloud Armor Managed Protection Plus*. Otherwise, you receive only a basic alert, without an attack signature or the ability to deploy a suggested rule.

Web Application Firewall (WAF) Rules

Google Cloud Armor comes with preconfigured WAF rules, which are complex web application firewall (WAF) rules with many signatures that are compiled from open source industry standards.

Each signature corresponds to an attack detection rule in the ruleset. Incoming requests are evaluated against the preconfigured WAF rules.

Each signature has also a *sensitivity level*, which ranges between zero (no rules are enabled by default) and four (all rules are enabled by default).

A lower sensitivity level indicates higher confidence signatures, which are less likely to generate a false positive. A higher sensitivity level increases security, but also increases the risk of generating a false positive.

When you select a sensitivity level for your WAF rule, you opt in signatures at the sensitivity levels less than or equal to the selected sensitivity level. In the following example, you tune a preconfigured WAF rule by selecting the sensitivity level of 1:

```
evaluatePreconfiguredWaf('sqli-v33-stable', {'sensitivity': 1})
```

Configure Custom Rules Language Attributes

In addition to using the preconfigured WAF rules, you can also define prioritized rules with configurable match conditions and actions in a security policy.

A rule takes effect, meaning that the configured action is applied, if the rule is the highest priority rule whose conditions match the attributes of the incoming request.

There are two kinds of match conditions:

- A *basic* match condition, which contains lists of IP addresses or lists of IP address ranges (a mixed list of addresses and ranges is allowed)

- An *advanced* match condition, which contains an expression with multiple subexpressions to match on a variety of attributes of an incoming request

The custom rules language is used to write the expressions in advanced match conditions for security policy rules. The Google Cloud Armor custom rules language is an extension of the Common Expression Language (CEL).

An expression requires two components:

- Attributes that can be inspected in rule expressions

- Operations that can be performed on the attributes as part of an expression

For example, the following expression uses the attributes `origin.ip` and `9.9.9.0/24` in the operation `inIpRange()`. In this case, the expression returns true if `origin.ip` is within the `9.9.9.0/24` IP address range:

```
inIpRange(origin.ip, '9.9.9.0/24')
```

Attaching Security Policies to Backend Services

Once created, a security policy is a Google Cloud resource that can be attached to one (or more) backend service(s) in order to enforce the rules expressed within the policy.

The following are the high-level steps for configuring Google Cloud Armor security policies to enable rules that allow or deny traffic to global external HTTP(S) load balancers (type 1) or global external HTTP(S) load balancers (classic) (type 2):

1. Create a Google Cloud Armor security policy.

2. Add rules to the security policy based on IP address lists, custom expressions, or preconfigured expression sets.

3. Attach the security policy to a backend service of the global external HTTP(S) load balancer or global external HTTP(S) load balancer (classic) for which you want to control access.

4. Update the security policy as needed.

In the example displayed in Figure 5-60, you create two Google Cloud Armor security policies and apply them to different backend services.

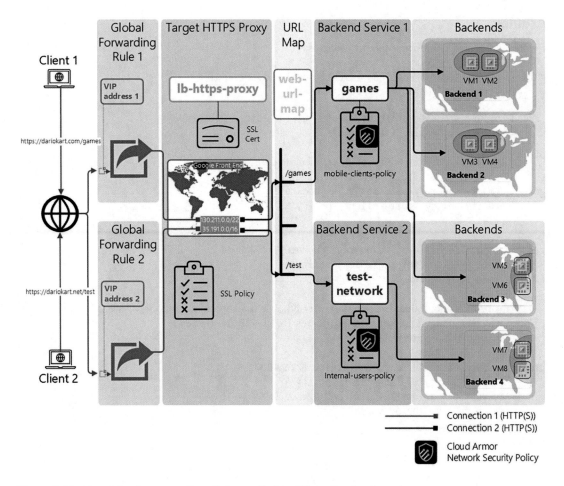

Figure 5-60. *Example of two security policies applied to different backend services*

In the example, these are the Google Cloud Armor security policies:

- `mobile-clients-policy`, which applies to external users of your game services

- `internal-users-policy`, which applies to your organization's test-network team

You apply `mobile-clients-policy` to the game service, whose backend service is called `games`, and you apply `internal-users-policy` to the internal test service for the testing team, whose corresponding backend service is called `test-network`.

If the backend instances for a backend service are in multiple regions, the Google Cloud Armor security policy associated with the service is applicable to instances in all regions. In the preceding example, the security policy `mobile-clients-policy` is applicable to instances 1, 2, 3, and 4 in `us-central1` and to instances 5 and 6 in `us-east1`.

Example

Create the Google Cloud Armor security policies:

```
gcloud compute security-policies create mobile-clients-policy \
    --description "policy for external users"

gcloud compute security-policies create internal-users-policy \
    --description "policy for internal test users"
```

Update the default rules to the security policies to deny traffic:

```
gcloud compute security-policies rules update 2147483647 \
    --security-policy mobile-clients-policy \
    --action "deny-404"

gcloud compute security-policies rules update 2147483647 \
    --security-policy internal-users-policy \
    --action "deny-502"
```

In the preceding commands, the first (and only) positional argument denotes the security policy priority, which is an integer ranging from 0 (highest) to 2147483647 (lowest).

Add rules to the security policies:

```
gcloud compute security-policies rules create 1000 \
    --security-policy mobile-clients-policy \
    --description "allow traffic from 192.0.2.0/24" \
    --src-ip-ranges "192.0.2.0/24" \
    --action "allow"

gcloud compute security-policies rules create 1000 \
    --security-policy internal-users-policy \
    --description "allow traffic from 198.51.100.0/24" \
    --src-ip-ranges "198.51.100.0/24" \
    --action "allow"
```

In the preceding commands, the two CIDR blocks 192.0.2.0/24 and 198.51.100.0/24 denote Internet reserved IP addresses scoped for documentation and examples.

Attach the security policies to the backend services:

```
gcloud compute backend-services update games \
    --security-policy mobile-clients-policy

gcloud compute backend-services update test-network \
    --security-policy internal-users-policy
```

Optionally, enable Adaptive Protection:

```
gcloud compute security-policies update mobile-clients-policy \
    --enable-layer7-ddos-defense

gcloud compute security-policies update internal-users-policy \
    --enable-layer7-ddos-defense
```

Configuring Cloud CDN

Cloud CDN (Content Delivery Network) is another network service, which uses Google's global edge network to serve content closer to your users, which reduces latency and delivers better website and application browsing experiences.

Cloud CDN uses the concept of a *cache*, which stores data so that future requests for that data can be served faster; the data stored in a cache might be the result of an earlier computation or a copy of data stored elsewhere.

Since the cache concept is a tenet of the HTTP protocol design specification, and since the cache data store is located in one of the many Google Front Ends in the Google's global edge network, Cloud CDN is naturally supported by the two global external HTTP(S) load balancers (types 1 and 2 in premium tier).

Cloud CDN content can be sourced from various types of backends:

- Instance groups

- Zonal network endpoint groups (NEGs)

- Serverless NEGs: One or more App Engine, Cloud Run, or Cloud Functions services

- Internet NEGs for external backends

- Buckets in Cloud Storage

In Cloud CDN, these backends are also called *origin servers*.

Interaction with HTTP(S) Load Balancer

A cache is a data store that uses infrastructure located in the Google Edge Network, as close as possible to the users of your application.

The cached content is a copy of cacheable content that is stored on origin servers. You will learn what "cacheable" means in the "Cacheable Responses" section. For the time being, assume that not all responses from the origin servers can be stored in a Cloud CDN cache.

You can toggle the use of Cloud CDN by enabling or disabling Cloud CDN in the configuration of your HTTP(S) load balancer's backend service (serving dynamic content) or backend bucket (serving static content) as shown in Figure 5-61 where the origin servers are a zonal network endpoint group.

Cloud CDN Interaction with Global External HTTP(S) Load Balancers ❶ ❷

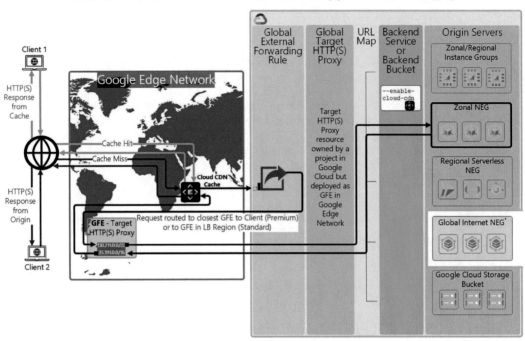

Figure 5-61. *Cache hit and cache miss*

The GFE determines whether a cached response to the user's request exists in the cache, and if it does, it returns the cached response to the user without any further action. This interaction is called *cache hit*, because Cloud CDN was able to serve the request from the user by retrieving the cached response directly from the cache, thereby avoiding an extra round-trip to the origin servers (backends), as well as the time spent regenerating the content. A cache hit is displayed with a green arrow in Figure 5-61.

Conversely, if the GFE determines that a cached response does not exist in the cache—for example, when the cache has no entries or when a request has been sent for the first time—the request is forwarded to the HTTP(S) load balancer and eventually reaches the origin servers (backends) for processing. Upon completion, the computed content is packaged in an HTTP(S) response and is sent back to the cache, which becomes replenished, and is then sent back to the user. This interaction is called a *cache miss*, because the GFE failed to retrieve a response from the cache and was forced to reach the origin servers in order to serve the request from the user. A cache miss is displayed with a red arrow in Figure 5-61.

If the origin server's response to this request is *cacheable*, Cloud CDN stores the response in the Cloud CDN cache for future requests. Data transfer from a cache to a client is called *cache egress*. Data transfer to a cache is called *cache fill*.

Enabling and Disabling Cloud CDN

As shown in Figure 5-61, Cloud CDN can be enabled (`--enable-cdn`) or disabled (`--no-enable-cdn`) by configuring the global external HTTPS load balancer's backend service or backend bucket as follows:

```
gcloud compute backend-services create YOUR_BACKEND_SERVICE \
    --[no-]enable-cdn
gcloud compute backend-services create YOUR_BACKEND_BUCKET \
    --[no-]enable-cdn
```

Optional flags:

- `--no-cache-key-include-protocol`

- `--no-cache-key-include-host`

- `--no-cache-key-include-query-string`

Additionally, upon enabling Cloud CDN you can choose whether Cloud CDN should cache all content, only static content, or selectively pick and choose which content to cache based on a setting in the origin server. This can be achieved using the `--cache-mode` optional flag, whose value can be one the following:

- `FORCE_CACHE_ALL`, which caches *all* content, ignoring any `private`, `no-store`, or `no-cache` directives in `Cache-Control` response headers.

- `CACHE_ALL_STATIC`, which automatically caches static content, including common image formats, media (video and audio), and web assets (JavaScript and CSS). Requests and responses that are marked as uncacheable, as well as dynamic content (including HTML), aren't cached.

- `USE_ORIGIN_HEADERS`, which requires the origin to set valid caching headers to cache content. Responses without these headers aren't cached at Google's edge and require a full trip to the origin on every request, potentially impacting performance and increasing load on the origin servers.

■ **Warning** Setting the `cache-mode` to `FORCE_CACHE_ALL` may result in Cloud CDN caching private, per-user (Personally Identifiable Information—PII) content. You should only enable this on backends that are not serving private or dynamic content, such as storage buckets. To learn more, visit `https://csrc.nist.gov/glossary/term/PII`.

Cacheable Responses

A cacheable response is an HTTP response that Cloud CDN can store and quickly retrieve, thus allowing for faster load times resulting in lower latencies and better user experiences. Not all HTTP responses are cacheable. Cloud CDN stores responses in cache if all the conditions listed in Figure 5-62 are true.

Attribute	Requirement
Served by	Backend service, backend bucket, or an external backend with Cloud CDN enabled
In response to	GET request
Status code	200, 203, 204, 206, 300, 301, 302, 307, 308, 404, 405, 410, 421, 451, or 501.
Freshness	The response has a Cache-Control header with a max-age or s-maxage directive, or an Expires header with a timestamp in the future. For cacheable responses without an age (for example, with no-cache), the public directive must be explicitly provided. With the CACHE_ALL_STATIC cache mode, if no freshness directives are present, a successful response with static content type is still eligible for caching. With the FORCE_CACHE_ALL cache mode, any successful response is eligible for caching. This might result in caching of private, per-user (user identifiable) content. You should only set FORCE_CACHE_ALL on backends that aren't serving private or dynamic content, such as Cloud Storage buckets. If negative caching is enabled and the status code matches one for which negative caching specifies a TTL, the response is eligible for caching, even without explicit freshness directives.
Content	Contains a valid Content-Length, Content-Range, or Transfer-Encoding: chunked header. For example, a Content-Length header that correctly matches the size of the response.
Size	Less than or equal to the maximum size. For responses with sizes between 10 MB and 5 TB, see the additional cacheability constraints described in byte range requests.

Figure 5-62. *Criteria for HTTP cacheable responses*

■ **Exam tip**   You don't need to memorize all the preceding criteria for the exam. However, the ones you should remember are the first two and the last, that is, Cloud CDN must be enabled for a backend service or a backend bucket; only responses to GET requests may be cached, and there is a limit to cacheable content size.

Using Cache Keys

Each cache entry in a Cloud CDN cache is identified by a cache key. When a request comes into the cache, the cache converts the URI of the request into a cache key and then compares it with keys of cached entries. If it finds a match, the cache returns the object associated with that key.

For backend services, Cloud CDN defaults to using the *complete* request URI as the cache key. For example, `https://dariokart.com/images/supermario.jpg` is the complete URI for a particular request for the `supermario.jpg` object. This string is used as the default cache key. Only requests with this exact string match. Requests for

- `http://dariokart.com/images/supermario.jpg`

- `https://dariokart.com/images/supermario.jpg?user=user1`

do not match.

For backend buckets, Cloud CDN defaults to using the URI *without the protocol or host*. By default, only query parameters that are known to Cloud Storage are included as part of the cache key (e.g., "generation").

Thus, for a given backend bucket, the following URIs resolve to the same cached object **/images/supermario.jpg**:

- `http://dariokart.com/`**`images/supermario.jpg`**

- `https://dariokart.com/`**`images/supermario.jpg`**

- `https://dariokart.com/`**`images/supermario.jpg`**`?user=user1`

- `http://dariokart.com/images/supermario.jpg?user=user1`

- `https://dariokart.com/images/supermario.jpg?user=user2`

- `https://media.dariokart.com/images/supermario.jpg`

- `https://www.dariokart.com/images/supermario.jpg`

■ **Exam tip**   You can change which parts of the URI are used in the cache key. While the filename and path must always be part of the key, you can include or omit any combination of protocol, host, or query string when customizing your cache key.

Customizing Cache Keys

You can override the default behavior of cache key definition for the backend service and backend bucket Google Cloud resources. The latter doesn't have flags to include (or exclude) *protocol* and *host* in a cache key, because protocol and host do not influence how objects are referenced within a Cloud Storage bucket.

This can be achieved using some of the flags that control HTTP constructs such as the query string, HTTP headers, and HTTP cookies as explained in the following sections.

Enabling Cloud CDN

First and foremost, you need to enable Cloud CDN on your HTTP(S) load balancer's backend service or backend bucket:

```
gcloud compute backend-services update YOUR_BACKEND_SERVICE \
    --enable-cdn
```

```
gcloud compute backend-buckets update YOUR_BACKEND_BUCKET \
    --enable-cdn
```

Updating Cache Keys to Remove Protocol, Host, and Query String

As you learned earlier, by default backend services configured to use Cloud CDN include all components of the request URI in cache keys. If you want to exclude the protocol, host, and query string, proceed as follows:

```
gcloud compute backend-services update YOUR_BACKEND_SERVICE \
    --no-cache-key-include-protocol
    --no-cache-key-include-host
    --no-cache-key-include-query-string
```

Updating Cache Keys to Add Protocol, Host, and Query String

These instructions readd the protocol, host, and query string to the cache key for an existing backend service that already has Cloud CDN enabled:

```
gcloud compute backend-services update YOUR_BACKEND_SERVICE \
    --cache-key-include-protocol \
    --cache-key-include-host \
    --cache-key-include-query-string
```

Updating Cache Keys to Use an Include or Exclude List of Query Strings

These instructions set CDN cache keys to use an include or exclude list with query string parameters.
Use this command to set the strings user and time to be in the include list:

```
gcloud compute backend-services update YOUR_BACKEND_SERVICE \
    --cache-key-include-query-string \
    --cache-key-query-string-whitelist user,time
```

Use this command to add the strings user and time to an exclude list:

```
gcloud compute backend-services update YOUR_BACKEND_SERVICE \
    --cache-key-include-query-string \
    --cache-key-query-string-blacklist user,time
```

■ **Note**   You can either specify --cache-key-query-string-whitelist or --cache-key-query-string-blacklist, not both. The characters '&' and '=' will be percent encoded and not treated as delimiters. These flags can only be applied to global backend services or global backend buckets.

Updating Cache Keys to Use HTTP Headers

These instructions set Cloud CDN cache keys to use HTTP headers:

```
gcloud compute backend-services update YOUR_BACKEND_SERVICE \
    --cache-key-include-http-header=[HEADER_FIELD_NAME,...]
gcloud compute backend-buckets update YOUR_BACKEND_BUCKET \
    --cache-key-include-http-header=[HEADER_FIELD_NAME,...]
```

Updating Cache Keys to Use Named Cookies

These instructions set Cloud CDN cache keys to use HTTP cookies:

```
gcloud compute backend-services update YOUR_BACKEND_SERVICE \
    --cache-key-include-named-cookie=[NAMED_COOKIE,...]
```

Cache Invalidation

After an object is cached, it remains in the cache until it expires or is evicted to make room for new content. You can control the expiration time through the standard HTTP header Cache-Control (www.rfc-editor. org/rfc/rfc9111#section-5.2).

Cache *invalidation* is the action of forcibly removing an object (a key-value pair) from the cache prior to its normal expiration time.

■ **Exam tip** The Cache-Control HTTP header field holds the directives (instructions) displayed in Figure 5-63—in both requests and responses—that control caching behavior. You don't need to know each of the sixteen Cache-Control directives, but it's important you remember the two directives no-store and private. The former indicates *not* to store any content in any cache—whether it be a private cache (e.g., local cache in your browser) or a shared cache (e.g., proxies, Cloud CDN, and other Content Delivery Network caches). The latter indicates to only store content in private caches.

Request	Response	Description
max-age	max-age	
max-stale	-	
min-fresh	-	
-	s-maxage	
no-cache	no-cache	
no-store	**no-store**	Don't store in any cache
no-transform	no-transform	
only-if-cached	-	
-	must-revalidate	
-	proxy-revalidate	
-	must-understand	
-	**private**	Store only in client (browser) cache
-	public	
-	immutable	
-	stale-while-revalidate	
stale-if-error	stale-if-error	

Figure 5-63. *Cache-Control directives*

Path Pattern

Each invalidation request requires a path pattern that identifies the exact object or set of objects that should be invalidated. The path pattern can be either a specific path, such as /supermario.png, or an entire directory structure, such as /pictures/*. The following rules apply to path patterns:

- The path pattern must start with /.

- It cannot include ? or #.

- It must not include an * except as the final character following a /.

- If it ends with /*, the preceding string is a prefix, and all objects whose paths begin with that prefix are invalidated.

- The path pattern is compared with the path component of the URL, which is everything between the hostname and any ? or # that might be present.

■ **Exam tip**   If you have URLs that contain a query string, for example, /images.php?image=supermario. png, you cannot selectively invalidate objects that differ only by the value of the query string. For example, if you have two images, /images.php?image=supermario.png and /images.php?image=luigi.png, you cannot invalidate only luigi.png. You have to invalidate all images served by images.php, by using /images.php as the path pattern.

The next sections describe how to invalidate your Cloud CDN cached content.

For example, if a file located at /images/luigi.jpg has been cached and needs to be invalidated, you can use several methods to invalidate it, depending on whether you want to affect only that file or a wider scope. In each case, you can invalidate for all hostnames or for only one hostname.

Invalidating a Single File

To invalidate a single file for all hosts, use the command

```
gcloud compute url-maps invalidate-cdn-cache YOUR_URL_MAP \
    --path "/images/luigi.jpg"
```

To invalidate a single file for a single host, add the --host flag as follows:

```
gcloud compute url-maps invalidate-cdn-cache YOUR_URL_MAP \
    --host HOSTNAME \
    --path "/images/luigi.jpg"
```

By default, the Google Cloud CLI waits until the invalidation has completed. To perform the invalidation in the background, append the --async flag to the command line.

Invalidate the Whole Directory

To invalidate the whole directory for all hosts, use the command

```
gcloud compute url-maps invalidate-cdn-cache YOUR_URL_MAP \
    --path "/images/*"
```

To invalidate the whole directory for a single host, add the `--host` flag as follows:

```
gcloud compute url-maps invalidate-cdn-cache YOUR_URL_MAP \
    --host HOSTNAME \
    --path "/images/*"
```

To perform the invalidation in the background, append the `--async` flag to the command line.

Invalidate Everything

To invalidate all directories for all hosts, use the command

```
gcloud compute url-maps invalidate-cdn-cache YOUR_URL_MAP \
    --path "/*"
```

To invalidate all directories for a single host, add the `--host` flag as follows:

```
gcloud compute url-maps invalidate-cdn-cache YOUR_URL_MAP \
    --host HOSTNAME \
    --path "/*"
```

To perform the invalidation in the background, append the `--async` flag to the command line.

Signed URLs

Signed URLs give time-limited resource access to anyone in possession of the URL, regardless of whether the user has a Google Account.

A signed URL is a URL that provides limited permission and time to make a request. Signed URLs contain authentication information in their query strings, allowing users without credentials to perform specific actions on a resource. When you generate a signed URL, you specify a user or service account that must have sufficient permission to make the request associated with the URL.

After you generate a signed URL, anyone who possesses it can use the signed URL to perform specified actions (such as reading an object) within a specified period of time.

Configuring Signed Request Keys

You enable support for Cloud CDN signed URLs and signed cookies by creating one or more keys on a Cloud CDN–enabled backend service, backend bucket, or both.

For each backend service or backend bucket, you can create and delete keys as your security needs dictate. Each backend can have up to three keys configured at a time. We suggest periodically rotating your keys by deleting the oldest, adding a new key, and using the new key when signing URLs or cookies.

You can use the same key name in multiple backend services and backend buckets because each set of keys is independent of the others. Key names can be up to 63 characters. To name your keys, use the characters A–Z, a–z, 0–9, _ (underscore), and - (hyphen).

When you create keys, be sure to keep them secure because anyone who has one of your keys can create signed URLs or signed cookies that Cloud CDN accepts until the key is deleted from Cloud CDN. The keys are stored on the computer where you generate the signed URLs or signed cookies. Cloud CDN also stores the keys to verify request signatures.

To keep the keys secret, the key values aren't included in responses to any API requests. If you lose a key, you must create a new one.

■ **Exam tip**   Keep the generated key file private, and do not expose it to users or store it directly in source code. Consider using a secret storage mechanism such as Cloud Key Management Service to encrypt the key and provide access to only trusted applications.

First, generate a strongly random key and store it in the key file with the following command:

```
head -c 16 /dev/urandom | base64 | tr +/ -_ > KEY_FILE_NAME
```

To add the key to a backend service:

```
gcloud compute backend-services \
    add-signed-url-key BACKEND_NAME \
    --key-name KEY_NAME \
    --key-file KEY_FILE_NAME
```

To add the key to a backend bucket:

```
gcloud compute backend-buckets \
    add-signed-url-key BACKEND_NAME \
    --key-name KEY_NAME \
    --key-file KEY_FILE_NAME
```

To list the keys on a backend service or backend bucket, run one of the following commands:

```
gcloud compute backend-services describe BACKEND_NAME
```

```
gcloud compute backend-buckets describe BACKEND_NAME
```

When URLs signed by a particular key should no longer be honored, run one of the following commands to delete that key from the backend service or backend bucket. This will prevent users from consuming the URL that was signed with KEY_NAME:

```
gcloud compute backend-services \
    delete-signed-url-key BACKEND_NAME --key-name KEY_NAME
```

```
gcloud compute backend-buckets \
    delete-signed-url-key BACKEND_NAME --key-name KEY_NAME
```

Signing URLs

Use these instructions to create signed URLs by using the gcloud compute sign-url command as follows:

```
gcloud compute sign-url \
  "URL" \
  --key-name KEY_NAME \
```

```
--key-file KEY_FILE_NAME \
--expires-in TIME_UNTIL_EXPIRATION \
[--validate]
```

This command reads and decodes the base64url encoded key value from `KEY_FILE_NAME` and then outputs a signed URL that you can use for GET or HEAD requests for the given URL.

For example, the command

```
gcloud compute sign-url \
  "https://dariokart.com/media/video.mp4" \
  --key-name my-test-key \
  --expires-in 1h \
  --key-file sign-url-key-file
```

creates a signed URL that expires in one hour. For more information about time format, visit `https://cloud.google.com/sdk/gcloud/reference/topic/datetimes`.

■ **Exam tip** The URL must be a valid URL that has a path component. For example, `http://dariokart.com` is invalid, but `https://dariokart.com/` and `https://dariokart.com/whatever` are both valid URLs.

If the optional `--validate` flag is provided, this command sends a HEAD request with the resulting URL and prints the HTTP response code.

If the signed URL is correct, the response code is the same as the result code sent by your backend.

If the response code isn't the same, recheck KEY_NAME and the contents of the specified file, and make sure that the value of TIME_UNTIL_EXPIRATION is at least several seconds.

If the `--validate` flag is not provided, the following are not verified:

- The inputs

- The generated URL

- The generated signed URL

The URL returned from the Google Cloud CLI can be distributed according to your needs.

■ **Note** We recommend signing only **HTTPS** URLs, because HTTPS provides a secure transport that prevents the signature component of the signed URL from being intercepted. Similarly, make sure that you distribute the signed URLs over secure transport protocols such as TLS/HTTPS.

Custom Origins

A *custom origin* is an Internet network endpoint group (NEG), that is, a backend that resides outside of Google Cloud and is reachable across the Internet.

Specifying a Custom Origin

Similar to configuring Cloud CDN with your endpoints deployed in Google Cloud, you can use the network endpoint group (NEG) API to add your server as a custom origin for Cloud CDN.

To specify the custom origin, use an Internet NEG. An Internet NEG has one of the endpoint types specified in Figure 5-64.

Endpoint address	Type	Definition	When to use
Hostname and an optional port	INTERNET_FQDN_PORT	A publicly resolvable fully qualified domain name (FQDN), and an optional port, for example backend.example.com:443 (default ports: 80 for HTTP and 443 for HTTPS)	Use this endpoint when your external backend can be resolved by using an FQDN with public DNS.
IP address and an optional port	INTERNET_IP_PORT	A publicly accessible IP address and an optional port, for example 192.0.2.8 or 192.0.2.8:443 (default ports: 80 for HTTP and 443 for HTTPS)	Use this endpoint to specify a publicly accessible IP address and a port to connect to.

Figure 5-64. *Internet network endpoint group (NEG) types*

The best practice is to create the Internet NEG with the INTERNET_FQDN_PORT endpoint type and an FQDN (Fully Qualified Domain Name) value as an origin hostname value. This insulates the Cloud CDN configuration from IP address changes in the origin infrastructure. Network endpoints that are defined by using FQDNs are resolved through public DNS. Make sure that the configured FQDN is resolvable through Google Public DNS.

After you create the Internet NEG, the type cannot be changed between INTERNET_FQDN_PORT and INTERNET_IP_PORT. You need to create a new Internet NEG and change your backend service to use the new Internet NEG.

Figure 5-65 shows an Internet NEG used to deploy an external backend with HTTP(S) load balancing and Cloud CDN.

Cloud CDN Interaction with Global External HTTP(S) Load Balancers ❶ ❷ and Internet NEGs

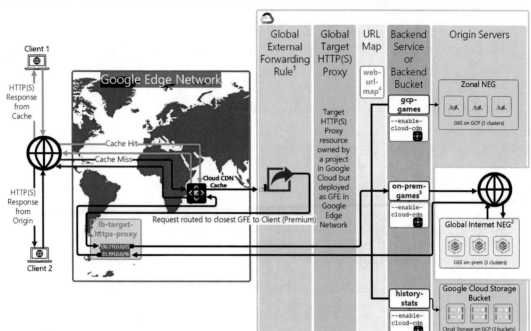

¹ The forwarding rule's network tier must be PREMIUM
² The Internet NEG must have an endpoint, whose type is INTERNET_FQDN_PORT, e.g. backend.dariokart.com:443
³ The backend service leverages a custom request header configured to match the endpoint in footnote 2 to route incoming traffic to the Internet NEG
⁴ The URL Map is configured with a matching rule to map incoming traffic directed to the Internet NEG to the on-prem-games backend service

Figure 5-65. *An example of a custom origin in a hybrid topology*

Best Practices

In this last section, you will learn a few load balancing best practices I want to share based on my experience and my research with GCP.

Use TLS Everywhere

Reduce the attack surface of your workloads by implementing TLS everywhere.

Google doesn't charge for TLS, so you should take advantage of this "bonus" feature while keeping your sensitive data always encrypted in transit.

Restrict Ingress Traffic with Cloud Armor and Identity-Aware Proxy (IAP)

Use Cloud Armor to secure at the edge by filtering ingress traffic, and enforce *context-aware* access controls for your workloads with Identity-Aware Proxy (IAP).

Leverage the OSI layer 3–7 protection and the geolocation and WAF (web application firewall) defense capabilities offered by Cloud Armor.

When Cloud Armor combines forces with IAP, you are significantly strengthening your workloads' security posture.

Identity-Aware Proxy is a Google Cloud service that accelerates you on your way to a Zero Trust Security Model.

Enable Cloud CDN for Cacheable Content

If the content served by your backends is cacheable, enable Cloud CDN (Content Delivery Network). The enablement of Cloud CDN is easy, and your users will be happy with a superior navigation experience.

Enable HTTP/2 As Appropriate

You learned in the "Configuring External HTTP(S) Load Balancers" section that the HTTP/2 protocol is supported by all four HTTP(S) load balancers, that is, types 1, 2, 5, and 6.

When compared to HTTP/1.1, the HTTP/2 protocol has the main advantage of supporting the QUIC (Quick UDP Internet Connections) protocol and the gRPC high-performance Remote Procedure Call (RPC) framework.

All of this results in better performance, lower latency, and better user experiences.

■ **Exam tip**   QUIC is a transport layer protocol (layer 4) developed by Google, which is faster, more efficient, and more secure than earlier protocols, for example, TCP. *For the exam, you need to know that QUIC is only supported by global HTTP(S) load balancers, that is, types 1 and 2.* For increased speed, QUIC uses the UDP transport protocol, which is faster than TCP but less reliable. It sends several streams of data at once to make up for any data that gets lost along the way, a technique known as *multiplexing*. For better security, everything sent over QUIC is automatically encrypted. Ordinarily, data has to be sent over HTTPS to be encrypted. But QUIC has TLS encryption built-in by default.

QUIC results in lower latency due to less handshakes.

Optimize Network for Performance or Cost Based on Your Requirements

When traffic egresses the Google global backbone, you incur outbound data transfer costs. As a result, to architect your workload for cost-effectiveness and performance, you should consider using the Google premium network tier because this tier minimizes egress-related costs by letting your traffic stay in the Google global backbone as long as possible.

However, you may use free tier services for nonmission-critical workloads. As a result, in order to reduce costs—at the expense of performance and resilience—you may choose to configure your load balancer to use the standard network tier, which uses the Internet more than the Google global backbone.

Nevertheless, Google Cloud gives you the option to choose between premium network tier and standard network tier on a per–load balancer basis or a per-project basis (i.e., all your load balancers in your projects will default to your chosen network tier).

Leverage User-Defined HTTP Request Headers to Manage Metadata

Your workload backends can leverage metadata sent in the form of HTTP request headers (e.g., client geolocation, cache-control properties, etc.) to make decisions.

Take advantage of the URL map advanced HTTP capabilities to route traffic to the proper backend services or backend buckets.

Exam Questions

Question 5.1 (Backend Services)

You are configuring the backend service for a new Google Cloud HTTPS load balancer. The application requires high availability and multiple subnets and needs to scale automatically. Which backend configuration should you choose?

- **A.** A zonal managed instance group

- **B.** A regional managed instance group

- **C.** An unmanaged instance group

- **D.** A network endpoint group

Rationale

A is not correct because it would only allow the use of a single zone within a region.

B is CORRECT because it allows the application to be deployed in multiple zones within a region.

C is not correct because it does not allow for autoscaling.

D is not correct because traffic cannot be distributed across multiple subnets and is a singular NEG as opposed to multiple NEGs.

Question 5.2 (Backend Services, Max CPU %, Capacity)

You have the Google Cloud load balancer backend configuration shown in Figure 5-66. You want to reduce your instance group utilization by 20%. Which settings should you use?

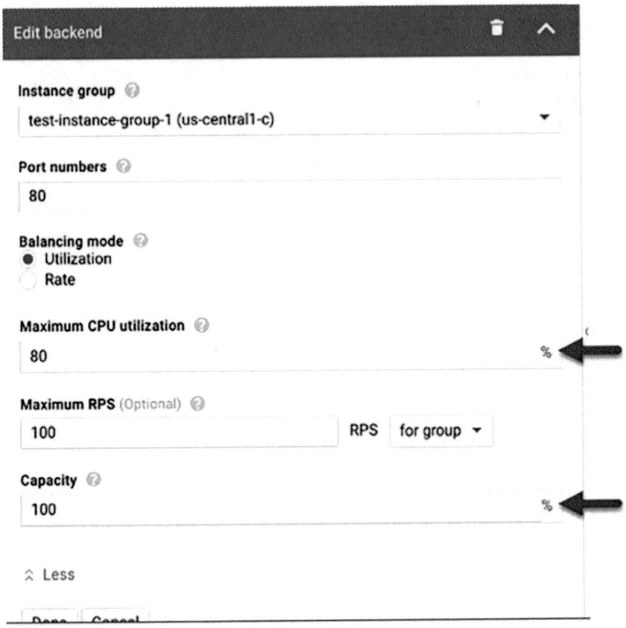

Figure 5-66. *Load balancer backend configuration*

A. Maximum CPU utilization: 60 and Maximum RPS: 80

B. Maximum CPU utilization: 80 and Capacity: 80

C. Maximum RPS: 80 and Capacity: 80

D. Maximum CPU: 60, Maximum RPS: 80, and Capacity: 80

Rationale

A is not correct because this reduces both the CPU utilization and requests per second, resulting in more than a 20% reduction.

B is CORRECT because you are changing the overall instance group utilization by 20%.

C is not correct because this reduces the requests per second by more than 20%.

D is not correct because this reduces both max CPU and RPS, resulting in greater than 20%.

Question 5.3 (Backend Services, Canary A/B Testing)

Your company offers a popular gaming service. The service architecture is shown in Figure 5-67. Your instances are deployed with private IP addresses, and external access is granted through a global load balancer. Your application team wants to expose their test environment to select users outside your organization. You want to integrate the test environment into your existing deployment to reduce management overhead and restrict access to only select users. What should you do?

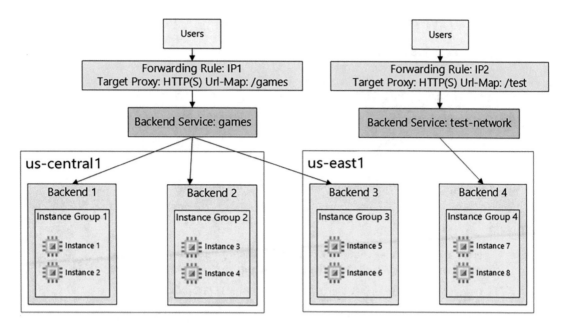

Figure 5-67. *Gaming service architecture*

A. Create a new load balancer, and update VPC firewall rules to allow test clients.

B. Create a new load balancer, and update the VPC Service Controls perimeter to allow test clients.

C. Add the backend service to the existing load balancer, and modify the existing Cloud Armor policy.

D. Add the backend service to the existing load balancer, and add a new Cloud Armor policy and target test-network.

Rationale

A is not correct because the HTTPS load balancer acts as a proxy and doesn't provide the correct client IP address.

B is not correct because VPC Service Controls protects Google Managed Services.

C is not correct because this change would allow everyone to access the test service.

D is CORRECT because this provides integration and support for multiple backend services. Also, a Cloud Armor Network Security Policy is attached to backend services in order to whitelist/blacklist client CIDR blocks, thus allowing traffic to specific targets. In this case, a Cloud Armor Network Security Policy would allow (whitelist) incoming requests originated by the selected testers' IP ranges to reach the test-network backend and deny them (blacklist) access to the game backends.

Question 5.4 (HTTPS Load Balancer, Cloud CDN)

One of the secure web applications in your GCP project is currently only serving users in North America. All of the application's resources are currently hosted in a single GCP region. The application uses a large catalog of graphical assets from a Cloud Storage bucket. You are notified that the application now needs to serve global clients without adding any additional GCP regions or Compute Engine instances. What should you do?

A.   Configure Cloud CDN.

B.   Configure a TCP proxy.

C.   Configure a network load balancer.

D.   Configure dynamic routing for the subnet hosting the application.

Rationale

A is CORRECT because Cloud CDN will front (cache) static content from a Cloud Storage bucket and move the graphical resources closest to the users.

B,C are not correct because Cloud CDN requires and HTTPS proxy.

D is not correct because dynamic routing will not help serve additional web clients.

Question 5.5 (HTTPS Load Balancer, Autoscale)

You have implemented an HTTP(S) load balancer to balance requests across Compute Engine virtual machine instances. During peak times, your backend instances cannot handle the number of requests per second (RPS), which causes some requests to be dropped. Following Google-recommended practices, you want to efficiently scale the instances to avoid this scenario in the future. What should you do?

A.   Use unmanaged instance groups, and upgrade the instance machine type to use a higher-performing CPU.

B.   Use unmanaged instance groups, and double the number of instances you need at off-peak times.

C.   Use managed instance groups, and turn on autoscaling based on the average CPU utilization of your instances.

D.   Use managed instance groups, turn on autoscaling for HTTP(S) load balancing usage (RPS), and set target load balancing usage as a percentage of the serving rate.

Rationale

A is not correct because the stated limitation is not the result of CPU utilization, and this method is inefficient.

B is not correct because doubling the number of instances is inefficient.

C is not correct because the stated limitation is on requests per second, not CPU utilization.

D is CORRECT because the autoscaling method leverages the load balancer and efficiently scales the instances.

CHAPTER 6

■ ■ ■

Configuring Advanced Network Services

You learned in Chapter 5 how Google Cloud load balancing comprises an ecosystem of products and services. Load balancing alone includes nine different types of load balancers, and most of them are available in the two network service tiers, that is, premium and standard.

While load balancing focuses on the performance and reliability aspects of your workloads, there are other important factors you need to consider when designing the network architecture of your workloads.

In this chapter, our focus will shift toward security. I already mentioned it once, but you should also have started to notice how security and networking are two sides of the same coin: there is no well-architected workload designed without addressing network and security—altogether.

In this chapter, you will learn how to configure three advanced network services, that is, Cloud DNS, Cloud NAT, and Packet Mirroring policies.

These three advanced network services supplement nicely the capabilities offered by the GCP load balancers and when properly used will reinforce the security posture of your workloads.

Let's get started!

Configuring and Maintaining Cloud DNS

DNS is a hierarchical distributed database that lets you store IP addresses and other data and look them up by name. Cloud DNS lets you publish your zones and records in DNS without the burden of managing your own DNS servers and software.

Cloud DNS offers both *public* zones and *private* managed DNS zones.

A public zone hosts DNS records that are visible to the Internet, whereas a private zone hosts DNS records that are visible only inside your organization. This is done by setting up one or more VPC networks and by connecting them to your organization's data centers with VLAN attachments or IPsec tunnels.

Cloud DNS supports Identity and Access Management (IAM) permissions at the project level and individual DNS zone level. This approach allows for separation of duties at the level that best suits your security requirements.

Managing Zones and Records

A managed zone is the container for all of your DNS records that share the same domain name, for example, dariokart.com. Managed zones are automatically assigned a set of name servers when they are created to handle responding to DNS queries for that zone. A managed zone has quotas for the number of resource records that it can include.

© Dario Cabianca 2023
D. Cabianca, *Google Cloud Platform (GCP) Professional Cloud Network Engineer Certification Companion*, Certification Study Companion Series, https://doi.org/10.1007/978-1-4842-9354-6_6

Creating Public Zones

To create a new managed zone, run the dns managed-zones create command with the --visibility flag set to public:

```
gcloud dns managed-zones create your-public-zone \
    --dns-name=dariokart.com \
    --description="A public zone" \
    --visibility=public
```

■ **Note** Cloud DNS creates NS (Name Server) and SOA (Start of Authority) records for you automatically when you create the zone. Do not change the name of your zone's NS record, and do not change the list of name servers that Cloud DNS selects for your zone.

Creating Private Zones

A private managed zone is a container of DNS records that is only visible from one or more VPC networks that you specify.

To create a private zone, run the dns managed-zones create command with the --visibility flag set to private:

```
gcloud dns managed-zones create your-private-zone \
    --dns-name=dariokart.private \
    --description="A private zone" \
    --visibility=private \
    --networks=default
```

■ **Note** As you learned in Chapter 3, every Google Cloud new project has a default network (an auto-mode VPC) that has one subnet in each region. The subnet CIDR blocks have IPv4 ranges only and are automatically assigned for you. The subnets and all subnet ranges fit inside the 10.128.0.0/9 CIDR block.

If you receive an accessNotConfigured error, you must enable the Cloud DNS API.

To change the networks to which a private zone is visible:

```
gcloud dns managed-zones update your-private-zone \
    --networks=default,your-app-shared-vpc
```

Creating Forwarding Zones

A *forwarding zone* overrides normal DNS resolution of the specified zones. Instead, queries for the specified zones are forwarded to the listed forwarding targets:

```
  gcloud dns managed-zones create your-forwarding-zone \
      --dns-name=dariokart.com \
      --description="A forwarding zone" \
```

```
--networks=default,your-app-shared-vpc \
--visibility=private \
--forwarding-targets=8.8.8.8,8.8.4.4
```

In the preceding example

- `--dns-name` is the domain name to be resolved by the forwarding zone.

- `--networks` is the list of networks that are authorized to query the zone.

- `--visibility` indicates whether the forwarding zone is public or private.

- `--forwarding-targets` is a list of static IP addresses. These IP addresses can be RFC 1918 addresses if they are reachable on the same VPC network or on a network connected via VPN or Interconnect. Otherwise, they must be publicly routable IP addresses.

Creating Peering Zones

When two networks are peered, they do not automatically share DNS information. With DNS peering, you can have one network (consumer network) forward DNS requests to another network (producer network). You can do this by creating a peering zone in the consumer network that forwards matching DNS requests to the producer network.

■ **Exam tip**   VPC network peering is not the same as DNS peering. VPC network peering allows VMs in multiple projects (even in different organizations) to reach each other, but it does not change name resolution. Resources in each VPC network still follow their own resolution order.

In contrast, through DNS peering, you can allow requests to be forwarded for specific zones to another VPC network. This lets you forward requests to different Google Cloud environments, regardless of whether the VPC networks are connected.

VPC network peering and DNS peering are also set up differently. For VPC network peering, both VPC networks need to set up a peering relationship to the other VPC network. The peering is then automatically bidirectional.

DNS peering unidirectionally forwards DNS requests and does not require a bidirectional relationship between VPC networks. A VPC network referred to as the DNS consumer network performs lookups for a Cloud DNS peering zone in another VPC network, which is referred to as the DNS producer network. Users with the IAM permission dns.networks.targetWithPeeringZone on the producer network's project can establish DNS peering between consumer and producer networks. To set up DNS peering from a consumer VPC network, you require the DNS peer role for the producer VPC network's host project. We will discuss DNS peering in detail shortly, but if you can't wait to see how this works, have a look at Figure 6-3.

Managing Records

Managing DNS records for the Cloud DNS API involves sending *change* requests to the API. This page describes how to make changes, consisting of additions and deletions to or from your *resource record sets* collection. This page also describes how to send the desired changes to the API using the import, export, and transaction commands.

Before learning how to perform an operation on a DNS resource record, let's review the list of resource record types. Figure 6-1 displays the complete list.

Type	Description
A	The host's numeric IP address, in dotted decimal format.
AAAA	The host's numeric IP address, in IPv6 hexadecimal format.
CAA	The Certificate Authorities that are authorized to issue certificates for this domain.
CNAME	The canonical name for which the DNS name is an alias. A **Canonical Name record** (abbreviated as **CNAME record**) is a type of resource record in the Domain Name System (DNS) which maps one domain name (an alias) to another (the Canonical Name). ***CNAME records must always point to another domain name, never directly to an IP address.***
DNSKEY	The DNSSEC key from another operator for secure transfer. This record set type can only be added to a DNSSEC-enabled zone in Transfer state.
DS	The DNSSEC Key fingerprint for secure delegated zone. This record set type does not activate DNSSEC for a delegated zone unless you enable (and activate) DNSSEC for this zone.
IPSECVPNKEY	The IPSec public VPN key. DNSSEC is recommended when using this record set type, but it is not enabled for this zone.
MX	A number and DNS name of a mail exchange server, indicating priority of the server. Servers with lower numbers are tried first. Make sure there is a space between the number and DNS name.
NAPTR	Name authority pointer rules used for mapping Uniform Resource Names.
NS	***The DNS name of the authoritative nameserver.*** Your NS records must match the nameservers for your zone. Note: A wildcard resource record set of type `NS` is not supported.Note: Managed private zones do not support custom resource record sets of type `NS`.
PTR	The resource's canonical name, typically used for reverse lookups.
SOA	Specifies authoritative information about a DNS zone, including the primary name server, the email of the domain administrator, the domain serial number, and several timers relating to refreshing the zone.
SPF	The SPF record set type is deprecated. Use TXT records starting with "v=spf1 " instead. SPF type records are not used by modern e-mail software.
SRV	The data that specifies the location, that is, the hostname and port number, of servers for a particular service. For more details, refer to RFC 2782.
SSHFP	The SSH server algorithm number, fingerprint type number, and key fingerprint. Use this record type if you have enabled DNSSEC for this zone.
TLSA	The DNS-based Authentication of Named Entities (DANE) TLSA Certificate Association information.
TXT	Text data, which can contain arbitrary text and can also be used to define machine-readable data, such as security or abuse prevention information. A TXT record may contain one or more text strings; the maximum length of each string is 255 characters. Mail agents and other software agents concatenate multiple strings. Enclose each string in quotation marks. For example: "Hello World!" "Bye World!"

Figure 6-1. *Resource record types*

You add or remove DNS records in a resource record set by creating and executing a transaction that specifies the operations you want to perform. A transaction is a group of one or more record changes that should be propagated altogether and atomically, that is, either all or nothing in the event the transaction fails. *The entire transaction either succeeds or fails, so your data is never left in an intermediate state.*

You start a transaction using the gcloud dns record-sets transaction start command as follows:

```
gcloud dns record-sets transaction start --zone=my-zone
```

where --zone is the name of the managed zone whose record sets you want to manage.

To add a record to a transaction, you use the transaction add command as follows:

```
gcloud dns record-sets transaction add 10.2.3.4
  --name=test.dariokart.com \
  --ttl=30 \
  --type=A \
  --zone=my-zone
```

where

- --name is the DNS or domain name of the record set to add.
- --ttl is the TTL (time to live in seconds) for the record set.
- --type is the record type described in Figure 6-1.
- --zone is the name of the managed zone whose record sets you want to manage.

To execute a transaction, you use the execute command as follows:

```
gcloud dns record-sets transaction execute --zone=my-zone
```

To add a wildcard transaction, use the transaction add command as follows:

```
gcloud dns record-sets transaction add --zone=my-zone-name \
  --name=*.dariokart.com. \
  --type=CNAME \
  --ttl=300 all.dariokart.com
```

where

- --name is the DNS or domain name of the record set to add.
- --ttl is the TTL (time to live in seconds) for the record set.
- --type is the record type described in Figure 6-1.
- --zone is the name of the managed zone whose record sets you want to manage.

To remove a record as part of a transaction, you use the remove command as follows:

```
gcloud dns record-sets transaction remove 10.2.3.4 \
  --name=test.dariokart.com \
  --ttl=30 \
  --type=A \
  --zone=my-zone
```

where

- --name is the DNS or domain name of the record set to remove.

- --ttl is the TTL (time to live in seconds) for the record set.

- --type is the record type described in the table.

To replace an existing record, issue the remove command followed by the add command.

■ **Note** You can also edit transaction.yaml in a text editor to manually specify additions, deletions, or corrections to DNS records. To view the contents of transaction.yaml, run

```
gcloud dns record-sets transaction describe
```

To import record sets, you can use import and export to copy record sets into and out of a managed zone. The formats you can import from and export to are either BIND zone file format or YAML records format:

```
gcloud dns record-sets import -z=examplezonename \
    --zone-file-format path-to-example-zone-file
```

To export a record set, use the dns record-sets export command. To specify that the record sets are exported into a BIND zone–formatted file, use the --zone-file-format flag. For example:

```
dariokart.com. 21600 IN NS ns-gcp-private.googledomains.com.
dariokart.com. 21600 IN SOA ns-gcp-private.googledomains.com.
cloud-dns-hostmaster.google.com. 1 21600 3600 259200 300
host1.dariokart.com. 300 IN A 192.0.2.91
```

■ **Exam tip** If you omit the --zone-file-format flag, the gcloud dns record-sets export command exports the record set into a YAML-formatted records file.

For example, the command

```
gcloud dns record-sets export dariokart.zone -z=examplezonename
```

would return the YAML-formatted output:

```
---
kind: dns#resourceRecordSet
name: dariokart.com.
rrdatas:
- ns-gcp-private.googledomains.com.
ttl: 21600
type: NS
---
kind: dns#resourceRecordSet
name: dariokart.com.
```

```
rrdatas:
- ns-gcp-private.googledomains.com. cloud-dns-hostmaster.google.com. 1 21600 3600 259200 300
ttl: 21600
type: SOA
---
kind: dns#resourceRecordSet
name: host1.dariokart.com.
rrdatas:
- 192.0.2.91
ttl: 300
type: A
```

To display the current DNS records for your zone, use the gcloud dns record-sets list command:

```
gcloud dns record-sets list --zone=my-zone
```

The command outputs the JSON response for the resource record set for the first 100 records (default). You can specify these additional parameters:

- limit: Maximum number of record sets to list.

- name: Only list record sets with this exact domain name.

- type: Only list records of this type. If present, the --name parameter must also be present.

Migrating to Cloud DNS

Cloud DNS supports the migration of an existing DNS domain from another DNS provider to Cloud DNS. This procedure describes how to complete the necessary steps.

Create a Managed Zone for Your Domain

To migrate an existing domain, first create a managed zone to contain your DNS records. When you create a zone, the new zone isn't used until you update your domain registration, point a resolver at it, or query one of your zone's name servers.

To create a zone, run the gcloud dns managed-zones create command you learned in the previous section:

```
gcloud dns managed-zones create --dns-name=dariokart.com.
--description="Migrated DNS zone" dariokart-migrated-zone
```

Export the DNS Configuration from Your Existing Provider

To export your zone file, see your provider's documentation. Cloud DNS supports the import of zone files in BIND or YAML records format.

For example, in AWS Route 53, which does not support export, you can use the open source cli53 tool.

Import Your Existing DNS Configuration to Cloud DNS

After you have exported the file from your DNS provider, you can use the `gcloud dns record-sets import` command to import it into your newly created managed zone.

Remember that the addition of the flag `--zone-file-format` tells Google Cloud that the input record set is in BIND format. As you already learned in the previous section, if you omit this flag Google Cloud expects the input file to be in YAML format instead.

■ **Warning**   If your import file contains NS or SOA records for the apex of the zone, they will conflict with the preexisting Cloud DNS records. To use the preexisting Cloud DNS records (recommended), ensure that you remove the NS or SOA records from your import file. However, there are use cases for overriding this behavior, which goes beyond the scope of the exam.

To import record sets correctly, you must remove the apex records:

```
gcloud dns record-sets import -z=dariokart-migrated-zone
--zone-file-format "/misc/dariokart_exported_zone_file"
```

Verify the Migration

To monitor and verify that the Cloud DNS name servers have picked up your changes, you can use the Linux `watch` and `dig` commands.

First, look up your zone's Cloud DNS name servers using the `gcloud dns managed-zones describe` command:

```
gcloud dns managed-zones describe dariokart-migrated-zone
```

An example of the output is

```
nameServers:
- ns-cloud-a1.googledomains.com.
- ns-cloud-a2.googledomains.com.
- ns-cloud-a3.googledomains.com.
- ns-cloud-a4.googledomains.com.
```

Finally, check if the records are available on the name servers:

```
watch dig example.com @ZONE_NAME_SERVER
```

Replace ZONE_NAME_SERVER with one of the name servers returned when you ran the previous command.

Update Your Registrar's Name Server Records

Sign in to your registrar provider and change the authoritative name servers to point to the name servers that you saw in step 1. At the same time, make a note of the time to live (TTL) that your registrar has set on the records. That tells you how long you have to wait before the new name servers begin to be used.

Wait for Changes and Then Verify

To get the authoritative name servers for your domain on the Internet, run the following Linux commands:

```
dig +short NS dariokart.com
```

If the output shows that all changes have propagated, you're done. If not, you can check intermittently, or you can automatically run the command every two seconds while you wait for the name servers to change. To do that, run the following:

```
watch dig +short NS dariokart.com
```

If you're using Windows, you can use the nslookup command.

DNS Security Extensions (DNSSEC)

The Domain Name System Security Extensions (DNSSEC) is a feature of the Domain Name System (DNS) that authenticates responses to domain name lookups. It does not provide privacy protections for those lookups, but prevents attackers from manipulating or poisoning the responses to DNS requests.

There are three places where you must enable and configure DNSSEC for it to protect domains from spoofing and poisoning attacks:

1. The DNS zone for your domain must serve special DNSSEC records for public keys (DNSKEY), signatures (RRSIG), and nonexistence (NSEC or NSEC3 and NSEC3PARAM) to authenticate your zone's contents. Cloud DNS manages this automatically if you enable DNSSEC for a zone.

2. The top-level domain (TLD) registry (for example.com, this would be .com) must have a DS (Delegation Signer) record that authenticates a DNSKEY record in your zone. Do this by activating DNSSEC at your domain registrar.

3. For full DNSSEC protection, you must use a DNS resolver that validates signatures for DNSSEC-signed domains. You can enable validation for individual systems or your local caching resolvers if you administer your network's DNS services. You can configure systems to use public resolvers that validate DNSSEC, notably Google Public DNS and Verisign Public DNS.

The second point limits the domain names where DNSSEC can work. Both the registrar and registry must support DNSSEC for the TLD that you are using. If you cannot add a DS record through your domain registrar to activate DNSSEC, enabling DNSSEC in Cloud DNS has no effect.

Before enabling DNSSEC, check the following resources:

- The DNSSEC documentation for both your domain registrar and TLD registry

- The Google Cloud community tutorial's domain registrar–specific instructions

- The ICANN (Internet Corporation for Assigned Names and Numbers) list of domain registrar DNSSEC support to confirm DNSSEC support for your domain

If the TLD registry supports DNSSEC, but your registrar does not (or does not support it for that TLD), you might be able to transfer your domains to a different registrar that does. After you have completed that process, you can activate DNSSEC for the domain.

Forwarding and DNS Server Policies

You can configure *one* DNS server policy for each Virtual Private Cloud (VPC) network. The policy can specify inbound DNS forwarding, outbound DNS forwarding, or both. In this section, inbound server policy refers to a policy that permits inbound DNS forwarding. Outbound server policy refers to one possible method for implementing outbound DNS forwarding. It is possible for a policy to be both an inbound server policy and an outbound server policy if it implements the features of both.

Inbound Server Policy

Each VPC network provides DNS name resolution services to the VMs that use it. When a VM uses its metadata server 169.254.169.254 as its name server, Google Cloud searches for DNS records according to the name resolution order.

By default, a VPC network's name resolution services—through its name resolution order—are only available to that VPC network itself. You can create an inbound server policy in your VPC network to make these name resolution services available to an on-premises network that is connected using Cloud VPN or Cloud Interconnect.

When you create an inbound server policy, Cloud DNS takes an internal IP address from the primary IP address range of each subnet that your VPC network uses. For example, if you have a VPC network that contains two subnets in the same region and a third subnet in a different region, a total of three IP addresses are reserved for inbound forwarding. Cloud DNS uses these internal IP addresses as entry points for inbound DNS requests.

Outbound Server Policy

You can change the name resolution order by creating an outbound server policy that specifies a list of alternative name servers. When you specify alternative name servers for a VPC network, those servers are the only name servers that Google Cloud queries when handling DNS requests from VMs in your VPC network that are configured to use their metadata servers (169.254.169.254).

■ **Note**   A DNS policy that enables outbound DNS forwarding disables resolution of Compute Engine internal DNS and Cloud DNS managed private zones. An outbound server policy is one of two methods for outbound DNS forwarding.

Integrating On-Premises DNS with Google Cloud

In a hybrid or a multi-cloud environment, DNS records for private (RFC 1918) resources often need to be resolved across environments.

Traditionally, on-premises DNS records are manually administered by using an authoritative DNS server, such as BIND in UNIX/Linux environments or Active Directory in Microsoft Windows environments. In contrast, Google Cloud DNS records are administered by fully managed DNS services like Cloud DNS.

Either way, a strategy on how to forward private DNS requests between environments is needed to make sure that services can be effectively and efficiently addressed from both on-premises environments and within Google Cloud.

As a Google Cloud Professional Cloud Network Engineer, you need to understand your business and technical requirements so that you can determine where an authoritative service for all domain resolution takes place.

> *Does it make sense to have an authoritative service for all domain resolution on-premises, in Google Cloud, or both?*

Let's discuss these three approaches and learn when either one of the three is better suited than the other.

Approach 1: Keep DNS Resolution On-Premises

The easiest way is to continue using your existing on-premises DNS server for authoritatively hosting all internal domain names. In that case, you can use an alternative name server to forward all requests from Google Cloud through *outbound DNS forwarding*.

This approach has the following advantages:

- You make fewer changes in business processes.

- You can continue to use your existing tools.

- You can use deny lists to filter individual DNS requests on-premises.

However, it has the following disadvantages:

- DNS requests from Google Cloud have higher latency.

- Your system relies on connectivity to on-premises environments for DNS operations.

- You might find it difficult to integrate highly flexible environments such as autoscaled instance groups.

- The system might not be compatible with products such as Dataproc because those products rely on reverse resolution of Google Cloud instance names.

Approach 2: Move DNS Resolution to Cloud DNS

Another approach is to migrate to Cloud DNS as an authoritative service for *all* domain resolution. You can then use private zones and *inbound DNS forwarding* to migrate your existing on-premises name resolution to Cloud DNS.

This approach has the following advantages:

- You don't need to maintain a high availability DNS service on-premises.

- Your system can use Cloud DNS to take advantage of centralized logging and monitoring.

However, it has the following disadvantages:

- DNS requests from on-premises have higher latency.

- Your system requires a reliable connection to your VPC network for name resolution.

Approach 3 (Recommended): Use a Hybrid Approach with Two Authoritative DNS Systems

Google Cloud recommends using a *hybrid* approach with two authoritative DNS systems. In this approach

- Authoritative DNS resolution for your private Google Cloud environment is done by Cloud DNS.

- Authoritative DNS resolution for on-premises resources is hosted by existing DNS servers on-premises.

The diagram in Figure 6-2 shows this setup.

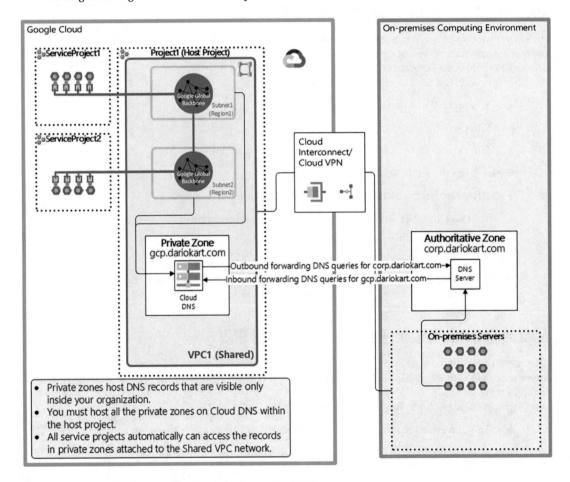

Figure 6-2. *Hybrid architecture with two authoritative DNS systems*

Split-Horizon DNS

Split-horizon DNS can provide a mechanism for security and privacy management by logical or physical separation of DNS resolution for internal network access (RFC 1918) and access from an unsecure, public network (e.g., the Internet).

Cloud DNS can be used as the authoritative name server to resolve your domains on the Internet through public DNS zones and use private DNS zones to perform internal DNS resolution for your private GCP networks.

Split-Horizon Use Cases

One common use case for split-horizon DNS is when a server has both a private IP address on a local area network (not reachable from most of the Internet) and a public address, that is, an address reachable across the Internet in general.

By using split-horizon DNS, the same name can lead to either the private IP address or the public one, depending on which client sends the query. This allows for critical local client machines to access a server directly through the local network, without the need to pass through a router. Passing through fewer network devices has the twofold benefit of reducing the network latency and freeing up limited router bandwidth for traffic that requires the Internet, for example, access to external or cloud-resident resources.

DNS Peering

In large Google Cloud environments, Shared VPC is a very scalable network design that lets an organization connect resources from multiple projects to a common Virtual Private Cloud (VPC) network, so that they can communicate with each other securely and efficiently using internal IPs. Typically shared by many application teams, a central team (or platform team) often manages the Shared VPC's networking configuration, while application teams use the network resources to create applications in their own service projects.

In some cases, application teams want to manage their own DNS records (e.g., to create new DNS records to expose services, update existing records, etc.). There's a solution to support fine-grained IAM policies using Cloud DNS peering. In this section, we will explore how to use it to give your application teams autonomy over their DNS records while ensuring that the central networking team maintains fine-grained control over the entire environment.

Understanding the Cloud DNS Peering Solution

Imagine that you, as an application team (service project) owner, want to be able to manage your own application (service project) DNS records without impacting other teams or applications. DNS peering is a type of zone in Cloud DNS that allows you to send DNS requests from a specific subdomain (e.g., c.dariokart.com) to another Cloud DNS zone configured in another VPC.

The example in Figure 6-3 shows a developer in project-c who needs to resolve a hostname with subdomain (suffix) p.dariokart.com. The project has its own private zone, which contains DNS records for domain names with suffix c.dariokart.com.

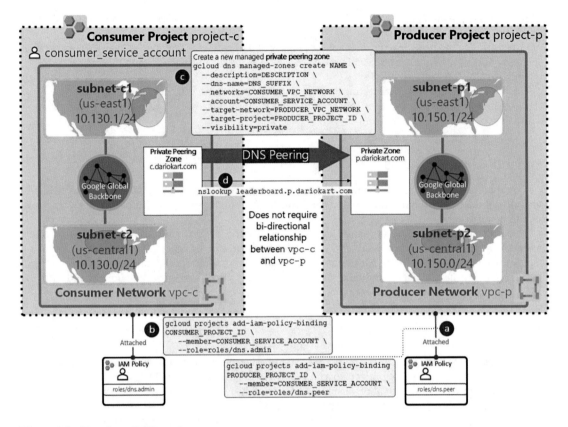

Figure 6-3. *Creating a DNS peering zone*

With DNS peering, you can create a Cloud DNS *private peering zone* and configure it to perform DNS lookups in a VPC network where the records for that zone's namespace are available.

The VPC network where the DNS private peering zone performs lookups is called the DNS *producer network*, as indicated in Figure 6-3. The project that owns the producer network is called the producer project, referred to as project-p in the figure.

The VPC network where DNS queries originate is called the DNS *consumer network*. The project that owns the consumer network is called the consumer project, referred to as project-c in the same figure.

Figure 6-3 shows you how to create a DNS peering zone with the gcloud CLI.

First, as indicated in step a, the service account associated to the consumer network (vpc-c) must be granted the roles/dns.peer role in the producer project, that is, project-p.

Next, as indicated in step b, the same service account must be granted the roles/dns.admin role in the consumer project, that is, project-c.

Finally, you create a new managed private peering zone by running the gcloud dns managed-zones create as indicated in Figure 6-3.

When the setup is completed, any DNS query to resolve a hostname with suffix p.dariokart.com, for example, leaderboard.p.dariokart.com, is sent to the DNS private zone in the producer VPC, as shown in step d.

■ **Exam tip**   You may wonder how a DNS private peering zone setup is any different than any other DNS private zone. After all, the `gcloud dns managed-zones create` command shows no indication that the new zone uses DNS peering. The answer is "hidden" in step a. By granting the `roles/dns.peer` IAM role to the consumer service account, we are basically giving this principal access to target networks with DNS peering zones. In fact, the only permission included in such IAM role is the permission `dns.networks.targetWithPeeringZone`. Put differently, principals with the IAM permission `dns.networks.targetWithPeeringZone` on the producer network's project can establish DNS peering between consumer and producer networks.

Cloud DNS peering is not to be confused with VPC peering, and it doesn't require you to configure any communication between the source and destination VPC. All the DNS flows are managed directly in the Cloud DNS backend: each VPC talks to Cloud DNS, and Cloud DNS can redirect the queries from one VPC to the other.

So, how does DNS peering allow application teams to manage their own DNS records?

The answer is by using DNS peering between a Shared VPC and other Cloud DNS private zones that are managed by the application teams. Figure 6-4 illustrates this setup.

For each application team that needs to manage its own DNS records, you provide them with

- Their own private DNS subdomain, for example, `t1.dariokart.com`

- Their own Cloud DNS private zone(s) in a dedicated project (`DNSproject1`), plus a standalone VPC (`dns-t1-vpc`) with full IAM permissions

You can then configure DNS peering for the specific DNS subdomain to their dedicated Cloud DNS zone—you just learned how to configure DNS peering with the steps (a-b-c-d) illustrated in Figure 6-3.

In the application team's standalone VPC (`dns-t1-vpc`), they have Cloud DNS IAM permissions only on their own Cloud DNS instance and can manage only their DNS records.

A central team, meanwhile, manages the DNS peering and decides which Cloud DNS instance is authoritative for which subdomain, thus allowing application teams to only manage their own subdomain.

By default, all VMs that consume the Shared VPC use Cloud DNS in the Shared VPC as their local resolver. This Cloud DNS instance answers for all DNS records in the Shared VPC by using DNS peering to the application teams' Cloud DNS instances or by forwarding to on-premises for on-premises records.

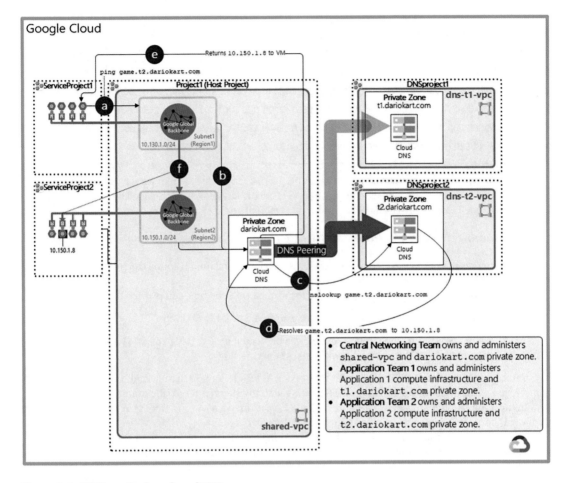

Figure 6-4. *DNS peering in a shared VPC*

To summarize, shared-vpc acts as the DNS consumer network and dns-t1-vpc and dns-t2-vpc act as the DNS producer networks.

As a result, the flow is the following:

- (Step a) A VM in ServiceProject1 tries to ping game.t2.dariokart.com.

- (Step a) The VM uses Cloud DNS as its local DNS resolver.

- (Step a) The VM tries to resolve game.t2.dariokart.com, which is a DNS record owned by team 2.

- (Step b) The VM then sends the DNS request to the Shared VPC Cloud DNS.

- (Step c) This Cloud DNS is configured with **DNS peering** and sends everything under the t2.dariokart.com subdomain to Cloud DNS in DNSproject2.

- (Step d) Team 2 is able to manage its own DNS records, but only in its dedicated DNS project, that is, DNSproject2. It has a private zone there for *.t2.dariokart.com and an A record for game.t2.dariokart.com that resolves to 10.150.1.8.

- (Step e) The VM receives its DNS answer.

- (Step f) The VM finally tries to ping 10.150.1.8 using the built-in VPC route. If the corresponding firewall rules are open, the request is successful!

Private DNS Logging

Cloud DNS logging is disabled by default on each Google Cloud VPC network. By enabling monitoring of Cloud DNS logs, you can increase visibility into the DNS names requested by the clients within your VPC network. Cloud DNS logs can be monitored for anomalous domain names and evaluated against threat intelligence.

You should make sure that Cloud DNS logging is enabled for all your Virtual Private Cloud (VPC) networks using *DNS policies*. Cloud DNS logging records queries that the name servers resolve for your Google Cloud VPC networks, as well as queries from external entities directly to a public DNS zone. Recorded queries can come from virtual machine (VM) instances, GKE containers running in the same VPC network, peering zones, or other Google Cloud resources provisioned within your VPC.

To determine whether Cloud DNS logging is enabled for a VPC network, first determine the name of the DNS policy associated to your VPC:

```
gcloud dns policies list
  --project frontend-devs-7734
  --format='value(name)'
  --filter='networks[].networkUrl ~ your-app-shared-vpc'
```

The command output should return the name of the associated DNS policy:

your-shared-vpc-dns-policy

Then, run the gcloud dns policies describe command as indicated as follows:

```
gcloud dns policies describe your-shared-vpc-dns-policy
  --format="value(enableLogging)"
```

The command output should return the status of the Cloud DNS logging feature (True for enabled, False for disabled).

Configuring Cloud NAT

You learned in the previous chapter that every VPC network has an "implied allow egress rule" firewall rule, which permits outgoing connections (the other implied firewall rule blocks incoming connections). This firewall rule alone is not enough for your VMs (or other compute resource instance types) to reach the Internet.

Wouldn't it be nice for your internal VMs to reach the Internet without requiring to use an external IP address?

That's where Cloud NAT comes into play. Cloud NAT is a distributed, software-defined managed service, which lets certain compute resources without external IP addresses create outbound connections to the Internet.

These compute resources are

- VMs without external IP addresses
- Private Google Kubernetes Engine (GKE) clusters
- Cloud Run instances through Serverless VPC Access
- Cloud Functions instances through Serverless VPC Access
- App Engine standard environment instances through Serverless VPC Access

Architecture

Cloud NAT is not based on proxy VMs or network appliances. Rather, it configures the *Andromeda* software-defined network that powers your VPC, so that it provides Source Network Address Translation (SNAT) for VMs without external IP addresses. Cloud NAT also provides Destination Network Address Translation (DNAT) for established inbound response packets. Figure 6-5 shows a comparison between traditional NAT proxies and Google Cloud NAT.

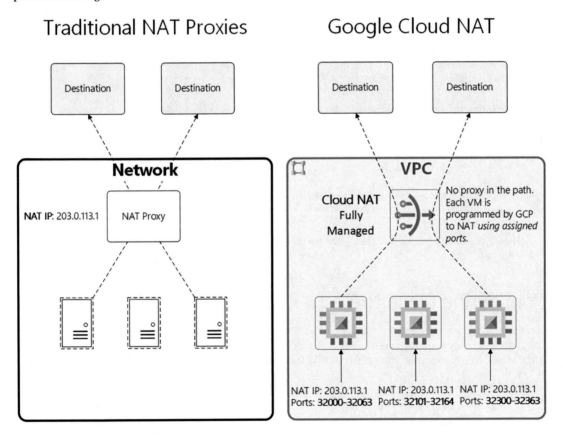

Figure 6-5. *Traditional NAT vs. Cloud NAT*

With Cloud NAT, you achieve a number of benefits, when compared to a traditional NAT proxy. As you can see, these benefits match the five pillars of the *well-architected framework*.

First and foremost, with Cloud NAT you achieve **better security** because your internal VMs (or other compute resource instance types) are not directly exposed to potential security threats originating from the Internet, thereby minimizing the attack surface of your workloads.

You also get **higher availability** because Cloud NAT is fully managed by Google Cloud. All you need to do is to configure a NAT gateway on a Cloud Router, which provides the control plane for NAT, holding configuration parameters that you specify.

Finally, you also achieve **better performance and scalability** because Cloud NAT can be configured to automatically scale the number of NAT IP addresses that it uses, and it does not reduce the network bandwidth per VM.

Creating a Cloud NAT Instance

Use the command `gcloud compute routers nats create` to add a Cloud NAT instance to a Compute Engine router. The syntax of this command is shown in Figure 6-6.

NAME

> gcloud compute routers nats create - add a NAT to a Compute Engine router

SYNOPSIS

> ```
> gcloud compute routers nats create NAME --router = ROUTER ( --auto-allocate-nat-external-ips  |
>    --nat-external-ip-pool = IP_ADDRESS ,[ IP_ADDRESS ,...]) ( --nat-all-subnet-ip-ranges   |
>    --nat-custom-subnet-ip-ranges = SUBNETWORK [: RANGE_NAME ],[...]   | --nat-primary-subnet-ip-ranges )
> [ --async ] [ --[no-]enable-dynamic-port-allocation ] [ --enable-endpoint-independent-mapping ]
> [ --enable-logging ] [ --icmp-idle-timeout = ICMP_IDLE_TIMEOUT ] [ --log-filter = LOG_FILTER ]
> [ --max-ports-per-vm = MAX_PORTS_PER_VM ] [ --min-ports-per-vm = MIN_PORTS_PER_VM ]
> [ --region = REGION ] [ --rules = RULES ]
> [ --tcp-established-idle-timeout = TCP_ESTABLISHED_IDLE_TIMEOUT ]
> [ --tcp-time-wait-timeout = TCP_TIME_WAIT_TIMEOUT ]
> [ --tcp-transitory-idle-timeout = TCP_TRANSITORY_IDLE_TIMEOUT ]
> [ --udp-idle-timeout = UDP_IDLE_TIMEOUT ] [ GCLOUD_WIDE_FLAG ... ]
> ```

DESCRIPTION

> `gcloud compute routers nats create` is used to create a NAT on a Compute Engine router.

Figure 6-6. *gcloud command to create a Cloud NAT instance*

You can specify which subnets are allowed to use the Cloud NAT instance by selecting *exactly* one of these flags:

- `--nat-all-subnet-ip-ranges`, which allows *all* IP ranges of *all* subnets in the region, including primary and secondary ranges, to use the Cloud NAT instance

- `--nat-custom-subnet-ip-ranges=SUBNETWORK[:RANGE_NAME],[...]`, which lets you specify a list of the subnet's primary and secondary IP ranges allowed to use the Cloud NAT instance

  - SUBNETWORK: Specifying a subnetwork name includes only the primary subnet range of the subnetwork.

- SUBNETWORK:RANGE_NAME: Specifying a subnetwork and secondary range name includes only that secondary range. It does not include the primary range of the subnet.

- --nat-primary-subnet-ip-ranges, which allows *only primary IP ranges of all subnets in the region* to use the Cloud NAT instance

Addressing and Port Allocations

When you create a Cloud NAT gateway, you can choose to have the gateway automatically allocate regional external IP addresses. Alternatively, you can manually assign a fixed number of regional external IP addresses to the gateway.

You can configure the number of source ports that each Cloud NAT gateway reserves to each VM for which it should provide NAT services. You can also configure *static port allocation*, where the same number of ports is reserved for each VM, or *dynamic port allocation*, where the number of reserved ports can vary between the minimum and maximum limits that you specify.

For example, in Figure 6-5 the VM with (RFC 1918 IP address) IP3 always gets ports in the range 32,000–32,063; the VM with IP4 always gets ports in the range 32,101–32,164; and the VM with IP45 always gets ports in the range 32,300–32,363.

The VMs for which NAT should be provided are determined by the subnet IP address ranges that the gateway is configured to serve.

■ **Exam tip**   Each NAT IP address on a Cloud NAT gateway offers 64,512 TCP source ports and 64,512 UDP source ports. TCP and UDP each support 65,536 ports per IP address, but Cloud NAT doesn't use the first 1024 well-known (privileged) ports.

Static Port Allocation

When you configure static port allocation, you specify a *minimum number of ports per VM instance.*

Because all VMs are allocated the same number of ports, static port allocation works best if all VMs have similar Internet usage. If some VMs use more ports than others, the ports in the Cloud NAT gateway might be underused. If Internet usage varies, consider configuring dynamic port allocation.

Dynamic Port Allocation

When you configure dynamic port allocation, you specify a *minimum number of ports per VM instance and a maximum number of ports per VM instance.*

The NAT gateway automatically monitors each VM's port usage and "elastically" modifies the number of ports allocated to each VM based on demand. You don't need to monitor the port usage or adjust the NAT gateway configuration.

Customizing Timeouts

Cloud NAT uses predefined timeout settings based on the connection type.

A connection is a unique 5-tuple consisting of the NAT source IP address and source port tuple combined with a unique destination 3-tuple.

Use the `gcloud compute routers nats create` command to create a NAT gateway with custom timeout settings:

```
gcloud compute routers nats create NAT_CONFIG \
  --router=NAT_ROUTER \
  --region=REGION \
  --auto-allocate-nat-external-ips \
  --nat-custom-subnet-ip-ranges=SUBNETS_RANGES_LIST \
  --udp-idle-timeout=60s \
  --tcp-established-idle-timeout=60s \
  --tcp-transitory-idle-timeout=60s \
  --tcp-time-wait-timeout=60s \
  --icmp-idle-timeout=60s
```

Replace the following:

- NAT_CONFIG: The name of your NAT configuration.

- NAT_ROUTER: The name of your Cloud Router.

- REGION: The region of the NAT to create. If not specified, you might be prompted to select a region (interactive mode only).

- SUBNETS_RANGES_LIST: A comma-separated list of subnet names. For example:

  - SUBNET_NAME_1,SUBNET_NAME_2: Includes only the primary subnet range of SUBNET_NAME_1 and SUBNET_NAME_2.

  - SUBNET_NAME:SECONDARY_RANGE_NAME: Includes the secondary range SECONDARY_RANGE_NAME of subnet SUBNET_NAME. It does not include the primary range of SUBNET_NAME.

  - SUBNET_NAME_1,SUBNET_NAME_2:SECONDARY_RANGE_NAME: Includes the primary range of SUBNET_NAME_1 and the specified secondary range SECONDARY_RANGE_NAME of subnet SUBNET_NAME_2.

Logging and Monitoring

Cloud NAT logging allows you to log NAT connections and errors.

When you enable Cloud NAT logging, a single log entry can be generated for each of the following scenarios:

- When a network connection is created

- When a packet is dropped because no port was available for NAT

You can choose to log both kinds of events or only one or the other.

All logs are sent to Cloud Logging.

■ **Note** Dropped packets are logged only if they are egress (outbound) TCP and UDP packets. No dropped incoming packets are logged. For example, if an inbound response to an outbound request is dropped for any reason, no error is logged.

Enabling Cloud NAT Logging

To enable logging for an existing Cloud NAT instance, including address translation events and errors, use the --enable-logging flag as follows:

```
gcloud compute routers nats update NAT_GATEWAY \
    --router=ROUTER_NAME \
    --region=REGION \
    --enable-logging
```

where

- NAT_GATEWAY denotes the name of the NAT gateway.

- ROUTER_NAME denotes the name of the Cloud Router that hosts the NAT gateway.

- REGION denotes the region of the Cloud Router.

Filtering NAT Logs

To log only Network Address Translation events:

```
gcloud compute routers nats update NAT_GATEWAY \
    --router=ROUTER_NAME \
    --region=REGION \
    --enable-logging \
    --log-filter=TRANSLATIONS_ONLY
```

To log only errors:

```
gcloud compute routers nats update NAT_GATEWAY \
    --router=ROUTER_NAME \
    --region=REGION \
    --enable-logging \
    --log-filter=ERRORS_ONLY
```

To clear a log filter, thereby accepting all logs:

```
gcloud compute routers nats update NAT_GATEWAY \
    --router=ROUTER_NAME \
    --region=REGION \
    --log-filter=ALL
```

Verifying NAT Logging Status

To determine logging status:

```
gcloud compute routers nats describe NAT_GATEWAY \
    --router=ROUTER_NAME \
    --region=REGION
```

Viewing NAT Logs

To view NAT logs in JSON format and limit the output to ten entries:

```
gcloud logging read 'resource.type=nat_gateway' \
    --limit=10 \
    --format=json
```

An output example is shown as follows:

```
{
insertId: "1the8juf6vab1t"
jsonPayload: {
        connection: {
            Src_ip: "10.0.0.1"
            Src_port: 45047
            Nat_ip: "203.0.113.17"
            Nat_port: 34889
            dest_ip : "198.51.100.142"
            Dest_port: 80
            Protocol: "tcp"
        }
        allocation_status: "OK"
        Gateway_identifiers: {
            Gateway_name: "my-nat-1"
            router_name: "my-router-1"
            Region: "europe-west1"
        }
        Endpoint: {
            Project_id: "service-project-1"
            Vm_name: "vm-1"
            Region: "europe-west1"
            Zone: "europe-west1-b"
        }
        Vpc: {
            Project_id: "host-project"
            Vpc_name: "network-1"
            Subnetwork_name: "subnetwork-1"
        }
        Destination: {
            Geo_location: {
                Continent: "Europe"
                Country: "France"
                Region: "Nouvelle-Aquitaine"
                City: "Bordeaux"
            }
        }
}
logName: "projects/host-project/logs/compute.googleapis.com%2Fnat_flows"
receiveTimestamp: "2018-06-28T10:46:08.123456789Z"
resource: {
```

```
        labels: {
               region: "europe-west1-d"
               project_id: "host-project"
               router_id: "987654321123456"
               gateway_name: "my-nat-1"
        }
        type: "nat_gateway"
}
labels: {
        nat.googleapis.com/instance_name: "vm-1"
        nat.googleapis.com/instance_zone: "europe-west1-b"
        nat.googleapis.com/nat_ip: "203.0.113.17"
        nat.googleapis.com/network_name: "network-1"
        nat.googleapis.com/router_name: "my-router-1"
        nat.googleapis.com/subnetwork_name: "subnetwork-1"
}
timestamp: "2018-06-28T10:46:00.602240572Z"
}
```

Monitoring

Cloud NAT exposes key metrics to Cloud Monitoring that give you insights into your fleet's usage of NAT gateways.

Metrics are sent automatically to Cloud Monitoring. There, you can create custom dashboards, set up alerts, and query the metrics.

The following are the required Identity and Access Management (IAM) roles:

- For Shared VPC users with VMs and NAT gateways defined in different projects, access to the VM level metrics requires the `roles/monitoring.viewer` IAM role for the project of each VM.

- For the NAT gateway resource, access to the gateway metrics requires the `roles/monitoring.viewer` IAM role for the project that contains the gateway.

Cloud NAT provides a set of predefined dashboards that display activity across your gateway:

- Open connections

- Egress data processed by NAT (rate)

- Ingress data processed by NAT (rate)

- Port usage

- NAT allocation errors

- Dropped sent packet rate

- Dropped received packet rate

You can also create custom dashboards and metrics-based alerting policies.

Restrictions per Organization Policy Constraints

An Organization Policy Administrator (roles/orgpolicy.policyAdmin) can use the constraints/compute.restrictCloudNATUsage constraint to *limit which subnets can use the Cloud NAT instance.*

You also learned in the "Creating a Cloud NAT Instance" section how network administrators can create Cloud NAT configurations and specify which subnets can use the gateway. By default, there are no limits to what subnets the administrator creates or which of them can use a Cloud NAT configuration.

Configuring Network Packet Inspection

Network packet inspection is an advanced network monitoring capability that clones the traffic of specified VMs in your VPC network and forwards it for examination.

Network packet inspection uses a technique called *Packet Mirroring* to capture all traffic and packet data, including payloads and headers. The capture can be configured for both egress and ingress traffic, only ingress traffic, or only egress traffic.

The mirroring happens on the virtual machine (VM) instances, not on the network. Consequently, Packet Mirroring consumes additional bandwidth on the VMs.

Packet Mirroring is useful when you need to monitor and analyze your security status. Unlike VPC Flow Logs, Packet Mirroring exports *all* traffic, not only the traffic between sampling periods. For example, you can use security software that analyzes mirrored traffic to detect all threats or anomalies. Additionally, you can inspect the full traffic flow to detect application performance issues.

Configuring Packet Mirroring

To configure Packet Mirroring, you create and enable a *packet mirroring policy* that specifies the mirrored *sources* and the collector *destination* of the traffic you need to monitor:

- **Mirrored sources** are the VMs whose packets (ingress, egress, or both) need to be inspected. These can be selected by specifying a source type, that is, any combination of the following: subnets, network tags, or VM names.

- **Collector destination** is an instance group which is configured as an internal TCP/UDP network load balancer (type 8) backend. VMs in the instance group are referred to as *collector instances.*

An internal load balancer for Packet Mirroring is similar to other type 8 load balancers, except that the forwarding rule must be configured for Packet Mirroring using the --is-mirroring-collector flag. Any nonmirrored traffic that is sent to the load balancer is dropped.

■ **Exam tip**   You need to know a few constraints on packet mirroring policies. For a given packet mirroring policy: (1) *All mirrored sources must be in the same project, VPC network, and Google Cloud region.* (2) *Collector instances must be in the same region as the mirrored sources' region.* (3) *Only a single collector destination can be used.*

As you can see, there are a number of preliminary steps you need to complete in order to create a packet mirroring policy. These include

1. **Permissions**: For Shared VPC topologies, you must have the `compute.packetMirroringUser` role in the project where the collector instances are created and the `compute.packetMirroringAdmin` in the project where the mirrored instances are created.

2. **Collector instances**: You must create an instance group, which will act as the destination of your mirrored traffic.

3. **Internal TCP/UDP network load balancer**: You must create a type 8 load balancer, configured to use the collector instances as backends.

4. **Firewall rules**: Mirrored traffic must be allowed to go from the mirrored source instances to the collector instances, which are the backends of the internal TCP/UDP network load balancer.

Upon completion of the four preliminary steps, you can create a packet mirroring policy using the command `gcloud compute packet-mirrorings create` as explained in the following:

```
gcloud compute packet-mirrorings create POLICY_NAME \
    --region=REGION \
    --network=NETWORK_NAME \
    --collector-ilb=FORWARDING_RULE_NAME \
    [--mirrored-subnets=SUBNET,[SUBNET,...]] \
    [--mirrored-tags=TAG,[TAG,...]] \
    [--mirrored-instances=INSTANCE,[INSTANCE,...]] \
    [--filter-cidr-ranges=ADDRESS_RANGE,[ADDRESS_RANGE,...]] \
    [--filter-protocols=PROTOCOL,[PROTOCOL,...]] \
    [--filter-direction=DIRECTION]
```

Replace the following:

- POLICY_NAME: The name of the packet mirroring policy.

- REGION: The region where the mirrored sources and collector destination are located.

- NETWORK_NAME: The network where the mirrored sources are located.

- FORWARDING_RULE_NAME: The name of the forwarding rule that is configured as a mirroring collector. Google Cloud sends all mirrored traffic to the associated internal TCP/UDP network load balancer.

- SUBNET: The name of one or more subnets to mirror. You can provide multiple subnets in a comma-separated list. Google Cloud mirrors existing and future instances in the subnet.

- TAG: One or more network tags. Google Cloud mirrors instances that have the network tag. You can provide multiple tags in a comma-separated list.

- INSTANCE: The fully qualified ID of one or more instances to mirror. You can provide multiple instances in a comma-separated list.

- ADDRESS_RANGE: One or more IP CIDR ranges to mirror. You can provide multiple ranges in a comma-separated list.

- PROTOCOL: One or more IP protocols to mirror. Valid values are tcp, udp, icmp, esp, ah, ipip, sctp, or an IANA (Internet Assigned Numbers Authority) protocol number. You can provide multiple protocols in a comma-separated list. If the filter-protocols flag is omitted, all protocols are mirrored.

- DIRECTION: The direction of the traffic to mirror relative to the VM. By default, this is set to both, which means that both ingress and egress traffic are mirrored. You can restrict which packets are captured by specifying ingress to capture only ingress packets or egress to capture only egress packets.

In the next section, you will learn some of the most relevant reference topologies you can use for your workloads' network packet inspection requirements.

Packet Mirroring in Single and Multi-VPC Topologies

Packet mirroring can be configured in a number of ways, based on where you want the mirrored sources and collector instances to be.

Mirrored Sources and Collector Instances Located in the Same VPC

This is the simplest configuration because VPC colocation results in one single project, which owns mirrored sources and collector instances. Figure 6-7 illustrates this topology.

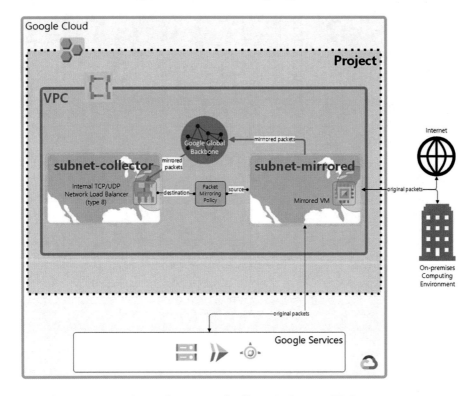

Figure 6-7. *Packet mirroring policy with source and collector in the same VPC*

In Figure 6-7, the packet mirroring policy is configured to mirror `subnet-mirrored` and send mirrored traffic to the internal TCP/UDP network load balancer configured in `subnet-collector`. Google Cloud mirrors the traffic on existing and future VMs in the `subnet-mirrored`. This includes all traffic to and from the Internet, on-premises hosts, and Google services.

Mirrored Sources and Collector Instances Located in Peered VPCs

In this reference topology (Figure 6-8), two packet mirroring policies are required because mirrored sources exist in different VPC networks:

1. `policy-1` collects packets from VMs in `subnet-mirrored-1` in the VPC1 network, owned by `Project1`, and sends them to a collector internal load balancer in the `subnet-collector` subnet.

2. `policy-2` collects packets from VMs in `subnet-mirrored-2` in the VPC2 network, owned by `Project2`, and sends them to the collector internal load balancer in the `subnet-collector` subnet in VPC1.

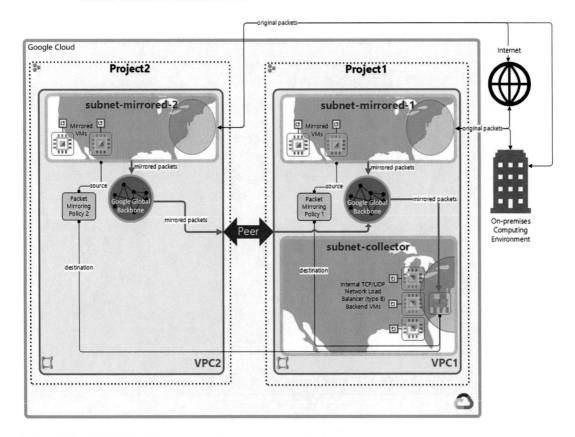

Figure 6-8. *Packet mirroring policy with source and collector in peered VPCs*

The two VPCs VPC1 and VPC2 are peered. All resources are located in the same region us-central1, which complies with the third constraint you just learned in the previous exam tip.

The packet mirroring policy policy-1 is similar to the policy in Figure 6-7 in that policy-1 is configured to collect traffic from subnet-mirrored-1 and send it to the forwarding rule of the internal load balancer in subnet-collector—mirrored sources and collector instances are all in the same VPC.

However, this is not the case for policy-2 because this policy is configured with mirrored sources (all VMs in subnet-mirrored-2) and collector instances (the backend VMs of the load balancer) in different VPC networks.

As a result, policy-2 can be created by the owners of Project1 or the owners of Project2 under one of the following conditions:

- The owners of Project1 must have the compute.packetMirroringAdmin role on the network, subnet, or instances to mirror in Project2.

- The owners of Project2 must have the compute.packetMirroringUser role in Project1.

Collector Instances Located in Shared VPC Service Project

In the scenario illustrated in Figure 6-9, the collector instances (the internal TCP/UDP network load balancer's backend VMs) are in a service project that uses subnet-collector in the host project.

■ **Note** The collector instances are in a service project, which means they are billed to the billing account associated to the service project, even though they consume subnet-collector in the host project. This is how Shared VPC works.

In this reference topology, the packet mirroring policy has also been created in the service project and is configured to mirror ingress and egress traffic for all VMs that have a network interface in subnet-mirrored.

■ **Exam tip** In this topology, service or host project users can create the packet mirroring policy. To do so, users must have the compute.packetMirroringUser role in the service project where the collector destination is located. Users must also have the compute.packetMirroringAdmin role on the mirrored sources.

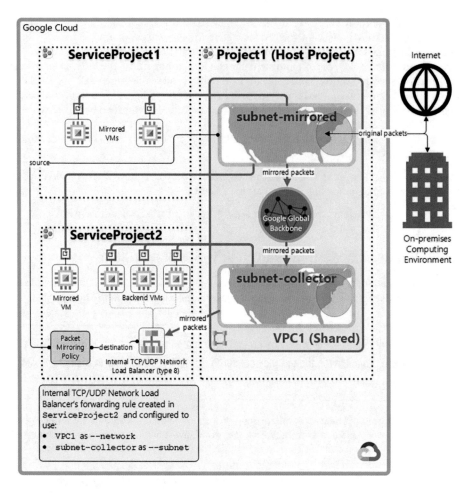

Figure 6-9. *Packet mirroring policy with collector in a service project*

Collector Instances Located in Shared VPC Host Project

In the scenario illustrated in Figure 6-10, we moved the collector instances to the host project.

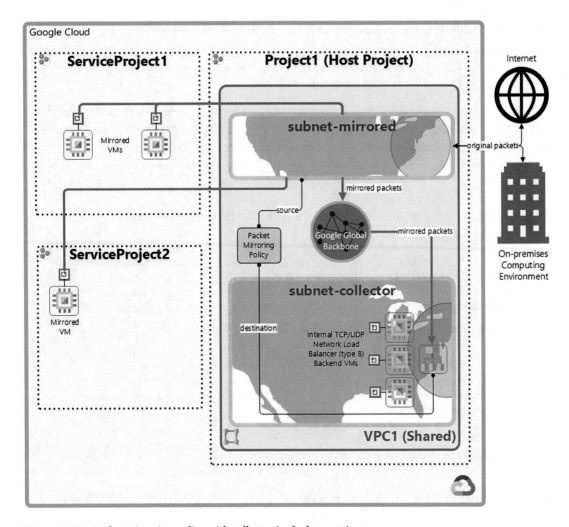

Figure 6-10. *Packet mirroring policy with collector in the host project*

This reference topology is a perfect use case of a Shared VPC for what it was intended to do. You learned in Chapter 2 that the idea of a Shared VPC is all about separation of duties, by letting developers manage their own workloads in their own service project without worrying about network setups, and network engineers manage the network infrastructure in the host project. Packet inspection is a network concern. As a result, it makes sense to let network engineers own the collector instances (i.e., the backend VMs along with all the internal TCP/UDP network load balancer resources) and the packet mirroring policies in the host project.

■ **Exam tip**   In this topology, service or host project users can create the packet mirroring policy. To do so, users in the service project must have the `compute.packetMirroringUser` role in the host project. This is because the collector instances are created in the host project. Alternatively, users in the host project require the `compute.packetMirroringAdmin` role for mirrored sources in the service projects.

Mirror Sources and Collector Instances Using Multi-NIC VMs

VMs with multiple network interfaces can be used as mirrored sources in a packet mirroring policy. However, because a policy can mirror resources from a single network at a time, you cannot create a single policy to mirror traffic *for all* network interfaces of a VM.

■ **Exam tip**   If you need to mirror more than one network interface (NIC) of a multi-NIC VM, you must create one packet mirroring policy for each NIC. This is because each NIC connects to a unique VPC network.

Capturing Relevant Traffic Using Packet Mirroring Source and Traffic Filters

You learned in the "Configuring Packet Mirroring" section how to create a packet mirroring policy with the `gcloud compute packet-mirrorings create` command.

To limit the amount of packets that need to be inspected, it is always a good practice to leverage the filtering flags, which we describe again for your convenience:

- `--filter-cidr-ranges`: One or more IP CIDR ranges to mirror. You can provide multiple ranges in a comma-separated list.

- `--filter-cidr-protocols`: One or more IP protocols to mirror. Valid values are tcp, udp, icmp, esp, ah, ipip, sctp, or an IANA protocol number. You can provide multiple protocols in a comma-separated list. If the filter-protocols flag is omitted, all protocols are mirrored.

- `--filter-cidr-direction = ingress | egress | both (default)`

A proper use of the filters will also save you money in egress cost.

Routing and Inspecting Inter-VPC Traffic Using Multi-NIC VMs (e.g., Next-Generation Firewall Appliances)

A common use case is to inspect bidirectional traffic between two VPC networks by leveraging a group of network virtual appliances, that is, multi-NIC VMs.

■ **Exam tip**   A network interface card (NIC) can be connected to *one and one only* (VPC) network.

In this use case, the multi-NIC VMs are configured as backend instances in a managed instance group. These multi-NIC VMs can be commercial solutions from third parties or solutions that you build yourself.

The managed instance group (MIG) is added to the backend service of an internal TCP/UDP network load balancer (referenced by the regional internal forwarding rule `ilb-a`). See Figure 6-11.

Since each backend VM has two NICs, and since each NIC maps *one to one* to exactly one VPC, the same group of VMs can be used by the backend service of another internal TCP/UDP network load balancer (referenced in Figure 6-11 by the regional internal forwarding rule `ilb-b`).

In the VPC network called `vpc-a`, the internal network TCP/UDP load balancer referenced by the regional internal forwarding rule `ilb-a` distributes traffic to the `nic0` network interface of each VM in the backend MIG.

Likewise, in the VPC network called vpc-b, the second internal network TCP/UDP load balancer referenced by the regional internal forwarding rule ilb-b distributes traffic to a different network interface, nic1.

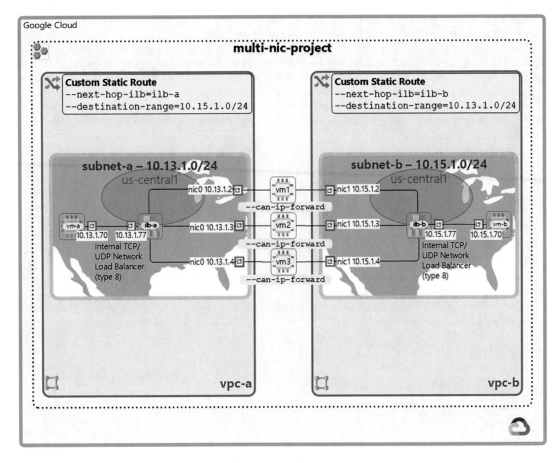

Figure 6-11. *Inter-VPC traffic inspection with multi-NIC load balancing*

As you can see, this is another way to let two VPCs exchange traffic with each other. This is achieved by leveraging two *custom static routes*, whose next hop is the forwarding rule of their internal TCP/UDP network load balancer and whose destination is the CIDR block of the subnet in the other VPC.

■ **Exam tip** The multi-NIC VMs must be allowed to send and receive packets with nonmatching destination or source IP addresses. This can be accomplished by using the --can-ip-forward flag in the gcloud compute instances create command: https://cloud.google.com/sdk/gcloud/reference/compute/instances/create#--can-ip-forward.

Configuring an Internal Load Balancer As a Next Hop for Highly Available Multi-NIC VM Routing

You learned in the "Network Load Balancers" section in Chapter 5 that an internal TCP/UDP network load balancer (type 8) is a regional, software-defined, pass-through (layer 4) load balancer that enables you to run and scale your services behind an internal (RFC 1918) IP address.

With a group of multi-NIC VMs identically configured like in an instance group, you can create an internal TCP/UDP network load balancer in each VPC a VM's NIC is attached to—as mentioned in the exam tip, a NIC can be attached to *one, and one only, VPC*. Then, you can create in each VPC a custom static route with your load balancer as the next hop and the CIDR of another VPC as destination.

For example, if all your backend VMs have two NICs each—say nic0 and nic1—you can create two internal TCP/UDP network load balancers, one in the first VPC (attached to nic0) and the other in the second VPC (attached to nic1).

This topology allows you to do the following:

1. **Use case 1**: To implement a highly available NAT, as explained in Chapter 3 (see Figure 3-94).

2. **Use case 2**: To integrate third-party appliances in a highly available, scaled-out manner. These can act as gateways or as firewalls with advanced packet inspection capabilities (e.g., Intrusion Prevention Systems—IPS), which can help you improve your workloads' security posture.

In this section, we'll walk you through the high-level process to configure two internal TCP/UDP network load balancers to address use case 2.

This can be achieved by building a solution that sends bidirectional traffic through two load balancers that use the same group of multi-NIC VMs as backends, as illustrated in Figure 6-12. Let's get started.

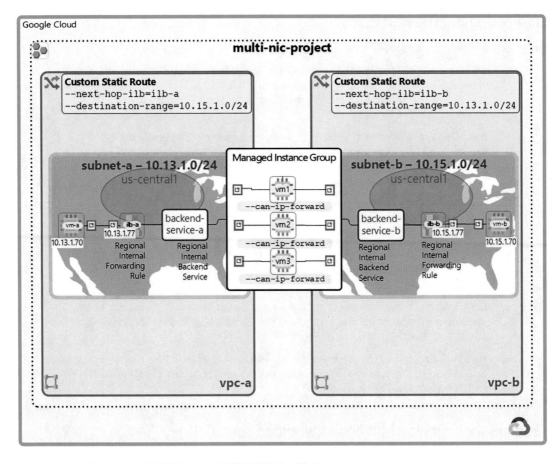

Figure 6-12. *Next-hop multi-NIC internal TCP/UDP load balancing*

Configuring the Networks

This reference topology uses two custom-mode VPC networks named vpc-a and vpc-b, each with one subnet.

Each backend VM has two network interfaces, one attached to each VPC network (nic0 attached to VPC vpc-a, nic1 attached to VPC vpc-b).

The subnets, subnet-a and subnet-b, use the 10.13.1.0/24 and 10.15.1.0/24 primary IP address ranges, respectively, and they both reside in the us-central1 region.

■ **Exam tip** In this reference topology, the subnets attached to each NIC must all share the same region, for example, us-central1, because *VMs are zonal resources*.

Configuring the Firewall Rules

This reference topology uses the following firewall rules:

- fw-allow-vpc-a-from-both: An ingress rule, applicable to all targets in the vpc-a network. This rule allows traffic from sources in both the 10.13.1.0/24 and 10.15.1.0/24 IP address ranges. These two ranges cover the primary internal IP addresses of VMs in both subnets.

- fw-allow-vpc-b-from-both: An ingress rule, applicable to all targets in the vpc-b network. This rule allows traffic from sources in both the 10.13.1.0/24 and 10.15.1.0/24 IP address ranges. These two ranges cover the primary internal IP addresses of VMs in both subnets.

- fw-allow-vpc-a-ssh: An ingress rule applied to the VM instances in the vpc-a VPC network. This rule allows incoming SSH connectivity on TCP port 22 from any address.

- fw-allow-vpc-b-ssh: An ingress rule applied to the VM instances in the vpc-b VPC network. This rule allows incoming SSH connectivity on TCP port 22 from any address.

- fw-allow-vpc-a-health-check: An ingress rule for the backend VMs that are being load balanced. This rule allows traffic from the Google Front Ends (130.211.0.0/22 and 35.191.0.0/16).

- fw-allow-vpc-b-health-check: An ingress rule for the backend VMs that are being load balanced. This rule allows traffic from the Google Front Ends (130.211.0.0/22 and 35.191.0.0/16).

Creating the Common Managed Instance Group (MIG)

This reference topology uses an instance template, which is a resource necessary to create a managed instance group in us-central1. The instance template uses the iptables software as a third-party virtual appliance, which enables the multi-NIC configuration.

In the order:

1. Create a startup script that will install the iptables software on any backend VM. This script named config.sh will be passed to the gcloud compute instance-templates create command using the --metadata flag in the next step:

```
#!/bin/bash
# Enable IP forwarding:
echo 1 > /proc/sys/net/ipv4/ip_forward
echo "net.ipv4.ip_forward=1" > /etc/sysctl.d/20-iptables.conf
# Read VM network configuration:
md_vm="http://metadata.google.internal/computeMetadata/v1/instance/"
md_net="$md_vm/network-interfaces"
nic0_gw="$(curl $md_net/0/gateway -H "Metadata-Flavor:Google" )"
nic0_mask="$(curl $md_net/0/subnetmask -H "Metadata-Flavor:Google")"
nic0_addr="$(curl $md_net/0/ip -H "Metadata-Flavor:Google")"
nic0_id="$(ip addr show | grep $nic0_addr | awk '{print $NF}')"
nic1_gw="$(curl $md_net/1/gateway -H "Metadata-Flavor:Google")"
```

```
nic1_mask="$(curl $md_net/1/subnetmask -H "Metadata-Flavor:Google")"
nic1_addr="$(curl $md_net/1/ip -H "Metadata-Flavor:Google")"
nic1_id="$(ip addr show | grep $nic1_addr | awk '{print $NF}')"
# Source based policy routing for nic1
echo "100 rt-nic1" >> /etc/iproute2/rt_tables
sudo ip rule add pri 32000 from $nic1_gw/$nic1_mask table rt-nic1
sleep 1
sudo ip route add 35.191.0.0/16 via $nic1_gw dev $nic1_id table rt-nic1
sudo ip route add 130.211.0.0/22 via $nic1_gw dev $nic1_id table rt-nic1
# Use a web server to pass the health check for this example.
# You should use a more complete test in production.
sudo apt-get update
sudo apt-get install apache2 -y
sudo a2ensite default-ssl
sudo a2enmod ssl
echo "Example web page to pass health check" | \
tee /var/www/html/index.html
sudo systemctl restart apache2
```

2. Create a common instance template named third-party-template-multinic, which will be used to create new VMs in *both* the vpc-a and vpc-b VPC networks, when an autoscaling event is triggered:

```
gcloud compute instance-templates create third-party-template-multinic \
    --region=us-central1 \
    --network-interface subnet=subnet-a,address="" \
    --network-interface subnet=subnet-b \
    --tags=allow-ssh,allow-health-check,my-network-tag \
    --image-family=debian-10 \
    --image-project=debian-cloud \
    --can-ip-forward \
    --metadata=startup-script="$(< config.sh)"
```

■ **Exam tip** The **--can-ip-forward** flag is required for the instance template creation. This setting lets each backend VM forward packets with any source IP in the vpc-a and vpc-b VPCs, not just the ones whose source IP matches one of the VM's NICs.

---

3. Create a common managed instance group named **third-party-instance-group** that will also be used by the two backend services, one in the vpc-a and the other one in the vpc-b VPC networks:

```
gcloud compute instance-groups managed create third-party-instance-group \
    --region=us-central1 \
    --template=third-party-template-multinic \
    --size=3
```

Creating the Forwarding Rules

You learned the components of a regional internal TCP/UDP network load balancer (type 8) in Chapter 5 (Figure 5-51).

In this reference topology, there are two type 8 load balancers, one in the vpc-a VPC and another one in the vpc-b VPC.

These are the operations you need to implement to create them.

1. Create a new HTTP health check named **hc-http-80** to test TCP connectivity to the VMs on port 80:

```
gcloud compute health-checks create http hc-http-80 \
    --region=us-central1 \
    --port=80
```

2. Use the previously created health check to create two internal backend services in the us-central1 region: one named backend-service-a in the vpc-a VPC, and the other one named backend-service-b in the vpc-b VPC (see Figure 6-12).

```
gcloud compute backend-services create backend-service-a \
    --load-balancing-scheme=internal \
    --health-checks-region=us-central1 \
    --health-checks=hc-http-80 \
    --region=us-central1 \
    --network=vpc-a \
    --session-affinity=CLIENT_IP
gcloud compute backend-services create backend-service-b \
    --load-balancing-scheme=internal \
    --health-checks-region=us-central1 \
    --health-checks=hc-http-80 \
    --region=us-central1 \
    --network=vpc-b \
    --session-affinity=CLIENT_IP
```

3. Add to each of the two backend services the managed instance groups you created in step 3 (**third-party-instance-group**), which contains the third-party virtual appliances as backends:

```
gcloud compute backend-services add-backend backend-service-a \
    --instance-group=third-party-instance-group \
    --instance-group-region=us-central1 \
    --region=us-central1
gcloud compute backend-services add-backend backend-service-b \
    --instance-group=third-party-instance-group \
    --instance-group-region=us-central1 \
    --region=us-central1
```

4. Create two regional, internal forwarding rules: one associated with the **subnet-a** and the other one associated with the **subnet-b**. Connect each forwarding rule to its respective backend service, that is, backend-service-a and backend-service-b:

```
gcloud compute forwarding-rules create ilb-a \
    --load-balancing-scheme=internal \
    --ports=80 \
    --network=vpc-a \
    --subnet=subnet-a \
    --region=us-central1 \
    --backend-service=backend-service-a \
    --address=10.13.1.77

gcloud compute forwarding-rules create ilb-b \
    --load-balancing-scheme=internal \
    --ports=80 \
    --network=vpc-b \
    --subnet=subnet-b \
    --region=us-central1 \
    --backend-service=backend-service-b \
    --address=10.15.1.77
```

Creating the Custom Static Routes That Define the Load Balancers As the Next Hops

1. This is the key configuration step that enables routing between the two VPCs, resulting in a fully integrated, highly available solution with the third-party multi-NIC appliances:

```
gcloud compute routes create ilb-nhop-dest-10-15-1 \
    --network=vpc-a \
    --destination-range=10.15.1.0/24 \
    --next-hop-ilb=ilb-a \
    --next-hop-ilb-region=us-central1
gcloud compute routes create ilb-nhop-dest-10-13-1 \
    --network=vpc-b \
    --destination-range=10.13.1.0/24 \
    --next-hop-ilb=ilb-b \
    --next-hop-ilb-region=us-central1
```

■ **Note** With the optional --tags flag, one or more network tags can be added to the route to indicate that the route applies only to the VMs with the specified tag. Omitting this flag tells Google Cloud that the custom static route applies to all VMs in the specified VPC network, whose value is set using the --network flag. In this example, the route applies to all VMs in each VPC. Remember, routes (just like firewall rules) are global resources that are defined at the VPC level.

This last step concluded the actual configuration of this reference topology. Let's validate the setup.

Creating the First VM

Let's now create a VM with the IP address 10.13.1.70 in the subnet-a (10.13.1.0/24). The creation of the VM installs the Apache web server, which will serve incoming traffic on the TCP port 80:

```
gcloud compute instances create vm-a \
    --zone=us-central1-a \
    --image-family=debian-10 \
    --image-project=debian-cloud \
    --tags=allow-ssh \
    --subnet=subnet-a \
    --private-network-ip 10.13.1.70 \
    --metadata=startup-script='#! /bin/bash
    sudo apt-get update
    sudo apt-get install apache2 -y
    sudo a2ensite default-ssl
    sudo a2enmod ssl
    vm_hostname="$(curl -H "Metadata-Flavor:Google" \
    http://metadata.google.internal/computeMetadata/v1/instance/name)"
    echo "Page served from: $vm_hostname" | \
    tee /var/www/html/index.html
    sudo systemctl restart apache2'
```

Creating the Second VM

Similarly, let's create another VM with the IP address 10.15.1.70 in the subnet-b (10.15.1.0/24). The creation of the VM installs the Apache web server, which will serve incoming traffic on the TCP port 80:

```
gcloud compute instances create vm-b \
    --zone=us-central1-b \
    --image-family=debian-10 \
    --image-project=debian-cloud \
    --tags=allow-ssh \
    --subnet=subnet-b \
    --private-network-ip 10.15.1.70 \
    --metadata=startup-script='#! /bin/bash
    sudo apt-get update
    sudo apt-get install apache2 -y
    sudo a2ensite default-ssl
    sudo a2enmod ssl
    vm_hostname="$(curl -H "Metadata-Flavor:Google" \
    http://metadata.google.internal/computeMetadata/v1/instance/name)"
    echo "Page served from: $vm_hostname" | \
    tee /var/www/html/index.html
    sudo systemctl restart apache2'
```

Verifying Load Balancer Health Status

Before testing, let's make sure both internal TCP/UDP network load balancers are healthy:

```
gcloud compute backend-services get-health backend-service-a \
    --region us-central1
gcloud compute backend-services get-health backend-service-b \
    --region us-central1
```

You should see a message that confirms both load balancers are in a healthy status.

Testing Connectivity from the Testing VM

Connect to vm-a using the SSH protocol and try to "curl" to vm-b:

```
gcloud compute ssh vm-a --zone=us-central1-a
curl http://10.15.1.70
exit
```

Testing Connectivity from the Production VM

Connect to vm-b using the SSH protocol and try to "curl" to vm-a:

```
gcloud compute ssh vm-b --zone=us-central1-b
curl http://10.13.1.70
exit
```

Exam Questions

Question 6.1 (Cloud DNS)

You are migrating to Cloud DNS and want to import your BIND zone file.
  Which command should you use?

  A. `gcloud dns record-sets import ZONE_FILE --zone MANAGED_ZONE`

  B. `gcloud dns record-sets import ZONE_FILE --replace-origin-ns --zone MANAGED_ZONE`

  C. `gcloud dns record-sets import ZONE_FILE --zone-file-format --zone MANAGED_ZONE`

  D. `gcloud dns record-sets import ZONE_FILE --delete-all-existing --zone MANAGED_ZONE`

Rationale

A is not correct because the default behavior of the command is to expect ZONE_FILE in YAML format.

B is not correct because the --replace-origin-format flag indicates that NS records for the origin of a zone should be imported if defined, which is not what the question asked.

C is CORRECT because the --zone-file-format flag indicates that the input records file is in BIND zone format. If omitted, the ZONE_FILE is expected in YAML format.

D is not correct because the --delete-all-existing flag indicates that all existing record sets should be deleted before importing the record sets in the records file, which is not what the question asked.

Question 6.2 (Cloud NAT)

You decide to set up Cloud NAT. After completing the configuration, you find that one of your instances is not using the Cloud NAT for outbound NAT.

What is the most likely cause of this problem?

A. The instance has been configured with multiple interfaces.

B. An external IP address has been configured on the instance.

C. You have created static routes that use RFC 1918 ranges.

D. The instance is accessible by a load balancer external IP address.

Rationale

A is not correct because the fact that the instance uses multi-NIC is not related with its inability to use the Cloud NAT for outbound NAT.

B is CORRECT because the existence of an external IP address on an interface always takes precedence and always performs one-to-one NAT, without using Cloud NAT.

C is not correct because the custom static routes don't use the default Internet gateway as the next hop.

D is not correct because the question asked to select the cause of the inability of the instance to use the Cloud NAT for outbound traffic. However, this answer describes a scenario for inbound traffic.

Question 6.3 (Cloud DNS)

Your organization uses a hub and spoke architecture with critical Compute Engine instances in your Virtual Private Clouds (VPCs). You are responsible for the design of Cloud DNS in Google Cloud. You need to be able to resolve Cloud DNS private zones from your on-premises data center and enable on-premises name resolution from your hub and spoke VPC design.

What should you do?

A. Configure a private DNS zone in the hub VPC, and configure DNS forwarding to the on-premises server. Then configure DNS peering from the spoke VPCs to the hub VPC.

B. Configure a DNS policy in the hub VPC to allow inbound query forwarding from the spoke VPCs. Then configure the spoke VPCs with a private zone, and set up DNS peering to the hub VPC.

C. Configure a DNS policy in the spoke VPCs, and configure the on-premises DNS as an alternate DNS server. Then configure the hub VPC with a private zone, and set up DNS peering to each of the spoke VPCs.

D. Configure a DNS policy in the hub VPC, and configure the on-premises DNS as an alternate DNS server. Then configure the spoke VPCs with a private zone, and set up DNS peering to the hub VPC.

Rationale

A is not correct because the answer does not allow to resolve GCP hostnames from on-premises, which is one of the two requirements.

B is CORRECT because both requirements are met. `https://cloud.google.com/dns/docs/best-practices#hybrid-architecture-using-hub-vpc-network-connected-to-spoke-vpc-networks`

C and D are not correct because you don't need to configure the on-premises DNS as an alternate DNS server to meet the requirements.

CHAPTER 7

■ ■ ■

Implementing Hybrid Connectivity

Cloud computing unlocks a significant number of capabilities due to its ability to deliver an unprecedented level of computing power at a relatively low cost.

It's no secret that every large enterprise is moving away from its corporate data centers and has invested in a cloud adoption program.

However, a cloud adoption program faces a number of challenges mainly due to the choice technology and business leaders need to make to balance the right mix of innovation while maintaining the "business as usual."

Innovation maps to delivering cloud-native solutions, which leverage modern compute products and services, for example, serverless products like Cloud Run, Cloud Functions, or App Engine.

"Business as usual" maps to migrating to the cloud existing applications that generate business value.

Put differently, unless you are a small startup beginning from scratch, chances are you need a plan to move your applications to the cloud. Unplugging the connectivity to your data center and by magic turning the switch on to enable your applications in the cloud is not a realistic option.

That's why Google Cloud has developed a number of offerings that let your company's data centers (or your local development environment) connect to Google Cloud in a variety of different ways, ranging from solutions that prioritize performance, reliability, and reduced latencies to others that prioritize cost savings and easy setups.

In this chapter, you will learn what these connectivity offerings are, how to configure them, and most importantly how to choose which one(s) best suits the requirements for your workload.

Configuring Cloud Interconnect

Cloud Interconnect extends your company's on-premises networks to your company's Google Cloud VPCs with a solution that provides low latency, high availability, and reliability.

Cloud Interconnect connections are called *circuits* and deliver internal (RFC 1918) IP address communication, that is, internal IP addresses are directly accessible from both networks.

■ **Exam tip**   Cloud Interconnect circuits do not traverse the Internet and, by default, do not encrypt data in transit.

© Dario Cabianca 2023
D. Cabianca, *Google Cloud Platform (GCP) Professional Cloud Network Engineer Certification Companion*, Certification Study Companion Series, https://doi.org/10.1007/978-1-4842-9354-6_7

Cloud Interconnect comes in two "flavors":

- **Dedicated Interconnect**, which provides a *direct* physical connection between your on-premises networks and Google's global backbone.

- **Partner Interconnect**, which provides an *indirect* connection between your on-premises networks and Google's global backbone. This is achieved by leveraging a supported service provider.

Dedicated Interconnect Connections and VLAN Attachments

Dedicated Interconnect provides direct physical connections between your on-premises network and Google's global backbone network. Dedicated Interconnect enables you to transfer large amounts of data between networks, which can be more cost-effective than purchasing additional bandwidth over the public Internet.

Prerequisites

As a Google Cloud professional cloud network engineer, you are responsible for making sure the following prerequisites are met before ordering Dedicated Interconnect:

- Your network must physically meet Google's global backbone in a colocation facility. Use the `gcloud compute interconnects locations list` command to list the colocation facilities close to you.

- You must provide your own routing equipment. Your on-premises router is typically located in the colocation facility. However, you can also extend your connection to a router outside of the colocation facility.

- In the colocation facility, your network devices must support the following technical requirements:

  - 10 Gbps circuits, single-mode fiber, 10GBASE-LR (1310 nm) or 100 Gbps circuits, single-mode fiber, 100GBASE-LR4

  - IPv4 link-local addressing

  - LACP (Link Aggregation Control Protocol), even if you're using a single circuit

  - EBGP-4 (External Border Gateway Protocol version 4 - `https://www.ietf.org/rfc/rfc4271.txt`) with multi-hop

  - 802.1Q VLANs

How It Works

You provision a Dedicated Interconnect connection between the Google global backbone and your own network. The diagram in Figure 7-1 shows a single Dedicated Interconnect connection between a Virtual Private Cloud (VPC) network and your on-premises network.

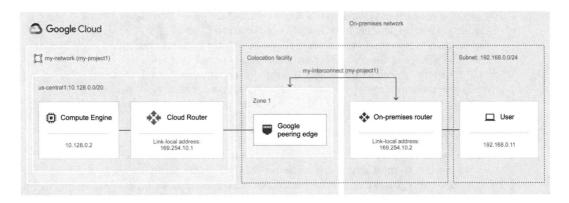

Figure 7-1. *Example of a Dedicated Interconnect connection. Portions of this page are reproduced under the CC-BY license and shared by Google:* `https://cloud.google.com/network-connectivity/docs/interconnect/concepts/dedicated-overview`

For the basic setup shown in Figure 7-1, a Dedicated Interconnect connection is provisioned between the Google global backbone and the on-premises router in a common colocation facility.

VLAN Attachments

VLAN attachments (also known as `interconnectAttachments`) determine which Virtual Private Cloud (VPC) networks can reach your on-premises network through a Dedicated Interconnect connection.

Billing for VLAN attachments starts when you create them and stops when you delete them.

A VLAN attachment is always associated to a Cloud Router. This Cloud Router creates a BGP session for the VLAN attachment and its corresponding on-premises peer router. The Cloud Router receives the routes that your on-premises router advertises. These routes are added as *custom dynamic routes* in your VPC network. The Cloud Router also advertises routes for Google Cloud resources to the on-premises peer router.

■ **Note**   It is possible to associate multiple, different VLAN attachments to the same Cloud Router.

Configuring Dedicated Interconnect

The following are the steps to configure a Dedicated Interconnect connection:

1. **Ordering a Dedicated Interconnect connection**: Submit an order, specifying the details of your Interconnect connection. Google then emails you an order confirmation. After your resources have been allocated, you receive another email with your LOA-CFAs (Letter of Authorization and Connecting Facility Assignment).

2. **Retrieving LOA-CFAs**: Send the LOA-CFAs to your vendor. They provision the connections between the Google peering edge and your on-premises network. Google automatically starts testing the light levels on each allocated port after 24 hours.

3. **Testing the connection**: Google sends you automated emails with configuration information for two different tests. First, Google sends an IP address configuration to test light levels on every circuit in an Interconnect connection. After those tests pass, Google sends the final IP address configuration to test the IP connectivity of each connection's production configuration. Apply these configurations to your routers so that Google can confirm connectivity. If you don't apply these configurations (or apply them incorrectly), Google sends an automated email with troubleshooting information. After all tests have passed, your Interconnect connection is ready to use.

4. **Creating a VLAN attachment**: When your Interconnect connection is ready to use, you need to connect Virtual Private Cloud (VPC) networks to your on-premises network. To do that, first create a VLAN attachment, specifying an existing Cloud Router that's in the VPC network that you want to reach.

5. **Configuring on-premises routers**: After you create a VLAN attachment, to start sending traffic between networks, you need to configure your on-premises router to establish a BGP session with your Cloud Router. To configure your on-premises router, use the VLAN ID, interface IP address, and peering IP address provided by the VLAN attachment.

The process is illustrated in Figure 7-2, with emphasis on the gcloud CLI commands you need to know for the exam.

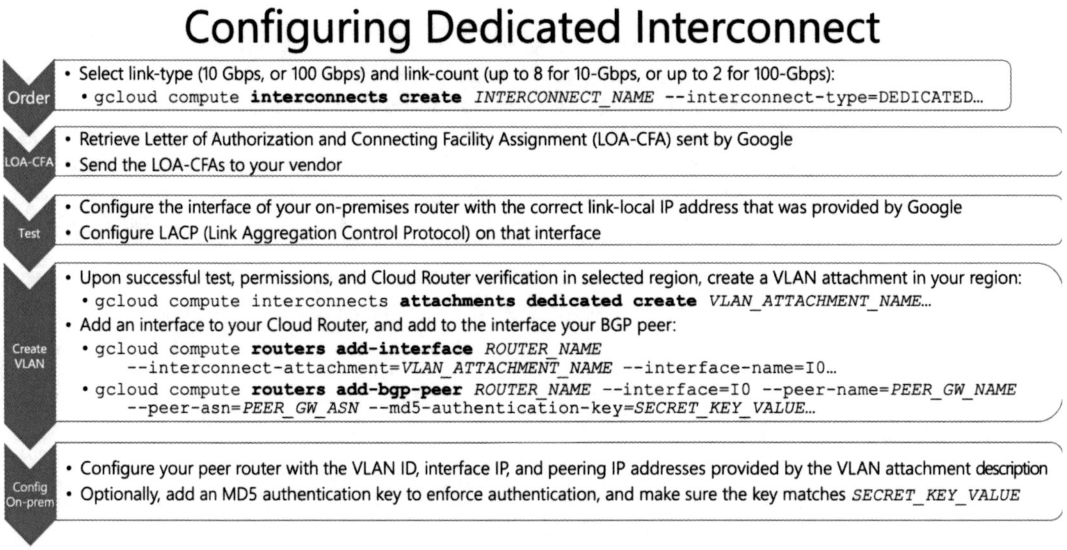

Configuring Dedicated Interconnect

Order
- Select link-type (10 Gbps, or 100 Gbps) and link-count (up to 8 for 10-Gbps, or up to 2 for 100-Gbps):
  - `gcloud compute` **`interconnects create`** `INTERCONNECT_NAME --interconnect-type=DEDICATED...`

LOA-CFA
- Retrieve Letter of Authorization and Connecting Facility Assignment (LOA-CFA) sent by Google
- Send the LOA-CFAs to your vendor

Test
- Configure the interface of your on-premises router with the correct link-local IP address that was provided by Google
- Configure LACP (Link Aggregation Control Protocol) on that interface

Create VLAN
- Upon successful test, permissions, and Cloud Router verification in selected region, create a VLAN attachment in your region:
  - `gcloud compute interconnects` **`attachments dedicated create`** `VLAN_ATTACHMENT_NAME...`
- Add an interface to your Cloud Router, and add to the interface your BGP peer:
  - `gcloud compute` **`routers add-interface`** `ROUTER_NAME`
    `--interconnect-attachment=VLAN_ATTACHMENT_NAME --interface-name=I0...`
  - `gcloud compute` **`routers add-bgp-peer`** `ROUTER_NAME --interface=I0 --peer-name=PEER_GW_NAME`
    `--peer-asn=PEER_GW_ASN --md5-authentication-key=SECRET_KEY_VALUE...`

Config On-prem
- Configure your peer router with the VLAN ID, interface IP, and peering IP addresses provided by the VLAN attachment description
- Optionally, add an MD5 authentication key to enforce authentication, and make sure the key matches `SECRET_KEY_VALUE`

Figure 7-2. Process to configure a Dedicated Interconnect connection

Ordering a Dedicated Interconnect Connection

When you order a Dedicated Interconnect connection, you have to choose the capacity of your connection. You can request the following capacities:

- 1 x 10 Gbps (10 Gbps) circuit up to 8 x 10 Gbps (80 Gbps) circuits

- 1 x 100 Gbps (100 Gbps) circuit up to 2 x 100 Gbps (200 Gbps) circuits

---

■ **Note**　The link type that you select when you create an Interconnect connection cannot be changed later. For example, if you select a 10 Gbps link type and need a 100 Gbps link type later, you must create a new Interconnect connection with the higher capacity.

To create a Dedicated Interconnect connection, use the `gcloud compute interconnects create` as indicated as follows:

```
gcloud compute interconnects create INTERCONNECT_NAME \
    --customer-name=NAME \
    --interconnect-type=DEDICATED \
    --link-type=LINK_TYPE \
    --location=LOCATION_NAME \
    --requested-link-count=NUMBER_OF_LINKS \
  [--noc-contact-email=EMAIL_ADDRESS] \
  [--description=STRING]
```

Substitute the following values:

- INTERCONNECT_NAME: A name for the Interconnect connection; this name is displayed in the Google Cloud console and is used by the Google Cloud CLI to reference the connection, such as my-interconnect.

- NAME: The name of your organization to put in the LOA as the party authorized to request a connection.

- LINK_TYPE

    - If you want your Interconnect connection to be made up of 10 Gbps circuits, replace LINK_TYPE with LINK_TYPE_ETHERNET_10G_LR.

    - If you want your connection to be made up of 100 Gbps circuits, replace LINK_TYPE with LINK_TYPE_ETHERNET_100G_LR.

- LOCATION_NAME: Specifies the location where the Interconnect connection is created; to list the names of locations, use the `gcloud compute interconnects locations list` command we introduced in the "Prerequisites" section.

- NUMBER_OF_LINKS: Number of circuits of type link-type; this field combined with --link-type determines your total connection capacity. For example, for 2 x 100 Gbps (200 Gbps) circuits, this number would be 2.

- EMAIL_ADDRESS and STRING: Optional; for the NOC (Network Operations Center) contact, you can specify only one email address—you don't need to enter your own address because you are included in all notifications. If you are creating a connection through workforce identity federation, providing an email address with the --noc-contact-email flag is required.

For redundancy, Google recommends to create a duplicate Interconnect connection that is in the same location but in a different edge availability domain (metro availability zone).

After you order an Interconnect connection, Google emails you a confirmation and allocates ports for you. When the allocation is complete, Google generates LOA-CFAs for your connections and emails them to you.

All the automated emails are sent to the NOC (Network Operations Center) technical contact and the email address of the Google Account used when ordering the Interconnect connection. You can also get your LOA-CFAs by using the Google Cloud console.

You can use the Interconnect connection only after your connections have been provisioned and tested for light levels and IP connectivity.

Retrieving LOA-CFAs

After you order a Dedicated Interconnect connection, Google sends you and the NOC (technical contact) an email with your Letter of Authorization and Connecting Facility Assignment (LOA-CFA) (one PDF file per connection). You must send these LOA-CFAs to your vendor so that they can install your connections. If you don't, your connections won't get connected.

If you can't find the LOA-CFAs in your email, retrieve them from the Google Cloud console (in the Cloud Interconnect page, select Physical connections). This is one of the very few operations that require the use of the console. You can also respond to your order confirmation email for additional assistance.

After the status of an Interconnect connection changes to PROVISIONED, the LOA-CFA is no longer valid, necessary, or available in the Google Cloud console.

■ **Note** To retrieve the LOA-CFAs, you must be granted the permission compute.interconnects. create, which is available in the following IAM roles: roles/owner, roles/editor, roles/compute. networkAdmin.

Testing a Single-Circuit Connection (One 10 Gbps or 100 Gbps Circuit)

Google polls its edge device every 24 hours, checking for a light on the port to your on-premises router. Receiving light indicates that your connection has been established. After detecting this light, Google sends you an email containing an IP address that Google uses to ping your on-premises router to test the circuit.

You must configure the interface of your on-premises router with the correct link-local IP address and configure LACP (Link Aggregation Control Protocol) on that interface. Even though there is only one circuit in your Interconnect connection, you must still use LACP.

■ **Note** LACP is required because it allows you to adjust the capacity of an Interconnect connection without disrupting traffic. An Interconnect connection can be shared by multiple VLAN attachments.

The example in Table 7-1 shows an IP address configuration similar to the one that Google sends you for the test. Replace these values with the values that Google sends you for your network.

Table 7-1. *Example of an LACP configuration*

Google's Link-Local IP Address	Your Router's Link-Local IP Address	Subnet Size
169.254.0.1	169.254.0.2	/30

Apply the test IP address that Google has sent you to the interface of your on-premises router that connects to Google. For testing, you must configure this interface in access mode with no VLAN tagging.

Google tests your connection by pinging the link-local IP address with LACP enabled. Google tests once, 30 minutes after detecting light, and then every 24 hours thereafter.

After a successful test, Google sends you an email notifying you that your connection is ready to use.

If a test fails, Google automatically retests the connection once a day for a week.

After all tests have passed, your Interconnect connection can carry traffic, and Google starts billing it. However, your connection isn't associated with any Google Virtual Private Cloud (VPC) networks. The next step will show you how to attach a VPC network to your Dedicated Interconnect connection.

Creating a VLAN Attachment

VLAN attachments are a way to tell your Cloud Router which VPC network is allowed to connect to your on-premises networks.

There are a few checks you need to complete before creating a VLAN attachment in your Dedicated Interconnect connection.

First, your Dedicated Interconnect connection must have passed all tests and must be ready to use. From a cost standpoint, billing for VLAN attachments starts when you create them and stops when you delete them.

Second, you must have the following IAM permissions:

- `compute.interconnectAttachments.create`
- `compute.interconnectAttachments.get`
- `compute.routers.create`
- `compute.routers.get`
- `compute.routers.update`

or the following IAM roles:

- `roles/owner`
- `roles/editor`
- `roles/compute.networkAdmin`

Third, you must have an existing Cloud Router in the VPC network and region that you want to reach from your on-premises network—Cloud Router is a regional resource. If you don't have an existing Cloud Router, you must create one.

■ **Exam tip** The Cloud Router can use any private autonomous system number (64512–65535 or 4200000000–4294967294) or the Google public ASN, that is, 16550.

After all three checks are completed, you can create a VLAN attachment using the following command:

```
gcloud compute interconnects attachments dedicated create my-attachment \
    --router my-router \
    --interconnect my-interconnect \
    --candidate-subnets 169.254.0.0/29,169.254.10.0/24 \
    --bandwidth 400m \
    --vlan 7 \
    --region us-central1
```

At a minimum, you must specify the name of your Direct Interconnect connection and the name of your Cloud Router resources, which are passed to the flags `--interconnect` and `--router`, respectively.

If you don't specify a region, you may be prompted to enter one. Again, this is because a Cloud Router is a regional resource, and a VLAN attachment is always associated to a Cloud Router.

The optional `--candidate-subnets` flag is a list of up to 16 CIDR blocks—all in the link-local address space `169.254.0.0/16`, which was sent by Google to ping your on-premises router in the previous step. You can use this list to restrict the CIDR blocks Google can use to allocate a BGP IP address for the Cloud Router in your Google Cloud project and your router on-premises.

■ **Exam tip**   The BGP IP CIDR blocks that you specify as values of the `--candidate-subnets` flag must be unique among all Cloud Routers in all regions of a VPC network.

The optional `--bandwidth` flag denotes the maximum provisioned capacity of the VLAN attachment. In the example, its value is set to 400 Mbps. As of the time writing this book (April 2023), you can only choose from the following discrete list: 50m (50 Mbps), 100m, 200m, 300m, 400m, 500m, 1g, 2g, 5g, 10g (default), 20g, 50g (50 Gbps). This ability to "tweak" the capacity of a VLAN attachment is possible because the LACP protocol is required, as we observed in the previous section.

The optional `--vlan` flag denotes the VLAN ID for this attachment and must be an integer in the range 2–4094. You cannot specify a VLAN ID that is already in use on the Interconnect connection. If your VLAN ID is in use, you are asked to choose another one. If you don't enter a VLAN ID, an unused, random VLAN ID is automatically selected for the VLAN attachment.

Upon creation of the VLAN attachment, use the describe command to extract the VLAN ID, the Cloud Router IP address, and the customer router IP address:

```
gcloud compute interconnects attachments describe my-attachment \
    --region us-central1
```

You will need these values to configure your Cloud Router and your on-premises router. Here is an example of an output:

```
cloudRouterIpAddress: 169.254.180.81/29
creationTimestamp: '2022-03-13T10:31:40.829-07:00'
customerRouterIpAddress: 169.254.180.82/29
id: '7'
interconnect: https://www.googleapis.com/compute/v1/projects/my-project/global/
interconnects/myinterconnect
kind: compute#interconnectAttachment
name: my-attachment
operationalStatus: ACTIVE
```

```
privateInterconnectInfo:
  tag8021q: 1000
region: https://www.googleapis.com/compute/v1/projects/my-project/regions/us-central1
router: https://www.googleapis.com/compute/v1/projects/my-project/regions/us-central1/
routers/my-router
```

Associate your newly created VLAN attachment to your Cloud Router by adding an interface that connects to it. The interface IP address is automatically configured using your attachment's cloudRouterIpAddress:

```
gcloud compute routers add-interface my-router \
    --region us-central1 \
    --interface-name my-router-i1 \
    --interconnect-attachment my-attachment
```

Last, associate a BGP peer to your Cloud Router by adding the customer router to the newly added interface:

```
gcloud compute routers add-bgp-peer my-router \
    --interface my-router-i1 \
    --peer-asn 65201 \
    --peer-name bgp-for-my-interconnect \
    --region us-central1 \
    --advertised-route-priority 1000 \
    --md5-authentication-key 'secret_key_value'
```

The first three flags, that is, --interface, --peer-asn, and --peer-name, are mandatory. This makes sense because you are adding a peer router to your Cloud Router's interface, which is associated to your VLAN attachment. As a result, you must provide at a minimum the interface name, your peer ASN, and your peer name.

For the peer ASN, use the same number that you used to configure your on-premises router. The peer IP address is automatically configured using your attachment's customerRouterIpAddress.

The --advertised-route-priority optional flag denotes the base priority of routes advertised to the BGP peer. As you learned in Chapter 2, the value must be in the 0–65535 range.

The --md5-authentication-key optional flag can be added if you want to use MD5 authentication.

■ **Exam tip**   By default, any VPC network can use Cloud Interconnect. To control which VPC networks can use Cloud Interconnect, you can set an organization policy.

Configuring On-Premises Devices

After you create a VLAN attachment, you need to configure your on-premises router to establish a BGP session with your Cloud Router. To configure your on-premises router, use the VLAN ID, interface IP address, and peering IP address provided by the VLAN attachment. You can optionally configure your BGP sessions to use MD5 authentication. If you added MD5 authentication to the BGP session on Cloud Router, you must use the same authentication key when you configure BGP on your on-premises router.

The setup varies based on what topology you want to use:

- **Layer 3 (network) only topology (recommended)**: A Dedicated Interconnect connection or connections terminating on an on-premises router. The router performs BGP peering with Cloud Router.

- **Layer 2 (data link)/layer 3 (network) topology**: A Dedicated Interconnect connection or connections terminating on an on-premises switch connected to an on-premises router. The router performs BGP peering with Cloud Router.

Figure 7-3 illustrates the simplest setup at a logical level, using a layer 3 topology.

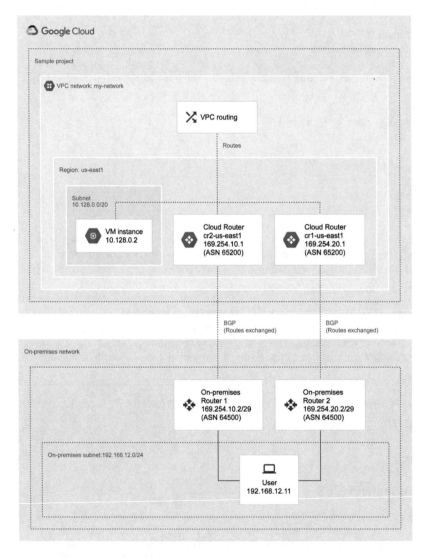

Figure 7-3. *Reference Dedicated Interconnect layer 3 topology. Portions of this page are reproduced under the CC-BY license and shared by Google:* `https://cloud.google.com/network-connectivity/docs/interconnect/how-to/dedicated/configuring-onprem-routers`

Partner Interconnect Connections and VLAN Attachments

There are scenarios where your data center is in a location that can't physically reach a Dedicated Interconnect colocation facility. You still want to use the benefits of private, broadband connectivity, but you are limited by the geography of your company's data centers. That's where Partner Interconnect comes into play.

Partner Interconnect provides connections between your on-premises network and Google's global backbone network through a supported service provider.

Prerequisites

The only two prerequisites are

1. **Supported service provider**: You must select a supported service provider to establish connectivity between their network and your on-premises network. The list of supported service providers is available at `https://cloud.google.com/network-connectivity/docs/interconnect/concepts/service-providers#by-location`.

2. **Cloud Router**: You must have a Cloud Router in the region where your selected service provider operates.

How It Works

You select a service provider from the previous list and establish connectivity.

Next, you create a VLAN attachment in your Google Cloud project, but this time you specify that your VLAN attachment is for a Partner Interconnect connection. This action generates a unique pairing key that you use to request a connection from your service provider. You also need to provide other information such as the connection location and capacity.

After the service provider configures your VLAN attachment, you activate your connection to start using it. Depending on your connection, either you or your service provider then establishes a Border Gateway Protocol (BGP) session. Figure 7-4 illustrates this setup.

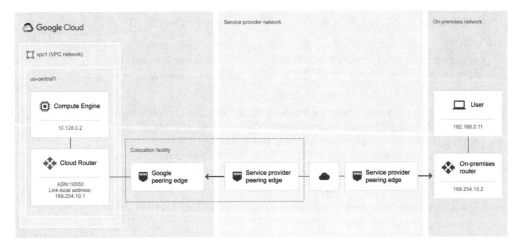

Figure 7-4. *Example of a Partner Interconnect connection. Portions of this page are reproduced under the CC-BY license and shared by Google: `https://cloud.google.com/network-connectivity/docs/interconnect/concepts/partner-overview`*

VLAN Attachments

The main difference here is that with Partner Interconnect, a VLAN attachment generates a pairing key that you share with your service provider.

■ **Note** Unlike Dedicated Interconnect, with Partner Interconnect you delegate to a service provider the task of setting up the connectivity between your on-premises router and the Cloud Router in your Google Cloud project.

The pairing key is a unique key that lets the service provider identify and connect to your Virtual Private Cloud (VPC) network and associated Cloud Router. The service provider requires this key to complete the configuration of your VLAN attachment.

Configuring Partner Interconnect

The following are the steps to configure a Partner Interconnect connection:

1. **Establishing connectivity with a supported service provider**: Select a Google Cloud supported service provider from the list of supported service providers, and establish connectivity between your on-premises network(s) and the supported service provider.

2. **Creating a VLAN attachment**: Create a VLAN attachment for a Partner Interconnect connection, which results in a pairing key that you share with your service provider as previously discussed.

3. **Ordering a connection to Google Cloud from your service provider**: Go to your service provider portal and order a connection to Google Cloud by submitting the pairing key and other connection details, that is, the connection capacity and location. Wait until your service provider configures your connection; they must check that they can serve your requested capacity. After their configuration is complete, you receive an email notification from Google.

4. **Activating your connection**: After the service provider configures your connection, you must activate it. Activating the connection and checking its activation status enables you to verify that you established connectivity with the expected service provider.

5. **Configuring on-premises routers**: For layer 2 (data link layer) connections, you must establish a BGP session between the VPC network's Cloud Router in your region and your on-premises router. For layer 3 connections (network layer), the service provider establishes a BGP session with the VPC network's Cloud Router in your region. This configuration is automated and doesn't require any action from you.

The process is illustrated in Figure 7-5, with emphasis on the gcloud CLI commands you need to know for the exam.

Configuring Partner Interconnect

Connect with Partner	• Choose a supported service provider (partner) • Establish connectivity between your on-premises network(s) and the partner network

Create VLAN	• Create a VLAN attachment and store the resulting pairing key:
	  • `gcloud compute interconnects` **attachments partner create** `VLAN_ATTACHMENT_NAME`
	    `--router=ROUTER_NAME --edge-availability-domain=any`

Order Connection	• Use the pairing key, the desired VLAN attachment capacity, and region to order a connection to Google Cloud • After partner has established a connection to Google Cloud, VLAN attachment state PENDING_PARTNER→PENDING_CUSTOMER

Activate Connection	• Activate the connection (Layer 3 - Network):
	  • `gcloud compute interconnects` **attachments partner update** `VLAN_ATTACHMENT_NAME --enable-admin`
	• Activate the connection (Layer 2 – Data Link) by supplying the peer router ASN to your Cloud Router:
	  • `gcloud compute` **routers update-bgp-peer** `ROUTER_NAME --peer-asn=ON_PREM_ASN --peer-name=…`

Configure On-prem	• Configure your peer router with the VLAN ID, interface IP, and peering IP addresses provided by the VLAN attachment description • Optionally, add an MD5 authentication key to enforce authentication

Figure 7-5. *Process to configure a Partner Interconnect connection*

Establishing Connectivity with a Supported Service Provider (Partner)

This is the first "link" in the connection chain. Your company may have already connectivity with a supported service provider, in which case you can move to the next step. Otherwise, you must establish connectivity with your selected partner. This process may take a few weeks.

Creating a VLAN Attachment

For Partner Interconnect, the only item in the checklist you must complete—in addition to the necessary permissions and the connectivity to a selected service provider—is to have an existing Cloud Router in the VPC network and region that you want to reach from your on-premises network. If you don't have an existing Cloud Router, you must create one.

■ **Exam tip** Unlike Dedicated Interconnect, Partner Interconnect requires that your Cloud Router uses the Google public ASN, that is, 16550 (www.whatismyip.com/asn/16550/).

It is best practice to utilize *multiple* VLAN attachments into your VPC network to maximize throughput and increase cost savings. For each BGP session, Google Cloud recommends using the same MED values to let the traffic use equal-cost multipath (ECMP) routing over all the configured VLAN attachments.

The following example creates a VLAN attachment in edge availability domain `availability-domain-1` and is associated with the Cloud Router `my-router`, which is in the region `us-central1`:

```
gcloud compute interconnects attachments partner create my-attachment \
    --region us-central1 \
    --router my-router \
    --edge-availability-domain any
```

The only required flags are

- `--router`, which denotes your router (prerequisite 2).
- `--edge-availability-domain = any | availability-domain-1 | availability-domain-2`, which denotes your choice of a set of redundant hardware. In each metropolitan area where the service provider can connect to Google, there are two sets of redundant hardware. To configure high availability with a redundant VLAN attachment, by selecting any you must wait until your service provider configures your first VLAN attachment. This is because the keyword any indicates either one of the two options (`availability-domain-1`, `availability-domain-2`), and you won't know which one was chosen by your service provider until the setup is complete.

The outcome of creating a Partner VLAN attachment is a pairing key that you must share with your service provider to bridge the connections.

Use the `gcloud compute interconnects attachments describe` command to obtain the pairing key as illustrated in the following:

```
gcloud compute interconnects attachments describe my-attachment \
    --region us-central1
```

Here is an example of an output:

```
adminEnabled: false
edgeAvailabilityDomain: AVAILABILITY_DOMAIN_1
creationTimestamp: '2017-12-01T08:29:09.886-08:00'
id: '7976913826166357434'
kind: compute#interconnectAttachment
labelFingerprint: 42WmSpB8rSM=
name: my-attachment
pairingKey: 7e51371e-72a3-40b5-b844-2e3efefaee59/us-central1/1
region: https://www.googleapis.com/compute/v1/projects/customer-project/regions/us-central1
router: https://www.googleapis.com/compute/v1/projects/customer-project/regions/us-central1/
routers/my-router
selfLink: https://www.googleapis.com/compute/v1/projects/customer-project/regions/us-
central1/interconnectAttachments/my-attachment
state: PENDING_PARTNER
type: PARTNER
```

Remember not to share the pairing key with anyone you don't trust. The pairing key is sensitive data.

The state of the VLAN attachment is PENDING_PARTNER until the service provider completes your VLAN attachment configuration. After the configuration is complete, the state of the attachment changes to ACTIVE or

`PENDING_CUSTOMER.`

■ **Note** Billing for VLAN attachments starts when your service provider completes their configurations, whether or not you preactivated your attachments. Your service provider configures your attachments when they are in the PENDING_CUSTOMER or ACTIVE state. Billing stops when you or the service provider deletes the attachments (when they are in the DEFUNCT state).

If you use a layer 2 connection, you can improve the security posture of your BGP sessions by enforcing MD5 authentication.

■ **Exam tip** To build fault tolerance—with a second VLAN attachment—repeat the same process for the redundant VLAN attachment. Make sure you use the same Cloud Router and the same metropolitan area, but use a different edge availability domain.

Ordering a Connection to Google Cloud

Upon creating a VLAN attachment, you can contact the service provider of your choice serving your region. At a minimum, you need to have ready

- The pairing key resulting from the creation of the VLAN attachment
- The VLAN attachment region
- The VLAN attachment connection capacity

Since you want to minimize the latency between your Google Cloud workloads and resources on-premises, the best practice is to choose the region of a location that is close to your data center.

The capacity can range from 50 Mbps to 50 Gbps. Choose the capacity that best suits your workloads' performance and reliability requirements based on your service provider's offerings. Obviously, the higher the capacity, the higher the price.

Upon ordering the connection, your service provider will start configuring your VLAN attachment. When the configuration is complete, you get a confirmation email from Google, and the state of your attachment changes from PENDING_PARTNER to PENDING_CUSTOMER.

Behind the scenes, Google automatically configures an interface and a BGP peering session on the associated Cloud Router in the region you chose.

Activating Your Connection

When the state has changed to PENDING_CUSTOMER, the ball is in your court, and you need to activate your connection in order to use it. You activate your connection by updating your VLAN attachment with the --
admin-enabled flag:

```
gcloud compute interconnects attachments partner update my-attachment \
    --region us-central1 \
    --admin-enabled
```

For layer 3 (network) connections, you are good to go.

For layer 2 (data link) connections, you must add the ASN of your on-premises router to your Cloud Router. Here is how you do it with the gcloud CLI.

Get the name of your Cloud Router BGP peer:

```
gcloud compute routers describe my-router \
```

```
    --region us-central1
```

Here is an example of an output:

```
bgp:
  advertiseMode: DEFAULT
  asn: 16550
bgpPeers:
- interfaceName: auto-ia-if-my-attachment-c2c53a710bd6c2e
  ipAddress: 169.254.67.201
  managementType: MANAGED_BY_ATTACHMENT
  name: auto-ia-bgp-my-attachment-c2c53a710bd6c2e
  peerIpAddress: 169.254.67.202
creationTimestamp: '2018-01-25T07:14:43.068-08:00'
description: 'test'
id: '4370996577373014668'
interfaces:
- ipRange: 169.254.67.201/29
  linkedInterconnectAttachment: https://www.googleapis.com/compute/alpha/projects/customer-
project/regions/us-central1/interconnectAttachments/my-attachment-partner
  managementType: MANAGED_BY_ATTACHMENT
  name: auto-ia-if-my-attachment-c2c53a710bd6c2e
kind: compute#router
name: partner
network: https://www.googleapis.com/compute/v1/projects/customer-project/global/
networks/default
region: https://www.googleapis.com/compute/v1/projects/customer-project/regions/us-central1
selfLink: https://www.googleapis.com/compute/v1/projects/customer-project/regions/us-
central1/routers/my-router
```

The name is denoted in bold.
Next, use this name and the on-premises router ASN to update your Cloud Router as follows:

```
gcloud compute routers update-bgp-peer my-router \
    --peer-name auto-ia-bgp-my-attachment-c2c53a710bd6c2e \
    --peer-asn=ON_PREM_ASN \
    --region us-central1
```

Configuring On-Premises Devices

Unlike Dedicated Interconnect, when using Partner Interconnect, your on-premises router physically meets the service provider devices rather than a Google Edge device. To configure your on-premises router, follow the guidance that you received from your service provider.

Figure 7-6 illustrates the simplest setup at a logical level, using a layer 3 topology.

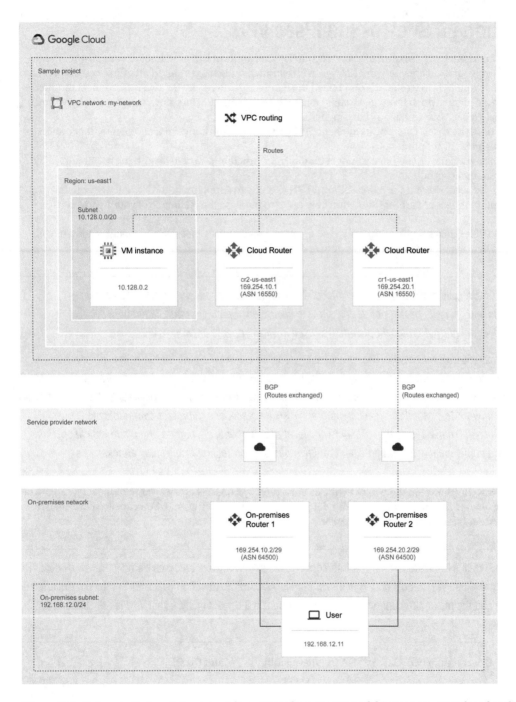

Figure 7-6. *Reference Partner Interconnect layer 3 topology. Portions of this page are reproduced under the CC-BY license and shared by Google:* https://cloud.google.com/network-connectivity/docs/ interconnect/how-to/partner/configuring-onprem-routers

Configuring a Site-to-Site IPsec VPN

There are scenarios where you want to connect your VPC networks in Google Cloud to your on-premises data center—or your local area network (LAN)—with a limited budget in mind. In other use cases, you may determine that your hybrid workloads don't need the bandwidth offered by the two Interconnect products you just learned about, which leverage circuits ranging from 10 Gbps to 100 Gbps. In some situations, you may even realize that your workloads have higher tolerance for latency.

For all these use cases, Google Cloud offers *Cloud VPN* as an alternative or a complementary option to the Interconnect family of products.

In the former scenario, you have a budget in mind, and you don't want to absorb the cost incurred by using an Interconnect product.

In the latter scenario, you want to use Cloud VPN as a way to supplement the connectivity offered by Dedicated Interconnect or Partner Interconnect in order to increase the resilience of your hybrid connectivity.

Cloud VPN leverages an IPsec tunnel to securely connect your VPC networks in Google Cloud to your on-premises data center or your local area network (LAN).

■ **Note** From Wikipedia, **IPsec** *(Internet Protocol Security) is a secure network protocol suite that authenticates and encrypts packets of data to provide secure encrypted communication between two computers over an Internet Protocol network. It is used in virtual private networks (VPNs).*

IPsec includes protocols for establishing mutual authentication between agents at the beginning of a session and negotiation of cryptographic keys to use during the session. IPsec can protect data flows between a pair of hosts (host-to-host), between a pair of security gateways (network-to-network), or between a security gateway and a host (network-to-host). IPsec uses cryptographic security services to protect communications over Internet Protocol (IP) networks. It supports network-level peer authentication, data origin authentication, data integrity, data confidentiality (encryption), and replay protection (protection from replay attacks).

Traffic traveling between the two networks is encrypted by one VPN gateway and then decrypted by the other VPN gateway. This action protects your data as it travels over the Internet. You can also connect two VPC networks with each other with Cloud VPN.

■ **Exam tip** Unlike Dedicated or Partner Interconnect, Cloud VPN always encrypts traffic in transit by design. This is because Cloud VPN is built on top of IPsec tunnels. Also, traffic traveling over an IPsec tunnel traverses the Internet, and the maximum bandwidth of an IPsec tunnel is 3 Gbps. Finally, Cloud VPN is not supported in standard tier.

Cloud VPN comes in two "flavors": HA (high availability) VPN and Classic VPN.

The former is the recommended choice from Google, due to its higher reliability (99.99% SLA) and its adaptability to topology changes.

High Availability VPN (Dynamic Routing)

HA VPN is a type of Cloud VPN that always utilizes *at least* two IPsec tunnels.

Two tunnels are required to provide high availability: in the event one becomes unresponsive, you have the other available to carry traffic.

These two IPsec tunnels connect your VPC network to another network, which can be on-premises, in Google Cloud, or even in another Cloud, for example, AWS.

■ **Exam tip**   The two IPsec tunnels must originate from the same region.

Put differently, with HA VPN you cannot have a tunnel originating from an HA VPN gateway with a network interface in `us-east1` and another tunnel originating from another network interface (associated to the same HA VPN gateway) in `us-central1`.

HA VPN provides an SLA of 99.99% service availability.

How It Works

When you create an HA VPN gateway, Google Cloud automatically reserves two external IPv4 addresses, one for each (of the two) network interfaces. The two IPv4 addresses are chosen from a unique address pool to support high availability.

When you delete the HA VPN gateway, Google Cloud releases the IP addresses for reuse.

The best way to understand how an HA VPN gateway works is with an illustration (Figure 7-7).

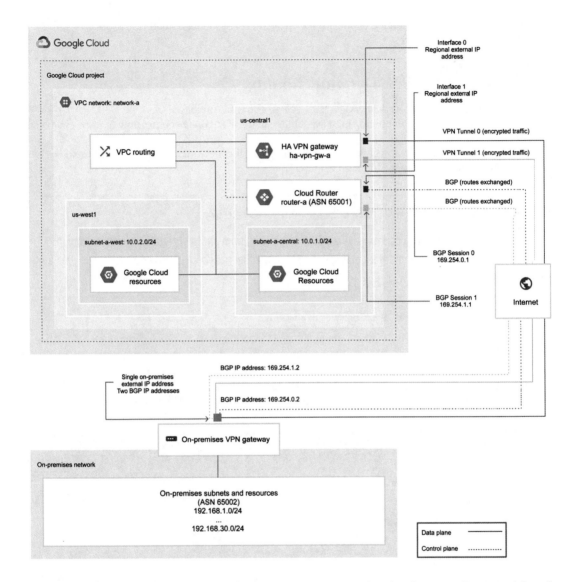

Figure 7-7. *HA VPN simplest topology. Portions of this page are reproduced under CC-BY license and shared by Google:* `https://cloud.google.com/network-connectivity/docs/vpn/concepts/topologies`

Figure 7-7 shows the simplest HA VPN topology, with one HA VPN gateway equipped with two network interfaces—each associated with its own regional external IP address.

The HA VPN gateway connects to *one peer* on-premises router, which has *one external IP address* (i.e., one network card).

The HA VPN gateway uses two tunnels, which are connected to the single external IP address on the peer router.

In Google Cloud, the REDUNDANCY_TYPE for this configuration takes the value SINGLE_IP_INTERNALLY_REDUNDANT.

The topology in Figure 7-7 provides 99.99% availability on Google Cloud, but there is a single point of failure on-premises.

Other topologies can offer a higher level of resilience on-premises, for example, by adding an extra network interface to the peer on-premises router (TWO_IPS_REDUNDANCY) or by using two peer routers each with two network interfaces (FOUR_IPS_REDUNDANCY).

Configuring an HA VPN Gateway and a Tunnel Pair to a Peer VPN Gateway

In the upcoming sections, we will walk you through the process to create an HA VPN gateway with the configuration described in Figure 7-7.

In order to perform this configuration, you must have the roles/compute.networkAdmin IAM role or a custom role that includes all the permissions in the roles/compute.networkAdmin IAM role.

Figure 7-8 illustrates the high-level process, with emphasis on the gcloud CLI commands you need to know for the exam.

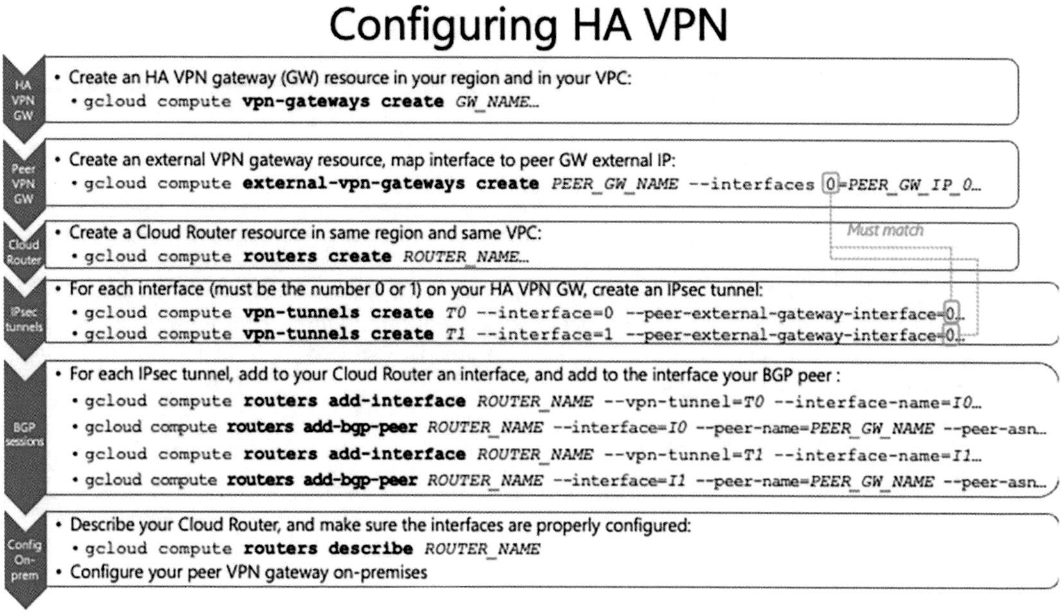

Configuring HA VPN

HA VPN GW
- Create an HA VPN gateway (GW) resource in your region and in your VPC:
  - gcloud compute **vpn-gateways create** *GW_NAME...*

Peer VPN GW
- Create an external VPN gateway resource, map interface to peer GW external IP:
  - gcloud compute **external-vpn-gateways create** *PEER_GW_NAME* --interfaces 0=*PEER_GW_IP_0...*

Cloud Router
- Create a Cloud Router resource in same region and same VPC:
  - gcloud compute **routers create** *ROUTER_NAME...*

Must match

IPsec tunnels
- For each interface (must be the number 0 or 1) on your HA VPN GW, create an IPsec tunnel:
  - gcloud compute **vpn-tunnels create** *T0* --interface=0 --peer-external-gateway-interface=0...
  - gcloud compute **vpn-tunnels create** *T1* --interface=1 --peer-external-gateway-interface=0...

BGP sessions
- For each IPsec tunnel, add to your Cloud Router an interface, and add to the interface your BGP peer :
  - gcloud compute **routers add-interface** *ROUTER_NAME* --vpn-tunnel=T0 --interface-name=I0...
  - gcloud compute **routers add-bgp-peer** *ROUTER_NAME* --interface=I0 --peer-name=*PEER_GW_NAME* --peer-asn...
  - gcloud compute **routers add-interface** *ROUTER_NAME* --vpn-tunnel=T1 --interface-name=I1...
  - gcloud compute **routers add-bgp-peer** *ROUTER_NAME* --interface=I1 --peer-name=*PEER_GW_NAME* --peer-asn...

Config On-prem
- Describe your Cloud Router, and make sure the interfaces are properly configured:
  - gcloud compute **routers describe** *ROUTER_NAME*
- Configure your peer VPN gateway on-premises

Figure 7-8. *Process to create the simplest HA VPN topology*

Creating an HA VPN Gateway

The first step is to create the actual HA VPN gateway Google Cloud resource:

```
gcloud compute vpn-gateways create GW_NAME \
    --network=NETWORK \
    --region=REGION \
    --stack-type=IP_STACK
```

Substitute as indicated in the following:

- GW_NAME: The name of the gateway

- NETWORK: The name of your Google Cloud network

- REGION: The Google Cloud region where you create the gateway and tunnel

- IP_STACK (optional): The IP stack to use. Specify either IPV4_ONLY or IPV4_IPV6. If you do not specify this flag, the default stack type is IPV4_ONLY.

An example output is

```
Created [https://www.googleapis.com/compute/v1/projects/PROJECT_ID/regions/us-central1/
vpnGateways/ha-vpn-gw-a].
NAME            INTERFACE0      INTERFACE1      NETWORK     REGION
ha-vpn-gw-a     203.0.113.16    203.0.113.23    network-a   us-central1
```

As expected, the output shows the two interfaces, each associated to its own regional (us-central1), external IPv4 address.

Creating a Peer VPN Gateway Resource

Since your peer gateway operates on-premises, you cannot create this exact resource from Google Cloud. What Google Cloud allows you to do is to create a resource referred to as external-vpn-gateway, which provides information to Google Cloud about your peer VPN gateway. This resource is essentially the representation of your physical (or software-defined) peer gateway on-premises. The following command creates the representation in Google Cloud of your peer, on-premises gateway, equipped with one network interface as per our configuration in Figure 7-7:

```
gcloud compute external-vpn-gateways create PEER_GW_NAME \
    --interfaces 0=PEER_GW_IP_0
```

Substitute as indicated in the following:

- PEER_GW_NAME: A name representing the peer gateway

- PEER_GW_IP_0: The external IP address for the interface from the peer gateway

An example output is

```
Created [https://www.googleapis.com/compute/v1/projects/PROJECT_ID/global/
externalVpnGateways/peer-gw].
NAME        INTERFACE0
peer-gw     PEER_GW_IP_0
```

Creating a Cloud Router

Next, you must create a cloud router for the region where your HA VPN gateway operates, that is, us-central1:

```
gcloud compute routers create ROUTER_NAME \
    --region=REGION \
```

```
--network=NETWORK \
--asn=GOOGLE_ASN
```

Substitute as follows:

- ROUTER_NAME: The name of the Cloud Router, which must be in the same region as your HA VPN gateway

- REGION: The Google Cloud region where you created your HA VPN gateway and you will create your IPsec tunnel

- NETWORK: The name of your Google Cloud VPC network

- GOOGLE_ASN: Any private ASN (64512 through 65534, 4200000000 through 4294967294) that you are not already using in the peer network

---

■ **Exam tip**   The Google ASN is used for all BGP sessions on the same Cloud Router, and it cannot be changed later.

An example output is

```
Created [https://www.googleapis.com/compute/v1/projects/PROJECT_ID/regions/us-central1/
routers/router-a].
NAME        REGION        NETWORK
router-a    us-central1   network-a
```

Creating IPsec Tunnels

Now that you have your HA VPN gateway, the representation of your peer on-premises gateway, and your Cloud Router, you can establish two IPsec tunnels, one for each interface on the HA VPN gateway.

When creating IPsec tunnels, specify the peer side of the IPsec tunnels as the external VPN gateway that you created earlier.

In our simplest scenario, both IPsec tunnels connect to interface 0 of the external VPN gateway:

```
gcloud compute vpn-tunnels create TUNNEL_NAME_IF0 \
    --peer-external-gateway=PEER_GW_NAME \
    --peer-external-gateway-interface=PEER_EXT_GW_IF0  \
    --region=REGION \
    --ike-version=IKE_VERS \
    --shared-secret=SHARED_SECRET \
    --router=ROUTER_NAME \
    --vpn-gateway=GW_NAME \
    --interface=INT_NUM_0
gcloud compute vpn-tunnels create TUNNEL_NAME_IF1 \
    --peer-external-gateway=PEER_GW_NAME \
    --peer-external-gateway-interface=PEER_EXT_GW_IF0 \
    --region=REGION \
    --ike-version=IKE_VERS \
    --shared-secret=SHARED_SECRET \
    --router=ROUTER_NAME \
    --vpn-gateway=GW_NAME \
    --interface=INT_NUM_1
```

Substitute as follows:

- TUNNEL_NAME_IF0 and TUNNEL_NAME_IF1: A name for each tunnel; naming the tunnels by including the gateway interface name can help identify the tunnels later.

- PEER_GW_NAME: The name of the external peer gateway created earlier.

- PEER_EXT_GW_IF0: The interface number configured earlier on the external peer gateway.

- Optional: The --vpn-gateway-region is the region of the HA VPN gateway to operate on. Its value should be the same as --region. If not specified, this option is automatically set. This option overrides the default compute/region property value for this command invocation.

- IKE_VERS: 1 for IKEv1 or 2 for IKEv2. If possible, use IKEv2 for the IKE version. If your peer gateway requires IKEv1, replace --ike-version 2 with --ike-version 1. To allow IPv6 traffic, you must specify IKEv2.

- SHARED_SECRET: Your preshared key (shared secret), which must correspond with the preshared key for the partner tunnel that you create on your peer gateway; for recommendations, see generate a strong preshared key.

- INT_NUM_0: The number 0 for the first interface on the HA VPN gateway that you created earlier.

- INT_NUM_1: The number 1 for the second interface on the HA VPN gateway that you created earlier.

An example output is

```
Created [https://www.googleapis.com/compute/v1/projects/PROJECT_ID/regions/us-central1/vpnTunnels/
tunnel-a-to-on-prem-if-0].
NAME                        REGION       GATEWAY       VPN_INTERFACE   PEER_GATEWAY   PEER_INTERFACE
tunnel-a-to-on-prem-if-0    us-central1  ha-vpn-gw-a   0               peer-gw        0

Created [https://www.googleapis.com/compute/v1/projects/PROJECT_ID/regions/us-central1/vpnTunnels/
tunnel-a-to-on-prem-if-1].
NAME                        REGION       GATEWAY       VPN_INTERFACE   PEER_GATEWAY   PEER_INTERFACE
tunnel-a-to-on-prem-if-1    us-central1  ha-vpn-gw-a   1               peer-gw        0
```

Establishing BGP Sessions

To keep our configuration as simple as possible, we opt for

- Assigning IPv4 BGP addresses

- Letting Google Cloud automatically choose the link-local BGP IP addresses

In the upcoming commands, replace the following:

- ROUTER_INTERFACE_NAME_0 and ROUTER_INTERFACE_NAME_1: A name for the Cloud Router BGP interface; it can be helpful to use names related to the tunnel names configured previously.

- IP_ADDRESS_0 and IP_ADDRESS_1 (manual configuration): The BGP IP address for the HA VPN gateway interface that you configure; each tunnel uses a different gateway interface.

- MASK_LENGTH: 30; each BGP session on the same Cloud Router must use a unique /30 CIDR from the 169.254.0.0/16 block.

- TUNNEL_NAME_0 and TUNNEL_NAME_1: The tunnel associated with the HA VPN gateway interface that you configured.

- AUTHENTICATION_KEY (optional): The secret key to use for MD5 authentication.

For each of the two IPsec tunnels, you must

- Add an interface to your Cloud Router associated to the IPsec tunnel

- Add a BGP peer to the interface

Let's start with the first IPsec tunnel:

```
gcloud compute routers add-interface ROUTER_NAME \
    --interface-name=ROUTER_INTERFACE_NAME_0 \
    --mask-length=MASK_LENGTH \
    --vpn-tunnel=TUNNEL_NAME_0 \
    --region=REGION
gcloud compute routers add-bgp-peer ROUTER_NAME \
    --peer-name=PEER_NAME_0 \
    --peer-asn=PEER_ASN \
    --interface=ROUTER_INTERFACE_NAME_0 \
    --region=REGION
    --md5-authentication-key=AUTHENTICATION_KEY
```

Substitute PEER_NAME_0 with a name for the peer VPN interface, and substitute PEER_ASN with the ASN configured for your peer VPN gateway.

Let's repeat the same for the second IPsec tunnel:

```
gcloud compute routers add-interface ROUTER_NAME \
    --interface-name=ROUTER_INTERFACE_NAME_1 \
    --mask-length=MASK_LENGTH \
    --vpn-tunnel=TUNNEL_NAME_1 \
    --region=REGION
gcloud compute routers add-bgp-peer ROUTER_NAME \
    --peer-name=PEER_NAME_1 \
    --peer-asn=PEER_ASN \
    --interface=ROUTER_INTERFACE_NAME_1 \
    --region=REGION
    --md5-authentication-key=AUTHENTICATION_KEY
```

Substitute PEER_NAME_1 with a name for the peer VPN interface, and substitute PEER_ASN with the ASN configured for your peer VPN gateway.

Configure On-Premises Devices

To validate the Cloud Router configuration, use the gcloud compute routers describe command as follows:

```
gcloud compute routers describe ROUTER_NAME \
    --region=REGION
```

If everything worked successfully, an example output should look like

```
bgp:
  advertiseMode: DEFAULT
  asn: 65001
bgpPeers:
- interfaceName: if-tunnel-a-to-on-prem-if-0
  ipAddress: 169.254.0.1
  name: bgp-peer-tunnel-a-to-on-prem-if-0
  peerAsn: 65002
  peerIpAddress: 169.254.0.2
- interfaceName: if-tunnel-a-to-on-prem-if-1
  ipAddress: 169.254.1.1
  name: bgp-peer-tunnel-a-to-on-prem-if-1
  peerAsn: 65004
  peerIpAddress: 169.254.1.2
creationTimestamp: '2018-10-18T11:58:41.704-07:00'
id: '4726715617198303502'
interfaces:
- ipRange: 169.254.0.1/30
  linkedVpnTunnel: https://www.googleapis.com/compute/v1/projects/PROJECT_ID/regions/us-
central1/vpnTunnels/tunnel-a-to-on-prem-if-0
  name: if-tunnel-a-to-on-prem-if-0
- ipRange: 169.254.1.1/30
  linkedVpnTunnel: https://www.googleapis.com/compute/v1/projects/PROJECT_ID/regions/us-
central1/vpnTunnels/tunnel-a-to-on-prem-if-1
  name: if-tunnel-a-to-on-prem-if-1
  kind: compute#router
  name: router-a
  network: https://www.googleapis.com/compute/v1/projects/PROJECT_ID/global/networks/
network-a
  region: https://www.googleapis.com/compute/v1/projects/PROJECT_ID/regions/us-central1
  selfLink: https://www.googleapis.com/compute/v1/projects/PROJECT_ID/regions/us-central1/
routers/router-a
```

This completes the setup from Google Cloud. The final step is to configure your peer VPN gateway on-premises. You will need assistance from your on-premises network administrator to properly configure it and fully validate the IPsec tunnels and their fault tolerance.

Classic VPN (e.g., Route-Based Routing, Policy-Based Routing)

Unlike HA VPN, Classic VPN gateways have a single interface, a single external IP address, and support tunnels that use static routing (policy-based or route-based).

Dynamic routing (BGP) is still available for Classic VPN, but only for IPsec tunnels that connect to third-party VPN gateway software running on Google Cloud VM instances.

Classic VPN gateways provide an SLA of 99.9% service availability and do not support IPv6.

Table 7-2 shows a comparison between the two Cloud VPN types.

Table 7-2. *HA VPN and Classic VPN comparison*

Feature	HA VPN	Classic VPN
SLA	Provides a 99.99% SLA when configured with two interfaces and two external IP addresses	Provides a 99.9% SLA
Creation of external IP addresses and forwarding rules	External IP addresses created from a pool; no forwarding rules required	External IP addresses and forwarding rules must be created
Supported routing options	Only dynamic routing (route-based, i.e., BGP)	Static routing (policy-based, route-based). Dynamic routing is only supported for tunnels that connect to third-party VPN gateway software running on Google Cloud VM instances
Two tunnels from one Cloud VPN gateway to the same peer gateway	Supported	Not supported
API resources	Known as the `vpn-gateway` resource	Known as the `target-vpn-gateway` resource
IPv6 traffic	Supported (dual stack IPv4 and IPv6 configuration)	Not supported
Use cases	• Source or Destination NAT (NAT-Src, NAT-Dst) needs to occur while it traverses the VPN • Overlapping subnets/IP addresses between the two LANs • Hub and spoke VPN topology • Design requires primary and backup VPN • Dynamic routing protocol support (e.g., BGP) • Need to access multiple subnets or networks at the remote site, across the VPN	• Need to access only one subnet, or one network at the remote site, across the VPN • Your on-premises VPN devices don't support BGP

It is best practice to migrate your production traffic from Classic VPN to HA VPN, whenever possible.

The only scenario when you should retain Classic VPN is when your on-premises VPN devices don't support BGP and thus can't be used with HA VPN.

However, you should consider upgrading those devices to solutions that support BGP, which is a more flexible and reliable solution than static routing.

Policy-Based Routing

Policy-based routing is a technique that forwards and routes data packets based on policies or filters. Network administrators can selectively apply policies based on specific parameters such as source and destination IP address, source or destination port, traffic type, protocols, access list, packet size, or other criteria and then route the packets on user-defined routes.

Route-Based Routing

In contrast to policy-based routing, a route-based VPN works on IPsec tunnel interfaces as the endpoints of your virtual network. All traffic passing through an IPsec tunnel interface is routed into the VPN. Rather than relying on an explicit policy to dictate which traffic enters the VPN, static and/or dynamic IP routes are formed to direct the desired traffic through the IPsec tunnel interface.

■ **Exam tip**   A route-based VPN is required when there is a requirement for redundant VPN connections, or there is a need for dynamic routing within an IPsec tunnel.

Configuring Cloud Router

You learned about Cloud Router in the "Dynamic Routes" section in Chapter 3.

Every time your workload requires dynamic routing capabilities, you need a Cloud Router.

Cloud Router leverages the Border Gateway Protocol (BGP) to advertise IP address ranges. Custom dynamic routes are programmed and exchanged based on the BGP advertisements that it receives from a peer router, which can reside in Google Cloud, on-premises, or in another cloud (e.g., AWS or Azure).

Instead of a physical device or appliance, each Cloud Router consists of software tasks that act as BGP speakers and responders.

A Cloud Router also serves as the control plane for Cloud NAT. Cloud Router provides BGP services for the following Google Cloud products:

- Dedicated Interconnect

- Partner Interconnect

- HA VPN

- Classic VPN with dynamic routing only

- Router appliance (part of Network Connectivity Center)

When you connect an on-premises or multi-cloud network to Google Cloud, Cloud Router uses BGP to dynamically exchange routes between your Google Cloud VPC network and the remote network. Prefix and next hop changes automatically propagate between your VPC network and the other network without the need for static routes.

As you learned in the previous section, you can also use Cloud Router to connect two VPC networks in Google Cloud. In this scenario, you connect the VPC networks by using two HA VPNs and two Cloud Routers, one HA VPN and its associated Cloud Router on each network.

■ **Exam tip**   Direct peering and carrier peering do not use Cloud Routers.

Border Gateway Protocol (BGP) Attributes (e.g., ASN, Route Priority/ MED, Link-Local Addresses)

You are not required to be an expert in BGP in order to pass the exam.

However, a high-level understanding of what BGP does and how it works with a Cloud Router will definitely help you answer some of the questions.

Cloud Router advertises VPC subnet routes and custom prefixes to its BGP peers.

Unless you configure custom route advertisements, Cloud Router only advertises VPC subnet routes. Custom route advertisements also allow you to configure a Cloud Router to omit advertising VPC subnet routes.

The dynamic routing mode of a VPC network—which can be toggled with the --bgp-routing-mode flag—determines which VPC subnet routes are advertised by the Cloud Routers in that network.

The dynamic routing mode also controls how each Cloud Router applies learned prefixes as custom dynamic routes in a VPC network.

As you learned in the configuration of Dedicated Interconnect, Partner Interconnect, and HA VPN, you can also enhance the security of your Cloud Router BGP sessions by enforcing MD5 authentication.

The following sections describe the key attributes you need to know for the exam.

Autonomous System Number (ASN)

If you are using Dedicated Interconnect, you are required to use either a private ASN not already in use *or* the Google public ASN (i.e., 16550). A private ASN ranges from 64512 to 65534 or from 4200000000 to 4294967294 inclusive.

If you are using Partner Interconnect, you must use the Google public ASN to configure your Cloud Router.

Your on-premises ASN can be public or private.

Route Priorities and Multi-exit Discriminators (MEDs)

When a prefix is advertised by a Cloud Router to a BGP peer, a *priority* is always added to the prefix during the BGP session.

As you learned in Chapter 2, the advertised priority for a prefix is implemented as a MED, that is, the sum of the base priority for the prefix and the inter-region cost, if applicable.

The base priority is an integer number in the range 0 to 65535 inclusive and can be set with the --advertised-route-priority flag in the gcloud compute routers **add-bgp-peer/update-bgp-peer** commands, as illustrated in the following:

```
gcloud compute routers update-bgp-peer ROUTER_NAME \
    --peer-name=BGP_PEER_NAME \
    --advertised-route-priority=B
```

The preceding command updates the base priority for routes advertised by *ROUTER_NAME* to its BGP peer *BGP_PEER_NAME* with the integer number *B*.

■ **Note** The default base priority in GCP is 100.

For a visual representation on how MED applies to route priorities, we are going to use the example in Chapter 3, section "Updating the Base Priority for Advertised Routes."

Assuming the *inter-region* cost is denoted by the letter C, here is a summary of how the MED is calculated, based on whether your Cloud Router's VPC network operates in regional or global BGP routing mode:

- **Regional dynamic routing mode**: The Cloud Router *only* advertises prefixes of subnet ranges in the same region in its VPC. Each range is advertised as a prefix with priority: `MED = B` (Figure 7-9).

- **Global dynamic routing mode**: The Cloud Router advertises prefixes of subnet ranges in the same region in its VPC. Each range is advertised as a prefix with priority: `MED = B`. Additionally, the Cloud Router advertises prefixes of subnet ranges in different regions in its VPC. Each range is advertised as a prefix with priority: `MED = B+C` (Figure 7-10).

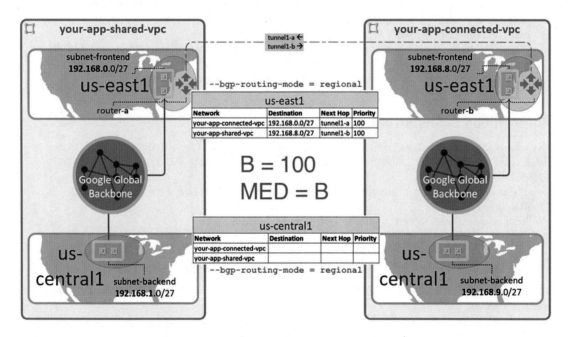

Figure 7-9. *MED for VPCs configured with regional BGP routing mode*

Notice in Figure 7-9 how the two Cloud Routers `router-a` and `router-b` advertise prefixes of subnet routes *in their own region only*, that is, `us-east1`.

There are no prefixes of subnet routes in the `us-central1` route table.

This is because the two VPC networks `your-app-shared-vpc` and `your-app-connected-vpc` are configured with *regional* BGP routing mode.

Figure 7-10 shows the effect of updating them with *global* BGP routing mode.

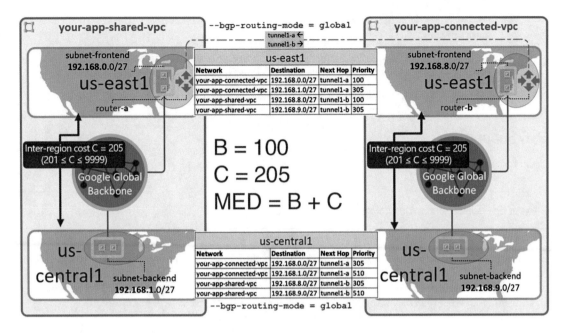

Figure 7-10. MED for VPCs configured with global BGP routing mode

This time, the two cloud routers `router-a` and `router-b` advertise prefixes of subnet routes *in all regions of their respective VPC*.

As a result, both route tables are populated with prefixes of subnet routes.

Notice how the priorities for prefixes of subnets in `us-central1` (as shown in the lower table in Figure 7-10) carry the extra inter-region cost `C=205`.

■ **Exam tip** The inter-region cost is an integer number between 201 and 9999, inclusive. It is defined by Google and is specific to the exact combination of the two regions, that is, the region of the subnet whose prefix is being advertised (e.g., `us-east1`) and the region of the BGP peer router (e.g., `us-central1`). This number may vary over time based on factors such as network performance, latency, distance, and available bandwidth between regions.

When your BGP peer routers receive the advertised prefixes and their priorities, they create routes that are used to send packets to your VPC network.

BGP Peering IP Addresses

BGP sessions for the following network connectivity products use link-local IPv4 addresses in the 169.254.0.0/16 range as BGP peering IP addresses:

- For Dedicated Interconnect, you can either specify candidate link-local addresses for BGP peering addresses, or Google Cloud can select unused link-local addresses automatically.

- For Partner Interconnect, Google Cloud selects unused link-local IPv4 addresses automatically.

- For HA VPN and Classic VPN using dynamic routing, you can specify the BGP peering IP addresses when you create the BGP interface on the Cloud Router.

Router appliances use internal IPv4 addresses of Google Cloud VMs as BGP IP addresses.

IPv6 Support

Cloud Router can exchange IPv6 prefixes, but only over BGP IPv4 sessions.

■ **Exam tip** Cloud Router does not support BGP IPv6 sessions natively.

For Cloud Router to be able to exchange IPv6 prefixes, the subnets must be configured to operate in dual stack mode (by using the flag --stack-type=IPV4_IPV6 in the gcloud compute networks subnets create/update commands), and you must enable IPv6 prefix exchange in an existing BGP IPv4 session by toggling the --enable-ipv6 flag in the gcloud compute routers update-bgp-peer command.

By default, internal IPv6 subnet ranges are advertised automatically.

External IPv6 subnet ranges are not advertised automatically, but you can advertise them manually by using custom route advertisements.

You can enable IPv6 prefix exchange in BGP sessions that are created for HA VPN tunnels.

Default Route Advertisements via BGP

You learned in Chapter 2 that the VPC network is the only required argument when you create a Cloud Router.

A Cloud Router's default route advertisement behavior depends on whether the VPC associated to your Cloud Router is configured with BGP routing mode set to regional or global.

You can toggle this behavior by setting the --bgp-routing-mode flag to regional (default) or global in the gcloud compute networks create/update commands:

- **Regional dynamic routing mode**: Each Cloud Router in the VPC network advertises primary and secondary subnet ranges *in the same region as the Cloud Router*. Internal IPv6 subnet ranges *in the same region as the Cloud Router* are also advertised, provided the conditions described in the IPv6 support sections are met.

- **Global dynamic routing mode**: Each Cloud Router in the VPC network advertises primary and secondary IPv4 subnet ranges *from all regions in the VPC network*. Internal IPv6 subnet ranges *from all regions in the VPC network* are also advertised, provided the conditions described in the IPv6 support sections are met.

If you advertise privately used public IPv4 addresses, on-premises systems might not be able to access Internet resources which use those public IPv4 addresses.

Subnet route advertisements are updated automatically.

Custom Route Advertisements via BGP

With custom route advertisement, you control which prefixes and which subnet routes a Cloud Router can advertise to its BGP peers.

This control can be defined on a Cloud Router basis (gcloud compute routers create/update) or on a BGP-peer basis (gcloud compute routers update-bgp-peer) and can be achieved by setting the flag --advertisement-mode to CUSTOM when you use the verbs create, update, or update-bgp-peer on a Cloud Router.

When you use any of the three commands as follows:

- gcloud compute routers create ROUTER_NAME --**advertisement-mode=CUSTOM**

- gcloud compute routers update ROUTER_NAME --**advertisement-mode=CUSTOM**

- gcloud compute routers update-bgp-peer ROUTER_NAME --peer-name=BGP_PEER_ NAME --**advertisement-mode=CUSTOM**

you can choose

1. The list of prefixes you want your Cloud Router to advertise

2. Whether you want all the subnet routes in your Cloud Router's VPC to be advertised

The list of prefixes can be specified by using the --set-advertisement-ranges or the --add-advertisement-ranges flags, which take a list of valid CIDR blocks as value.

The subnet routes can be excluded from the advertised routes with the command --remove-advertisement-groups=ALL_SUBNETS.

■ **Note** Remember, the subnet routes to be excluded can be only the ones in your Cloud Router's region or all the subnet routes in all regions spanned by your Cloud Router's VPC. This set of subnet routes is based on whether your Cloud Router's VPC network BGP routing mode is set to regional or global.

Deploying Reliable and Redundant Cloud Routers

Cloud Router is a key Google Cloud product specifically designed to enable dynamic routing capabilities for your workloads' hybrid and multi-cloud connectivity requirements.

As a Google Cloud professional cloud network engineer, you are responsible for ensuring the network architecture you are designing is aligned with the five pillars of the well-architected framework.

As a result, you should architect your Cloud Router strategy at a minimum for resilience, for reliability, for high availability, and for security.

In this section, you will learn how to achieve these goals.

Resilience

It is best practice to enable Bidirectional Forwarding Detection (BFD) on your Cloud Routers and on your peer BGP routers (on-premises or in other clouds) if they support this feature.

BFD is a UDP-based detection protocol that provides a low-overhead method of detecting failures in the forwarding path between two adjacent routers.

When configured with default settings, BFD detects failure in 5 seconds, compared to 60 seconds for BGP-based failure detection. With BFD implemented on Cloud Router, end-to-end detection time can be as short as 5 seconds.

Enabling BFD on both sides will make your network more resilient.

You can enable BFD on your Cloud Router by setting the `--bfd-session-initialization-mode` flag to `ACTIVE` in the `gcloud compute routers add-bgp-peer/update-bgp-peer` commands, as shown in the following code snippet:

```
gcloud compute routers update-bgp-peer ROUTER_NAME \
    --project=PROJECT_ID \
    --peer-name=PEER_NAME \
    --interface=INTERFACE \
    --ip-address=IP_ADDRESS \
    --peer-asn=PEER_ASN \
    --peer-ip-address=PEER_IP_ADDRESS \
    --region=REGION \
    --bfd-session-initialization-mode=BFD_SESSION_INITIALIZATION_MODE\
    --bfd-min-receive-interval=BFD_MIN_RECEIVE_INTERVAL \
    --bfd-min-transmit-interval=BFD_MIN_TRANSMIT_INTERVAL \
    --bfd-multiplier=BFD_MULTIPLIER
```

Substitute as indicated in the following:

- ROUTER_NAME: The name of your Cloud Router

- PROJECT_ID: The project that contains your Cloud Router

- PEER_NAME: The name of your BGP peer

- INTERFACE: The name of the interface for this BGP peer

- IP_ADDRESS: The IP address for your Cloud Router

- PEER_ASN: The BGP autonomous system number (ASN) for this BGP peer

- PEER_IP_ADDRESS: The link-local address of the peer router belonging to the range 169.254.0.0/16

- REGION: The region where the Cloud Router's VPC network is located

- BFD_SESSION_INITIALIZATION_MODE: The session initialization mode for this BGP peer. Must be one of

- ACTIVE: The Cloud Router will initiate the BFD session for this BGP peer.

- PASSIVE: The Cloud Router will wait for the BGP peer router to initiate the BFD session for this BGP peer.

- DISABLED: BFD is disabled for this BGP peer.

■ **Exam tip** You don't need to know all the BFD settings to pass the exam. What you need to know instead is that enabling BFD is one way to achieve resilience, and the way you do it is by setting the BFD_SESSION_INITIALIZATION_ MODE to ACTIVE. To learn how to configure BFD in detail, use the Google Cloud documentation: `https://cloud.google.com/network-connectivity/docs/router/concepts/bfd#bfd-settings`.

Reliability

Enable graceful restart on your on-premises BGP device. With graceful restart, traffic between networks isn't disrupted in the event of a Cloud Router or on-premises BGP device failure—as long as the BGP session is reestablished within the graceful restart period.

For high reliability, set up redundant routers and BGP peers, even if your on-premises device supports graceful restart. In the event of nontransient failures, you are protected even if one path fails.

Last, to ensure that you do not exceed Cloud Router limits, use Cloud Monitoring to create alerting policies. For example, you can use the metrics for learned routes to create alerting policies for the limits for learned routes.

High Availability

If graceful restart is not supported or enabled on your device, configure two on-premises BGP devices with one tunnel each to provide redundancy. If you don't configure two separate on-premises devices, Cloud VPN tunnel traffic can be disrupted in the event of a Cloud Router or an on-premises BGP device failure.

Notice that in this configuration, the redundant on-premises BGP device provides failover only and not load sharing.

Security

Enable MD5 authentication on your BGP peers, if they support this feature.

This will add an extra layer of security to your BGP sessions.

■ **Exam tip**   By default, BGP sessions are not authenticated.

Exam Questions
Question 7.1 (Interconnect Attachments)

You need to give each member of your network operations team least-privilege access to create, modify, and delete Cloud Interconnect VLAN attachments.

What should you do?

- **A.**   Assign each user the editor role.

- **B.**   Assign each user the `compute.networkAdmin` role.

- **C.**   Give each user the following permissions only: `compute.interconnectAttachments.create`, `compute.interconnectAttachments.get`.

- **D.**   Give each user the following permissions only: `compute.interconnectAttachments.create`, `compute.interconnectAttachments.get`,

    `compute.routers.create`,
    `compute.routers.get`,
    `compute.routers.update`.

Rationale

A is incorrect because the editor role is too permissive. The editor role contains permissions to create and delete resources for most Google Cloud services.

B is CORRECT because it contains the minimum set of permissions to create, modify, and delete Cloud Interconnect VLAN attachments. You learned this in the "VLAN Attachments" section. The keyword to consider in this question is the ability to delete VLAN attachments, whose permission is included in the `compute.networkAdmin` role, but is not included in the permissions in answer D.

C is incorrect because it doesn't include the permission to delete VLAN attachments.

D is incorrect because it doesn't include the permission to delete VLAN attachments.

Question 7.2 (Cloud VPN)

You need to configure a static route to an on-premises resource behind a Cloud VPN gateway that is configured for policy-based routing using the gcloud command.
    Which next hop should you choose?

    A.   The default Internet gateway

    B.   The IP address of the Cloud VPN gateway

    C.   The name and region of the Cloud VPN tunnel

    D.   The IP address of the instance on the remote side of the VPN tunnel

Rationale

A is incorrect because the packets are directed to your on-premises resource, which is located behind a Cloud VPN gateway.

B is incorrect because the name of the tunnel is required, and not the IP address of the Cloud VPN gateway.

C is CORRECT because you can use the `gcloud compute routes create` command with the flags `--next-hop-vpn-tunnel` and `--next-hop-vpn-tunnel-region`.

D is incorrect because the custom static route won't be able to directly reach the on-premises resource without going through the VPN gateways.

Question 7.3 (Cloud VPN)

You are in the early stages of planning a migration to Google Cloud. You want to test the functionality of your hybrid cloud design before you start to implement it in production. The design includes services running on a Compute Engine virtual machine instance that need to communicate to on-premises servers using private IP addresses. The on-premises servers have connectivity to the Internet, but you have not yet established any Cloud Interconnect connections. You want to choose the lowest cost method of enabling connectivity between your instance and on-premises servers and complete the test in 24 hours.

Which connectivity method should you choose?

A. Cloud VPN

B. 50 Mbps Partner VLAN attachment

C. Dedicated Interconnect with a single VLAN attachment

D. Dedicated Interconnect, but don't provision any VLAN attachments

Rationale

A is CORRECT because it's the cheapest and the quickest option to set up that meets the requirements.

B, C, D are incorrect because Dedicated and Partner Interconnect are not as cheap as Cloud VPN, and their setup will likely take more than 24 hours.

Question 7.4 (Partner Interconnect)

You want to use Partner Interconnect to connect your on-premises network with your VPC. You already have an Interconnect partner.
What should you do first?

A. Log in to your partner's portal and request the VLAN attachment there.

B. Ask your Interconnect partner to provision a physical connection to Google.

C. Create a Partner Interconnect–type VLAN attachment in the Google Cloud console and retrieve the pairing key.

D. Run `gcloud compute interconnect attachments partner update <attachment> / --region <region> --admin-enabled`.

Rationale

A is incorrect because you request the VLAN attachment from Google Cloud, and not from your partner's portal.

B is incorrect because after establishing connectivity with a supported service provider (partner)—as explained in Figure 7-5—the next step is to create a VLAN attachment and retrieve the pairing key resulting from the VLAN attachment creation. You will need the pairing key to provision a physical connection to Google Cloud using the partner's portal.

C is CORRECT because you need to create a VLAN attachment from Google Cloud, as explained in Figure 7-5, where the gcloud CLI is used. You can also use the Google Cloud console.

D is incorrect because the specified gcloud command is used to activate the Partner Interconnect connection, as explained in Figure 7-5.

Question 7.5 (Cloud Router)

You are configuring a new instance of Cloud Router in your organization's Google Cloud environment to allow connection across a new Dedicated Interconnect to your data center. Sales, marketing, and IT each have a service project attached to the organization's host project.

Where should you create the Cloud Router instance?

- **A.** VPC network in all projects
- **B.** VPC network in the IT project
- **C.** VPC network in the host project
- **D.** VPC network in the sales, marketing, and IT projects

Rationale

A is incorrect because your Cloud Router should be centralized and not distributed across all VPC networks.

B is incorrect because the IT service project admin doesn't need to create other VLAN attachments or Cloud Routers in the IT service project.

C is CORRECT because you must create VLAN attachments and Cloud Routers for an Interconnect connection only in the Shared VPC host project.

D is incorrect because service project admins don't need to create other VLAN attachments or Cloud Routers in the service projects.

CHAPTER 8

■ ■ ■

Managing Network Operations

This is the last chapter of our study. You've come a long way from the beginning of this book, where you learned the tenets of "well architecting" a Google Cloud network. You then learned in Chapter 3 how to implement Virtual Private Cloud (VPC) networks. The concept of a VPC as a logical routing domain is the basis of every network architecture in the cloud. As a natural progression, in Chapters 5 and 6 you learned how to leverage the wide spectrum of network services, which uniquely differentiate Google Cloud from other public cloud service providers. Last, you learned in Chapter 7 how to implement hybrid topologies—which are prevalent in any sector—along with all considerations related to resilience, fault tolerance, security, and cost.

Now that you have all your network infrastructure set up and running, what's next?

Well, you (and your team of Google Cloud professional network engineers) are in charge of maintaining this infrastructure to make sure it operates in accordance with the SLOs (Service Level Objectives) for your workloads.

In this chapter, you will learn how to use the products and services offered by Google Cloud to assist you in this compelling task.

Logging and Monitoring with Google Cloud's Operations Suite

Cloud Operations is a family of products (Figure 8-1) that help you monitor, log, troubleshoot, and perform advanced observability tasks on your workloads at scale.

Cloud Operations is integrated with a number of Google Cloud data and analytics products. This out-of-the-box integration can accelerate troubleshooting incidents or performance issues impacting your workloads.

© Dario Cabianca 2023
D. Cabianca, *Google Cloud Platform (GCP) Professional Cloud Network Engineer Certification Companion*, Certification Study Companion Series, https://doi.org/10.1007/978-1-4842-9354-6_8

Cloud Operations

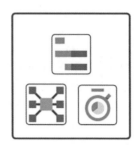

Cloud Logging   Cloud Monitoring   Observability
  • Cloud Trace
  • Cloud Profiler
  • Cloud Debugger

Figure 8-1. *Cloud Operations suite overview*

However, Cloud Operations is a lot more than just a suite of products to troubleshoot incidents. When combined with Google Cloud data engineering, data analytics, and machine learning products, Cloud Operations can proactively detect anomalies, identify trends, reveal security threats, and most importantly respond to them in a timely fashion.

Reviewing Logs for Networking Components (e.g., VPN, Cloud Router, VPC Service Controls)

In this section, you will learn about Cloud Logging. You will understand what it does, when to use it, and how to leverage its built-in features to collect and explore logs, specifically for networking components.

Cloud Logging

As illustrated in Figure 8-2, Cloud Logging is a fully managed service that allows you to collect, store, and route (forward) logs and events from Google Cloud, from other clouds (e.g., AWS, Azure, etc.), and from on-premises infrastructure. As of the writing of this book, you can collect logging data from over 150 common application components.

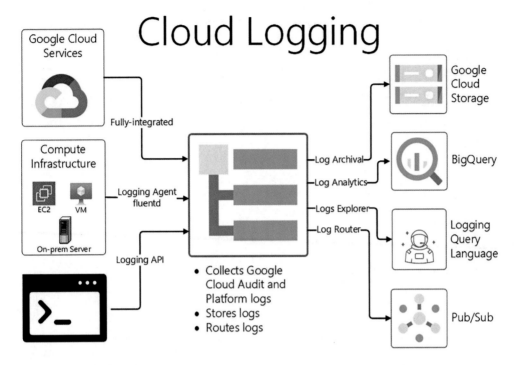

Figure 8-2. *Cloud Logging overview*

Cloud Logging includes built-in storage for logs called *log buckets*, a user interface called the Logs Explorer, and an API to manage logs programmatically (see Figure 8-3). Cloud Logging lets you read and write log entries, query your logs with advanced filtering capabilities, and control how and where you want to forward your logs for further analysis or for compliance.

By default, your Google Cloud project *automatically* stores all logs it receives in a Cloud Logging log bucket referred to as _Default. For example, if you create a Cloud Router, then all logs your Cloud Router generates are automatically stored for you in this bucket. However, if you need to, you can configure a number of aspects about your log storage, such as which logs are stored, which are discarded, and where the logs are stored.

```
itsmedario@cloudshell:~ (vpc-host-nonprod-pu645-uh372)$ gcloud logging buckets list
LOCATION: global
BUCKET_ID: _Default
RETENTION_DAYS: 30
RESTRICTED_FIELDS:
INDEX_CONFIGS:
LIFECYCLE_STATE: ACTIVE
LOCKED:
CREATE_TIME:
UPDATE_TIME:

LOCATION: global
BUCKET_ID: _Required
RETENTION_DAYS: 400
RESTRICTED_FIELDS:
INDEX_CONFIGS:
LIFECYCLE_STATE: ACTIVE
LOCKED: True
CREATE_TIME:
UPDATE_TIME:
itsmedario@cloudshell:~ (vpc-host-nonprod-pu645-uh372)$ ▮
```

Figure 8-3. *Listing log buckets in* `vpc-host-nonprod` *project*

As you can see in Figure 8-3, the `vpc-host-nonprod` project contains two log buckets, `_Default` and `_Required`. They are both globally scoped and have a retention of 30 days and 400 days, respectively. The `_Required` log bucket is also automatically generated by Google. This bucket is locked to indicate that it cannot be updated.

■ **Exam tip**   By locking a log bucket, you are preventing any updates on the bucket. This includes the log bucket's retention policy. As a result, *you can't delete the bucket until every log in the bucket has fulfilled the bucket's retention period.* Also, locking a log bucket is irreversible.

You can also route, or forward, log entries to the following destinations, which can be in the same Google Cloud project or in a different Google Cloud project:

- **Cloud Logging log buckets**: Provides built-in storage in Cloud Logging. A log bucket can store logs collected by multiple Google Cloud projects. You specify the data retention period, the data storage location, and the log views on a log bucket. Log views let you control which logs in a log bucket a user is authorized to access. Log buckets are recommended storage when you want to troubleshoot your applications and services, or you want to quickly analyze your log data. Analysis on your log bucket data can be performed by enabling Log Analytics and then by linking the log bucket to BigQuery.

- **Pub/Sub topics**: Provides support for third-party integrations, such as Splunk. Log entries are formatted into JSON and then delivered to a Pub/Sub topic. You can then use Dataflow to process your log data and stream it to other destinations.

- **BigQuery datasets**: Provides storage of log entries in BigQuery datasets. You can use big data analysis capabilities on the stored logs. If you need to combine your Cloud Logging data with other data sources, then you can route your logs to BigQuery. An alternative is to store your logs in log buckets that are upgraded to use Log Analytics and then are linked to BigQuery—these are known as external tables in BigQuery.

- **Cloud Storage buckets**: Provides inexpensive, archival storage of log data in Cloud Storage. Log entries are stored as JSON files.

Log Types

Logs are classified in the following categories (not mutually exclusive):

- **Platform logs**: These are logs written by the Google Cloud services you use in your project. These logs can help you debug and troubleshoot issues and help you better understand the Google Cloud services you're using. For example, VPC Flow Logs record a sample of network flows sent from and received by VMs.

- **Component logs**: These are similar to platform logs, but they are generated by Google-provided software components that run on your systems. For example, GKE provides software components that users can run on their own VM or in their own data center. Logs are generated from the user's GKE instances and sent to a user's cloud project. GKE uses the logs or their metadata to provide user support.

- **Security logs**: These logs help you answer "who did what, where, and when" and are comprised of

  - **Cloud Audit Logs**, which provide information about administrative activities and accesses within your Google Cloud resources. Enabling audit logs helps your security, auditing, and compliance entities monitor Google Cloud data and systems for possible vulnerabilities or external data misuse, for example, data exfiltration.

  - **Access Transparency logs**, which provide you with logs of actions taken by Google staff when accessing your Google Cloud content. Access Transparency logs can help you track compliance with your legal and regulatory requirements for your organization.

- **User-written logs**: These are logs written by custom applications and services. Typically, these logs are written to Cloud Logging by using one of the following methods:

  - Ops agent or the Logging agent (based on the *fluentd* open source data collector)

  - Cloud Logging API

  - Cloud Logging client libraries, for example, the gcloud CLI

- **Multi-cloud logs** and **hybrid cloud logs**: These refer to logs from other cloud service providers like Microsoft Azure, or AWS, and also logs from your on-premises infrastructure.

Cloud Logging Deep Dive

Let's see how you can read logs from your project.

In this example, I'll create a Cloud Router (Figure 8-4), and I'll show you how to read logs from the _Default bucket (Figure 8-5).

```
gianni@cloudshell:~ (vpc-host-nonprod-pu645-uh372)$ gcloud compute routers create gianni-router --network=your-app-shared-vpc
Did you mean region [us-east1] for router: [gianni-router] (Y/n)?  Y

Creating router [gianni-router]...done.
NAME: gianni-router
REGION: us-east1
NETWORK: your-app-shared-vpc
gianni@cloudshell:~ (vpc-host-nonprod-pu645-uh372)$ █
```

Figure 8-4. *User* `gianni@dariokart.com` *creates a Cloud Router*

To read logs, use the `gcloud logging read` command as shown in Figure 8-5.

```
itsmedario@cloudshell:~ (vpc-host-nonprod-pu645-uh372)$ gcloud logging read "resource.type=gce_router" | more
---
insertId: -4fir6id4ssk
logName: projects/vpc-host-nonprod-pu645-uh372/logs/cloudaudit.googleapis.com%2Factivity
operation:
  id: operation-1675740086987-5f413a49eeb98-0d375884-0cf18aca
  last: true
  producer: compute.googleapis.com
protoPayload:
  '@type': type.googleapis.com/google.cloud.audit.AuditLog
  authenticationInfo:
    principalEmail: gianni@dariokart.com
    principalSubject: user:gianni@dariokart.com
  methodName: v1.compute.routers.insert
  request:
    '@type': type.googleapis.com/compute.routers.insert
  requestMetadata:
    callerIp: 34.73.31.102
    callerSuppliedUserAgent: google-cloud-sdk gcloud/416.0.0 command/gcloud.compute.routers.create
      invocation-id/1a0d9a16517a42f6b4cf0da743b076c6 environment/devshell environment-version/None
      interactive/True from-script/False python/3.9.2 term/screen (Linux 5.15.65+),gzip(gfe)
    destinationAttributes: {}
    requestAttributes: {}
  resourceName: projects/vpc-host-nonprod-pu645-uh372/regions/us-east1/routers/gianni-router
  serviceName: compute.googleapis.com
receiveTimestamp: '2023-02-07T03:21:28.416634865Z'
resource:
  labels:
    project_id: vpc-host-nonprod-pu645-uh372
    region: us-east1
    router_id: '1780416684994887000'
  type: gce_router
```

Figure 8-5. *Cloud Audit log entry (request) for router creation operation*

In the first rectangle, you can see the filter I used "`resource.type=gce_router`" to select only logs applicable to cloud routers.

As you can see, a Cloud Audit log was captured, which included detailed information on who (gianni@dariokart.com) performed the action (`type.googleapis.com/compute.routers.insert`) and when, along with a wealth of useful metadata.

In the fourth rectangle, you can see the resulting Cloud Router resource name.

The second page of the log entry (Figure 8-6) shows the response.

The rectangle shows that the resource `gianni-router` was successfully created, and it's in running status.

■ **Note** When a request requires a long-running operation, Cloud Logging adds multiple log entries. The `operation` node in Figure 8-5 includes a `last:true` key-value pair to indicate that this is the last entry logged.

For details about how a log entry is structured, visit `https://cloud.google.com/logging/docs/reference/v2/rest/v2/LogEntry`.

```
    network: https://compute.googleapis.com/compute/v1/projects/vpc-host-nonprod-pu645-uh372/global/networks/your-app-shared-vpc
  requestMetadata:
    callerIp: 34.73.31.102
    callerSuppliedUserAgent: google-cloud-sdk gcloud/416.0.0 command/gcloud.compute.routers.create
      invocation-id/1a0d9a16517a42f6b4cf0da743b076c6 environment/devshell environment-version/None
      interactive/True from-script/False python/3.9.2 term/screen (Linux 5.15.65+),gzip(gfe)
    destinationAttributes: {}
    requestAttributes:
      auth: {}
      time: '2023-02-07T03:21:27.467676Z'
  resourceLocation:
    currentLocations:
    - us-east1
  resourceName: projects/vpc-host-nonprod-pu645-uh372/regions/us-east1/routers/gianni-router
  response:
    '@type': type.googleapis.com/operation
    id: '8820032687760506200'
    insertTime: '2023-02-06T19:21:27.417-08:00'
    name: operation-1675740086987-5f413a49eeb98-0d375884-0cf18aca
    operationType: insert
    progress: '0'
    region: https://www.googleapis.com/compute/v1/projects/vpc-host-nonprod-pu645-uh372/regions/us-east1
    selfLink: https://www.googleapis.com/compute/v1/projects/vpc-host-nonprod-pu645-uh372/regions/us-east1/operations/operation-1675740086987-5f413
a49eeb98-0d375884-0cf18aca
    selfLinkWithId: https://www.googleapis.com/compute/v1/projects/vpc-host-nonprod-pu645-uh372/regions/us-east1/operations/8820032687760506200
    startTime: '2023-02-06T19:21:27.426-08:00'
    status: RUNNING
    targetId: '1780416684994887000'
    targetLink: https://www.googleapis.com/compute/v1/projects/vpc-host-nonprod-pu645-uh372/regions/us-east1/routers/gianni-router
    user: gianni@dariokart.com
  serviceName: compute.googleapis.com
--More--
```

Figure 8-6. *Example of Cloud Audit log entry (response)*

To avoid incurring charges, I am going to delete the Cloud Router, and I will verify that this operation (deletion) is properly logged. Figure 8-7 shows you how to delete the Cloud Router. Notice that the `--region` flag is provided because a Cloud Router is a regional resource.

```
gianni@cloudshell:~ (vpc-host-nonprod-pu645-uh372)$ gcloud compute routers delete gianni-router --region=us-east1
The following routers will be deleted:
 - [gianni-router] in [us-east1]

Do you want to continue (Y/n)?  Y

Deleted [https://www.googleapis.com/compute/v1/projects/vpc-host-nonprod-pu645-uh372/regions/us-east1/routers/gianni-router]
gianni@cloudshell:~ (vpc-host-nonprod-pu645-uh372)$
```

Figure 8-7. *User `gianni@dariokart.com` deletes a Cloud Router*

Figure 8-8 shows one of the two log entries (the last) for the delete operation.

```
itsmedario@cloudshell:~ (vpc-host-nonprod-pu645-uh372)$ gcloud logging read --freshness=t10m | more
---
insertId: uj2be6duvzk
logName: projects/vpc-host-nonprod-pu645-uh372/logs/cloudaudit.googleapis.com%2Factivity
operation:
  id: operation-1675742762612-5f4144419b8fd-fc2ea059-ace7b38d
  last: true
  producer: compute.googleapis.com
protoPayload:
  '@type': type.googleapis.com/google.cloud.audit.AuditLog
  authenticationInfo:
    principalEmail: gianni@dariokart.com
    principalSubject: user:gianni@dariokart.com
  methodName: v1.compute.routers.delete
  request:
    '@type': type.googleapis.com/compute.routers.delete
  requestMetadata:
    callerIp: 34.73.31.102
    callerSuppliedUserAgent: google-cloud-sdk gcloud/416.0.0 command/gcloud.compute.routers.delete
      invocation-id/bff399a31e07472ea06d4017d16be267 environment/devshell environment-version/None
      interactive/True from-script/False python/3.9.2 term/screen (Linux 5.15.65+),gzip(gfe)
    destinationAttributes: {}
    requestAttributes: {}
  resourceName: projects/vpc-host-nonprod-pu645-uh372/regions/us-east1/routers/gianni-router
  serviceName: compute.googleapis.com
receiveTimestamp: '2023-02-07T04:06:04.530630282Z'
resource:
  labels:
    project_id: vpc-host-nonprod-pu645-uh372
    region: us-east1
    router_id: '1780416684994887000'
  type: gce_router
```

Figure 8-8. *Cloud Audit log entry (request) for router deletion operation*

Note in Figure 8-8 the use of the flag `--freshness=t10m` to retrieve the latest log entries within the past ten minutes.

Before moving to the next section, and for the sake of completeness, I want to quickly show you an alternative—equally expressive—approach to reading logs by using the provided user interface, referred to as the Logs Explorer.

■ **Note** My preference, and general recommendation for the exam, is that you get very familiar with the gcloud CLI, instead of the tools offered by the console, like Logs Explorer. This is because the exam is focused on gcloud, and there's a reason behind it. User interfaces available in the console change frequently, whereas the gcloud CLI and the Google Cloud REST APIs don't change as frequently as user interfaces. Also, gcloud code is a natural path into Infrastructure as Code (e.g., Terraform), which is strongly encouraged. Nevertheless, there are a few compelling use cases where the console is required because the gcloud CLI doesn't offer the expected functionality.

With that being said, in Figure 8-9 I included a screenshot of my Log Explorer session during my troubleshooting of the global external HTTP(S) load balancer (classic) with NEGs you learned in Chapter 5.

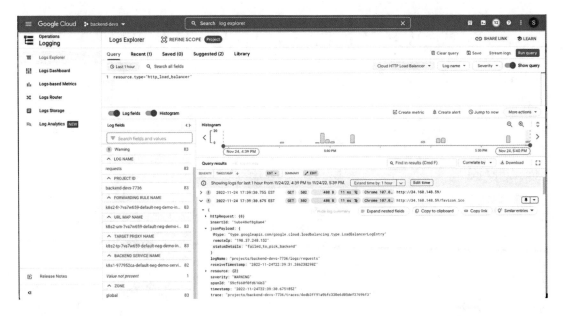

Figure 8-9. *Logs Explorer*

Monitoring Networking Components (e.g., VPN, Cloud Interconnect Connections and Interconnect Attachments, Cloud Router, Load Balancers, Google Cloud Armor, Cloud NAT)

In this section, you will learn how to use the second product of the Cloud Operations suite, that is, Cloud Monitoring.

Cloud Monitoring

Cloud Monitoring uses the logs managed by Cloud Logging to automatically capture metrics, for example, `firewall/dropped_bytes_count`, `https/backend_latencies`, and many others.

Metrics are grouped by cloud services (e.g., GCP services, AWS services), by agents, and by third-party applications. For a comprehensive list of metrics, visit `https://cloud.google.com/monitoring/api/metrics`.

Cloud Monitoring also allows you to create custom metrics based on your workloads' unique business and technical requirements.

Using the metrics explorer and the monitoring query language, you can analyze your workload's metrics on the fly, discovering correlations, trends, and abnormal behavior.

You can leverage these insights to build an overall view of health and performance of your workloads' code and infrastructure, making it easy to spot anomalies using Google Cloud visualization products.

This is all great information, but you cannot just sit and watch, right? You need a more proactive approach for your SRE team, so that when an abnormal behavior (or an incident) is detected, you can promptly respond to it.

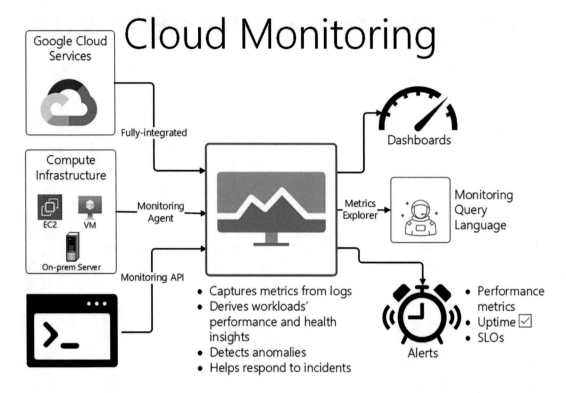

Figure 8-10. *Cloud Monitoring overview*

This is when Cloud Monitoring alerts come into play. With alerts, you can create policies on performance metrics, uptime, and Service Level Objectives (SLOs). These policies will ensure your SRE team and network engineers are promptly notified and are ready to respond when your workloads don't perform as expected.

Figure 8-10 summarizes the Cloud Monitoring capabilities.

In the next section, we'll use a simple example to show you how Cloud Monitoring can notify your SRE team and help them respond to incidents.

Cloud Monitoring Deep Dive

As per the exam objectives for this chapter, we will choose a network Google Cloud resource—for the sake of simplicity, a route—we will set up a custom metric specific to this resource, and we will monitor this resource with an alerting policy.

```
{
  "name": "detect_route_changes",
  "filter": "resource.type=\"gce_route\" AND (protoPayload.methodName:compute.routes.delete OR protoPayload.methodName:compute.routes.insert)"
~
~
~
~
~
~
~
~
~
~
~
~
~
~
~
"detect-route-changes.json" 4L, 181B                                                    3,142
```

Figure 8-11. *A JSON file defining the filter for a custom metric*

Finally, we will test the alerting policy by performing an action that triggers an alert and notifies the selected recipients in the channel configured for the alerting policy.

First, let's create a custom metric that measures the number of times a route was changed (created or deleted) in our shared VPC.

You can create a custom metric using the `gcloud logging metrics create` command, which requires you to define your metric during the creation process.

You can pass the definition of your custom metric by using the `--log-filter` flag or the `--config-from-file` flag. The former accepts the filter inline; the latter expects the path to a JSON or a YAML file such as the one in Figure 8-11, which includes the metric definition. To learn how this JSON or YAML file needs to be structured, visit

https://cloud.google.com/logging/docs/reference/v2/rest/v2/projects.metrics#resource:-logmetric

Figure 8-11 shows our JSON file. Notice how the filter property is expressed to tell the policy to raise an alert for resources whose type is a `gce_route` and whenever a route is deleted or inserted:

`"filter": "resource.type=\"gce_route\" AND (protoPayload. methodName:compute.routes.delete OR protoPayload.methodName: compute.routes.insert)"`

Next, we create the custom metric (Figure 8-12).

```
itsmedario@cloudshell:~/policies (vpc-host-nonprod-pu645-uh372)$ gcloud logging metrics create determine-route-changes --config-from-file="./detect
-route-changes.json"
Created [determine-route-changes].
itsmedario@cloudshell:~/policies (vpc-host-nonprod-pu645-uh372)$
```

Figure 8-12. *Creating a custom metric*

The custom metric alone doesn't alert anyone. All it does is measure the number of times a route was deleted or created in our shared VPC.

For this custom metric to be effective, it must be associated with an alerting policy, which needs to know at a minimum

1. To whom a notification should be sent

2. When to raise an alert for this metric

The first item requires you to create a notification channel (Figure 8-13).

```
itsmedario@cloudshell:~/policies (vpc-host-nonprod-pu645-uh372)$ gcloud alpha monitoring channels create \
> --display-name='dariokart_channel' \
> --type=email \
> --channel-labels=email_address=joseph@dariokart.com
Created notification channel [projects/vpc-host-nonprod-pu645-uh372/notificationChannels/14524290954872698375]
itsmedario@cloudshell:~/policies (vpc-host-nonprod-pu645-uh372)$
```

Figure 8-13. *Creating a notification channel*

Note, the gcloud command in Figure 8-13 is in the alpha testing phase.

■ **Note**   Alpha is a limited availability test before releases are cleared for more widespread use. Google's focus with alpha testing is to verify functionality and gather feedback from a limited set of customers. Typically, alpha participation is by invitation and subject to pre-general availability terms. Alpha releases may not contain all features, no SLAs are provided, and there are no technical support obligations. However, alphas are generally suitable for use in test environments. Alpha precedes beta, which precedes GA (general availability).

The second item is addressed by defining a triggering condition when you create the alerting policy.

To walk you through the process—this time, as an exception—I'll use the console. Go to Cloud Logging, and select the log-based metric section. This will bring you to the page displayed in Figure 8-14.

Figure 8-14. *Custom metric as it appears in the console*

Click the vertical ellipsis icon as indicated in Figure 8-14 with the arrow, and select "Create alert from metric," as indicated in Figure 8-15.

Figure 8-15. *Creating an alert from metric*

In the next screen, select "Notifications and name," check "dariokart_channel," and click OK, as indicated in Figure 8-16.

Figure 8-16. *Adding a notification channel to an alerting policy*

Upon confirming your channel, you get a notification that multiple channels are recommended for redundancy (Figure 8-17).

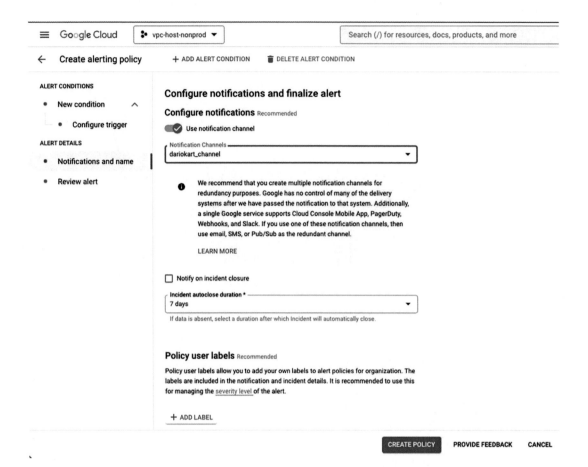

Figure 8-17. *Configuring a monitoring alerting policy*

Last, scroll down, assign a name to the alerting policy, and click "Create Policy," as indicated in Figure 8-18.

Our monitoring alerting policy is ready to go.

Before testing our alerting policy, let's have a look at it.

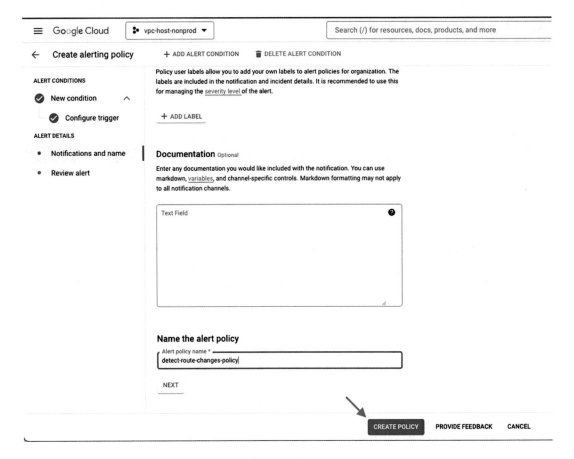

Figure 8-18. *Assigning a name to monitoring alerting policy*

In Figure 8-19, you can see our newly created alerting policy's details.

```
itsmedario@cloudshell:~ (vpc-host-nonprod-pu645-uh372)$ gcloud alpha monitoring policies list
---
alertStrategy:
  autoClose: 604800s
combiner: OR
conditions:
- conditionThreshold:
    aggregations:
    - alignmentPeriod: 600s
      crossSeriesReducer: REDUCE_SUM
      perSeriesAligner: ALIGN_DELTA
    comparison: COMPARISON_GT
    duration: 0s
    filter: metric.type="logging.googleapis.com/user/determine-route-changes"
    trigger:        When to raise an alert for this metric
      count: 1
  displayName: New condition
  name: projects/vpc-host-nonprod-pu645-uh372/alertPolicies/5778410432798651649/conditions/5778410432798652322
creationRecord:
  mutateTime: '2023-02-08T04:07:51.385342103Z'
  mutatedBy: itsmedario@dariokart.com
displayName: detect-route-changes-policy
enabled: true
mutationRecord:
  mutateTime: '2023-02-08T04:07:51.385342103Z'
  mutatedBy: itsmedario@dariokart.com
name: projects/vpc-host-nonprod-pu645-uh372/alertPolicies/5778410432798651649
notificationChannels:
- projects/vpc-host-nonprod-pu645-uh372/notificationChannels/14524290954872698375   To whom a notification
itsmedario@cloudshell:~ (vpc-host-nonprod-pu645-uh372)$                               should be sent
```

Figure 8-19. *A description of an alerting policy*

First, our project policy list is comprised of one policy only.

■ **Note** To understand each element of an alerting policy and a metrics threshold, visit respectively: https://cloud.google.com/monitoring/api/ref_v3/rest/v3/projects. alertPolicies#resource:-alertpolicy

https://cloud.google.com/monitoring/api/ref_v3/rest/v3/projects.alertPolicies#metr icthreshold

---

Second, our policy has one condition, which is based on our custom metric. The condition also uses a threshold, which tells you any count greater than zero should trigger an alert.

This is formalized in the filter, the trigger, and the comparison properties of the conditionThreshold object.

Now that you understand how to create a monitoring alerting policy and its components, we can finally test it by deliberately creating an event that will trigger an alert.

Our custom metric measures the number of times a route has changed (created or deleted) in our shared VPC. The easiest way to test this policy is by deleting an existing route. Let's try!

```
gianni@cloudshell:~ (vpc-host-nonprod-pu645-uh372)$ gcloud compute routes create goto-restricted-apis --network=your-app-shared-vpc --destination-r
ange=199.36.153.4/30 --next-hop-gateway=default-internet-gateway
ERROR: (gcloud.compute.routes.create) Could not fetch resource:
 - The resource 'projects/vpc-host-nonprod-pu645-uh372/global/routes/goto-restricted-apis' already exists

gianni@cloudshell:~ (vpc-host-nonprod-pu645-uh372)$ gcloud compute routes delete goto-restricted-apis
The following routes will be deleted:
 - [goto-restricted-apis]

Do you want to continue (Y/n)?  Y

Deleted [https://www.googleapis.com/compute/v1/projects/vpc-host-nonprod-pu645-uh372/global/routes/goto-restricted-apis].
gianni@cloudshell:~ (vpc-host-nonprod-pu645-uh372)$ █
```

Figure 8-20. *Deleting a route*

In Figure 8-20, I first made sure that the route I wanted to delete existed in our shared VPC. Upon confirming its existence, I used the `gcloud compute routes delete` command to delete the custom static route `goto-restricted-apis`.

Shortly after, I used the Cloud Monitoring dashboard to verify whether the alerting policy detected a triggering event.

Figure 8-21. *Cloud Monitoring dashboard*

As you can see in Figure 8-21, the event was captured (as pointed to by the arrow). The rectangle shows the condition threshold, as defined in our alerting policy.

As a result, an incident was added (Figure 8-22), and an email alert was sent to the recipient(s) of the notification channel, as shown in Figure 8-23.

Figure 8-22. *Incident creation*

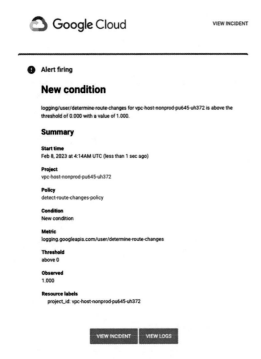

Figure 8-23. *Incident alert notification*

Before moving to the next section, here's a quick note about costs.

The good news is that there are no costs associated with using alerting policies. For more information, visit https://cloud.google.com/monitoring/alerts#limits.

This concludes our section about logging and monitoring network components using the Cloud Operations suite. In the next section, you will learn how to address security-related network operations.

Managing and Maintaining Security

Security, like the other four pillars of the well-architected framework, is a cross-cutting concern. Regardless of the architecture your workload is based upon, each component will require adequate protection to secure the data and the infrastructure used.

In this section, we will address how network operations can be effectively managed to secure the perimeter (with firewalls) and the identities (with IAM) for your workloads.

Firewalls (e.g., Cloud-Based, Private)

You learned about firewall rules in Chapter 2 as an effective means to secure your VPC network perimeter by allowing or denying traffic in or from your VPC based on a number of network-specific constructs (e.g., source and destination protocol, port, etc.).

A unique feature of Google Cloud firewall rules is that you can configure the source and target of your firewall rules with a service account. This alone is a powerful capability, because you can better segment sources and targets of your network using an identity, instead of a network construct like a CIDR block or a network tag.

"With great power comes great responsibility"—this adage applies well to firewall rules in that you really want to make sure only authorized principals are allowed to access the service account used in the source or target definitions of a firewall rule.

Network Firewall Policies

Another unique—yet powerful—feature of Google Cloud firewalls is *network firewall policies*.

Network firewall policies let you group firewall rules so that you can update them all at once, effectively controlled by Identity and Access Management (IAM) roles. These policies contain rules that can explicitly deny or allow connections, as do Virtual Private Cloud (VPC) firewall rules.

Network firewall policies come in three "flavors":

- Hierarchical

- Global

- Regional

Hierarchical firewall policies can be applied at the organization and folder levels, whereas global and regional network firewall policies can be applied at the VPC level, as illustrated in Figure 8-24.

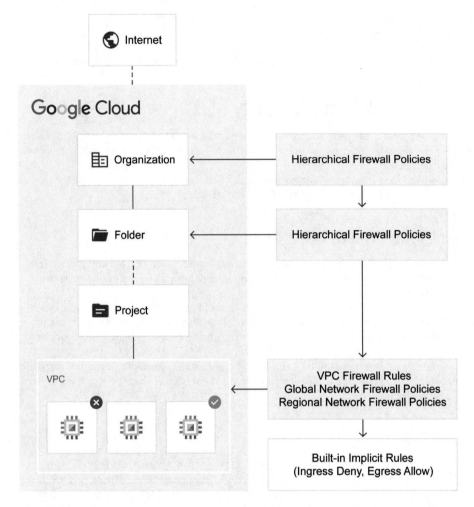

Figure 8-24. Network firewall policies overview. Portions of this page are reproduced under the CC-BY license and shared by Google: `https://cloud.google.com/firewall`

Diagnosing and Resolving IAM Issues (e.g., Shared VPC, Security/ Network Admin)

Identity and Access Management (IAM) lets you create and manage permissions for Google Cloud resources. IAM unifies access control for Google Cloud services into a single pane of glass and presents a consistent set of operations.

IAM is always concerned about

Is A allowed to perform verb B on resource C?

A denotes a principal—also referred to as an identity—and can be a user (a human principal), a service account (a nonhuman principal), a group, or a domain.

■ **Note**   A service account is a "tricky" type of identity in that it is simultaneously an identity and a resource.

B denotes the verb or the action A wants to perform on resource C. In this context, the verb is expressed as a Google Cloud permission, for example, `compute.instanceGroups.create`.

■ **Exam tip**   Remember the difference between a permission and a role. The former always denotes a single verb, whereas the latter denotes a group of permissions. For example, a permission can be `compute.instances.create`, while a role (including the permission) can be Compute Admin (`roles/ compute.admin`).

C denotes the Google Cloud resource the actor A wants to perform an action on. The term *resource* is not intended to be used in its generic form (e.g., an object or an entity). Instead, I used the term resource deliberately because C is really a REST (**Re**presentational **S**tate **T**ransfer) resource. As a result, C is always uniquely identified by a URI (Uniform Resource Identifier).

Whether you are a software (cloud) engineer, a software (cloud) architect, a database administrator, or simply a user of an application, chances are you ran into a permission issue, for example, you encountered the number 403 forbidden while browsing the Web.

Google Cloud provides an effective tool to quickly diagnose and resolve IAM permission issues. The tool is called the *Policy Troubleshooter* and can be accessed using the Google Cloud console, the gcloud CLI, or the REST API.

Policy Troubleshooter

Given the aforementioned three inputs, that is, A, B, and C, Policy Troubleshooter examines all Identity and Access Management (IAM) policies that apply to the resource (C). It then determines whether the principal's roles include the permission on that resource and, if so, which policies bind the principal to those roles.

When used from the console, Policy Troubleshooter also determines whether there are any deny policies that could impact the principal's access. The gcloud CLI and the REST API don't provide information about deny policies.

Let's see how it works with an example.

I want to verify whether user gianni is allowed to delete subnet-backend in our shared VPC. Simply put:

- A = `gianni@dariokart.com`
- B = `compute.subnetworks.delete`
- C = `subnet-backend`

Since I want to find out about *allow* and *deny resource policies* for `subnet-backend`—not just the IAM (allow) policies, I am going to use the Policy Troubleshooter from the console.

From the "IAM & Admin" menu in the left bar, select "Policy Troubleshooter" and fill out the form as follows.

The resource field in Figure 8-25 dynamically populates the resources the selected principal—`gianni@ dariokart.com`—has visibility on.

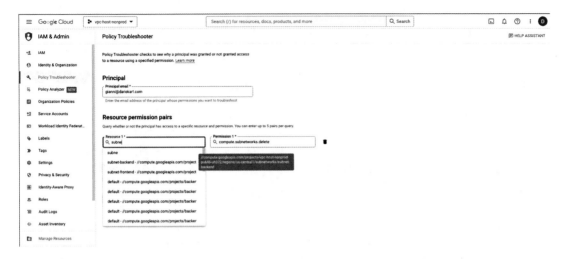

Figure 8-25. *Selecting the resource in Policy Troubleshooter form for gianni*

Figure 8-26 shows the selection of the permission for the same principal.

Figure 8-26. *Selecting the permission in Policy Troubleshooter form for gianni*

When I clicked the "Check Access" button, the Policy Troubleshooter confirmed that the principal gianni@dariokart.com has permission to delete subnet-backend as shown in Figure 8-27.

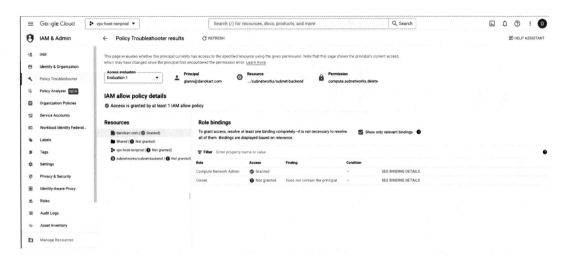

Figure 8-27. *Policy Troubleshooter results page for gianni*

If you remember the way our shared VPC was set up in Chapter 3, this makes sense because principal gianni@dariokart.com was granted the compute.networkAdmin role at the organization level (Figure 3-57), which includes the permission to delete subnets.

Figure 8-28 shows the outcome of this verification.

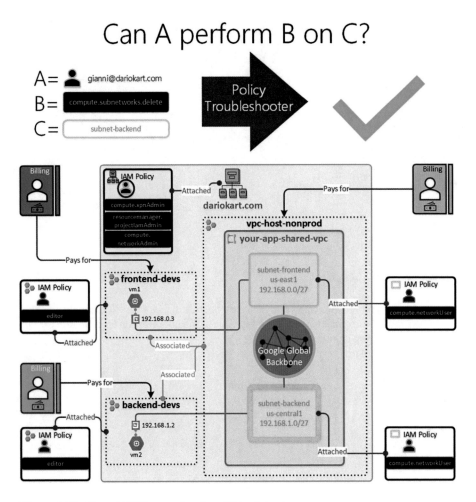

Figure 8-28. *Shared VPC access for* gianni@dariokart.com

Since the role roles/compute.networkAdmin contains the permission compute.subnetworks.delete (see Figure 8-29), and since this role is bound to the principal gianni@darikart.com at the organization level, it makes sense that this principal is allowed to delete subnet-backend in the vpc-host-nonprod project.

∨   compute.subnetworks.*

       compute.subnetworks.create

       compute.subnetworks.delete

       compute.subnetworks.expandIpCidrRange

       compute.subnetworks.get

       compute.subnetworks.getIamPolicy

       compute.subnetworks.list

       compute.subnetworks.mirror

  👥 compute.subnetworks.setIamPolicy

       compute.subnetworks.

         setPrivateIpGoogleAccess

       compute.subnetworks.update

       compute.subnetworks.use

       compute.subnetworks.useExternalIp

Figure 8-29. *Subnet permissions allowed in role* `compute.networkAdmin`

■ **Note**   To see what permissions are included in a role, visit `https://cloud.google.com/compute/docs/access/iam`.

Next, let's test the same permission on the same resource from the standpoint of another principal. In Figure 8-30, I am selecting one of the two service project administrators, for example, `samuele@dariokart.com`.

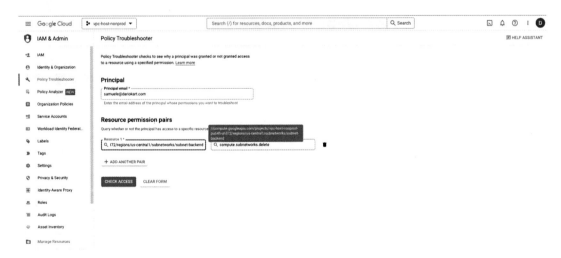

Figure 8-30. *Selecting the resource in Policy Troubleshooter form for samuele*

When I clicked the "Check Access" button, the Policy Troubleshooter confirmed that the principal samuele@dariokart.com does not have permission to delete subnet-backend as shown in Figure 8-31.

Figure 8-31. *Policy Troubleshooter results page for samuele*

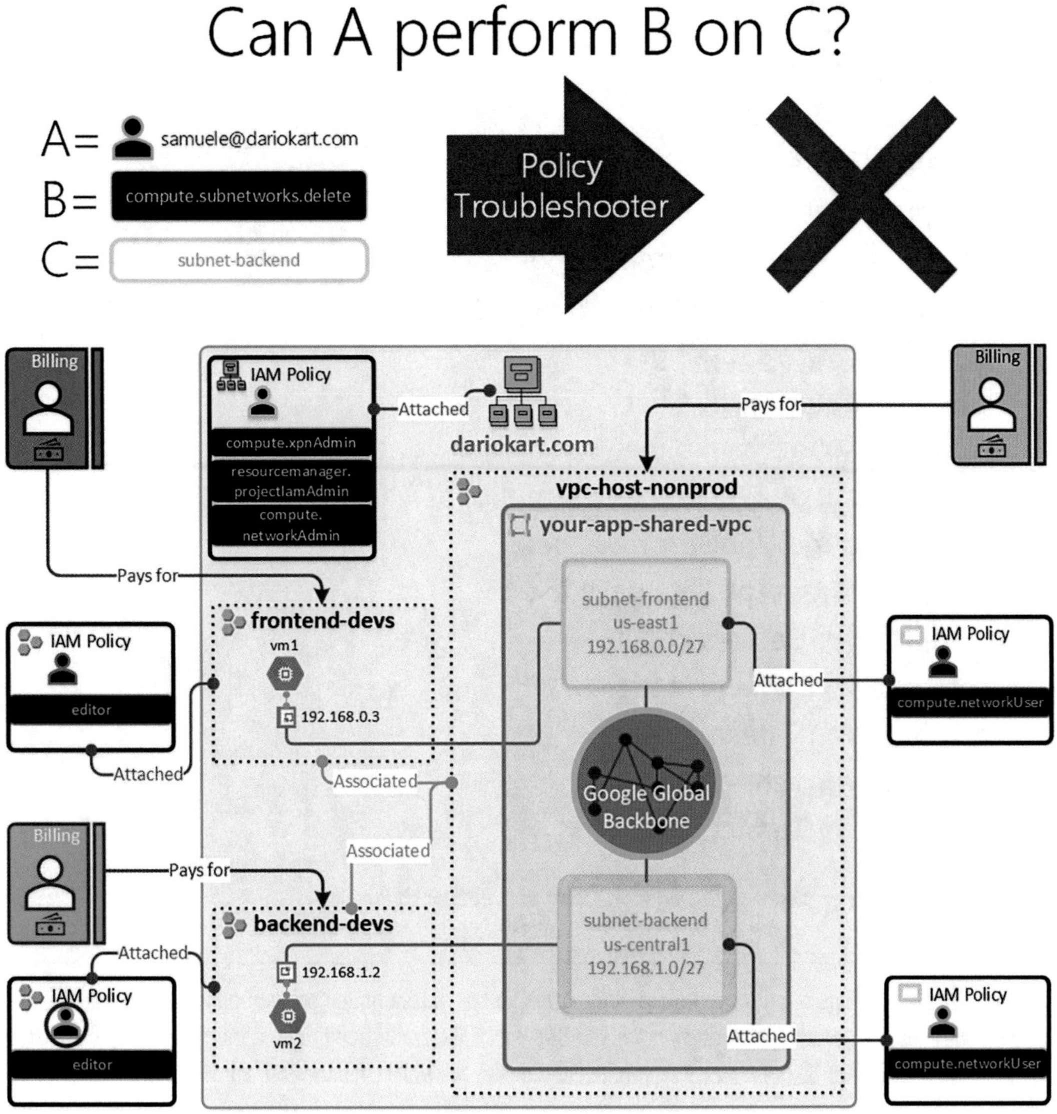

Can A perform B on C?

Figure 8-32. *Shared VPC access for samuele@dariokart.com*

This outcome makes sense as well, because as shown in Figure 8-32 the principal samuele@dariokart.com has the editor role in the backend-devs project and the compute.networkUser role in subnet-backend. The latter role doesn't include the permission to delete subnets as shown in Figure 8-33.

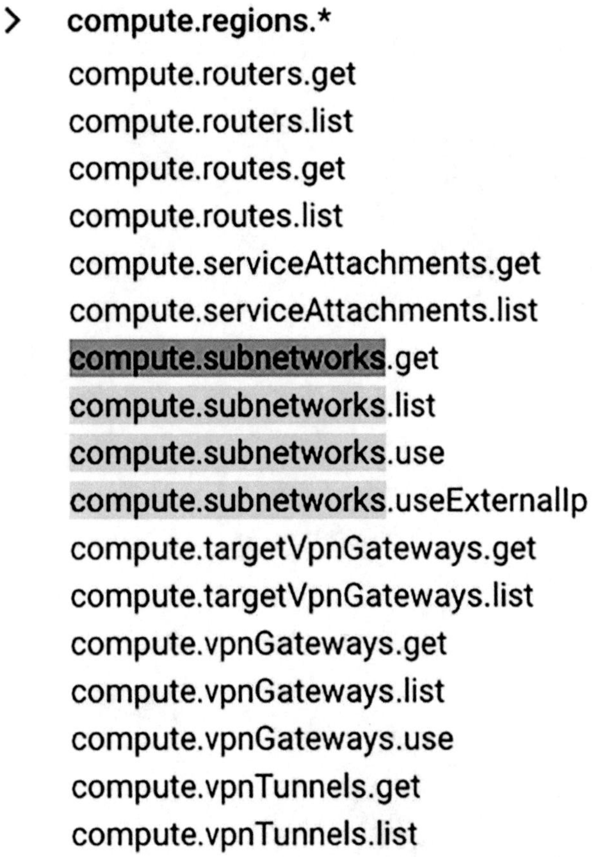

> **compute.regions.***

compute.routers.get

compute.routers.list

compute.routes.get

compute.routes.list

compute.serviceAttachments.get

compute.serviceAttachments.list

compute.subnetworks.get

compute.subnetworks.list

compute.subnetworks.use

compute.subnetworks.useExternalIp

compute.targetVpnGateways.get

compute.targetVpnGateways.list

compute.vpnGateways.get

compute.vpnGateways.list

compute.vpnGateways.use

compute.vpnTunnels.get

compute.vpnTunnels.list

Figure 8-33. Subnet permissions allowed in role compute.networkUser

---

■ **Exam tip**   The compute.networkAdmin role gives you permissions to create, modify, and delete networking resources, *except for firewall rules and SSL certificates*. You need to be a member of the compute. securityAdmin role to be able to create, modify, and delete firewall rules and SSL certificates.

In this section, you learned how to manage network security operations for firewalls and IAM. You learned how network firewall policies are an effective way to control firewall rules at different levels of your organization. You also learned how to use the Policy Troubleshooter to diagnose and resolve IAM permission issues. In the next section, we will shift our focus on best practices to resolve common connectivity issues.

Maintaining and Troubleshooting Connectivity Issues

This section highlights best practices on how to address common connectivity issues.

Draining and Redirecting Traffic Flows with HTTP(S) Load Balancing

Connection draining is a process that ensures that existing, in-flight HTTP(S) requests are given time to complete when a VM is removed from an instance group or when an endpoint is removed from a zonal network endpoint group (NEG).

How It Works

Connection draining uses a timeout setting on the load balancer's backend service, whose duration must be from 0 to 3600 seconds inclusive.

For the specified duration of the timeout, existing requests to the removed VM or endpoint are given time to complete. The load balancer does not send new TCP connections to the removed VM. After the timeout duration is reached, all remaining connections to the VM are closed.

The events that trigger connection draining are

- Manual removal of a VM from an instance group

- Programmatic removal of VM from a managed instance group (MIG) by performing a `resize()`, `deleteInstances()`, `recreateInstances()`, or `abandonInstances()` REST API call

- Removal of an instance group from a backend service

- Deletion of a VM as part of autoscaling

- MIG update using the managed instance group updater

- Manual removal of an endpoint from a zonal NEG

It can take up to 60 seconds after your specified timeout duration has elapsed for the VM in the (managed) instance group to be terminated.

■ **Exam tip**   If you enable connection draining on multiple backend services that share the same instance groups or NEGs, the largest timeout value is used.

Enabling Connection Draining

Enable connection draining on a new or existing backend service by using the `--connection-draining-timeout` flag, as shown in the following examples.

For an existing global load balancer:

```
gcloud compute backend-services update BACKEND_SERVICE \
    --global \
    --connection-draining-timeout=CONNECTION_TIMEOUT_SECS
```

For an existing regional load balancer:

```
gcloud compute backend-services update BACKEND_SERVICE \
    --region=REGION \
    --connection-draining-timeout=CONNECTION_TIMEOUT_SECS
```

Replace the placeholders with valid values:

- BACKEND_SERVICE: The backend service that you're updating.

- REGION: If applicable, the region of the backend service that you're updating.

- CONNECTION_TIMEOUT_SECS: The number of seconds to wait before existing connections to instances or endpoints are terminated, between 0 and 3600 seconds, inclusive. A setting of 0 disables connection draining. The connection draining timeout applies to all backends of the backend service.

You can also use the `gcloud compute backend-services edit` command to update an existing backend service.

The difference between `gcloud compute backend-services edit` and `gcloud compute backend-services update` is that the former fetches the backend's configuration file from the server and presents it in a text editor that displays the configurable fields.

The specific editor is defined by the EDITOR environment variable.

Monitoring Ingress and Egress Traffic Using VPC Flow Logs

VPC Flow Logs collects a sample of network flows sent from and received by VMs, including VMs used as GKE nodes. These samples can be used for offline analysis including network monitoring, forensics, real-time security analysis, and cost optimization.

VPC Flow Logs can be viewed in Cloud Logging and can be routed to any supported destination sink.

How It Works

VPC Flow Logs collects samples of each VM's TCP, UDP, ICMP, ESP (Encapsulating Security Payload), and GRE (Generic Routing Encapsulation) protocol flows.

Samples of both inbound and outbound flows are collected as shown in Figure 8-34.

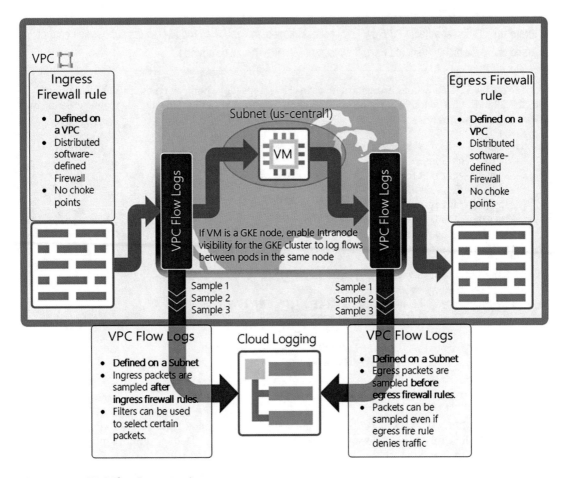

Figure 8-34. *VPC Flow Logs overview*

These flows can be between a VM and one of the following:

- Another VM in Google Cloud

- A host in your on-premises data center

- A Google service

- A host on the Internet

When a flow sample is collected, VPC Flow Logs generates a log for the flow. Each flow record is structured in accordance with a specific definition.

For details about the structure of a flow record, visit https://cloud.google.com/vpc/docs/flow-logs#record_format.

If you want to sample flow logs on a multi-NIC VM, you must enable VPC Flow Logs for any subnets attached to a NIC in the VM.

Enabling VPC Flow Logs

VPC Flow Logs are enabled at the subnet level, just like Private Google Access.

■ **Exam tip** When enabled, VPC Flow Logs collects flow samples *for all the VMs in the subnet.* You cannot pick and choose which VM should have flow logs collected—it's all or nothing.

You enable VPC Flow Logs using the `--enable-flow-logs` flag when you create or update a subnet with the gcloud CLI. The following code snippets show how to enable VPC Flow Logs at subnet creation and update time, respectively:

```
gcloud compute networks subnets create SUBNET_NAME \
    --enable-flow-logs \
    [--logging-aggregation-interval=AGGREGATION_INTERVAL] \
    [--logging-flow-sampling=SAMPLE_RATE] \
    [--logging-filter-expr=FILTER_EXPRESSION] \
    [--logging-metadata=LOGGING_METADATA] \
    [--logging-metadata-fields=METADATA_FIELDS] \
    [other flags as needed]

gcloud compute networks subnets update SUBNET_NAME \
    --enable-flow-logs \
    [--logging-aggregation-interval=AGGREGATION_INTERVAL] \
    [--logging-flow-sampling=SAMPLE_RATE] \
    [--logging-filter-expr=FILTER_EXPRESSION] \
    [--logging-metadata=LOGGING_METADATA] \
    [--logging-metadata-fields=METADATA_FIELDS] \
    [other flags as needed]
```

Replace the following:

- AGGREGATION_INTERVAL: The aggregation interval for flow logs in that subnet. The interval can be set to any of the following: 5 sec (default), 30 sec, 1 min, 5 min, 10 min, or 15 min.

- SAMPLE_RATE: The flow sampling rate. Flow sampling can be set from 0.0 (no sampling) to 1.0 (all logs). The default is 0.5 to indicate that 50% of the collected flow log samples are ingested into Cloud Logging.

- FILTER_EXPRESSION: An expression that defines what logs you want to keep. For details, visit `https://cloud.google.com/vpc/docs/flow-logs#filtering`.

- LOGGING_METADATA: The metadata annotations that you want to include in the logs.

  - `include-all` to include all metadata annotations

  - `exclude-all` to exclude all metadata annotations (default)

  - `custom` to include a custom list of metadata fields that you specify in METADATA_FIELDS

- METADATA_FIELDS: A comma-separated list of metadata fields you want to include in the logs, for example, src_instance and dst_instance. It can only be set if LOGGING_METADATA is set to `custom`.

Cost Considerations

As you can see in Figure 8-34, the two arrows ingest flow log samples into Cloud Logging at a frequency specified by the AGGREGATION_INTERVAL variable.

You can also control the amount of sampling (from zero to one inclusive) with the SAMPLE_RATE variable, but if you are not careful, there may be a large volume of data collected for each VM in your subnet. These may result in significant charges.

Luckily, the console provides a view of the estimated logs generated per day based on the assumption that the AGGREGATION_INTERVAL is the default value of five seconds. The estimate is also based on data collected over the previous seven days. You can use this estimated volume to have an idea on how much enabling VPC Flow Logging would cost you.

Viewing Flow Logs

You learned that VPC Flow Logs are collected and initially stored in Cloud Logging. There are a number of ways to view logs in Cloud Logging as shown in Figure 8-1. What really matters for the purpose of the exam is to understand what logging query filter to use based on your use case. Let's see a few.

To view flow logs *for all subnets in your project* (that have VPC Flow Logs enabled), use this logging query:

```
resource.type="gce_subnetwork"
logName="projects/PROJECT_ID/logs/compute.googleapis.com%2Fvpc_flows"
```

To view flow logs *for a specific subnet in your project* (that have VPC Flow Logs enabled), use this logging query:

```
resource.type="gce_subnetwork"
logName="projects/PROJECT_ID/logs/compute.googleapis.com%2Fvpc_flows"
resource.labels.subnetwork_name="SUBNET_NAME"
```

To view flow logs *for a specific VM in your project* (whose NIC is attached to a subnet that has VPC Flow Logs enabled), use this logging query:

```
resource.type="gce_subnetwork"
logName="projects/PROJECT_ID/logs/compute.googleapis.com%2Fvpc_flows"
jsonPayload.src_instance.vm_name="VM_NAME"
```

To view flow logs *for a specific CIDR block*, use this logging query:

```
resource.type="gce_subnetwork"
logName="projects/PROJECT_ID/logs/compute.googleapis.com%2Fvpc_flows"
ip_in_net(jsonPayload.connection.dest_ip, CIDR_BLOCK)
```

To view flow logs *for a specific GKE cluster*, use this logging query:

```
resource.type="k8s_cluster"
logName="projects/PROJECT_ID/logs/vpc_flows"
resource.labels.cluster_name="CLUSTER_NAME"
```

To view flow logs *for only egress traffic from a subnet*, use this logging query:

```
logName="projects/PROJECT_ID/logs/compute.googleapis.com%2Fvpc_flows" AND
jsonPayload.reporter="SRC" AND
jsonPayload.src_vpc.subnetwork_name="SUBNET_NAME" AND
(jsonPayload.dest_vpc.subnetwork_name!="SUBNET_NAME" OR NOT jsonPayload.dest_vpc.
subnetwork_name:*)
```

To view flow logs *for all egress traffic from a VPC network*, use this logging query:

```
logName="projects/PROJECT_ID/logs/compute.googleapis.com%2Fvpc_flows" AND
jsonPayload.reporter="SRC" AND
jsonPayload.src_vpc.vpc_name="VPC_NAME" AND
(jsonPayload.dest_vpc.vpc_name!="VPC_NAME" OR NOT jsonPayload.dest_vpc:*)
```

To view flow logs *for specific ports and protocols*, use this logging query:

```
resource.type="gce_subnetwork"
logName="projects/PROJECT_ID/logs/compute.googleapis.com%2Fvpc_flows"
jsonPayload.connection.dest_port=PORT
jsonPayload.connection.protocol=PROTOCOL
```

This concludes the section about VPC Flow Logs. In the next section, you will learn when to enable firewall logs and firewall insights and which option better suits your network operations needs.

Monitoring Firewall Logs and Firewall Insights

Firewall rules provide a software-defined, distributed firewall that protects the perimeter of your VPC network. By doing so, they are the first form of defense from unauthorized access to your workloads.

In addition to isolating your VMs and compute resources (e.g., GKE clusters, etc.), they allow you to monitor inbound and outbound activity to and from your VMs.

In the first part of this section, you will learn how to configure firewall rules to log inbound and outbound events.

In the second part of this section, you will learn what to do to utilize firewall rules effectively and efficiently.

Firewall Rules Logging

Firewall Rules Logging lets you audit, verify, and analyze the effects of your firewall rules. For example, you can determine if a firewall rule designed to deny traffic is functioning as intended. Firewall Rules Logging is also useful if you need to determine how many connections are affected by a given firewall rule.

You enable Firewall Rules Logging individually for each firewall rule whose connections you need to log. Firewall Rules Logging is an option for any firewall rule, except the two implied rules, as noted as follows.

■ **Exam tip** You cannot enable Firewall Rules Logging for the implied deny ingress and implied allow egress rules. For more details about the implied rules, visit `https://cloud.google.com/vpc/docs/firewalls#default_firewall_rules`.

In Figure 8-35, you can see how each of the two firewall rules associated to the VPC has its own log stream, which ingests connection records to Cloud Logging.

In contrast to VPC Flow Logs, firewall rule logs are not sampled. Instead, connection records—whether the connections are allowed or denied—are continuously collected and sent to Cloud Logging.

As shown in Figure 8-35, each connection record includes the source and destination IP addresses, the protocol and ports, date and time, and a reference to the firewall rule that applied to the traffic.

The figure also reminds you—as you learned in Chapters 2 and 3—that firewall rules are defined at the VPC level because they are global resources. They also operate as distributed, software-defined firewalls. As a result, they don't become choke points as traditional firewalls.

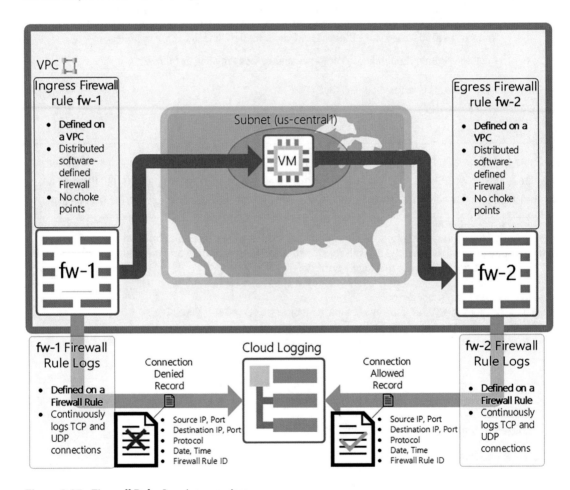

Figure 8-35. *Firewall Rules Logging overview*

To enable or disable Firewall Rules Logging for an existing firewall rule, follow these directions. When you enable logging, you can control whether metadata fields are included. If you omit them, you can save on storage costs.

To enable Firewall Rules Logging, use the --enable-logging flag as follows:

```
gcloud compute firewall-rules update RULE_NAME \
    --enable-logging \
    --logging-metadata=LOGGING_METADATA
```

Replace the following:

- RULE_NAME: The name of the firewall rule.

- LOGGING_METADATA: Whether Firewall Rules Logging includes metadata fields in firewall rule logs. You can configure this field only if logging is enabled. The value must be exclude-all or include-all. By default, metadata fields are included.

To disable Firewall Rules Logging, use the --no-enable-logging flag as follows:

```
gcloud compute firewall-rules update RULE_NAME \
    --no-enable-logging
```

■ **Exam tip** Firewall rule logs are created in the project that hosts the network containing the VM instances and firewall rules. With Shared VPC, VM instances are created and billed in service projects, but they use a Shared VPC network located in the host project. As a result, firewall rule logs are stored in the host project.

Firewall rule logs are initially stored in Cloud Logging. Here are some guidelines on how to filter the data in Cloud Logging to select the firewall rule logs that best suit your network operation needs.

To view all firewall logs, use this logging query:

```
resource.type="gce_subnetwork"
logName="projects/PROJECT_ID/logs/compute.googleapis.com%2Ffirewall"
```

To view firewall logs specific to a given subnet, use this logging query:

```
resource.type="gce_subnetwork"
logName="projects/PROJECT_ID/logs/compute.googleapis.com%2Ffirewall"
resource.labels.subnetwork_name="SUBNET_NAME"
```

To view firewall logs specific to a given VM, use this logging query:

```
resource.type="gce_subnetwork"
logName="projects/PROJECT_ID/logs/compute.googleapis.com%2Ffirewall"
jsonPayload.instance.vm_name="INSTANCE_ID"
```

To view firewall logs for connections from a specific country, use this logging query:

```
resource.type="gce_subnetwork"
logName="projects/PROJECT_ID/logs/compute.googleapis.com%2Ffirewall"
jsonPayload.remote_location.country=COUNTRY
```

where the variable COUNTRY denotes the ISO 3166-1alpha-3 code of the country whose connections you are inquiring about.

Firewall Insights

Firewall Insights analyzes your firewall rules and provides guidance on how you can optimize them. It produces insights, recommendations, and metrics about how your firewall rules are being used. Firewall Insights also uses machine learning to predict future firewall rules usage.

For example, by using Firewall Insights you learn which firewall rules are overly permissive, and you can leverage the generated recommendations to make them more strict.

Additional insights include firewall rules that overlap existing rules, rules with no hits, and unused firewall rule attributes such as IP address and port ranges. Insights are classified as follows:

- **Shadowed firewall rule insights**, which are derived from data about how you have configured your firewall rules. A shadowed rule shares attributes—such as IP address ranges—with other rules of higher or equal priority.

- **Overly permissive rule insights**, including each of the following:

  - Allow rules with no hits

  - Allow rules with unused attributes

  - Allow rules with overly permissive IP addresses or port ranges

- **Deny rule insights** with no hits during the observation period.

Firewall Insights uses the logs produced by Firewall Rules Logging to generate metrics. You can use these metrics to determine whether your firewall rules protect your workloads as expected and—most importantly—in accordance with the least privilege principle and cloud security best practices.

You can also use these metrics to discover malicious attempts to access your network and act on it by leveraging Cloud Monitoring.

Insights and recommendations are accessible through the gcloud CLI by using one of the three following commands, the first of which lists the names of the available insights whose type is `google.compute.firewall.Insight`:

- `gcloud recommender insights list --insight-type=google.compute.firewall.Insight --location=LOCATION`

- `gcloud recommender insights describe INSIGHT --insight-type=google.compute.firewall.Insight --location=LOCATION`

- `gcloud recommender insights mark-accepted INSIGHT --etag=ETAG --insight-type= google.compute.firewall.Insight --location=LOCATION`

Replace as follows:

- LOCATION: The location defining the scope of your insights, for example, `global`

- INSIGHT: The name of the insight resource

- ETAG: Fingerprint of the insight. Provides optimistic locking when updating states. For more info, visit `https://cloud.google.com/storage/docs/hashes-etags#etags`.

Insights and recommendations can also be viewed with the console in one of the following locations:

- On the Network Intelligence page

- On the details page for a VPC firewall rule

- On the details page for a VPC network interface

Firewall Insights metrics can be viewed using Cloud Monitoring.

Managing and Troubleshooting VPNs

To troubleshoot VPN connectivity, start by checking the status of your IPsec tunnels.

Since Classic VPN is going to be deprecated, we will focus on HA VPN.

There are two steps to view IPsec tunnel status. First, identify the tunnel name and region, and then use the describe command option to view tunnel details.

In the following commands, replace the following:

- PROJECT_ID: The ID of your project

- GW_NAME: The name of the gateway

- REGION: The region where the gateway or tunnel resides

- NAME: The name of the IPsec tunnel

To identify the name and region of the VPN tunnel whose status you need to check, use the `gcloud compute vpn-gateways describe` command as follows:

```
gcloud compute vpn-gateways describe GW_NAME \
  --region=REGION \
  --project=PROJECT_ID \
  --format='flattened(tunnels)'
```

To view IPsec tunnel details, use the `gcloud compute vpn-tunnels describe` command as follows:

```
gcloud compute vpn-tunnels describe NAME \
  --region=REGION \
  --project=PROJECT_ID \
  --format='flattened(status,detailedStatus)'
```

The output will return a message that shows the status of the investigated IPsec tunnel.

If the detailedStatus property value doesn't provide enough information to help you resolve the issue, you can perform root cause analysis by using the following checklist:

1. Verify that the remote peer IP address configured on the Cloud VPN gateway is correct.

2. Verify that traffic flowing from your on-premises hosts is reaching the peer gateway.

3. Verify that traffic is flowing between the two VPN gateways in both directions. In the VPN logs, check for reported incoming messages from the other VPN gateway.

4. Check that the configured IKE versions are the same on both sides of the tunnel.

5. Check that the shared secret is the same on both sides of the tunnel.

6. If your peer VPN gateway is behind one-to-one NAT, ensure that you have properly configured the NAT device to forward UDP traffic to your peer VPN gateway on ports 500 and 4500.

7. If the VPN logs show a *no-proposal-chosen* error, this error indicates that Cloud VPN and your peer VPN gateway were unable to agree on a set of ciphers. For IKEv1, the set of ciphers must match exactly. For IKEv2, there must be at least one common cipher proposed by each gateway. Make sure that you use supported ciphers to configure your peer VPN gateway.

8. Make sure that you configure your peer and Google Cloud routes and firewall rules so that traffic can traverse the tunnel. You might need to contact your network administrator for help.

If the issue still persists, use Cloud Logging with the gcloud CLI (or with Logs Explorer) as you learned in the first section of the chapter. Figure 8-36 shows a list of common Cloud VPN events you may want to consult for further troubleshoot analysis.

To view	Use this Logging Query
Cloud VPN initiates Phase 1 (IKE SA)	`resource.type="vpn_gateway" ("initiating IKE_SA" OR "generating IKE_SA_INIT request")`
Cloud VPN cannot contact remote peer	`resource.type="vpn_gateway" "establishing IKE_SA failed, peer not responding"`
IKE (Phase 1) authentication events	`resource.type="vpn_gateway" ("generating IKE_AUTH request" OR "parsed IKE_AUTH response")`
Successful IKE authentication	`resource.type="vpn_gateway" ("authentication of" AND "with pre-shared key successful")`
Phase 1 (IKE SA) established	`resource.type="vpn_gateway" ("IKE_SA" AND "established between")`
All Phase 2 (Child SA) events, including re-key events	`resource.type="vpn_gateway" "CHILD_SA"`
Peer asks for Phase 2 re-key	`resource.type="vpn_gateway" detected rekeying of CHILD_SA`
Peer asks to terminate Phase 2 (Child SA)	`resource.type="vpn_gateway" received DELETE for ESP CHILD_SA`
Cloud VPN asks to terminate Phase 2 (Child SA)	`resource.type="vpn_gateway" sending DELETE for ESP CHILD_SA`
Cloud VPN closes Phase 2 (Child SA), perhaps in response to the peer	`resource.type="vpn_gateway" closing CHILD_SA`
Cloud VPN closed Phase 2 itself	`resource.type="vpn_gateway" CHILD_SA closed`
If remote traffic selectors don't match	`resource.type="vpn_gateway" Remote traffic selectors narrowed`
If local traffic selectors don't match	`resource.type="vpn_gateway" Local traffic selectors narrowed`

Figure 8-36. *Cloud Logging filters for Cloud VPN events*

Troubleshooting Cloud Router BGP Peering Issues

The following sections include best practices to troubleshoot common issues related to BGP peering.

BGP Session Failed to Establish

Validate the settings on your Cloud Router and its peer BGP router(s). For detailed information, use Cloud Logging to view the Cloud Router logs.

IP Addresses for BGP Sessions

The IP addresses that you can use for a BGP session depend on which network connectivity product you use. For details, visit https://cloud.google.com/network-connectivity/docs/router/concepts/overview#bgp-ips.

Invalid Value for the Field resource.bgp.asn

You may get the following error:

"Invalid value for field resource.bgp.asn: ######. Local ASN conflicts with peer ASN specified by a router in the same region and network."

The Cloud Router is attempting to establish a BGP session with an on-premises device that has the same ASN as the Cloud Router. To resolve this issue, change the ASN of your device or Cloud Router.

iBGP Between Cloud Routers in a Single Region Doesn't Work

In contrast to BGP (which was designed to exchange routing and reachability information among autonomous systems (AS) on the Internet), iBGP (Interior Border Gateway Protocol) is used for routing *within* an autonomous system.

Monitoring, Maintaining, and Troubleshooting Latency and Traffic Flow

The last section of the book is about performance and latency. You have architected the network of your workloads for high availability, resilience, security, and cost-effectiveness—these are four of the five pillars of the well-architected framework, which has been the main theme of our journey.

Now, you need to make sure that your workloads operate and maintain the performance specified by the SLOs.

A key metric to measure performance is latency. Latency tells you what is the acceptable maximum time a request should take to be fulfilled by your workload. Latency has a direct impact on user experience. If your workload underperforms resulting in slow responses (i.e., high latency), users won't be happy and their experience will be negatively impacted. They may never visit your website again, which may have a monetary impact.

Google Cloud has developed and released Cloud Trace to help you measure latency. Cloud Trace is a distributed tracing system for Google Cloud, which helps you understand how long it takes your application to handle incoming requests from users or other applications and how long it takes to complete operations like RPC calls performed when handling the requests.

In the next section, you will learn how to use Cloud Trace to measure latency and determine bottlenecks in your workloads.

Testing Latency and Network Throughput

Let's start by reviewing the basics of distributed tracing, as described in the original paper from Google on the "Dapper" distributed tracing framework.

When a user request arrives, we create a *trace* that will describe how our workload responds.

Traces are composed of *spans*, which represent a specific request and response pair involved in serving the original user request.

In Figure 8-37, you can find an example. The parent (also referred to as root) span describes the latency observed by the end user and is drawn in the top part of the figure. Each of the child spans describes how a particular service in a distributed system was called and responded with latency data captured for each. Child spans are shown under the root span.

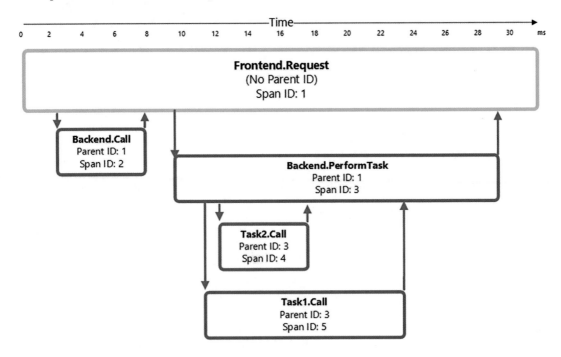

Figure 8-37. Traces and spans

All Cloud Run, Cloud Functions, and App Engine standard applications are automatically traced, and libraries are available to trace applications running elsewhere after minimal setup.

If your application doesn't run in any of the aforementioned services, it must be instrumented to submit traces to Cloud Trace. You can instrument your code by using the Google client libraries. However, it's recommended that you use *OpenTelemetry* to instrument your application. OpenTelemetry is an open source tracing package, which is actively in development and is the preferred package. For more information, visit https://opentelemetry.io/.

An alternative approach to instrumenting your application is to use the Cloud Trace API and write custom methods to send tracing data to Cloud Trace.

Either way, your application will need to be instrumented to create traces and send them to Cloud Trace for inspection and analysis. The resulting instrumentation code leverages HTTP headers to submit the trace data to Cloud Trace for further analysis.

Spans are created as needed programmatically. This allows Cloud Trace to explicitly measure the latency of the services that are part of our application.

To view your application's traces, you need to use the Google Cloud console.

From the product dashboard, go to the product menu and select Trace.

The trace list shows all the traces that were captured by Cloud Trace over the selected time interval, as shown in Figure 8-38.

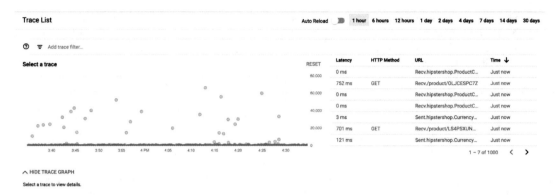

Figure 8-38. *Trace list. Portions of this page are reproduced under the CC-BY license and shared by Google:* `https://cloud.google.com/trace/docs/finding-traces#viewing_recent_traces`

You can filter by label to select only the traces for a given span (e.g., RootSpan: Recv as shown in Figure 8-39).

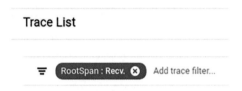

Figure 8-39. *Filtering traces by label. Portions of this page are reproduced under the CC-BY license and shared by Google:* `https://cloud.google.com/trace/docs/finding-traces#filter_traces`

You can use this filter to drill down a relevant trace and find latency data in the "waterfall chart" (Figure 8-40).

Selected trace details ▭

Selected trace ID
0af00b56371d452fac3efcc4dfc8eccd ✕

☐ Show Events ☐ Show Logs ❶ No Logs found for this trace

Sent.hipstershop.CurrencyService.Convert

Start Time: @0.00 ms. Timestamp: 2020-07-28
(15:16:56.379)

Summary

Name	RPCs	Total D
Sent.hipstershop.CurrencyService.Convert	1	3.951
grpc:/hipstershop.CurrencyService/Convert	1	1

Details ∨

Logs	View ❘ ❶
Report	View
Status Code	0
Status Message	"OK"

Labels

Label	Value
FailFast	true
Client	true
g.co/agent	opencensus-go [0.15.0]

Figure 8-40. Waterfall chart for a trace. Portions of this page are reproduced under the CC-BY license and shared by Google: `https://cloud.google.com/trace/docs/viewing-details#timeline`

On the top, you can see the root span, and all the child spans are below it. You can see the latency for each span in the chart to quickly determine the source of the latency in our application overall.

In this section, you learned how to use Cloud Trace to measure and analyze both the overall latency of user requests and the way services interact. This will help you find the primary contributor to latency issues.

Using Network Intelligence Center to Visualize Topology, Test Connectivity, and Monitor Performance

Network Intelligence Center provides a single pane of glass for managing Google Cloud network visibility, monitoring, and troubleshooting.

Network Intelligence Center includes the following modules:

- **Network topology**: To visualize the topology of your VPCs and their associated metrics

- **Connectivity tests**: To test network connectivity to and from your VPC

- **Performance dashboards**: To view packet loss and latency between zones where you have VMs

- **Firewall Insights**: To view usage of your VPC firewall rules and optimize their configuration

- **Network analyzer**: To view network and service issues, insights, and best practice recommendations from automatic discovery

Whether you want to diagnose connectivity issues to prevent outages, improve network security and compliance, or save time with intelligent monitoring, Network Intelligence Center has the tools you need to increase the security posture of your applications and infrastructure, whether they be in Google Cloud or in hybrid and multi-cloud environments.

Exam Questions
Question 8.1 (VPC Flow Logs, Firewall Rule Logs)

Your company is running out of network capacity to run a critical application in the on-premises data center. You want to migrate the application to GCP. You also want to ensure that the security team does not lose their ability to monitor traffic to and from Compute Engine instances.

Which two products should you incorporate into the solution? (Choose two.)

- **A.** VPC Flow Logs
- **B.** Firewall logs
- **C.** Cloud Audit logs
- **D.** Cloud Trace
- **E.** Compute Engine instance system logs

Rationale

A and B are CORRECT because the requirement is to let the security team keep their ability to monitor traffic to and from Compute Engine instances. VPC Flow Logs allows you to monitor a sample of flow logs that reach and leave each of the VMs in your subnet, provided the subnet has been configured to enable VPC Flow Logs. Firewall logs allow you to continuously detect TCP and UDP connection records for each of your firewall rules associated to your VPC.

C is incorrect because Cloud Audit logs are a specific type of logs that describe administrative activities and accesses within your Google Cloud resources. They don't provide connection details, packet information, and other network-specific component data, which are required to monitor traffic to and from Compute Engine instances.

D is incorrect because Cloud Trace is a product intended to measure latency between the components of your workloads, which is not a requirement in the question.

E is incorrect because Compute Engine instance system logs are intended for automated Google Cloud actions that modify the configuration of resources, which is not a requirement in the question.

Question 8.2 (Firewall Rule Logs)

You have created a firewall with rules that only allow traffic over HTTP, HTTPS, and SSH ports. While testing, you specifically try to reach the server over multiple ports and protocols; however, you do not see any denied connections in the firewall logs. You want to resolve the issue. What should you do?

A. Enable logging on the default Deny Any Firewall Rule.

B. Enable logging on the VM instances that receive traffic.

C. Create a logging sink forwarding all firewall logs with no filters.

D. Create an explicit Deny Any rule and enable logging on the new rule.

Rationale

A is incorrect because you cannot enable Firewall Rules Logging for the implied deny ingress and implied allow egress rules.

B is incorrect because enabling logging on the VMs won't tell you anything about allowed or denied connections, which is the requirement.

C is incorrect because a logging sink won't change the current scenario.

D is CORRECT because to capture denied connections, you need to create a new firewall rule with `--action=deny` and `--direction=ingress` and enable logging on it with the flag `--enable-logging`.

Question 8.3 (IAM)

You are trying to update firewall rules in a shared VPC for which you have been assigned only network admin permissions. You cannot modify the firewall rules.

Your organization requires using the least privilege necessary.

Which level of permissions should you request?

A. Security admin privileges from the Shared VPC admin.

B. Service project admin privileges from the Shared VPC admin.

C. Shared VPC admin privileges from the organization admin.

D. Organization admin privileges from the organization admin.

Rationale

A is CORRECT because the security admin role (`roles/securityAdmin`) gives you permissions to create, modify, and delete firewall rules and SSL certificates and also to configure Shielded VM settings.

B is incorrect because the service project admin by design doesn't give you permissions to manage network infrastructure—including firewall rules—in the host project, where the shared VPC is located.

C and D are incorrect because the specified IAM roles are both overly permissive.

Question 8.4 (IAM)

Your company has a security team that manages firewalls and SSL certificates. It also has a networking team that manages the networking resources. The networking team needs to be able to read firewall rules, but should not be able to create, modify, or delete them.

How should you set up permissions for the networking team?

A. Assign members of the networking team the `compute.networkUser` role.

B. Assign members of the networking team the `compute.networkAdmin` role.

C. Assign members of the networking team a custom role with only the `compute.networks.*` and the `compute.firewalls.list` permissions.

D. Assign members of the networking team the `compute.networkViewer` role, and add the `compute.networks.use` permission.

Rationale

A is incorrect because the compute.networkUser role doesn't give you permissions to manage networking resources.

B is CORRECT because `compute.networkAdmin` is the role with the least set of privileges that gives you permissions to manage network resources, and it lets you read firewall rules. If you need permissions to modify firewall rules (and SSL certificates), then the `compute.securityAdmin` role should be granted as well.

C is incorrect because the permission compute.firewalls.list lets you list firewall rules but not read them.

D is incorrect because the compute.networkViewer role won't let you modify network components.

Question 8.5 (Troubleshooting VPN)

Your on-premises data center has two routers connected to your GCP network through a VPN on each router. All applications are working correctly; however, all of the traffic is passing across a single VPN instead of being load-balanced across the two connections as desired.

During troubleshooting, you discover the following facts:

- Each on-premises router is configured with the same ASN.

- Each on-premises router is configured with the same routes and priorities.

- Both on-premises routers are configured with a VPN connected to a single Cloud Router.

- The VPN logs have no-proposal-chosen lines when the VPNs are connecting.

- BGP session is not established between one on-premises router and the Cloud Router.

What is the most likely cause of this problem?

- **A.** One of the VPN sessions is configured incorrectly.
- **B.** A firewall is blocking the traffic across the second VPN connection.
- **C.** You do not have a load balancer to load-balance the network traffic.
- **D.** BGP sessions are not established between both on-premises routers and the Cloud Router.

Rationale

A is CORRECT because the no-proposal-chosen error indicates that Cloud VPN and your peer VPN gateway were unable to agree on a set of ciphers. For IKEv1, the set of ciphers must match exactly. For IKEv2, there must be at least one common cipher proposed by each gateway. Make sure that you use supported ciphers to configure your peer VPN gateway.

B, C, and D are incorrect because the issue is a VPN misconfiguration.

Index

■ W, X

■ Y

■ Z

Printed in the United States
by Baker & Taylor Publisher Services